RENDER UNTO ROME

RENDER UNTO ROME

THE SECRET LIFE OF MONEY
IN THE CATHOLIC CHURCH

JASON BERRY

CROWN PUBLISHERS

New York

Copyright © 2011 by Jason Berry

All rights reserved.
Published in the United States by Crown Publishers,
an imprint of the Crown Publishing Group,
a division of Random House, Inc., New York.
www.crownpublishing.com

CROWN and the Crown colophon are registered trademarks
of Random House, Inc.

Library of Congress Cataloging-in-Publication Data
Berry, Jason.
Render unto Rome: the secret life of money in the Catholic Church /
Jason Berry.—1st ed.
p. cm.
1. Catholic Church—Finance.   I. Title.
BX1950.B47 2011
262'.020681—dc22   2010051105

ISBN 978-0-385-53132-0
eISBN 978-0-385-53133-7

PRINTED IN THE UNITED STATES OF AMERICA

Jacket design by David Tran
Jacket photograph: Istock.com

1   3   5   7   9   10   8   6   4   2

FIRST EDITION

In memoriam

Ariel Laforet Berry,
child of my heart

Gerald Renner,
colleague and friend

I am an old policeman guarding the gold reserves. If you tell an old policeman that the laws are going to change, he will realize that he is an old policeman, and he will do everything that he can to prevent them from changing . . . Once the new laws have become the Church's treasure, an enrichment of her gold reserves, there is still only one principle: loyalty in the Church's service. But this service means loyalty to her laws—like a blind man. Like the blind man that I am.

—Cardinal Alfredo Ottaviani, Prefect of the Holy Office,
to Mario von Galli in *The Council and the Future* (1966)

CONTENTS

PROLOGUE: PRINCES OF THE REALM 1

1: BOSTON IN THE FAULT LINES 19

2: ORIGINS OF THE VATICAN FINANCIAL SYSTEM 36

3: SEEDS OF REVOLT 69

4: THE VATICAN, THE VIGILS, AND THE REAL ESTATE 95

5: ITALIAN INTERVENTIONS 119

6: THE CASE OF THE MISSING MILLIONS 133

7: FATHER MACIEL, LORD OF PROSPERITY 156

8: BORRÉ IN ROME 197

9: SECRECY AND LAMENTATIONS 203

10: PROSECUTION AND SUPPRESSION 240

11: THE DEBTS OF APOSTOLIC SUCCESSION 277

12: ANOTHER CALIFORNIA 287

13: AMERICA AND THE VATICAN 325

EPILOGUE: BENEDICT XVI: POPE OF IRONIES 352

NOTES 361

ACKNOWLEDGMENTS 401

INDEX 407

RENDER UNTO ROME

PRINCES of the REALM

The church stood at the bottom of Bunker Hill in Charlestown, one of the city's oldest neighborhoods. Like much of Greater Boston, Charlestown was no longer hard-shell Irish. The wooden triple-deckers that housed large working families in decades past had become pearls for gentrification in 2004, despite the outlying streets that bore the scars of a drug economy.

The social mosaic at St. Catherine of Siena parish delighted Rose Mary Piper. She was in the winter of life, with four children grown and grandchildren nearing adulthood. The range of people in the pews, so different from that of the predominantly white parishes she had known, touched her identity as one soul united with a greater body of believers. From the housing projects along Mystic River came Puerto Ricans and people from the Dominican Republic to Sunday Mass, with their Spanish songs and bilingual bulletins, worshipping alongside people with Irish roots and then more cosmopolitan Bostonians like her son-in-law, Peter Borré, who lived in a nearby condo.

Rosie Piper knew the Latino women had it tough, like her ancestors who got off the ships from Ireland and made it in Staten Island, New York. To live is to change. When her husband was diagnosed with dementia, Rosie oversaw the selling of their home in Hilton Head, South Carolina.

For most of their long marriage, Bill Piper's career as a chemical engineer with DuPont had anchored them in Delaware. Rosie had enjoyed their time in the South. But with the realization that she alone could not manage his needs, she decided on the Boston area, where their two daughters had settled. Mary Beth, the rebellious one, no longer went to church; but her husband, Peter, attended Mass with Rosie.

Every Sunday, Rose Mary Piper put a $10 check in the collection basket, a practice ingrained with time. Peter gave cash. The worldview Peter Borré carried from his navy years turned on just authority. You went to church, prayed for those you loved, asked forgiveness for your sins, and donated money because it was the right thing to do. Until the scandal rocked Boston neither of them thought much about church finances, how a given dollar broke down—what percentage went to parish costs, what part for the parochial school and to help the poor; how much to the bishop, how much to Rome. You gave money and let the priest and bishop handle it. The Catholic Church was holy, true, apostolic, and wealthy enough to help many of those truly in need.

The revolution in Peter Borré's life began in 2004, when the Boston archdiocese imposed a sweeping closure plan on parish churches some months after a legal settlement with 552 clergy abuse victims. *Cardinal Law covered up for child molesters*, brooded Rosie Piper, *and now they sell churches!* Peter Borré, who led a comfortable life, was also offended, but he soon acquired a cold curiosity about the money. As Borré would learn, many American Catholics were riled about just stewardship: how bishops manage the finances. Huge legal settlements caused by bishops who recycled pedophiles, churches closed against the people's will, continuing reports of priests or lay staffers who stole parish funds—all fed a deep sense of betrayal. In 2010 an upsurge of clergy abuse cases showed bad decisions by Cardinal Joseph Ratzinger long before he became pope. As Benedict XVI met with victims and apologized, he nevertheless seemed detached, in a surreal way, from the obvious need for structural reform.

Since the harrowing struggle of Benedict XV during World War I, the role of the pope has enlarged, dramatically, from that of a supreme religious leader to that of an international advocate for peace. Following the Great War, a succession of popes emerged as moral statesmen on the global stage, slowly distancing themselves from a history of anti-Semitic views within the church and calling for dialogue and diplomacy over armed conflict, particularly in the nuclear age. The evolution of the papacy as a force for peace took a major step in 1958, when John XXIII, who as papal nuncio in Istanbul during the war had helped save Jews, abolished the phrase "treacherous Jews" from the Good Friday liturgy. He greeted a delegation of American Jews with an echo of the Old Testament account of Joseph in Egypt: "I am Joseph, your brother."[1]

His successor, Paul VI, made a point of often saying, "If you want peace, work for justice."[2] Even Pius XII—the focus of an ongoing debate among historians and Jewish leaders about his reticence during World War II toward condemning Hitler and the Nazis—was revered in postwar years as a voice of peace. Pius's questioned legacy results not just from revisionist historians. Ironically, John Paul II raised the expectations for a church more honest about itself in his call for "the purification of the memory."[3] A champion of human rights in the political sphere, John Paul in his many apologies for past church sins cited "sufferings inflicted upon Jews,"[4] though he mentioned no pope by name.

In his last dozen years, John Paul damaged his own legacy on human rights by failing to appropriately acknowledge the victims of clergy child abusers and to act forcefully on the clear signs of a criminal sexual underground in clerical culture. Benedict XVI inherited a Vatican tribunal system averse to punishing bishops who were sex offenders or complicit in concealing them. By failing to show resolve as a ruler and bring the worst bishops to justice, Benedict has invited scrutiny of the Vatican's legal system, such as it is. Vatican offices have largely rubber-stamped bishops' financial decisions. How that Vatican legal system functions is the central theme of this book.

Render unto Rome follows a series of property and financial decisions that link certain American bishops and Vatican officials; the book further examines how Father Marcial Maciel, the greatest fund-raiser of the modern church, became its greatest criminal. In following these narrative lines I have taken a deep look at the handling of church assets in Boston, Cleveland, and Los Angeles, interlaced with events from other dioceses and a recurrent focus on the Congregation for the Clergy, the Vatican office that monitors how bishops sell property. A key official in Clergy recently assisted a profiteering scheme on the sale of U.S. churches. A central figure in that scheme, Cardinal Angelo Sodano, was Vatican secretary of state for fourteen years under John Paul and slightly more than a year under Benedict. Sodano was also a tireless supporter of Father Maciel. The cardinal refused to be interviewed; however, FBI findings on the business dealings of his nephew were of great help, along with other sources, as I put a viewfinder on Sodano and his machinations. *Nipote*, in Italian, is the root word for "nepotism."

I have drawn a timely insight from *Worldly Goods*, James Gollin's 1971 book on Catholic Church finances. Gollin reported that the American church held between 50 and 60 percent of global church assets, but much of it lay in property that could not be sold. "Adding up the total wealth of the church is a game," he observed. "The essential thing is to understand how the wealth is managed."[5] As I have learned, that management varies greatly from one bishop to the next.

With 1.2 billion members, the Roman Catholic Church is the largest organization in the world, the most populous single entity that operates nearly everywhere. It is also a vastly decentralized church, with power invested in individual bishops. No matter how much a bishop relies on advisory boards or staff, his authority looks to Rome. Each bishop answers to the pope through officials in the Roman Curia. Few Catholics questioned this monarchical arrangement until the bishops' strategies to conceal sexual abuse unraveled in lawsuits, allowing the press to expose a netherworld of pathological secrecy.

"I'm constantly amazed by how little information some dioceses have on their finances," Patrick Schiltz, the dean of the University of St. Thomas Law School in St. Paul, Minnesota, told the *New York Times* in 2002. "They are like mom-and-pop operations."[6] Schiltz has since become a federal judge. Words like that from a legal scholar who had done defense work for dioceses in abuse cases hinted at a deeper dissatisfaction shared by many prominent Catholics.

"The church should open up its books," Erica P. John, an heir to the Miller brewing fortune and a major philanthropist, also told the *Times*. "We want transparency."[7] A family foundation established by John's late husband had been a bedrock supporter of Milwaukee's archdiocese when she discovered, in May 2002, that Archbishop Rembert Weakland had used $450,000 in church funds in 1998 to pay off a disgruntled male lover from years before.[8] Weakland was closing parishes at the time, citing a need for fiscal pragmatism, while his lawyers negotiated the secret settlement; he was also steering $1.5 million to Rome for an endowed chair in social teaching in his name at the Pontifical Gregorian University, and a $500,000 chair in liturgy and music, courtesy of an archdiocesan fund that relied on the John family foundation.[9] In a 2009 memoir, Weakland noted: "I knew that people's allegiance was primarily to the parish: their Catholicism was identified with it. The closing or merging of parishes would almost certainly reduce the number of practicing Catholics."[10] Weakland, who had a remarkable history of recycling child molesters, commissioned a $100,000 bronze relief for Milwaukee's Cathedral of St. John the Evangelist that gave honor to Saint John, Saint Anne, and himself.

The celibacy law, which any pope could make optional, has become an expensive yoke on the church. Since the 1960s many more men have left the priesthood than entered, most of them to marry; the priesthood has also acquired a vast gay subculture. The number of seminarians has plunged by 85 percent. One-fifth of America's 17,958 parishes have no priest. A key rationale in the eleventh-century papacy's imposition of celibacy was to prevent the children of priests and bishops from creating dynasties; the church was trying to secure its territories and a role for its legal system in European society. Ending clerical marriage was "an essential precondition for the liberation of Church property from lay control," writes the historian James A. Brundage.[11] Today, bishops have liquidated assets at a numbing pace to pay victims of priests who should have been prosecuted but mostly went to expensive treatment centers.

In the 1950s, the ratio of priest to parishioners was 1 to 650; today, it is 1 to 1,600.[12] Most priests strive to give the Gospel meaning in their parishioners' lives. They are also the parish fund-raisers; the priest shortage has escalated financial pressures and losses. Pastors rely on lay staff, many of whom have families and real salary needs, unlike priests and nuns of yesteryear.

A true financial profile of the church is elusive. Few dioceses post complete financial statements, nor does the United States Conference of Catholic Bishops (USCCB), which has a large building and staff in Washington, D.C. In 2002 the USCCB released a report that calculated $5.6 billion from Sunday collections, and all parish revenues of $7.6 billion.[13] Financial analyst Joseph Claude Harris, author of *The Cost of Catholic Parishes and Schools*, has studied the available figures on Sunday giving from people like Rose Mary Piper. "The largest church in the world has no definitive data on its American collection yield," states Harris. "A complete portrait of church financials would include *all* revenues and expenses., We have only a portion. Maybe there isn't a big demand. If every bishop wanted the information, the USCCB would do it."[14]

Harris revised the 2002 Sunday collection figures, using updated metrics on the number of U.S. Catholic households. For 2002, the year the abuse scandal became a national media narrative, he calculated the Sunday collections at $6.102 billion. In 2003, as the scandal coverage worsened, the weekly contribution *rose* by $38 million, to $6.140 billion. In 2004 there was an increase of $207 million to $6.347 billion. In 2005 the giving rose by another $194 million, reaching $6.541 billion. And for 2006, the last year for which Harris has data, he tallied an even greater jump, of $441 million, to $6.982 billion.[15]

An escalation of $880 million to the Sunday baskets during the worst religious scandal in American history is a testament to Catholics' faith "in the church"—but not in its power structure. A *USA Today* poll in June 2002 found that 89 percent of Catholics thought that a bishop who recycled a pedophile should be removed. Apart from Cardinal Bernard Law of Boston, few complicit bishops "stepped down." The increase in donations (in cash and other assets) suggests that Catholics looked past guilty bishops to support parishes and programs they wanted to preserve. But the abuse crisis was unrelenting.

Between 1950 and 2002 the church paid $353 million in victim settlements, legal defense, therapy for victims, and treatment for perpetrators, according to a study commissioned by the bishops. Insurance carriers paid $218.5 million, for a combined cost of $571.5 million.[16] The chain reaction of reporting ignited by the *Boston Globe* in 2002 caused many more victims to seek redress. Church expenses for 2002 through 2009 were $1.42 billion. The total cost (including priests' treatment) from 1950 through 2009 was $1.775 billion. The average annual loss (or expense) for the most recent seven-year period was $203 million.[17]

How does an organization recover from losses of this magnitude?

The short answer is by selling property; the long answer is through deficit financing.

The Roman Catholic Church in America is undergoing the most massive downsizing in its history. A religious infrastructure built up over the century between the presidencies of Abraham Lincoln and John F. Kennedy is liquidating assets at a startling pace. Abuse cases alone do not explain the "national fire sale" of bishops selling churches, to quote a notable critic, Peter Borré.

Since 1995 the bishops have closed 1,373 churches—more than one parish per week for fifteen years. As new parishes go up in suburbs, many old enclaves of Irish, Italian, and East European immigrants turn into ghettos.[18] As the European ethnics found more affluent environs, poor people of color moved into streets on a downward spiral. Cavernous churches face steep maintenance costs; parish schools are put to other uses. If a grim inevitability drives some church sales, few bishops relish abandoning at-risk neighborhoods where churches historically served as anchors for poor people in a hard struggle to keep afloat.

In every diocese, the parishes pay an assessment charge to the bishop, a fee of between 5 and 15 percent of the collection, based on revenue stream, operating costs, and ability to pay. Wealthier parishes pay more. The fee (which has a Latin name, *cathedraticum*) is a tax the parish pays the diocese. In this realm, the bishop is both tax collector and central banker. The diocese pools the assessment fees to earn interest; when a parish falls behind on payment, the bishop can charge interest for the late charges. He can devise ways for wealthier parishes to cover costs for poorer parishes. He can forgive poor parishes' assessment debts or charge interest until they are paid up. He can lend money to parishes for their projects at interest. He can send funds to other dioceses or foreign countries for causes he supports. The bishop also raises money for capital campaigns as suburbs expand or structures face renovation.

On becoming a bishop, a man—or his diocese—pays a fee to the Vatican called the *taxa*. "The amount varies according to the size of a diocese," explains Tom Doyle, a Dominican on leave from the priesthood who served as a canon lawyer at the Vatican embassy in the early 1980s. "I remember when Joe Bernardin of Chicago was made a cardinal, the *taxa* was $6,000. I thought Chicago got a good deal on that one."

These days, many dioceses have turned to the bond market to reconsolidate debt and for building projects. "Investors increasingly view the collection plate as a reliable source of cash flow," James Freeman wrote in the *Wall Street Journal*. "Church debt, which is increasingly packaged and sold as bond, has even offered sanctuary from otherwise turbulent credit markets."[19]

The bishop historically stands as a protector of immigrants and the poor, a role many hierarchs handle for the betterment of church and society. Cardinals are called Princes of the Church; each bishop functions as a prince of his own realm. In a monarchical power structure, money is a story of personality, how a given bishop tends to the infrastructure, funds, property, investments, social service programs, and parish life. But regardless of how they do the job, bishops are largely unaccountable for their decisions. The Vatican occasionally removes an incompetent bishop, but unless a hierarch speaks against dogma, he operates with little oversight. In the late 1990s Cardinal Anthony Bevilacqua of Philadelphia spent $5 million renovating an archdiocesan-owned vacation home on the New Jersey shore, his residence in Philadelphia, and three office buildings. Meanwhile, he closed fifteen inner-city parishes that had a combined deficit of $1.2 million. "Bevilacqua spent the approximately $5 million without making the expenditures public, bypassing his own advisers on some projects," wrote Ralph Cipriano in a *National Catholic Reporter* investigation.

> In one instance archdiocesan officials failed to notify city officials about renovations at archdiocesan headquarters, in violation of city law.
>
> In contrast to his public style, Bevilacqua is remote in his private life. He reportedly has lived alone in a 30-room, stone-clad Victorian villa that serves as the archbishop's official residence . . . with interior decorating, brass rails, Queen Anne chairs, gilt-edged mirrors, tasteful floral and pink draperies, pink brocade couches, poster beds with matching drapes and valances, brass chandeliers, brass sconces and polished stone statues of Italian greyhounds.[20]

People in the pews had no role in choosing Bevilacqua. The Vatican and other bishops did. Nor, as laypeople learned during Philadelphia's particularly harsh abuse crisis, could they remove him. Only the pope or a prosecutor could do that. The district attorney guided a lengthy investigation by a criminal grand jury in 2004–2005, which finally decided that Pennsylvania statutes did not support a prosecution of Bevilacqua for concealing pedophiles—the time frame was too far in the past. The 2005 grand jury report noted that the cardinal had a law degree: "What makes these actions all the worse, the grand jurors believe, is that the abuses that

Cardinal Bevilacqua and his aides allowed children to suffer—the molestations, the rapes, the lifelong shame and despair—did not result from failures or lapses, except of the moral variety. They were made possible by purposeful decisions, carefully implemented policies and calculated indifference."[21]

THE EMBEZZLEMENT DILEMMA

Catholics historically function in a culture of passivity, a mentality of pray, pay, obey that assumes that donations and decisions entrusted to ecclesial officials are executed for "the good of the church." That timeworn term is elastic with irony. As Catholics we know too little about how well, or poorly, bishops and religious leaders manage the money we give and the larger sphere of church assets. The world's largest organization is governed as a monarchy with no inherent structure for accountability, nor a true system of justice. Theft and embezzlements by American priests and lay workers account for substantial losses. Professor Charles E. Zech, an economist at Villanova University and director of the Center for the Study of Church Management, coauthored a report in which 85 percent of dioceses responding to the survey acknowledged having funds stolen. Eleven percent of the reported cases exceeded $500,000 in losses.[22]

In 2009, for example, a jury in West Palm Beach, Florida, convicted the Reverend Francis Guinan, age sixty-six, of grand theft after hearing testimony about how he took funds over many years from his parish, St. Vincent Ferrer. The judge sentenced Guinan to four years in prison. The assistant pastor, John Skehan, drew fourteen months after a guilty plea in which he promised to make $780,000 in restitution.[23] The two Irish-born clerics used church funds on expensive vacations, girlfriends, and lavish living. Dozens of cases of priests or lay workers who have stolen church funds have been reported in the American press. It is a problem that affects other denominations, too. In the reports on Catholic cases, one rarely reads of the priests being defrocked.

Consider Monsignor John Woolsey, an ousted pastor on Manhattan's Upper East Side who in 2006 agreed to a guilty plea of grand larceny for stealing more than $50,000 from parish funds. Prosecutors contended that Woolsey had stolen more than $800,000 in the previous seven years. The parish, Church of St. John the Martyr, sued its Travelers Crime Plus policy for denying its claim of $1.2 million in losses from Woolsey's theft. Woolsey spent a year in prison. Upon his release, a spokesman for the New York archdiocese said, "We will have to sit down with Msgr. Woolsey to discuss his future with him."[24]

Such news reports, and the Villanova study findings, did not surprise Michael W. Ryan, a retired U.S. Postal Inspection Service manager who for years conducted field audits to ensure the integrity of post offices' accounting systems. Across two decades, Ryan, a rock-ribbed Catholic and father of five, patiently wrote to bishops, cardinals, and the USCCB, proposing a plan to safeguard the collection plates. The bishops avoided him like the plague. Ryan's letters and the articles he has written can be accessed at www.churchsecurity.info.

"Assuming Sunday collection embezzlements are ongoing at 10 percent of the approximately 17,900 parishes at any given time," states Ryan, "the average parish loss falls somewhere in the neighborhood of $1,000 per week, or roughly $50,000 per year. That computes to an *annual* loss of about $90 million solely attributable to Sunday collection embezzlements." If one accepts Ryan's theory, it would mean that in roughly the same time span in which sex abuse cases cost the church $1.775 billion, the loss from embezzlement and theft by priests or lay staff was $2.16 billion.[25] Ryan's figures are raw estimates. Joseph Harris, who demands hard data, scoffs at them. But on this issue, Ryan has good company.

Leon Panetta, the Obama administration's CIA director (and President Clinton's former chief of staff), served from 2002 to 2004 on the National Review Board for the Protection of Children and Young People, composed of prominent lay Catholics who were chosen by the bishops' conference to research the abuse crisis and advise on reform procedures. Panetta has called for outside oversight of parish finances. "They've got to be able to move into the 21st century," he told USA Today, "and begin to apply some management practices that can help insure that they protect the trust of their parishioners."[26]

Terence McKiernan, a director of BishopAccountability.org, the library and online archive of the Catholic Church crisis, has tabulated intrachurch theft losses in press reports of sixty-nine cases, amounting to $38.5 million, based on indictments, convictions, and civil actions. In many reports, prosecutors allege a greater amount of embezzled funds. When those figures are added, the total leaps to $81.5 million. How much of that was recouped by insurance, and at what cost to premiums, we do not know. "Reported losses," says McKiernan, "are a fraction of the total. We're dealing with an unaudited, cash-based system. The great majority of theft goes unreported in parishes, dioceses, and institutions run by religious orders. The same organizational problems that make theft possible in the first place make it difficult to detect. The general terms of the Villanova study show from another perspective that it is impossible to count the funds embezzled each year."

"The complex that bishops have as *the* authority is that no one can give them constructive criticism," explains Mike Ryan. "I think the primary reason they refuse to accept and act on the need to safeguard Sunday collection funds is that they were pastors, back when, and they know that all hell will break loose if they change the present system where Father has access to a little 'walking around money' before the funds are deposited in the bank."

"Many priests and parishioners would not consider 'walking around money' to be theft," adds McKiernan. As Ryan points out, if funds are accurately deposited, a priest can write checks to cash. The parish finance council will monitor the accounts, with special focus on the cash account. The weekly collection should always be counted in the presence of two people with the total collection matching the amount that is deposited in the bank and shown on the deposit slip. For many years the bishops claimed that they could not impose binding standards for the removal of child molesters because every bishop was autonomous. They changed their position in 2002, adopting a youth protection charter. The same could be done with a policy to safeguard the collection plates. Were that to happen, argues Ryan, dioceses would see a surge of income. Alternatively, as McKiernan states, "losses can go unnoticed for decades."

When the losses spotlighted in the BishopAccountability.org database are weighed against the financial management of religious order provinces, the situation is more serious. In Philadelphia, a religious order's finances were as vulnerable to theft as those of a diocese. The Reverend Charles Newman, OFM, was charged by a county grand jury in 2007 of taking by theft and forgery a total of $1,033,748 from Archbishop Ryan High School (where he was teacher, principal, and finally president) and from his Franciscan order. Newman was accused of using some of the funds to groom and bribe a boy he sexually abused. The youth later died of a drug overdose. Newman pleaded guilty on the finance charge and in 2009 drew a sentence of three to six years in prison.[27]

FINANCIAL ACCOUNTABILITY

In a 1985 survey of empirical data, Andrew M. Greeley found that Catholics donated on average $320 per year to the church as opposed to $580 by Protestants. "The decline in Catholic contributions over the last quarter century is the result of a failure in leadership and an alienation of membership," noted Father Greeley, an esteemed sociologist, "not from the Catholic community or from sacramental participation but from support of the ecclesiastical institution."[28] In the quarter century since that survey, the alienation of Catholics from church leadership has worsened. A 1994 study found that the church lost $1.96 billion a year from "low giving"—what the bishops "could collect annually if Catholics gave at the average rate of all Americans" of other faiths.[29] In a 2000 study provocatively titled *Why Catholics Don't Give . . . and What Can Be Done About It*, Professor Charles Zech of Villanova assessed survey data in concluding that Catholics "felt they did not have sufficient influence in Church decision-making, lacked information on how Church funds were spent, and didn't think denominational leaders were accountable on how contributions were used."[30]

As custodians of a religious charity the bishops are under no obligation to produce profit and loss statements for stockholders or the IRS. The distinction mattered little until the battering that many prelates took in the media coverage of the abuse crisis and the spotlight on legal settlements, which raise questions about the use of donations for religious causes. In a shift toward transparency, many bishops now post diocesan financial statements on their Web sites. Jack Ruhl, a professor of accountancy and associate dean of Haworth College of Business at Western Michigan University, has done sustained research on Catholic Church financial disclosures. Ruhl reports:

> Of 194 dioceses and archdioceses, about 115 have audited or reviewed financial statements available online. Of the others, 39 do not release financial statements to the public. At 12 dioceses, you must make a written appeal to the chief financial officer and if he or she thinks your request is worth granting, they will grant it.

Another 28 dioceses publish some sort of financial report, which is different from financial statements, and which may or may not be audited. Only 5 of the 115 audited statements include parishes. The remaining 110 are primarily just the administrative offices. If the audited financials are just for the administrative offices, and not the parishes, those financials are almost worthless to someone who wants to understand the financial state of a diocese.

The highest level of assurance is provided by a full set of financial statements that have been audited by a public accounting firm.

A CPA firm will not provide an audit report without all of the figures for a statement. Ruhl credits the Archdioceses of Boston and Los Angeles and the Kalamazoo, Michigan, diocese for posting audited statements:

> A review is substantially less in scope than an audit. That's how the Chicago Archdiocese releases information.
>
> No assurance is provided by financial statements that have been compiled by a CPA firm. A compilation just requires the CPA to look for obvious errors. An example is the Archdiocese of New Orleans. The numbers may or may not even be close. There is not a full set of financial statements, nor are there notes to the financial statement.
>
> Atlanta, Austin, Arlington, and Anchorage have audited statements, but none includes parishes in the accounting entity. Austin states that its parishes and other agencies have been separately incorporated. I would be very certain that they have been separately incorporated as a shield from abuse settlements. Anchorage's statements are "special purpose," not prepared in accordance with generally accepted accounting principles.
>
> Finally, there are financial statements that are not even accompanied by a compilation report. Somebody has just put some numbers together. An example of that is the Archdiocese of Philadelphia.[31]

The church faces a major challenge in the retirement and elder care needs of priests and nuns, many of whom never paid into Social Security.

The Archdiocese of Los Angeles had a $98 million shortfall for clergy pension and retirement as of 2009. The Chicago archdiocese was short $103 million for these needs in 2010; the Boston archdiocese was short $104 million. This funding crisis for priests and nuns stems only in part from the loss of investment revenues in the Great Recession. Abuse litigation is a huge cost. So is a downturn in giving by people who leave the church, distrust bishops, or have been strained by the recession. In 2003 religious orders of men and women faced unfunded retirement costs of $8.7 million. Of 573 religious communities providing data to researchers, 38 were adequately funded for retirement.[32]

These are aching realities in light of the paramount role of religious sisters in developing a Catholic system of schools, hospitals, and orphanages. Today, that infrastructure has an impact well beyond the faithful. Catholic schools educate many inner-city youngsters from non-Catholic families. The church's commitment to the poor, immigrants, and people on the margins is enmeshed with U.S. social policy. Catholic Charities USA was a leader in helping Vietnamese refugees relocate in America in the late 1970s and in assisting Gulf Coast families who were thrown into an economic free-fall by the BP oil spill in 2010. The Reverend Fred Kammer, a Jesuit and former president of Catholic Charities USA, explains, "In the United States, the Roman Catholic Church runs the largest private school system, the largest private health care system, and the largest private social service system. We built parallel systems that were dependent almost entirely on religious"—meaning priests and nuns in religious orders, not diocesan clergy. "And those three systems are all now predominantly staffed by lay people. They serve lay people and non-Catholics. Now one can say this is 'a shortage of priests' if you look at it negatively. Or it's the era of the post–Vatican II church and the emergence of the Catholic lay person and the realization that baptism calls you to ministry. It's reality."[33]

Catholic Charities USA had a $3.8 billion budget in 2007. Forty percent of that came from state and local governments, and 11 percent from federal grants. More than $440 million was for programs assisting needy children and families, including foster and residential care.[34] Catholic Charities in each diocese functions with its own budget, programs, and fund-raising. Overall, Catholic Charities has more than 50,000 employees and 250,000 volunteers providing services that are integral to the nation's social safety net.

THE VATICAN

The Holy See issues a financial statement each July; however, it is not a clear picture of assets and worth. The two main categories are the Vatican city-state and the Apostolic Patrimony. The city-state revenues come from real estate, museums, gift shops, stamps, and coins. Apostolic Patrimony is the administration, or the Curia; it governs the 120 diplomatic missions, a publishing house, Vatican Radio, and the daily *L'Osservatore Romano*. The city-state revenues typically offset costs of Apostolic Patrimony. In 2006 the Vatican operating statement showed a surplus of $3.2 million, despite a loss of $9.5 million in the value of the euro against the dollar. "Most donations to the Vatican and some of its investments are in dollars, yet the Vatican's expenses are mainly in euros," reported Catholic News Service.[35] But the Holy See has a major asset omitted from its financial statement: the Vatican Bank.

In 1984 the Vatican Bank agreed to pay $242 million to three creditor banks as compensation for its role in assisting the money-laundering scheme of Roberto Calvi's Banco Ambrosiano, which collapsed under $1.2 billion in debts. The Vatican Bank is traditionally "off the books," a black hole in the Holy See financial statements. The Holy See's true net worth is invisible. Subtract liabilities from understated assets and you have an illusory bottom line. Nevertheless, the Holy See's 2007 balance sheet valued its total assets at 1.4 billion euros, or about 2.05 billion U.S. dollars. The statement showed the bulk of the Holy See's income from rental properties in Europe. "The net worth is small for a national government," comments Jack Ruhl. "But this is a gross understatement because they're listing the value of St. Peter's Basilica and other historic buildings at 1 euro each ($1.47)."

One asset stood out from the report: gold. "The Holy See owns almost a [metric] tonne of gold which in today's volatile market would be worth some £15 million," wrote Robert Mickens, Rome correspondent for *The Tablet*, England's independent Catholic magazine, in 2008.[36] "I have never seen gold as a separate line item on any financial statement," comments Ruhl. "People tend to speculate, rather than invest, in gold, because the gold market is a yo-yo. Still, given the undervalued assets, we can't tell how much the Holy See is worth." The Vatican city-state and Apostolic Patrimony appear to be comfortably secured, but the secret profits from the Vatican Bank obscure any real "transparency" by the Holy See.

Meanwhile, eight American dioceses, and the Northwestern province of the Society of Jesus, which includes Alaska, have tried bankruptcy filings to reduce what they would have to pay in lawsuits to abuse victims. As the reports on bankruptcy filings and the impact of civil litigation roll across the media screens, people wonder how a church so powerful could lose nearly $4 billion (embezzlements included) since 1965. The same bishops who recycled sex offenders have avoided a binding policy to secure Sunday collections. Church apologists say the huge settlements are unfair, but the Vatican's failure to regulate bishops stems from a flawed system of justice.

Corruption in the church is a reality as the wheel of history turns. Democracy has its history of nightmares too. The resilience of the church as a spiritual reality has produced a continuing force of pastoral care, relief work, and vital forms of assistance to the truly needy. "Look at what the church has done for direct services to AIDS victims in Africa, and disaster relief in Haiti and many countries as a first responder," explains Sister Christine Schenk, a nurse-midwife with a long history of social activism in Cleveland. A pivotal figure in the latter part of this book, Sister Schenk continues: "The church is one of the few transnational entities that connects religious people to something that's *not* about making a profit—helping the poor, educating and feeding people, healing the sick through health services by missionaries. You don't see much about this on the nightly news, but these are daily acts of witness in Christ's name. The church has a communications network to reach many of the world's dispossessed, people on the outer edge. This is not like Microsoft. It is going where Jesus calls. As crazy as the Vatican monarchical system can be with its top-down political model, the Catholic network of genuine service providers has a global reach to the needy, a real record of doing good in the world."

The sacramental imagination, and an ethos of responsibility to those on the outer edge, gives many of us who are appalled by the scandals of church officialdom some cause to keep faith. Saint Augustine called justice a virtue that gives every one his due. Internal justice is what the church severely needs.

Render unto Rome follows a line of reporting I began in *Lead Us Not into Temptation* (1992), a book that took seven years of research and exposed the contours of a national scandal. At the time, the scattered abuse cases available from Boston and Los Angeles persuaded me that if the internal documents of those archdioceses were ever released, a secret history of epic corruption would surface. Back then I doubted that such would ever happen. Journalists used my calculation of $400 million in losses from legal and medical costs for four hundred priests in covering the early phase of the crisis. The impact of the *Boston Globe* reporting in 2002 signaled more than a new chapter in an old scandal. Under public pressure, the bishops' conference finally released data: 4,392 priests had abused youngsters between 1950 and 2002.[37]

In 2004 I published *Vows of Silence* with Gerald Renner, the longtime religion editor of the *Hartford Courant.* In that newspaper we first reported on the Vatican's failure to act on pedophilia allegations that trailed Father Marcial Maciel, the founder of the Legion of Christ. In 2008 I released a documentary film based on that book and updated research. Chapter 7 of this book goes deeper, exploring Maciel's financial odyssey as a mirror on Vatican justice.

Render unto Rome concludes an investigative trilogy on the crisis of the Catholic Church. Since my first reports in 1985 on a priest who traumatized the Cajun diocese of Lafayette, Louisiana, I have followed an intervening path of cultural productions, jazz history, and a novel— works that draw a bead on life's uplifting mysteries, particularly in my flood-resurrected hometown of New Orleans. These pursuits, I confess, have imbued me with a certain optimism about the human experiment. This cast of mind was a source of some amusement to Gerald Renner, who shares in the dedication of this book. Jerry died of cancer in 2007, at seventy-six. I thought of him often in this current round of work. He was a reporter of rock-solid integrity; he also savored good bourbon. He had a grand Irish heart and was one of the finest men I have known.

CHAPTER 1

BOSTON IN THE FAULT LINES

Peter Borré was midway past sixty, and like most men who find domestic harmony, he had learned that women are usually right. This knowledge, gathered slowly, had taught him that it was useless to argue over certain realities.

The condo he and his wife shared in the old Naval Shipyard overlooked sailboat slips nestled by a pier off Boston Harbor. The view extended to a grand sweep of the city skyline. During World War II, forty thousand men had built destroyers in the vast complex; now, as with many industrial zones of urban America, a large part of the shipyard had become an upscale housing project. On the walls of their home hung color photographs his wife, Mary Beth, had taken of flowers in Finland, carved doors in Marrakech, an arched footbridge in Tahiti—pictures from their travels.

Borré had made his money in oil and gas, developing facilities to generate power and regional grids. He had a holding company for energy ventures. In the 1980s Borré had worked for Mobil on natural gas projects in West Africa and on marketing in Europe. Before that he had worked in government, starting in 1973 as an intelligence officer in the Energy Agency of the Nixon administration, advancing to assistant secretary for international affairs as Energy achieved department status under Jimmy

Carter, capped by a year under Ronald Reagan. But all the geopolitical experiences and business savvy had left him without leverage to engage his wife, a Democratic Party activist, about her spiritual life.

And so on Sundays, while Mary Beth watched *Meet the Press*, Peter Borré went to Mass with his mother-in-law, Rosie. Mary Beth had left the church well before the *Boston Globe* began its 2002 investigation of how Cardinal Bernard F. Law and a clutch of his auxiliary bishops recycled child-molester priests. The *Globe* ignited a chain reaction of media coverage in America that radiated to other countries, causing a crisis for which a frail and ailing John Paul II was in no way prepared. By winter of 2004, the media narrative on bishops concealing clergy predators began receding. The big story shifted to the Democratic presidential primaries, and a media frenzy over Mel Gibson's movie *The Passion of the Christ*. Mary Beth Borré, forty-nine, had worked as a field organizer in Bill Clinton's 1996 reelection. She had no interest in the front-runner, Senator John Kerry of Massachusetts. She had once worked on Kerry's annual fund-raiser, held on his birthday, which struck her as an act of outsized ego. Although addicted to news coverage, Mary Beth had tired of campaign work. In Boston, the "epicenter" of the abuse scandal, the church faced financial convulsions.

Mary Beth and her sister, Claudia, had settled their dad, Bill Piper, into a nursing home near Claudia's house in Winchester. After bouts of depression as the girls grew up, he was diagnosed with Parkinson's disease, then dementia, in retirement. Mary Beth's brothers, living in Delaware and California, had drifted from the church, and Claudia was a Unitarian. Mary Beth attended Mass once a year with her mother, at Christmas, as a gesture of continuity. She considered herself a spiritual person but despised organized religion.

Rosie lived with Mary Beth and Peter at the condo for six months while searching for a new home in greater Boston. After she found a place near Claudia's and the nursing home, Bill insisted on moving back in with Rosie.

Peter was seventeen years older than Mary Beth. Watching his response to the *Globe*'s coverage, she decided that his rarefied upbringing as an American in Rome, without exposure to nuns, had made Peter an Italian Catholic. He had an aesthetic idea of Catholicism in contrast to her more puritanical encounter with faith. Born in 1955, she was a high school senior in Hockessin, Delaware, when the Supreme Court's *Roe v. Wade* decision legalized abortion. Inspired by Gloria Steinem and Germaine Greer, Mary Beth Piper, the ripening feminist, gritted her teeth at the elderly pastor's sermons against abortion. Later, she realized that a younger priest in the parish rectory who had dyed blond hair and vestments that sported lightning bolts (sewn by his mother) was going through his own drama with the closet. At the time she was galvanized by the social changes running every night on TV news, the protests for civil rights, feminism, gay liberation, and against the Vietnam War. She bridled at religion classes about mysteries and the afterlife. She wanted to make sense of this life, now. The right to choose an abortion made sense to her and caused friction with her mother. They clashed when she tried leaving the house without a bra. "Mary Beth went from being a stick figure to an attractive girl who was well endowed," recalled Rosie, who was fourth-generation Irish from New York and had her standards. Bill, a Presbyterian, was a more detached dad, a bit of the soft touch. The distance Mary Beth felt from the church widened in college as she got to know gay people.

The abuse scandal darkened Peter Borré's thought field, presaging a slow shift in his views. When the early 2002 reports in the *Globe* uncovered Law's mishandling of one priest, then others, Borré fumed about "a few bad apples."

"It's about time," retorted Mary Beth.

Borré listened as she recalled the late 1980s, the early years of their marriage, when he had been traveling on business and she worked in an AIDS crisis program as the epidemic hit Boston. While counseling victims of the retrovirus, Mary Beth Borré heard stories of priests who shunned those seeking solace. She knew that for all of its hard-line stance on homosexuality, the church had a large closet of gay priests. Some of them were trying to help AIDS victims, but others held back, avoiding any involvement. She also heard from men with the virus who said that they were abused by priests as teenage boys. Many of her colleagues were ex-Catholics and ex-Jews, divorced from church or synagogue; they joked with one another about religious guilt as they followed a deep Judeo-Christian impulse to help people dying of the mysterious disease.

Fourteen years later, when Cardinal Law's world exploded in a scandal of covering up abusive priests, Mary Beth Borré figured he had it coming. As the scandal became the topic of everybody's conversation, Peter

Borré registered his wife's surgical insights and brooded about the church internal.

On September 18, 2002, the plaintiff attorney Mitchell Garabedian and his associate William H. Gordon secured a $10 million settlement for eighty-six victims of one priest, John Geoghan.[1] As the press coverage made reference to an earlier line of legal actions, Borré wondered how much the archdiocese had paid to settle claims in the late 1990s that were handled by Garabedian, and by a high-profile attorney at another firm, Roderick MacLeish Jr. (a grandson of the poet Archibald MacLeish). The attorneys had resolved cases for some seventy victims out of court, but with stipulations by the archdiocese that muzzled the survivors—the agreements sealed church documents from public view. Still, with so many cases, information surfaced in legal filings that drew the scrutiny of Kristen Lombardi in the weekly *Boston Phoenix*. Lawyers for the *Globe* asked the court for access to documents. Overruling church lawyers, Judge Constance Sweeney granted the request, which opened the gates for an epic investigation in 2002.[2]

Globe reporters excavated a criminal sexual underground involving dozens of clerics, based on the church personnel files surrendered to the subpoena demands by victims' lawyers. The media narrative seemed to crest when Cardinal Law resigned as archbishop shortly before Christmas in 2002.

But events charged on in a high-stakes legal war. On September 9, 2003, the church pulled back from a threatened bankruptcy filing to embrace an $85 million settlement with 542 victims. Law was down in Maryland, living with a community of nuns. "The agreement marked the dramatic conclusion to Archbishop Seán P. O'Malley's all-out push in his first weeks in Boston to bring closure to the abuse cases," the *Globe* reported.[3]

Seán O'Malley, a Capuchin monk with a snowy beard, was fifty-nine and the bishop of Palm Beach, Florida, when he received the papal appointment as Boston's archbishop. Wearing sandals and a brown robe with a rope belt, O'Malley cut an image quite the opposite of Law's imperial persona. No one blamed O'Malley for the crisis, but donations had plummeted by 43 percent in the preceding year, from $14 million to $8 million in 2003.[4] O'Malley faced huge barriers to restoring trust—and cash flow. In a letter issued on January 9, 2004, O'Malley announced that one-seventh of the archdiocesan buildings needed upgrading, a cost pegged at $104 million. The church had to assess its properties and streamline workings of the infrastructure. On February 2, 2004, O'Malley in a speech on the archdiocesan TV station revealed that the church faced a $4 million operating deficit and a $37 million loan from the Knights of Columbus to be repaid: "This has nothing to do with paying for abuse settlements, but has everything to do with providing vital services."

Nothing to do with abuse settlements, Borré repeated to himself.

Two months later, the Red Sox had wrapped up spring training when O'Malley approved the sale of the mansion on a hill in Brighton where Law had lived like a lord, with a staff trained to call him "Your Eminence." The cost for the cardinal's estate and forty-three acres: $107.4 million. The buyer was the neighbor across Commonwealth Avenue: Boston College, a pearl in the crown of Jesuit higher education.[5] By virtue of the size of its student body and faculty, and the scope of its graduate programs, BC should have been called a university, but BU had gotten there first. Nevertheless, in a city synonymous with Irish Catholicism, Boston College had a force of loyal alumni (many of them with Italian and Portuguese roots) who had produced an endowment that exceeded $1 billion. To Catholics outraged by Law's reshuffling of predators, selling the mansion carried symbolic weight. The palazzo of the cardinal who had resigned his archbishopric in shame joined the infrastructure of a Jesuit college that stood for a church with intellectual moorings and a focus on social justice.

Seasoned in the ways of oil companies, Peter Borré began thinking about an archbishop in the role of a CEO. If forced to do butcher's work, the prelate must be adroit enough to avoid spattering blood on the floor. Red ink was rising around Archbishop O'Malley. Following the news accounts, Borré knew the archdiocese was holding back information. His mind raced. *Where did the money go? What is O'Malley's plan? Is he leveling with us? How bad is it?*

Those questions might have hung in some cerebral side pocket, throwing cold shadows on his golden years until the day Peter Borré, the very opposite of a radical, got mad at a priest. When that happened, Mary Beth, who had wondered how her husband, with his complex molecular composition, might occupy himself in retirement, saw the swell of dark, silent anger and knew immediately they were in for a ride. Peter Borré was not a man to yell, yet she knew that despite his elegant manner, he was just the kind of Italian who would fight.

FAMILY VALUES

Mary Beth married her college sweetheart in 1976 at a guitar Mass. "It probably didn't seem like a concession to our families," she said, sighing, decades later. "If we'd only been a little older, when society accepted people living together, the relationship might have ended with a lot less anguish. I was surprised when my mom actually said that to me much later on." They divorced after four years—no children. Mary Beth was done with the church, done with religion. Too many of the moral teachings struck her as invasive, politics of the body, insensitive to ordinary people as they sought intimacy in life. She earned a B.S. in marketing at the University of Delaware.

In 1986 she was working for an oil company in Houston when friends introduced her to Peter, who was in town on a business trip. With dark hair going silver at the curls, a charming wit, and a razor-sharp mind, he made an immediate impression. He had three children from his first marriage, which had ended several years before. When Mary Beth told her mother she was taking a trip to Paris with her new (forty-eight-year-old) boyfriend, Rosie caught a train to New York to meet the man. She took note of his flawless manners and the silken gesture of slipping cash into the palm of her cabdriver.

He proposed after three months.

They married in 1987 at the Harvard Club in Boston.

Despite the French surname, Borré's forebears were Italian. His paternal grandfather, Agostino, was born in 1871, the year after nationalists captured territories long controlled by the papacy. In the convulsions of Italian statehood, Giuseppe Agostino Borré emigrated from Zerba, a mountain village in Piacenza province, north of Genoa, "at the urging of his brother Ernesto, who had come in 1882. Both came at about age nineteen and became chefs," explains Marie Roth, a cousin who researched the family lineage.[6] His maternal grandfather, Giuseppe Balboni, came from a village in Emilia in the Po Valley. Starting out as a pushcart peddler of fruit and vegetables, he ended up with a grocery store.

Born in Boston in 1938, Peter was a boy when his father, Peter senior, a lawyer and an army veteran, hired on for an American rebuilding project in Italy, in advance of the Marshall Plan. In August 1946 the family moved to Rome. Boxes bearing the remains of U.S. soldiers were stacked at the airport awaiting shipment home. The boy asked about the boxes.

His father answered, gently telling him about the war. His mother, Mary Albina, had completed a teaching degree and then gone to Harvard, earning a master's in English. She befriended the aging philosopher George Santayana (who famously said, "Those who cannot remember the past are condemned to repeat it") during his sunset years in Rome.

The bishops, monsignors, and priests who came to dinner were cultivated men whose intelligence impressed the boy. One visitor, Auxiliary Bishop John Wright from Boston, was a large, heavy man who enjoyed his wine and the discussions of American politics, Italian politics, and Vatican politics. Wright later became a cardinal at the Vatican and prefect of the Congregation for the Clergy.

Postwar Italy was a bleeding chaos of embedded Fascists, the largest Communist Party in Western Europe backed by Soviet Russia, a resurgent mafia in the south, and the Christian Democrats, a party supported by Pope Pius XII. The leader of the Christian Democrats, Alcide De Gasperi, had been an outspoken anti-Fascist before the war; he was imprisoned by Mussolini in 1927 and released to the custody of the previous pope, Pius XI, in 1929. De Gasperi spent the next fifteen years basically living in the Vatican Library. "Catholic, Italian and democratic, in that order" was his motto.[7] In 1945, as one of the first postwar prime ministers, he led a church-sponsored party with little organization apart from Catholic Action, a movement that Pius X had launched in 1905 to unite lay activism and the hierarchy's agenda. The little social cohesion left in postwar Italy lay with the 65,000 parish priests serving 24,000 parishes in 300 dioceses. Another 200,000 religious order priests and nuns staffed schools, hospitals, and charitable organizations.[8] As De Gasperi guided the Christian Democrats through three governments in as many years, dozens of parties were vying for power. The Truman administration braced for Italy's 1948 elections. "The American intervention in Italy was large and well-coordinated, very much the work of an 'efficient machine,'" wrote U.S. intelligence historian Thomas Powers.[9] "Cash, lots of it, would be needed to help defeat the communists," observed journalist Tim Weiner in a history of the CIA[10]—an estimated $10 million, according to the CIA station chief in Rome. Thus, Secretary of the Treasury John Snyder decided

to tap into the Exchange Stabilization Fund set up in the Depression to shore up the value of the dollar overseas through short-term currency trading, and converted during World War II as a depository for captured Axis loot. The fund held $200 million earmarked for the reconstruction of Europe. It delivered millions into the bank accounts of wealthy American citizens, many of them Italian Americans, who then sent the money to newly formed political fronts created by the CIA. Donors were instructed to place a special code on their income tax forms alongside their "charitable donation." The millions were delivered to Italian politicians and priests of Catholic Action, a political arm of the Vatican.[11]

Between the CIA and U.S. relief projects, America poured $350 million into Italy during the twelve months before the April 18, 1948, election. The Vatican Bank, which was founded in 1942 under Pius XII to consolidate the Holy See's finances during the worst of World War II, became a conduit for funds to the Christian Democrats. Pius "provided 100 million lire [$185,000] from his personal bank," writes John Cornwell, "a sum of money apparently raised from the sale of U.S. war matériel and earmarked for the Vatican to spend on anti-Communist activities."[12] The 1948 parliamentary elections were the first under Italy's postwar constitution since the fall of Fascism.

"The fate of Italy depends upon the forthcoming election and the conflict between Communism and Christianity, between slavery and freedom," declared Cardinal Francis J. Spellman of New York. On Vatican orders, Spellman entreated Italian Americans to write to relatives in the old country. Spellman, Gary Cooper, Bing Crosby, and the golden boy Frank Sinatra made radio broadcasts for De Gasperi's party.[13] The Vatican pulled out all the stops, "even to the extent of swinging open the doors of convents and marching cloistered nuns off to the polling places to vote for Christian Democrat candidates," reported journalist Nino Lo Bello.[14] The Christian Democrats won by a heavy margin in an election that also secured the party's narcotic dependency on CIA money. "The CIA's practice of purchasing elections and politicians with bags of cash was repeated in Italy—and in many other nations—for the next twenty-five years," writes Weiner.[15]

At the soirees that the Borrés hosted or attended, U.S. diplomats,

Italian politicians, and businessmen mingled with Vatican officials, bankers, and film directors. Peter, a pampered only child, grew up in that milieu.

Mussolini had given heavy state support to the 1930s Italian film industry. The dictator considered movies a powerful tool and ordered the production of proto-Fascist films for his propaganda machinery as he moved toward an alliance with Hitler.[16] After the war, as American dollars rolled into Rome, Borré père did legal work for MGM and other American studios lured by the cheap production costs and solid studio infrastructure Il Duce had built. The CIA encouraged American studios to distribute films in Western Europe as a counter to Communist politics. As American producers became flush with lire, Italian law barred them from taking the funds out of local banks for conversion into dollars. With a mountain of money that the Americans had to spend locally, Italy's postwar film industry rebounded as a Hollywood-on-the-Tiber. Charlton Heston won the 1959 Best Actor Oscar for *Ben-Hur*, and Peter Borré, who had just graduated from Harvard, earned lire as an Italian-English interpreter and gofer on the film's set.

The month after he had first arrived in Italy, seven-year-old Peter was enrolled in Rome's most prestigious Jesuit school, Istituto Massimo. The alumni included Pope Pius XII. Peter admired the teachers for their strong-minded sermons and lectures, vaunting Rome as the capital of the Catholic Church, emphasizing each man's responsibility to further the faith. The Jesuits stressed classical learning with a rigor that seems punishing by today's standards. The six-day-a-week schedule began with Mass at 7 a.m. and ran until 2:30 in the afternoon. Lunch was thirty minutes. In third grade he was speaking good Italian, studying Latin and algebra; in fifth grade he added Greek and French.

The school was in central Rome, near Piazza della Repubblica and Santa Maria degli Angeli (St. Mary of the Angels), a vast church begun in 1563 by Michelangelo within the ruins of the ancient baths built by Emperor Diocletian. Brown earth tones colored the shell, which opened into an interior of immense vaulted ceilings and light streams that washed the gigantic columns and multicolored marble floors. When Peter made occasional stops on silent afternoons, watching the people as they knelt in prayer, he drew a notion from the sheer size of the space, fortified by his school lessons, of his soul as a small but unique presence in the firmament.

On trips to St. Peter's Basilica he felt sorrow at Michelangelo's *Pietà*, the statue of Mary in grief for the Son come down from the cross. Here was faith, close and true.

He was fourteen when his father, though pleased with his academic skills and fluency in foreign languages, worried that he could barely write in English. And so his parents sent him back to New England for prep school.

The first Mass Borré attended in the town of Andover appalled him. The church reminded him of some garish county fair; the priest so stressed the importance of contributing money as to seem a bumpkin. The beauty and size of Rome's sacred spaces, inspiring his awe for a global faith, stood out in high relief from what he now took to be a religious backwater. He entered Harvard College at age sixteen. The disgruntlement over Boston Catholicism lingered through his undergraduate years; he was bored by sermons with all the Irish baggage that showed in the working-class people who heeded them and the homilies telling the faithful that they must pray, make confession, *follow the rules,* and give money. Borré's idea of faith looked back on the urbane clerics at his parents' dinners, the Jesuits with their emphasis on analytical thinking and a sacramental imagination shaped by the soaring beauty of Italian church interiors.

He was too young to appreciate the mystery of Jesus, a radical who scorned the powerful and embraced the outcasts of society, or to understand how spirituality matures through suffering, prayer, and ritual memory.

He felt as if he were living in a foreign country, and, of course, he was.

THE NEIGHBORHOOD

Many years after establishing his career in the energy industry, and residing for long periods in Washington, D.C., and New York City, Peter Borré had come to enjoy the life he and Mary Beth made in Boston.

Charlestown covers one square mile of a hilly peninsula cradled by the Mystic River on the north and the Charles on the southeastern side; the rivers converge at Boston Inner Harbor. The Borrés' condo looked out on the steel bridge that links Boston's North End to a neighborhood unusually rich in history.

In 1630, ten years after the first pilgrims reached Cape Cod, a brig carrying Puritans sailed out of England. John Winthrop, in a famous shipboard sermon, urged his followers to pull together in "patience, and liberty . . . [so] that we shall be as a city upon a hill."[17] Henry VIII's break with Rome had launched a state church from which Winthrop's followers soon split. They saw the pope as an anti-Christ and came to view Church of England liturgies as too much like the Mass.[18] Winthrop's people became separatists who spurned any official faith. Charlestown, briefly, was the capital of the infant colony, but Winthrop's idealized city gave way to a Bible Commonwealth as people settled across the Charles along the larger landmass girded by water. Roads followed farms, and villages mushroomed into the townships of a New England society bound by the Puritan covenant. The Congregational churches they fostered would each govern its own affairs, each choose its own pastor and spare interiors shorn of stained-glass windows and icons.[19]

The Massachusetts Bay Colony hatched its own pressures for conformity that sparked hysteria and executions in the Salem witch trials. Mid-seventeenth-century Charlestown "was breaking out of such isolation, becoming a trading center for the region," writes J. Anthony Lukas. "The less it resembled Winthrop's model, the more seductive became the memory of that archetypal New England town, harmonious, consensual, cemented by a single faith and devotion to a common cause."[20] On April 18, 1775, Paul Revere galloped through Charlestown to warn of the British troops advancing on Lexington. In the ensuing battle—the first in the War for Independence—Charlestown and Roxbury, which lay across the river to the south, formed a dual front. Fifteen thousand colonists took arms against five thousand soldiers for the Crown. At Bunker Hill the colonists lost 138 troops to 226 British dead. Most of Charlestown went down in flames. Yet in 1810 Charlestown had nearly five thousand people and was the state's third-largest town when the national navy opened a harbor shipyard. Builders began crafting vessels out of felled trees. In time, Charlestown became a neighborhood of Boston through annexation.

Compared with its seventeenth-century mission to California, the Catholic Church came late to Massachusetts. In the 1790s two French priests began proselytizing among pockets of Irish settlers and in the Indian villages of Maine, where earlier Canadian clerics had visited. Boston's first Catholic Church was built in 1803, a parish of mostly Irish surnames; the construction funds drew Protestant support, notably a $100 donation from former president John Adams. He had sent a consul to Rome, establishing a relationship with the Holy See short of full diplomatic ties. Boston's first bishop, a Frenchman, came in 1808.

A generation later, the bedraggled people who stepped off swollen ships from Ireland planted fear in the mind of Boston's fading homogeneous society. Bunched into shanties, clapboard houses, and brick tenements on back streets, the Irish scraped along the margins. In the late summer of 1825, local hooligans rampaged through Irish warrens, shattering windows, smashing furniture, driving the *Boston Advertiser* to decry "disgraceful riots." Charlestown drew its stability from the shipyard and Protestant artisans, merchants, and farmers. In October 1828 Catholics paraded behind a robed bishop to lay the cornerstone for a church. In 1830 people from Ireland numbered 8,000 in a city of 61,392.[21] Irish rowdies cavorted and fought near the docks.

In 1834 a nun wandered out of Charlestown's large Ursuline convent, where sixty young ladies studied under a dozen Parisian-trained Irish sisters. In a state of mental collapse, the woman ended up at her brother's house; she returned to the convent apparently of her own accord. As gossip coiled through the town, a Congregationalist minister named Lyman Beecher whipped up emotions already fed by lurid newspaper stories of the "kidnapped" girl in the nunnery. He accused the pope of wanting to colonize the Mississippi Valley. Town selectmen marched to the convent, demanding entry to investigate; a mob overran them, drove out the women, and set the place on fire. As the convent burned down, drunks fed a bonfire with books and furniture, dancing about in nuns' habits. Boston Protestants expressed outrage, but few rioters were arrested. A sham trial ended with no one convicted. In 1836 another mob torched most of the Irish neighborhoods. Violence ripped through Irish ghettos of New York, Philadelphia, and Detroit as roiling nativist fears targeted people who had fled deep hardship back home.[22]

A fungus that ravaged Ireland's large potato crop led to mass starvation and a diaspora of 3 million people between 1845 and 1870.[23] Thirty-nine percent of people born in Ireland no longer lived there by 1890; most of the emigrants fled to Britain, North America, or Australia. In the decade after 1846, ships bearing 130,000 Irish arrived at Boston. "Our country is literally being overrun with the miserable, vicious and unclean paupers of the old country," the *Bunker Hill Aurora* railed in 1848. As the Irish crept up from harbor streets toward triple-decker apartments on Bunker Hill, Protestants were moving back toward Somerville or across the bridge into Greater Boston. In 1880 the archbishop began a system of Catholic schools for Boston.[24] As Charlestown became heavily Irish, Boston's Italian population doubled, between 1881 and 1886, to 220,000. When Peter Borré's grandparents put down stakes in the 1880s, the Irish outnumbered the Italians three to one. Charlestown in the early 1900s was still heavily Irish.

Boston in the late 1930s used federal funds to build a housing project close to the Mystic River in Charlestown. The demolitions phase burdened St. Catherine of Siena's pastor with the task of "reconstructing a parish which was depopulated and nearly obliterated," according to a parish history. "On his shoulders came all the misery and distress of seeing hundreds of his faithful parishioners forced to leave their homes and dispersed throughout greater Boston."[25]

Charlestown after World War II was still largely Irish and working class. A culture of young Townies clashed with the cops and gangs from other neighborhoods. Charlestown lay in a congressional district that in 1946 drew twenty-nine-year-old John F. Kennedy as a candidate; handsome and rich, he lived in a fine hotel on Beacon Street. Kennedy downplayed his patrician gloss by shaking hands after dawn with shipyard workers and climbing the stairs of triple-deckers to meet stay-at-home mothers, emphasizing his service in World War II. Kennedy presented a check for $650,000 on behalf of his family to Archbishop Richard Cushing for a hospital in Brighton to be named for his brother Joseph Kennedy, who had gone down in a plane in World War II.[26] JFK won over a large share of Townies in winning the election. In April 1961, he welcomed fellow members of the Bunker Hill Council of the Knights of Columbus to a reception on the White House lawn, where they thrilled at "jawing with *their* President."[27]

Cushing became a cardinal and legendary fund-raiser as Boston Catholics gained prosperity. By 1967 he had overseen $300 million in construction projects, which included three hundred elementary or high schools, plus eighty-six new parishes. His insurance plan for archdiocesan property "saved his parishes ten million dollars in twenty years," according to a biographer.[28] Cushing donated $200,000 to assist renovations of a church in the hometown of Pope John XXIII and $1 million to help build a Catholic university in Taiwan.

By the mideighties, when Bernard Law became cardinal, black and Latino families had arrived in a new wave of immigration; the Charlestown housing projects took on a racial stigma. Whites who could afford to had been moving out since the midseventies, when a federal judge issued busing orders to desegregate Boston public schools, making Charlestown a flash point of white protests. As the white flight started to ease, younger people with good jobs began renovating the old apartment houses as spacious dwellings for smaller families. A short walk down the hill along the Mystic, an Irish drug mob homed in on poor streets, planting addiction and fueling crime in the ethnic mix. The Naval Shipyard put a gentrified edge to a neighborhood where three parishes lined the incline with less than a mile between them. A financial crisis had silently encroached under Cardinal Law, unbeknownst to Peter Borré as he and Rosie sat in the pews of Charlestown's poorest parish on a Sunday morning in 2004.

OPENING HIS LENS

After entering Harvard at age sixteen and graduating in 1959 with a degree in history, Peter Borré joined the U.S. Navy. He spent three years as a naval officer. In 1963 he earned a master's in international economics from Johns Hopkins University's School of Advanced International Studies (SAIS). Quarreling with his father, he refused to attend law school, but earned a second master's, in international finance, from Harvard Business School. The navy was his pivotal experience, a grounding in the discipline, teamwork, and chain of command on a ship as a system that worked. Three institutions shaped him: the U.S. Navy, the Catholic Church, and Harvard, in that order. Navy life formed a link in his mind with the church, a global institution that had weathered wars, scandal, and its share of crooked popes. The church's mission was of divine origin. Men could screw up anything.

Rosie Piper thrilled to the sermons of Father Bob Bowers, the fortysomething pastor with silver hair who spoke buoyantly about mutual obligations and the parish as a place where all peoples met; he was learning Spanish and creating outreach programs that made her feel good about being Catholic. She found herself oddly moved on the day two adopted boys of a gay couple made their First Communion. Gay marriage was a leap she could not make in her own mind. She had voted Republican much of her life, but civil unions with benefits seemed right. With so many kids out on the street, hooked on crack and fighting with guns, she reasoned that the children of that couple at least had the advantage of family, even if it was a different kind of family: they had two men who loved them, brushed their hair, put them in nice clothes, and prayed with them in church.

The society she found at St. Catherine of Siena, where "church" was greater than its rules, strengthened her sense of a spiritual home as she weighed the realities of her life against past expectations. Back in Delaware all those years ago, she had raised two sons and two daughters in the church, all of whom had left or detached from the faith. For some reason her eldest granddaughter, a University of Virginia undergraduate who had grown up in California, was a deeply devout Catholic. Rosie realized how much she had learned from her children, the tolerance they had taught her about a changing society—a tolerance sadly missing from the church she loved and which gave her spasms of agony. *Those bishops! Hiding sex criminals! All that lying! Somebody ought to show those men what's what!*

Attending Mass with Peter lent a measure of comfort to Rosie amid the reservoirs of patience she had to summon in dealing with Bill's dementia. Her son-in-law with his European air could be brusque, even arrogant, but Peter had a good heart. She was glad he and Mary Beth had found each other.

Peter Borré became active at St. Catherine of Siena by default. Since moving into the condo in 1987, he had logged hundreds of thousands of air miles on business. Now and then Mary Beth had gone with him, depending on the destination and her schedule. More often he was alone. On layovers from West Africa he had stayed most often in Paris, where he attended Les Augustins church. In London he sought out St. Martin-in-the-Fields, off Trafalgar Square. Back in Boston, he often made his way downtown to the Cathedral of the Holy Cross. But his attendance was sporadic, several Sundays running, then a stretch away.

Moving through his fifties, Borré had reached back for an essence of his earlier spiritual life, before the collapse of his first marriage. He blamed the divorce on his infidelity and the workaholic zeal of his thirties. In his twenties he had married the daughter of a European ambassador; she raised their son and two daughters during his time away. With a widening of his hindsight lens he had come to see those overlong travel stints as an escape mechanism. The divorce had left him riddled with self-disgust. In time, he cultivated a good relationship with his ex-wife; she had lived now for nearly three decades with a man on Martha's Vineyard. Repairing the bond with his children had come slowly, not without pain. They were grown now, and he had several grandchildren.

At Mass, he wanted to reclaim a spiritual equilibrium, the moral center he had lost. Nevertheless, each Sunday when the moment came to receive the Eucharist, the presence of Christ in the blessed wafer, Borré hung back. He sat in the pew as people moved past him into the Communion line.

Borré had recoiled from the idea of seeking an annulment for his first marriage, a process that would have made him legal, as it were, for Communion. Many Catholics view the annulment process as revisiting the traumas of a divorce. From his father's cynical take on the Rota, the Vatican court that held the final word on annulments, Borré thought the process was a racket. His father, as an American attorney well connected in Rome, had referred cases to canonists who had standing at the Rota; he had helped translate certain requests into Italian.

"There was a lot of dinner table talk about how phony the whole thing was—false affidavits about mental reservations a spouse had before getting married," recalls Borré. "It required a lot of collusion on the part of the other spouse, money changing hands in return for supporting affidavits. My dad had peripheral involvement in an infamous case. Lee Bouvier, sister of Jackie Kennedy, needed to annul her marriage so she could marry a Polish prince, Stanisław Radziwill. It would have looked bad for the Catholic president to have a divorced sister-in-law who had been a maid of honor at his wedding. It was a sordid matter, but the Sacra Rota came through and Lee became 'Princess Radziwill.' She was in Rome a lot in the Swinging Sixties. She and the prince divorced in the 1970s. By then it didn't matter as a political issue."

Still, many Catholics who go through annulments experience a feeling of cleansing; they can also remarry before a priest. The annulment involves a fee to the diocesan chancery, meeting with a canon lawyer, answering a lengthy questionnaire on causes of the divorce (with more intimate detail than many civil courts require), then the long wait to hear back from Rome. The escalation of annulments granted to American Catholics since the 1980s stirred suspicion at the Vatican. "The United States has the largest tribunal system in the world," a Vatican canonist told me during an interview in Rome in 2002. "To say that people were unqualified begs the issue. The U.S. tribunals violated *grandly*—terribly— the annulments of marriage."[29]

No one knows how many divorced Catholics remarry without an-nulments and take Communion. Most priests have no idea who in the Communion line may have canonically stained back pages nor a punitive inclination to use church law in withholding the Eucharist. Peter Borré, a prodigal son returned to the church, stuck to his guns. Eschewing the "caf-eteria Catholicism" of those who selectively follow church rules, he knew that by church law his second marriage was illicit. For all of his misgivings about annulments, he sat in the pew with his core of obedience, unable to shake a sense of being unworthy, an ironic law-and-order Catholic at Communion time, believing in the divine essence of the church and sal-vation in Jesus Christ, waiting, as if in Dante's *Purgatorio,* for absolution on some distant day.

> All men, though in a vague way, apprehend
> a good their souls may rest in, and desire it;
> each, therefore, strives to reach his chosen end.[30]

After Senator Kerry gained the nomination, Mary Beth was working in the garden of their Florida vacation home when the idea of George W. Bush getting reelected filled her with nausea; she telephoned a friend in the Kerry campaign to say, "I'm in." In short order she went to work in the Florida field organization for the presidential campaign.

Peter, gathering information about the archdiocese's financial prob-lems, was in a slow burn. For to him, the numbers did not add up.

CHAPTER 2

ORIGINS OF THE VATICAN FINANCIAL SYSTEM

On July 22, 2010, the Vatican announced a $250,000 gift by Pope Benedict XVI to rebuild a school in Port-au-Prince that had been lost in Haiti's horrific earthquake.[1] The Holy Father's international role in helping "the least of these" arose in the last century. But the Holy See is not a wealthy country like one of the Arab oil states. Its largesse relies on donors, large and small.

Peter's Pence is the Vatican's most important collection; it is taken once a year in late June, in parishes across the developed world. Promoted as the pope's fund for his assistance to people in dire need, Peter's Pence in 2009 took in $82.5 million.[2] Despite the Great Recession, the figure marked a nearly $7 million boost from 2008. Peter's Pence is by no means the only stream of financial support to the pope. In America, for example, the Papal Foundation (whose board members commit to paying $1 million over ten years) supports church projects in poor countries, under Vatican guidance, with gifts that range from $15,000 to $75,000, as listed on the foundation's website.[3]

Although the annual yield of Peter's Pence is published, how the Holy See uses those funds, the charitable outlay, is much less clear. A small office in the Secretariat of State in Vatican City tabulates the donations, sends letters of thanks to donors, and routes funds to other offices for disbursement. I sought information on Peter's Pence spending from the USCCB press office, which referred me to the Washington, D.C., office of the papal nuncio, Archbishop Pietro Sambi, who did not respond. In Rome, Alessandro Speciale, a correspondent for GlobalPost, the online foreign news service, reports: "A significant part of it goes to bishops from poor dioceses when they meet the pope in their *ad limina* (every fifth year) meetings and discuss projects they have for schools, hospitals, student grants, etcetera. Part of the money is channeled to an office called Cor Unum, part of it is spent directly by the Secretariat of State and part of it [is spent] through [the] apostolic office, which apparently deals mostly with Rome and Italy. Part of it is also used for the personal charity of the pope."[4]

Of the three major outlays of Peter's Pence funding, only Cor Unum publishes annual data. Cor Unum has several projects. The Sahel Foundation founded by John Paul II deals with agriculture and erosion; the Populorum Progressio assists indigenous peoples of Latin America and the Caribbean. In 2009 Cor Unum reported an outlay for emergency relief of $1.87 million in twenty-five countries; $2.3 million in general assistance for projects in forty-five countries; $2.3 million through the Sahel Foundation in nine countries; and $2.13 million spent in twenty countries in the initiative for Latin America and the Caribbean.

Cor Unum's four allocations—roughly $8.65 million—account for 10.5 percent of the $82.5 million collected through Peter's Pence. The Vatican has not released figures on how it spent the rest of Peter's Pence in 2009.

International philanthropy by the pope is a recent phenomenon in history. Across the last century Peter's Pence proved pivotal to the Holy See, but the money's major role was not to help the needy but to plug Vatican operating deficits. In 1985, a year after the Holy See agreed to pay three banks $242 million to resolve Vatican Bank complicity in the collapse of Roberto Calvi's Banco Ambrosiano, the Vatican Bank was unable to cover the Vatican operating deficit of $39.14 million. "The deficit has been mainly covered by the Peter's Pence and other free offerings to the Holy Father, which amount to $36,927,811," noted the General Final Balance Sheet.[5]

On November 18, 1987, Cardinal John Krol of Philadelphia spoke to a Vatican economic commission about the Holy See's finances. A son of

Polish immigrants, Krol was confident and socially conservative, but at the same time, in following the U.S. bishops' line against nuclear arms, a critic of the Reagan defense policy. Krol also raised major funds for the Polish resistance, thereby cementing good ties with John Paul II. That day in 1987 he complained of the Roman Curia's expanding bureaucracy. The Vatican city-state met its expenses, but the Curia ran way over budget. "None of these offices has anything to do with the IOR, sometimes called the Vatican Bank, which is truly a service agency operated autonomously under the direction of some cardinals and a director," said Krol, elliptically. (IOR stands for Istituto per le Opere di Religione—Institute for Religious Works—otherwise known as the Vatican Bank.) Krol omitted Archbishop Paul Marcinkus's role in allowing IOR to launder mob money for Michele Sindona and Roberto Calvi. Sindona had died in prison, poisoned, and Calvi had been found hanging from a bridge in London.[6] A native of Illinois, Marcinkus used diplomatic immunity to evade Italian subpoenas by staying inside Vatican City. When the storm passed, Marcinkus moved to Arizona and passed his sunset years playing golf. In the Vatican style of exquisite courtesy to hierarchs, Krol on that day in 1987 spoke not of the financial debacle caused by Marcinkus but of its prosaic offshoot: the Vatican operating deficit.

> Traditionally, Peter's Pence is to be collected for the Holy Father's charities, but with the reduction of the income and the increase of costs, a move was made first of all to take money from the Peter's Pence, and eventually to take all of the revenue from Peter's Pence. The Holy Father does receive, when people visit him, gifts of money. The gifts that are not earmarked for specific charities, also became available and were used to cover the deficits. As of this stage, the reserve—if it can be called that—is insufficient to cover the anticipated deficit.[7]

Krol did not want charitable donations sent to Peter's Pence from the various national churches diverted to cover salaries or costs of the Curial bureaucracy. On a 1987 budget of $132.6 million, the Holy See overspent by $63.8 million. "The resulting shortfall was covered by support from Peter's Pence amounting to $50,299,858.32," reported the 1987 Statement of Income and Expenditure. Moreover, $13.5 million came from "other sources . . . including the limited resources of accumulated reserves which have now been completely exhausted."[8] Krol was blunt on the matter of charitable money: "The Peter's Pence money must go back to the pope for the needs of the poor."[9]

In 1991 Cardinal Edmund C. Szoka, who had left his post as archbishop of Detroit to oversee Vatican City finances, told a conference of U.S. bishops that the Holy See's operating deficit was $86.3 million. "He said the practice of using Peter's Pence to help cover Vatican deficits, adopted as a matter of necessity in recent years, ought to stop," reported Catholic News Service.[10] Sandro Magister, the distinguished religion correspondent for Rome's *L'Espresso*, offered new insight in 2009. "Money is also sent by the religious congregations and foundations," he wrote. "According to a confidential [2007] report that the Vatican sent to the dioceses, these contributions amounted to $29.5 million." Magister zeroed in on a second source of funding for the pope, the Vatican Bank. Twenty years after the scandal, Magister echoed Krol:

> In March of every year, in fact, the IOR makes entirely available to the pope the difference between its income and expenditures the previous year. This total is kept secret, but it is believed to be close to the Peter's Pence. At least this was the case in the four years for which figures were leaked [before Italy adopted the euro]. It came to 60.7 billion Italian lire in 1992, 72 billion in 1993, 75 billion in 1994, and 78.3 billion in 1995. During those same years, the Peter's Pence was just slightly above these amounts.
>
> Given this state of affairs, 2007 should have brought Benedict XVI for his "charity" a sum total of about two hundred million dollars.[11]

The Vatican budget ran a deficit of about 2.4 million euros in 2007. "Chopped liver, by comparison," mused Magister.

"For many years the Vatican also subsidized the diocese of Rome," explains Jesuit Father Thomas J. Reese, a senior fellow at Georgetown University's Woodstock Center and author of *Inside the Vatican: The Politics and Organization of the Catholic Church*. "Now the diocese's budget is separate and doing well under Italy's tax check-off system, which allows every taxpayer to approve a payment to the church," Reese told me. "Even some Communists mark the box on their tax forms because they trust the church with their money more than they trust the state; so the Italian church has more money to donate to the Vatican. The sex abuse crisis may change that."

The Vatican Bank is an "off-the-books" asset: no accounting on the Holy See financial statement, nothing on the bank's profits, losses, or how much it gives the pope. Peter's Pence, however, powered papal finances before the Vatican Bank ever existed. As this charity evolved, it propped up the Vatican through decades of war and convulsions in Europe. The Vatican financial system is a product of charitable donations harnessed for capitalist investment.

THE WORLD OF PIO NONO

In 1849, when Catholic Church membership in America stood at 5 percent of its size today, the bishops collected just under $26,000 to help a financially crippled pope. The international funding drive revived a tradition called Peter's Pence. French Catholics led the benefactors until the late nineteenth century, giving way to the American church. But the 1849 American gift to Pius IX was substantial for the time. American Catholic support for Peter's Pence—particularly from New York, Philadelphia, Chicago, and Boston—rose with the tides of Irish, Italian, and other European immigrants settling in the cities. In the 1870s, with his papacy afloat on these donations, Pius IX railed against the unified Kingdom of Italy, demanding the return of a massive farming territory to the pope as an absolute monarch. As wrangling over the Papal States dragged on, Peter's Pence fed Vatican investments in Rome's booming real estate market.[12]

When the dispute over the lost territories was finally resolved to the Vatican's benefit, on the eve of the Great Depression, the Catholic Church in America stood as the Holy Father's chief benefactor. U.S. bishops raised money with the power of politicians, sending streams of support to the Holy Father.

The financial links that spanned the Atlantic were strained even before the global credit crisis erupted in 2008. At the onset of Benedict XVI's papacy in 2005, American dioceses were reeling from financial losses in the sex abuse cases. Bishops who faced mass lawsuits had resorted to bankruptcy filings in Portland, Spokane, San Diego, Tucson, and Davenport, Iowa (and later Wilmington, Delaware, and Milwaukee); they looked for no Vatican bailout. The money ran *to Rome*, always had. Still, Roman Curia officials monitored the bankruptcies and litigation losses. Under a 2002 agreement with the Vatican, a bishop seeking to liquidate assets over a value threshold of $5 million (or $10.3 million, depending on the size of his diocese) needed approval from the Congregation for the Clergy in Rome.[13]

Habits of the heart can defy easy explanation. Behind the financial ties lay a strange romance between New World faithful and the Old World's last sovereign monarchy, robed in messy Italian politics. But when the Vatican needed money, Catholic America delivered. The Vatican's financial dependency stood apart from the lawsuits and government probes over the last decade, in America and Ireland, that disgorged shocking church files on predatory priests. As the outlines surfaced of the church's greatest crisis since the Reformation, Pope John Paul II stood passive, other than to occasionally apologize or scold the media. In 2002, when clergy child-sex cases provoked an international scandal, John Paul, ailing with Parkinson's disease, blamed therapists for misleading bishops; Vatican cardinals blasted the media and lawyers. To concede failure by the pope was unspeakable, if not unthinkable.

The idea of an inerrant pope has a stormy history enmeshed with the development of church funding. In seventy years, the Vatican went from being a charity case to a Depression-era financial power, providing loans to Fascist Italy. As this strange odyssey unfolded, the image of the pope as a religious monarch with landed wealth changed into that of a preacher for global peace.

The seminal figure in our account is Pope Pius IX, "Pio Nono" as Italians called him, *nono* meaning "ninth." Pio Nono reacted to the loss of the Papal States by republican forces by demanding the return of the ancient agricultural territories as a right of monarchical absolutism. Pio Nono was the first celebrity pope, his persona garnering affection from Catholics in many countries. Like most celebrities he was in part a creation of publicity; his genial personality had a strange side that sometimes ran dark. Still, bishops and cardinals who traveled to Rome, bearing financial gifts, gained prestige for themselves back home.

Born on May 13, 1792, Giovanni Maria Mastai-Ferretti was the youngest of nine children. His father was a count in Senigallia on the Adriatic. Priests from aristocratic families had favored status in the Italian hierarchy; cardinals and archbishops were political figures in governing Rome and the historic Italian midlands known as the Papal States, where the church *was* the state. Two of Mastai-Ferretti's uncles were bishops; one served at St. Peter's Basilica. In adolescence Giovanni had seizures attributed to epilepsy. Whatever the neurology, his pleasant personality was subject to angry flares and a weird sense of humor. Family connections helped. A modest student in seminary, he was a priest at twenty-four and papal diplomat in four short years. In 1823 he was posted to Chile for two years. Back in Rome, he oversaw a hospice. In 1827, his thirty-fifth year, Mastai-Ferretti became archbishop of Spoleto in the Papal States, and in 1840, a cardinal.[14]

Reputedly tireless, pastoral, and known for good humor, Cardinal Mastai-Ferretti at age fifty-four was elected pope in the conclave of 1846, a compromise choice who impressed his cardinal peers with a balance of humility and gregariousness. Pope Pius IX entered his reign as a populist. Given to taking spontaneous walks through Rome, installing streetlights, offering an amnesty to rebels in the Papal States, releasing Jews from the onerous requirement of attending weekly sermons by priests, he set up a commission to study the condition of Jewish ghettos.[15] Pio Nono also held a rocklike belief in his worldly kingdom. He was eight in 1799 when Napoleon's troops invaded Rome and captured Pope Pius VI, who died a prisoner in France. By Pio Nono's time Italy had reverted to its status before the Napoleonic conquest: a patchwork of kingdoms and autonomous states, not a nation with a settled identity.

The French Revolution of 1789 had decapitated one king, but royalty still ruled many parts of Europe in the middle nineteenth century. Monarchs viewed the pope as the preeminent spiritual leader and a fellow sovereign. The papacy had a court with cardinals, bishops, and other officials in the retinue of papal advisers, girded by wealthy aristocrats, the "black Romans" who had financial interests in the city governed by the pope. The Papal Court relied on income from the Papal States, a fiefdom dating to the eighth century that stretched from Rome up the middle of the peninsula in a sinuous northwestern curl. Clerical overseers often shared power with local gentry. Seasonal day laborers worked many of the lands; a sharecropping belt ran from the edge of Tuscany down into Umbria.[16] Estates near Bologna, in the north, threw off profits from silk and tobacco; farther south, in the area around Rome, half of the population lived at the edge of destitution. Hierarchs censored the press and hired thugs to intimidate rebellious workers in quelling unrest.[17] Charles Dickens, on an 1844 trip to Rome, took chilly note of the "broken temples; broken tombs. A desert of decay, somber and desolate beyond all expression."[18]

To the south, Naples was ruled by a corrupt Bourbon king backed by a ruthless army. After an 1851 trip the British politician William Gladstone called the Naples monarchy "the negation of God erected into a system of government." Gladstone's comments had an impact on public opinion. The *New York Daily Times* denounced the king of Naples as "murder enthroned and crowned, the incarnated evil . . . the foulest and fiercest misrule that ever trampled a nation to dust."[19] America had trading ties with the Papal States, but only a vice-consul in Rome in 1847. Congress balked at formal ties with a religious state.[20]

In the north, Piedmont was ruled by Victor Emmanuel II, a soldier-king of reformist bent who was edging into an alliance with the prime minister of Sardinia, Count Camillo Cavour. The political architect for a united Italy, Cavour was pushing for a national currency. But integrating the monetary systems turned on geopolitical unity. In Sicily the charismatic warrior Giuseppe Garibaldi was leading forces to fight for Il Risorgimento, the unification of Italy. With troops at opposite ends of the peninsula pushing inward, the Papal States, an antique of sagging feudalism, kept losing money.

In 1832 the Rothschild bank of Paris had extended a loan to keep the papacy afloat. "Prohibited by law from owning land and kept out of the trades controlled by the guilds, the Jews found in finance and money-lending the only economic path to prosperity open to them," writes historian David I. Kertzer.[21] The Rothschilds wanted Jews freed from ghettos. In Pio Nono, they sized up a reformer they hoped would ease the harsh treatment of Jews.

The Venetian Republic had confined Jews to a ghetto in 1517. In 1555 Paul IV ordered Jewish segregation in cities he ruled. "For an extreme ascetic like him," explains historian James Carroll, "there was only one thing to do, which was to impose order in every way he could . . . *Oppose* Protestants outside the Church, *impose* discipline within the Church. But especially, *convert the Jews*."[22]

In 1848 Pio Nono agreed to a Papal States constitution with an elected chamber. But when Austrian forces headed south to seize a swath of the Italian peninsula, the pope, hoping to avoid war with a Catholic country, admonished people to be loyal to their princes. Garibaldi and others assembled an army to fight for a unified Italy. The economy heaved; the pope's prime minister was stabbed to death. As Garibaldi's troops captured Rome, the pope escaped in disguise as an ordinary priest, by carriage, to Gaeta, a fortress near Naples.

Pio Nono's hostility to Risorgimento was a huge roadblock to an Italian resolution. The peninsula was riven by dialects and area conflicts such that a national identity like France's was a distant goal. Regional leaders wanted to unite behind the pope as a spiritual sovereign, with governing power in a prime minister and a parliament. Demanding that Rome be *his* to govern, Pio Nono slammed negotiations shut. In July 1849, after France took Rome, the pope cast lines anew to the Rothschild bank. In Paris, the emperor Louis-Napoléon lobbied a loan in his behalf. But James Rothschild "raised the matter of the plight of the Jews in the Papal States, and demanded that before any loan was made, the Pope agree to free the Jews from the ghetto," writes David Kertzer.

> The Pope sent James a written assurance through his nuncio in Paris. He had the best intentions with respect to the Jews in the Papal States, he said, and he intimated that he would soon issue an edict abolishing the ghetto. But, he added, it would be unseemly—and indeed unthinkable—to directly link the making of a loan to such an edict.[23]

In January 1850 Rothschild approved a loan of 50 million francs. On April 12, Pio Nono returned to beaten-down Rome, reclaiming the city of his rule. But to his lender, he yielded no policy shift in return. In fact, he swung to the right, reverting to harsh controls on the Jewish ghettos as before.[24]

Just as he was anchoring himself on the wrong side of Italian history, Pio Nono emerged as a figure of sympathy *outside* Italy. Stirred by the spectacle of an exiled pope, Catholic patricians in Paris revived a medieval tradition, Peter's Pence (historically, a tax of one penny per household in England for the occupant of St. Peter's throne),[25] to directly assist the beleaguered Pio Nono. U.S. dioceses raised $25,978.24 in 1849 "for the relief of His Holiness."[26] The New York archdiocese contributed $6,200 and Philadelphia $2,800. The Catholic population (about 1.4 million) offered prayers for the pope whose tribulations made them feel closer to him. In helping him, they helped church and faith.[27]

For secretary of state, Pio Nono chose a shrewd young deacon from a well-connected family in Naples. Giacomo Antonelli was not a priest, yet Pius so valued his skills that he made him a cardinal, stirring jealousy among other ecclesial princes. Tall, lean, and "demonically astute," in the scalding words of one chronicler, Antonelli toiled in the shadows of Pio Nono's carousel personality. The cardinal had a brother in banking who provided commercial contacts beyond Italy. Guiding papal finances amid a sea change in European politics, Antonelli restructured the Holy See's debt, put the court and the Curia in separate budgets, and imposed tighter accounting procedures on the Papal States.[28] He installed his brother as head of the Pontifical Bank. "A greedy man," huffed one historian in describing Antonelli.[29] Another sibling gained the monopoly on Roman grain imports. "The Antonelli brothers fixed the price of corn, so that they and their middlemen amassed large fortunes . . . [in] one of the last cases of grand Papal nepotism," Anthony Rhodes writes. Pio Nono called Antonelli "my Barabbas."[30]

In 1857 Antonelli used Peter's Pence as collateral in negotiating a new loan with Rothschild. Nevertheless, Pius refused to order the return of a six-year-old Jewish child, Edgardo Mortara, who had been taken from his parents by police in Bologna after a servant claimed that she secretly baptized the boy when he was one and severely ill. Placed in the House of Catechumens (those studying for the faith), the boy visited Pio Nono. The pope took the child "into public audiences, playing hide and seek with him under his cloak."[31]

Outrage swelled in the international press; Pius browbeat Jewish leaders of Rome in an audience when they pleaded with him to return the boy to his family. "By the grace of God I have seen my duty, and I would rather cut off all my fingers than shrink from it," declared the pope. The boy entered a seminary. As a priest Mortara had fleeting family memories. He met his relatives as an adult and never truly reconciled with his family. (He died in 1940 in a Belgian monastery at age eighty-eight.) Revulsion rose in many countries for the pope's treatment of the Mortaras. "Even his critics, exasperated by his stubbornness and unimpressed by his modest intellect, admitted that it was impossible to dislike him," notes papal historian Eamon Duffy. "He was genial, unpretentious, wreathed in clouds of snuff." Years later, when his enemy Count Cavour died, the pope called him "truly Italian. God will assuredly pardon him, as we pardon him."[32]

In 1860 Cavour's coalition of Piedmont-Sardinia was allied with the nationalist Garibaldi's southern forces as the Risorgimento captured two-thirds of the Papal States. Garibaldi, who had once worked as a candle maker on Staten Island, became a hero in America. "The new birth of Italy is already the grandest event of the modern period," asserted the Dante scholar Charles Eliot Norton. "The claim for Peter's Pence may well remind us of the Crusades," the New York Times drily opined. "But today when the Holy City is attacked, it is by Catholics—Catholics from the South and from the North."[33]

Pio Nono shifted from benevolent despot to reactionary monarch. He struck back (without identifying Cavour, Garibaldi, or republicans)[34] in the 1864 Syllabus of Errors, an edict that cracked the whip against the emergence of European democracy. Garry Wills calls the Syllabus "grand in its crazy way" for its declaration that the pope should never have to "reconcile himself, or agree with, progress, liberalism, and modern civilization."[35]

Antonelli, however, had a new marketing asset: the papal image. The distribution of pictures and small cards bearing Pio Nono's face, combined with newspaper coverage, made him "a popular icon better known than that of any pope in history."[36] As bishops in Europe and America rallied to the cause, Peter's Pence averaged 8 million lire yearly from 1859 to 1870.[37] Although initially conceived to provide military defense for the pope, the money was his to use as he wished.

Despite Pius's intransigence on freeing Jews, Rothschild took a long view. His bank also lent to the royal house of Piedmont. For a French bank to have an embattled pope among its clients did not hurt, even if his betrayal did. With two-thirds of the Papal States controlled by Italian forces, Pio Nono stood helpless at the birth of the Kingdom of Italy. Thus, in 1861 he excommunicated its king, Victor Emmanuel II. Pio Nono rebuffed overtures by the new leaders for the Law of Guarantees, which pledged 3.5 million lire a year to papal coffers and defense of the Vatican. Count Cavour, the leader pushing for a rapprochement, called for "a free church in a free state." Antonelli the shrewd bargainer might have cut a better deal had he only had papal support. But Pio Nono believed in his kingship. He refused to concede his lost control of the territories.[38]

Money for daily operations, notably the salaries of Vatican lay workers, was a pressing need. The Holy See turned to French bishops, seeking subscription loans to be raised by the laity, a scheme quickly quashed for the conflict posed to Peter's Pence. Catholic financiers suggested a worldwide papal lottery; the Vatican said no. In this quagmire Antonelli gave the order for a massive minting of silver coins "with less than the prescribed amount of necessary metal."[39] French and Swiss banks rejected the quick-fix cheap coins. Money spread, inflation rose: the papacy by 1870 had a public debt of 20 million lire.

Amid the tribulations, Pio Nono kept his odd sense of humor. "How is it," the pope asked a British envoy in early 1866, "that the British can hang two thousand Negroes to put down an uprising in Jamaica, and receive only universal praise for it, while I cannot hang a single man in the Papal States without provoking worldwide condemnation?" At his own question he burst out laughing, repeating it, shaking a lone finger.[40] The envoy wondered if the pope was sane. In 1871 the pope ordered Italians not to vote in parliamentary elections, a decree that magnified his detachment from politics and undercut Vatican influence on party development as democratic changes swept through Europe.

French troops supplied the garrison that defended the pope. In 1869 Pio Nono summoned all of his bishops to a Vatican Council. He wanted their support for infallibility—that the pope could not err on a pronouncement of dogma, and could issue articles of faith entirely on his own, without the collegial advisory of cardinals and bishops. American bishops were not thrilled. Many of them were establishing dioceses in areas where raw sentiments flared against "popery"—the king of a religion who would menace America's democracy. "In my humble opinion," the bishop of Rochester, New York, writing from Rome, confided to a friend, "and almost every American Bishop whose opinion I have heard agrees with me, [infallibility] will be a great calamity for the Church." The bishop of Pittsburgh was more stark: "It will kill us."[41]

A mist of irony suffused the Vatican Council. Pius, the antirepublican, wanted the bishops *to vote*, as if in a parliament, for investing his office with a superhuman power. When an Italian cardinal spoke in opposition, Pio Nono bristled at his "error." Then he declared: "I, *I* am the tradition!"[42]

Such hubris may have sparked a revolt on a preliminary vote on the wording of the papal text, in which the first ballot had 88 votes against

Pius, 62 for, and about 85 bishops absent—on account of their leaving
Rome. The French troops packed up, heading out for war with Prussia.
The Vatican was unprotected. Fifty-seven bishops opposed to infallibility
left before voting. A lopsided number of bishops Pio Nono had appointed
in Italy and Spain rallied to his position; he won, 533–2.[43] But the margin
could not offset the misgivings of those who had left. "There was something hollow about this victory, which prevented even the hardliners from
showing ebullience," writes Wills.[44]

Antonelli the money manager warned the pope that infallibility would
alienate many people. "I have the Blessed Virgin on my side," rejoined
Pio Nono.[45] Indeed, the infallibility doctrine applied retroactively to
the pope's 1854 declaration of Mary's birth without original sin (the Immaculate Conception). Otherwise, none of his pronouncements after the
Vatican Council carried the stamp of infallibility. (To date, its only other
invocation was in 1950 when Pius XII announced that Mary ascended
bodily into heaven.) Such decrees of a spiritual realm stood apart from
an emerging age of science. As the geography controlled by the Supreme
Pontiff shrank to the size of a small town, the idea of papal perfection
enlarged his power, suggesting a reach no president, prime minister, or
dictator could rival.

As the papacy's financial struggle deepened, Pio Nono quipped, "I may
be infallible, but I am certainly bankrupt."[46] Infallibility, however, produced an ironic silver lining. As a popular misconception arose that the
pope could never make a mistake, the papacy became a symbol of pure
truth. Funds poured in from Catholics in Europe and the Americas, registering support for the pope.

The Vatican Council ended. Liberal Italy swallowed Rome and the
remaining Papal States. Shorn of the ancient lands, a king without an
army, Pio Nono crossed the Tiber into tiny Vatican City—the 108 acres
encompassing St. Peter's Basilica, the Apostolic Palace, gardens, and historic buildings—a self-proclaimed "Prisoner of the Vatican," vowing bit-
terly not to reenter Rome proper until Italy returned the land. This was
Pio Nono's full-throated sympathetic coda to the dying age of European
monarchy.

"The Achilles' heel of the Roman theory of infallibility is in the last
resort lack of faith," the eminent theologian Hans Küng would write many
years later in assessing Vatican I, as the council is called. "True, God acts

on the Church through the Holy Spirit . . . But the human beings who constitute the Church can err, miscalculate and blunder, mishear, misunderstand and go astray."[47]

Pio Nono, the blundering geopolitician, had won election as the infallible dogmatist. Priests in Ireland and Germany handed out palm cards of His Holiness in a dungeon on a straw bed, a prisoner of evil Italians.[48] Popular myth produced its opposite: a stunning 1.7 million lire for Peter's Pence yielded at an 1874 Catholic congress in Venice.[49] Incensed by Pio Nono's hostility, the Kingdom of Italy's parliament debated legislation to outlaw Peter's Pence; it failed to pass. Meanwhile, the idea of a spiritually perfect pope, standing on the rock of dogma in a fast-changing world, transformed the papal image from landed sovereign to sainted royalty at poverty's edge. The pope became a magnet for donations amid the spread of urban capitalism, despite a counterwind of dissent by theologians and intellectuals against infallibility to this day.

From his elegant bunker with the garden paths and great Vatican buildings, Pio Nono carved out a global map, creating more than two hundred new dioceses and appointing bishops to run them, a religious expansion in contrast to his tiny kingdom. He named more saints than all popes in the previous 150 years combined, a breathtaking pace unmatched until the twenty-seven-year pontificate of John Paul II. When a Jesuit adviser suggested a truce with Italy over reparations for the Papal States, Pio Nono sacked him, declaring, "In Rome, the Head of the Church must be either ruler or prisoner."[50]

The Cambridge historian John F. Pollard calculates that in the seven years following the 1870 fall of Rome, the Vatican saved 4.3 million lire annually from Peter's Pence income. Antonelli's investment strategy ignored Italy, still a semifeudal agrarian economy, for more industrialized countries. The nuncios, or papal ambassadors, played a pivotal role. Writes Pollard:

> Much of the Vatican's money was deposited in foreign banks, especially Rothschilds in Paris, the Société Générale in Brussels and the Bank of England; little or no money was sent to the United States at this juncture, though there is evidence that Antonelli did contemplate depositing money there. Antonelli used the papal nuncios as the agents of his financial operations abroad, especially

in the matter of seeking attractive bank accounts and stocks and bonds, rather than company shares. Two Roman financial middlemen . . . performed various necessary operations, smuggling in Peter's Pence when the Italian governmental authorities showed hostility, exchanging currencies, cashing stocks and bonds which formed part of Peter's Pence, and selling precious objects donated by the pious faithful.[51]

Pio Nono refused to negotiate reparations, stubbornly demanding the return of Rome and the ancient plantation belt, unfazed about the bleak peonage on which the lost kingdom had rested. Antonelli streamlined papal finances, steering investments into credit and commerce. Blind to the chance for a diplomatic rapprochement, Pio Nono rebuffed the king's family in their request that he preside at Victor Emmanuel's funeral in 1878. Two hundred thousand people thronged the streets for the procession as he was laid to rest in Rome's Pantheon—another chance to make peace squandered. Splits were surfacing in America, too. When Pittsburgh's bishop denied Italians a Mass for the king, they met in a Presbyterian church. In Chicago, four thousand Italians held a memorial parade with two hundred decorated carriages and a dozen marching bands, as the governor of Illinois and the mayor watched from a reviewing stand.[52]

What a paradox: Italian Americans in a parade of eulogy for the king of their unified homeland, many if not most of whom would attend Mass and say prayers for the pope, Pio Nono, a recalcitrant monarchist. Such people giving shape to U.S. cities wanted the social guarantees of a liberal democracy *and* the spiritual certitude of their faith. The loyal folk in the pews lived beyond the contradictions of a Vatican that was hostile to republican birth pangs in Italy. New World laity waited for the Old World hierarchy to find a faith in pluralism, even as they sent Peter's Pence donations over to Rome.

A few months after the king's death, Pio Nono died on February 7, 1878, at age eighty-six. Anticlerical protesters engulfed the funeral procession; a riot erupted at a bridge on the Tiber, and radicals almost dumped the pope's coffin into the river. Litigation over Pio Nono's personal estate by several family members ran nearly a decade in the Italian courts. Cardinals finally settled the claims.[53]

Cardinal Gioacchino Pecci, who was elected in the conclave after

Pio Nono's death, showed greater intellect and vision. Taking the name Leo XIII, he served for twenty-five years, sequestered in the Vatican. A voracious reader who pored through newspapers and novels, Leo had "superb eyes, brilliant like black diamonds," the novelist Émile Zola noted after a visit. Striving to bring the world and papacy into some accord, he sent nuncios to various countries and a small delegation to Washington.[54] Yet he also defended the Christian Social Party in Austria, whose leader pushed an anti-Semitic agenda that some of the Austrian bishops opposed.[55] A paradox deepened, as the United States recognized Liberal Italy as a nation, while priests, nuns, and editors of diocesan newspapers protested the Holy Father's isolation. Leo XIII cast lines to Germany and France to regain Rome and the lost lands. But by the lights of modern Europe, Italy belonged to Italy. As waves of Italians settled in America, Leo refused to negotiate the Law of Guarantees. Italian authorities put away funds in anticipation of an agreement.

In 1891 Leo XIII released *Rerum Novarum*, one of the papacy's most influential encyclicals. The pope aligned Catholic social teaching with workers' rights during an era of burgeoning trade unions. Leo's emphasis on the sanctity of private property put the church squarely against Marxism, signaling support for Italy's Catholic-owned banks and credit associations. In America, *Rerum Novarum* positioned many priests and even bishops behind organized labor.

Leo XIII held none of his predecessor's detachment about money, nor the assumption that God—or Antonelli, who had predeceased Pio Nono—would provide. Leo kept an iron trunk under his bed filled with gold, jewels, and cash. He chose Monsignor Enrico Folchi as *commissario* for finances. "Leo's repeated interference in the choice of investments, and particularly in the matter of making loans, including giving one to his nephew, Count Pecci," writes John Pollard, made Folchi's work less easy.[56] Pio Nono's cult of personality had dissolved with his death. To build his own persona, Leo XIII summoned several religious jubilees for which tens of thousands of people flocked to the Eternal City. Monsignor Folchi helped empty the white velvet bags filled with money given by pilgrims at the papal audiences, banked the cash, exchanged the foreign notes, and obeyed Leo on how much to spend for the Court, Curia, and Vatican offices.

In the 1880s Folchi positioned the Vatican as a major stockholder in

Banco di Roma which invested heavily in real estate. Elegant buildings in the Prati neighborhood, a ten-minute walk from St. Peter's, were built as government offices and residences for bureaucrats or politicians. As real estate boomed, Folchi sank Peter's Pence funds into Società Generale Immobiliare, a contractor that became Rome's major builder. With the pope still a symbolic prisoner, the Vatican invested in the utility company of its jailer-city. In 1885 Banco di Roma bought controlling interest in Rome's bus and streetcar service. Infallibility had its profit margin.

THE BUILDING BISHOPS

Washed in rivers of giving from distant dioceses, the Vatican had beauty when Boston seminarian William O'Connell studied in the 1880s at Pontifical North American College, the seminary Pio Nono founded. "Seminarians," writes James O'Toole in *Militant and Triumphant*, a biography of O'Connell, gained

> an abiding sense of what was called *Romanità*—"Roman-ness"— an intuitive belief that only from the pope and his expanding administrative apparatus could the definitive expression of Catholicism proceed. A few Roman alumni would adopt broader views once they returned home, but the majority tended to a more conservative, centralized outlook. "The Roman mind is the Church's mind and the mind of Christ," William O'Connell wrote later, having himself fully absorbed this attitude.[57]

Born in 1859, the second of six children of Irish-born parents, Will grew up in Lowell. His father toiled in the textile mills. Irish children typically married late, with other Irish, creating strong neighborhood bonds.[58] Will's four brothers went to work with their hands; the altar boy went to Boston College, earned academic medals, and spoke at graduation. With his archbishop's support, Will O'Connell sailed to Rome for seminary and found his stride at the North American College. As a priest he became its rector.

In 1901 O'Connell was consecrated a bishop in Rome and sent to Portland, Maine, in 1903 at age forty-four to assume his rank. In that small diocese—57 churches laced through forest land, 100 priests for 97,000

Catholics in a state of 700,000 people—he declared at his installation, "As I am American in patriotism, so am I, and shall ever be, Roman in faith and love of the church."[59] Dutiful and slightly stern, Bishop O'Connell visited churches and monitored the priests and parishes; if any finances seemed amiss he pressed his clergy for clarification. Obsessed about avoiding debt, he was determined to be a reliable contributor to the annual Peter's Pence, as the world's far-flung bishops registered their fealty to the Holy Father. Maine's small diocese averaged $3,000 annually for Peter's Pence in his five years there. In 1906 O'Connell went to Boston as coadjutor bishop, meaning that he would serve the ailing archbishop as Rome's designated successor.

With 850,000 Catholics, Boston was a huge career move for O'Connell. Back in Maine, however, the new bishop had an audit done and found a glaring deficit. Money was missing, a good deal of it. Outraged, Bishop Louis Walsh wrote to Archbishop O'Connell seeking restitution. In a terse reply, O'Connell admitted nothing, but sent a check for $25,576.09 to repair the hole. Walsh quietly balanced his books. If the Greek philosopher Heraclitus was correct in arguing that character is fate, what of O'Connell? "He formed the habit of failing to distinguish between himself as an individual and his role as trustee for the larger, ongoing organization that existed apart from him," writes O'Toole. In that sense of *l'église, c'est moi*, O'Connell followed in Pio Nono's footsteps. "The underside of his clear and aggressive public persona was a readiness to act like a law unto himself."[60] In 1911 he was made a cardinal.

Cardinal O'Connell was a commanding figure in the line of early prelates, mostly Irish American bishops who molded the Catholic Church into a potent institution between the Civil War and the baby boom of the 1950s. These were "the building bishops": John Hughes, Patrick Hayes, and Francis Spellman in New York; Dennis Dougherty in Philadelphia; John Ireland in St. Paul; James McIntyre (a former stockbroker) and Timothy Manning in Los Angeles; Patrick Feehan and George Mundelein in Chicago; Richard Cushing, who succeeded O'Connell in Boston. The list goes on. The bishops who spanned that era built an infrastructure of parishes and schools. Orphanages and hospitals were largely developed by orders of nuns, who also staffed the parish schools; the male religious orders, notably Jesuits, Dominicans, Salesians, Holy Cross fathers, and Christian Brothers, established high schools and colleges. But it was the bishops' financial and real estate decisions that boosted church wealth, funding ministries and schools, creating an infrastructure that shaped an American Catholic identity. Archbishop Feehan in Chicago built a record 140 parishes in his twenty-two years that culminated in 1902.[61]

At five foot eight and a rotund 250 pounds, O'Connell plunged into Boston life with a Romanità splendor of the church resurgent. He mingled with Brahmin civic leaders, politicians, visiting dignitaries, and presidents. He gave his views on certain laws, opposing both Prohibition and child labor laws (which he saw as undermining the authority of the family). An adroit fund-raiser, he harnessed the generosity of an Irish society ascending toward middle class. O'Connell traveled the city in a limousine, often with his adored poodles. He built the twenty-five-room Renaissance palazzo for his residence in Brighton. As Boston's first cardinal he filled the role of Prince of the Church to the approval of people who had real memory of hard poverty. His stature was their stature. He made lengthy European trips in each of the first seven years of his cardinalate, cultivating Vatican ties. The long winter vacations in the Bahamas came later.

Every pastor of the nearly two hundred churches needed his permission to pay any expense exceeding $100, meaning each substantial repair to a rectory or school had to pass muster with him. Pastors delivered their ledgers for annual inspection at the chancery. Wisely, he routed donations from key parishes into facilities or charities in those neighborhoods to show lay people proof of their giving. He bought a Catholic weekly, *The Pilot*, turning it into an archdiocesan paper that publicized his appearances (an early editor was the future New York cardinal Francis Spellman). To Rome, he sent Peter's Pence at $20,000 annually in his first decade as prelate.[62] As Boston's first cardinal (and America's second) O'Connell was a throwback to Antonelli the backroom man, reborn in an America of Ireland rising. The fusion of two roles, financial and religious, fanned hostilities toward popery, but "the building bishops" of O'Connell's generation withstood nativist bigotry, tapping strength in numbers to create a vast system of social and medical services for the poor long before federal programs like welfare or Medicaid.

O'Connell personified a form of governing that held allegiance to Rome and America in equal measure. Like the other building bishops, he saw himself through a prism of the medieval church—the bishop as

benevolent lord, with laypeople as vassals. As Catholics thrived in a plu-
ralist society with a court system, elections, and a free press, O'Connell
and the twentieth-century bishops molded a medieval idea of power, an
insular worldview remarkable both for its long resilience and for its cata-
lytic role in the recent abuse scandals and financial crisis.

A dress rehearsal began in 1907. The values of an Irish ward heeler
melded with Romanità when the cardinal appointed Father James
O'Connell, a nephew, as his secretary. In 1912 O'Connell, by then a monsignor, moved up to chancellor, the chief financial officer. He "relished
being his uncle's hatchet man," writes John Cooney.[63] The cardinal's
nephew kept the archdiocesan bank accounts, corresponded with pastors,
and oversaw church insurance policies and the archdiocese's investment
portfolio—a lot of power for one young man.

Just when O'Connell fell in love with the wife of a New Jersey doctor is
unclear, but on April 8, 1913, she got a quickie divorce in South Dakota
and landed in Indiana the next day to marry the monsignor before a justice of the peace. They were both twenty-eight. For seven and a half years,
O'Connell "lived a bizarre and schizophrenic existence, switching back
and forth between two entirely different lives," using the surname Roe at
home in Manhattan on East Thirty-sixth Street (his mother-in-law lived
with them) and shuttling to Boston for his church duties. The couple had
no children. They lived well. James O'Toole writes:

> In the summer of 1913 they sailed to Europe for a delayed honey-
> moon, declaring $1,600 worth of purchases after returning . . . Mr.
> Roe speculated in real estate, almost certainly with money that
> Monsignor O'Connell was embezzling from the church. The need
> to support his life in New York gave him the motive for such a
> crime just as surely as his access to large sums in Boston gave him
> the opportunity. Father [John] Mullen later claimed that an un-
> named Boston banker estimated the pilfering at three-quarters of
> a million dollars.[64]

But it was a second priest, one David Toomey, whose secret life set
the wheels of fate in motion. Father Toomey, the *Pilot* editor, was James
O'Connell's close friend—so close that he visited the O'Connells/Roes on
their European honeymoon. Mrs. Roe well knew who her husband was.

When David Toomey fell in love and married Florence Fossa, a friend of the Roes', he bluffed his bride, insisting he was some kind of secret agent in those stretches of work away. Toomey was Cardinal O'Connell's confessor. He literally absolved the cardinal of his sins. In a scene befitting a comic film, a suspicious Florence trails David to Boston, where she discovers not only that he is a priest but that he is *two-timing* her with his secretary at *The Pilot*! Bursting in on them, Florence ignites an ugly row: the cops come; Florence ends up one-on-one with the cardinal, disgorging the sordid truth about both priests, deriding Monsignor James as "that dirty skunk." The cardinal calms her, then excuses himself as the church lawyer steps in.

Today we would call Florence's $7,500 settlement "hush money."

And Toomey? Down came the sledgehammer of canon law, excommunicating him from priesthood and church. Florence washed her hands of him.[65]

On James, the avuncular cardinal stood passive as fallout from Toomey's disaster wafted through the priestly circles. The papal nuncio in Washington, D.C., met with Florence. Rome demanded the chancellor's ouster. After an amazing seven-year run in his double life, James O'Connell resigned by letter in November 1920 to "secure a respite from the arduous duties."[66] He went down to New York. The O'Connells lived comfortably ever after. Nothing broke in the press; the nephew was never prosecuted for embezzlement. But New England bishops wanted His Eminence out. Why had the cardinal tolerated his nephew's immoral life? The New England bishops confronted O'Connell in a private meeting; his denial inflamed them.

Bishop Walsh of Maine went to Rome bearing a letter signed by the region's brother bishops, calling for O'Connell's ouster. Walsh presented the letter to Pope Benedict XV along with a $17,000 gift from his small diocese. The pope's gravitas on receiving the news left Walsh encouraged, as he sailed back to America, that Boston's corrupt cardinal would soon be gone.

Benedict XV had come through the horrors of World War I with a vision of the papacy as a moral force for the cause of peace; this was a dramatic shift from the more insular concerns of past popes. His predecessor, Pius X, was a great reactionary who persecuted forward-looking theologians for the opaque heresy called "Modernism" (a throwback to Pio Nono's *Syllabus of Errors*); yet Pius X fostered a mild détente with Italy through continued support via Banco di Roma. He relaxed the Vatican prohibition against Italian Catholics voting in parliamentary elections. Pius X rejuvenated European parish life with Gregorian chant and improvements in liturgical music. The only Italian pope since the early nineteenth century to have grown up a peasant, Pius X was the only pontiff of the last two centuries (as of this writing) to become a saint. He is credited with miraculous healing. He died in 1914, one month into the world war. Cardinal Giacomo della Chiesa succeeded him, a Genoese aristocrat who had done diplomatic service in Spain. Della Chiesa took the name Benedict XV.

As he called off the Modernist witch hunt, Benedict XV staked out a position of neutrality for the Holy See in calling for an end to a war marked by "hideous butchery."[67] The French, who had twenty-five thousand priests in active service, were hostile to Vatican neutrality; they saw it as favoring the German coalition that was using submarine attacks. In 1916 Benedict denounced the arms trade as "contrary to the law of nations."[68] Trying to bring Austro-Hungarian and German bishops to support a negotiated peace, Benedict saw a sharp drop in Peter's Pence. Fewer bishops visited Rome; papal audiences shrank in size. Banco di Roma losses were sapping the Holy See's financial base.

American Catholics sent $300,000 a year to Peter's Pence during the war, giving Benedict funds for hospitals and relief projects; his gifts were in the $20,000 range. He provided small loans to Italy and authorized two thousand priests to mobilize as medical orderlies. In August 1917 Benedict issued a Peace Note, calling for negotiations to halt the "useless carnage," laying out a seven-point plan for disarmament to include an international court of justice. Furious, Italian generals called for his execution. German officials withdrew interest as the battling gained momentum. On October 24, 1917, Austro-Hungarian troops, backed by Germans, smashed Italy's defenses at Caporetto, blasting through with a ferocity that saw 300,000 die in a nightmare of slaughtered corpses sunk in muck, bunched along roads, and wedged among dead horses; bodies choked the swollen rivers as 600,000 civilians fled in terror.[69]

In Milan, a wounded soldier who had resumed his post as a newspaper editor, one Benito Mussolini, derided "His Holiness Pope Pilate XV." Mussolini called for a leader with "the delicate touch of an artist and the heavy fist of a warrior . . . A man who knows the people, loves the people and can direct and bend it—with violence if necessary."[70] Italy's industrialization mobilized nearly a million workers to manufacture matériel and vehicles. As the German alliance went down, a fleeting sense of triumph swept Italy; the papacy was dependent on American support. For Italy, the costs of maintaining a large navy and army began squeezing the economy.

As nations gathered for the 1919 Treaty of Versailles, Benedict was distressed at being denied a place. President Woodrow Wilson adopted several of the pope's 1917 planks in his Fourteen Points for Peace, and later visited the pope. Versailles instead produced a treaty distorted by fines that drove Germany deeper into poverty, laying punishment over defeat rather than fostering a peaceful rebuilding, as the pope helplessly looked on. In an encyclical, Benedict brooded on the "immense areas utterly desolate, uncultivated and abandoned . . . innumerable widows and orphans bereft of everything."[71]

Italy was reeling from inflation and Mussolini's Fascists were gaining ground using terrorist tactics against Catholics and leftists when Bishop Walsh of Maine gave Benedict the news of Cardinal O'Connell and his corrupt nephew.

Rarely does the pope remove an ecclesial prince or even a bishop. Temptations of hubris—pride rationalizing a cover-up for "the good of the church"—are enormous. Imagine, too, Benedict's frustration at handcuffed diplomacy from Pio Nono's intransigence of a bygone era: he was still a geographic prisoner. In 1920, after 10 million deaths in the Great War, Benedict held a huge ceremony at the Vatican to make Joan of Arc a saint. He hoped it would ease tensions between France's monarchists and the modern Catholics sympathetic to a "free church in a free state." Eighty French officials attended the sainthood rites. Against this backdrop, when the Holy Father turned his attention to the matter of Boston's cardinal, it must have seemed small-scale.

Benedict soon sent word: the U.S. bishops must agree on the cardinal's guilt before a Vatican intervention. In a war-tested response, the pope was telling the princes and bishops who powered his financial base to decide if *they* wanted what amounted to a court-martial. Abuses revealed in "the internal forum" were not public. Sins of the nephew had not made the press. To punish Cardinal O'Connell would not mean disclosing the facts; far from it: avoiding scandal to the church was paramount. But *some* reason must be given. Removing a prince also meant finding him a face-saving job in the Vatican. Here was the papal mind: the rare punishment of a prince must be soft-gloved and as subtle as possible.

By throwing the decision back on the bishops, did Benedict assume they would stall? In the logic of apostolic succession, the bishops considered themselves the descendants of Jesus's apostles. Who among them compared with Judas? In 1921 O'Connell sent a whopping $60,000 to Peter's Pence. Time passed. O'Connell stayed in Boston. An affair of state, his funeral in 1944 drew 25,000 mourners who sat in Holy Cross Cathedral, with 10,000 more outside.[72]

The fears of some bishops that infallibility would wreck the church did not materialize. Antipapal rhetoric ran like brushfire as bishops established dioceses from the Reconstruction years into the 1920s economic boom. In affirming freedom for all churches rather than the superiority of any one, the U.S. Constitution liberated ethnic immigrants to *worship* rather than work for their lives under a clergy overseer or distant pope. The democracy Pio Nono so reviled gave the American church a new lease on life. Mass attendance in Italy, France, and Spain declined in the early 1900s amid a hardening anticlericalism, while in America a church with blue-collar foundations had a 75 percent attendance at weekly Mass. With a papal endorsement in *Rerum Novarum*, labor unions won the support of American priests and a good number of bishops.

In 1916 the newly installed archbishop of Chicago, George Mundelein, sent $62,000 to Benedict for Peter's Pence.[73] Mundelein created his own banking system with procedures for pastors to build or expand on churches, schools, and parish complexes. No parish could exceed $200,000 in debt; the chancery had to approve all construction costs. Mundelein floated church-backed bond issues. With a banker's eye, he pooled surplus parish funds, facilitating loans from wealthier to poorer parishes. "Mundelein treated most pastors like financial idiots," states his biographer Edward Kantowicz."[74] As cardinal he made the archdiocese a financial powerhouse. Mundelein presided over Chicago's expansion; his contributions to Peter's Pence ran to six figures through the 1920s. But of all the American contributions in that era, the largest came in 1921—the year Boston's scandal-tainted O'Connell sent $60,000—when Archbishop Dennis Dougherty of Philadelphia, on becoming the third U.S. cardinal, sent a stunning $1 million in Peter's Pence. In the aftershocks of World War I, Benedict needed every dollar of it.[75]

Like Boston, Philadelphia was about one-fourth Irish, yet more tightly woven and more prosperous, as financial writer Charles R. Morris reports in *American Catholic*. The percentage of Irish in the general population before the Civil War was roughly the same in the two cities (about 20 percent), but the Irish accounted for 18 percent of grocers in Philadelphia, as opposed to just a single percent in Boston.[76] The Irish flourished in Philadelphia's construction trades; an entrepreneur by the name of Rafferty organized thirty-five parish loan societies with funding of at least $15 million. With solid blue-collar and middle-class well-kept neighborhoods, topped off by wealthier precincts, Catholic Philadelphia threw out a huge welcome for Archbishop Dennis Dougherty. A native of Scranton, Dougherty studied in Rome, was made a bishop there and dispatched to the Philippines, then served in Buffalo before he detrained at Philadelphia on a winter day in 1918 with 150 priests in escort. En route to the cathedral, he was cheered by 150,000 Catholics as he "sat in an open limousine, ruddy and smiling, behind an entourage of roaring motorcycles, fifty brass bands, and seventy-five automobiles," writes Morris. "Old ladies broke through the police line all along the way to run up and kiss the ring." Civic leaders turned out, four thousand strong, "including the governor-elect, the state attorney general, the mayor and all the important ministers and rabbis . . . that night for a grand reception."[77]

Spectacles like that do not happen today. The abuse crisis and issues of financial honesty have sapped the American hierarchy of the moral stature by which an archbishop comes a hero to his grateful city. In another time, Mundelein, O'Connell, Spellman, and the building bishops bestrode the public square as symbols of a triumphal church. Dougherty made his archdiocese one of Pennsylvania's largest landowners. The cardinal bought acreage in outlying areas before suburbanization, anticipating tracts to one day site a parish, and leased sections "back to the previous owners until he was ready to use [them]—the strategy of a cash-rich, long-term player." Dougherty foresaw the trend of developers allocating large tracts in a subdivision for a parish, calculating that home owners wanted churches: build, and they will come. Dougherty was his own developer, selling land to a planned parish, which the archdiocese financed, with any excess property sold for whatever the market would bear. Dougherty jocoseriously called himself "God's bricklayer." God's banker is just as apt. Charles Morris calls him "something of a tycoon" in real estate. When he died in 1951 the archdiocese, virtually debt free, had assets with fair market values in the "several hundred million range."[78]

The support ethnic Americans gave to their parishes registered an approval of Romanità, its trappings of royalty and the beauty of liturgical rituals that ran through the year. The church was a spiritual anchor with aesthetic grace to uplift people from the grit and stresses of workaday life. As the generations advanced to the middle class, embezzlement by clerics like the Boston cardinal's nephew and priests' sexual transgressions were aberrations quietly covered "for the good of the church." Philadelphia under Dougherty, Chicago under Mundelein, Boston under O'Connell, and large dioceses in California, the Northeast, and the Midwest signaled Catholic triumphalism.

THE FAUSTIAN PACT WITH FASCISM

Liberal Italy had ended Pio Nono's suppression of Jews. Under Benedict XV, "the anti-Semitic campaign in the papally-linked press was soon suppressed," writes David Kertzer.[79] As the first pope in a global war, Benedict XV controlled little land; he made quiet moves through intermediaries for a financial resolution with Italy over the lost territory, while Italy blunted his overtures to Britain and France for peace negotiations. After the war, Benedict broadened the church's global role, sending missionaries to poor countries. In Italy, he saw Socialists and Communists gaining strength, stirring fears of Russian persecution of the church under Lenin's Communist regime. In Italy, the pope gave covert support to unions and peasant groups that coalesced behind a Catholic political movement. Money, or the lack of it, still hounded the pope. In 1919 he sent an emissary to America seeking a $1 million loan. The bishops were hard-pressed, but the Knights of Columbus provided $250,000 in a lavish ceremony; dressed in knightly regalia, they received Holy Communion from the Supreme Pontiff in the Apostolic Palace.

In 1920, with papal finances still a juggling act, a charismatic priest named Luigi Sturzo, who had won a mayoralty in Sicily, galvanized a national movement, Partito Popolare Italiano, also known as the Catholic Party. In an extraordinary surge, Sturzo's PPI won 1.1 million votes to capture a fifth of the Chamber of Deputies, becoming Italy's second-largest party almost overnight. A brilliant organizer, Sturzo pushed land reform and workers' rights. The *Chicago Tribune*'s legendary correspondent George Seldes was struck by Sturzo's pacifism and loyalty to the pope.[80] As violence spread against churches and Catholic groups, Benedict wanted Italy to ensure security. The war had boosted his prestige; twenty-seven countries had posted ambassadors to the Holy See.

In 1921, the year Benedict sent 5 million lire for famine relief in Russia, Mussolini and thirty-five Fascists won seats in the chamber. Mussolini (who had called priests "black microbes") considered the church his chief threat as he used terrorism to cement a political base. "His *squadristi* descended upon towns and villages, burning, looting, killing," wrote Seldes. "Catholics as well as Socialists were always the victims."[81] The prime minister, who had secretly facilitated Fascists' weapons purchases, sent feelers to Benedict, seeking support from Sturzo to form a new government. Averse to taking a direct role in electoral politics, Benedict knew that Fascist attacks on Catholic groups, which had deposits and loans at Banco di Roma and many smaller banks with predominantly Catholic clientele, were killing innocent people as part of a broader assault on the church. The pope steered funds to assist cash-strapped Catholic newspapers. But he held back from endorsing Father Sturzo's PPI. Many bishops shrank from a Catholic party amid the Fascist assaults. For all of his resolve in shaping a vocabulary for peace, Benedict's detachment from the Catholic Party stemmed from the papacy's long political isolation. But between Fascism and pluralism, why *not* take a stand? In the 1920s Catholic independent parties offered a democratic alternative to Fascists and Nazis.

While his thugs murdered with impunity, Mussolini decried Bolshevism and advocated land reform. In January 1922, with Sturzo steering his party on a middle course, Benedict, "the pope of missions," died at age sixty-seven, of pneumonia caused by flu. He was one of history's greatest popes. The February conclave elected Achille Ratti, a former Vatican archivist whose career Benedict had transformed by dispatching him to Poland as the papal nuncio, then naming him archbishop of Milan. Ratti in Kraków witnessed the Bolshevist fist bent on crushing the church. In Bologna, during a 1921 commemoration of Italy's victory in the Great War, he allowed Fascists to drape a banner in the cathedral. Behind his bookish background, the eleventh pope to take the name Pius was a stern authoritarian skeptical of a "free church in a free state." Pius XI wanted

Catholic solidarity behind his office, a lordly vision that saw democracy as a sideshow. He was also determined to end the stalemate with Italy.

"A myth is a faith, a passion," Mussolini declared. "Our myth is the greatness of our nation."[82] In 1922, with a ragtag army of 30,000 Fascisti, Mussolini marched into Rome, a power strut that Italy's generals could have halted well before its arrival in symbolic triumph, but in a country so politically fragmented, Mussolini's militant charisma straddled many lines. Substantially poorer than France and Britain, Italy faced severe unrest: 400,000 engineering workers occupied factories in September 1920.[83] The society hungered for order, a center, stability to feed prosperity. "Violence is a brutal necessity to which we have been driven," Mussolini told parliamentarians in 1922. "We are prepared to disarm if you, too, are prepared to disarm."[84]

As snakes peel their skin, Mussolini the arriviste prime minister shed his raw anticlericalism. He awarded stipends for parish priests; he advocated restoring religious education in public schools and a crucifix in every class. Mussolini had his three out-of-wedlock children baptized; he married their mother. Where Liberal Italy held to a negotiating posture no prewar pontiff would embrace, the Fascist strongman saw a Catholic-majority country and decided to convert it to his agenda. In the mating ritual of demagogue and pontiff, Mussolini met secretly with Cardinal Pietro Gasparri, the secretary of state, in 1923, and sent a message: if His Holiness broke with the Catholic Party, Il Duce would seed government funds in the faltering Banco di Roma, where Vatican investments teetered. Pius XI ordered Father Sturzo to quit the PPI. Sturzo withdrew from politics; later on he moved to America.

When the Fascists murdered the leader of the Reformist Socialist Party, the PPI withdrew from the parliament in protest, throwing Mussolini's government into a crisis. Just when a movement was gelling around the Catholic Party for an alliance against Fascism, Pius XI denounced any collaboration between Catholics and the left. The pope equated Lenin's persecutions in Russia with even a democratic form of Socialism in Italy. Despite Catholic parties in Italy and Germany pushing for alliances with the moderate left against the Fascist right, Pius wanted the church as the absolute center of Catholic lives. Politics, coalitions, closing ranks to thwart political gangsters, all eluded the pope's purview. Imagine Mussolini's delight: *the pope was hammering his Catholic enemies*. Pius saw Fascism as corrupt, but considered it the lesser of two evils whose leader signaled a receptivity to restoring the church's high role in society. Aloof from ground-level politics, Pius failed to see the value of pluralism over a unilateral dealing with Il Duce for Catholic interests. When Sturzo's party collapsed, Catholic trade unions and peasant groups became more vulnerable. Seventy-four small banks with Catholic clientele folded. The killings continued.

After installing Fascist officers at Banco di Roma, Mussolini shored up its holdings, which helped stabilize Vatican finances. He gained support on Wall Street and with the Hoover administration for a break on Italy's war debt. The State Department took an "at least he's our bastard" approach to Mussolini, prizing rough unity over the Fascist homicides. King George V gave Mussolini a medal in Rome. Such cynicism on human rights would plague Anglo-American foreign policy for generations. Deported by Mussolini, George Seldes published *Sawdust Caesar*, a prophetic 1935 biography of Il Duce.

In pushing for church unity, Pius XI showed a comfort with power. Exasperated by retrograde French monarchists in a group called Action Française, Pius XI excommunicated the leader (an anti-Semite at that) and his followers. He summoned the superior of the French seminary in Rome and told him to fire the rector, an AF sympathizer. "Yes, Holy Father," answered the old priest. "I'll see what I can do." Grabbing his beard, the pope snarled, "I said, '*Fire him!*' "[85]

For a pope with such a volatile streak, the reliance on American finances must have been humbling. In 1928 Cardinal Mundelein arranged a $300,000 loan from the Chicago archdiocese for the Holy See. In Rome, a young Boston monsignor, Francis Spellman, had a minor post (overseeing playgrounds built by the Knights of Columbus) that positioned him to befriend wealthy Americans who spent winters in the Eternal City. Spellman facilitated financial gifts to Vatican officials on up to the pope. "Holy Father asked me for three autos," Spellman wrote in his diary on February 8, 1929.[86] But the days of papal begging for limousines were about to end.

Cardinal Gasparri met with Mussolini at his residences over several years, negotiating in fits and starts. On February 11, 1929, Gasparri, as papal surrogate, signed the Lateran Pacts with Prime Minister Mussolini in a brief ceremony. Vatican City became a sovereign, neutral state with ownership of fourteen churches and properties in Rome. Catholicism became Italy's official religion. The Holy See would control the appointment of bishops. In compensation for parts of Rome and the Papal States, Italy paid the equivalent of $92 million. The Vatican agreed to reinvest about 60 percent of it into government bonds.

"Italy has been given back to God and God to Italy," the Vatican paper *L'Osservatore Romano* exulted. Pius was pleased that Mussolini was overpowering Communism in Italy. But the Lateran treaty was Faustian at both ends. Mussolini tightened his grip on Italy, gaining respect on the world stage, while bankrolling his adversary, whose office magnified in global public opinion. Mussolini won a huge boost in Catholic popularity, particularly where he most needed it, in northern Italy. Pius gushed that Mussolini was "a man sent by providence."[87] As if heeding the whispers of Pio Nono's ghost, he signed the death warrant of the PPI, but as time passed he watched in horror as Fascism forged its creed. "Like the Christian ideal, the Fascist ideal is one in a state of perpetual becoming," a party secretary declared.[88] An ex-Fascist likened the radiant banners, mass marches, and solemn torch-lit rites to "a religion, a divinity all its own: the State, with its own Supreme worship . . . to which everything should be sacrificed." In 1931 Mussolini pulled Boy Scouts from parishes into Fascist groups, saying, "Youth shall be ours." Pius used an encyclical to condemn Fascism as "Pagan worship of the State."[89]

He was absolutely correct but by then in a quagmire of his own making.

Gasparri retired in 1930. In the next few years Pius, through his secretary of state, Eugenio Pacelli, oversaw concordats with European countries to secure papal authority in naming bishops, state support for clergy salaries, and autonomy for Catholic Action. Pius XI saw this movement of laypeople guided by bishops and clergy as a crusade waged by a Christian army against immorality in popular culture. "One of its tasks," Peter Godman writes of Catholic Action, "was to regain the allegiance and sympathies of the working classes alienated by Communism."[90] But in promoting an ethos of social cohesion through the church, Pius XI turned his back on party politics at a time when pluralism was the last hedge against the boot heel. When Cardinal Pacelli, a skilled diplomat and future pope, signed the 1933 concordat with Germany, the centrist Catholic Party there was in eclipse. As Pacelli ruefully joked to a British envoy, the Nazis "would probably not violate all of the articles of this Concordat at the same time."[91]

After its long estrangement from Liberal Italy, the Vatican became a financial partner of Fascist Italy. Pius launched a major construction project to remediate decades of deferred maintenance and expansion of the Vatican infrastructure, work that pumped Rome's sagging economy. His pivotal move was the hiring of Bernardino Nogara to manage the many millions. Papa Ratti, as Italians called Pius, was from Milan, the industrial and fashion center. The Milanese looked down on Romans as lazy, unproductive bureaucrats—"*Roma ladrona*," Rome the big thief. For financial advice Pius turned to a small group of Milanese, including his brother, a count, who became a key figure in the Vatican's civil administration. Among the Milanese, Nogara came with a good pedigree. An engineer who had managed mining operations in Britain and Bulgaria before the war, he had gone on to Istanbul as a vice president of the Banca Commerciale Italiana, and later worked on the Economic Council of the 1919 Versailles Treaty conference. A specialist in international currency, Nogara was a devout Catholic who kept a copy of *The Divine Comedy* at his bedside. He was on good terms with the Ratti family, and among his own siblings, two brothers were seminary rectors, a sister was the mother superior at a convent, and another brother supervised the Vatican Museums. When Pius XI asked the fifty-nine-year-old Nogara to run the newly established Special Administration, managing the Lateran windfall of $92 million of which $39.7 million went to the Vatican (the other $52.4 million went into government bonds at 5 percent), Nogara reportedly insisted that his investment not be constrained by religious or doctrinal issues, and that he be free to invest Vatican funds anywhere in the world he so chose. Pius said yes.[92]

Nogara guided investments in stocks, bonds, currency exchanges, and gold, amassing profits for the Holy See's muscular new wealth as the global financial crisis squeezed Italy. Mussolini created an Institute for Industrial Reconstruction (IRI) which issued bonds (backed by banks and insurance and mortgage companies) through which the state gained control of key industries. Nogara became an IRI adviser and made Vatican investments in the safest bonds.

"Whenever I read the words: *The sacrifice of our Father Abraham,* I cannot help but be deeply moved," Pius XI exclaimed tearfully to a group of visiting Belgians on September 6, 1938. "Mark well, we call Abraham our Patriarch, our ancestor. Anti-Semitism is irreconcilable with this lofty thought, the noble reality which this prayer expresses . . . But anti-Semitism is inadmissible. Spiritually, we are all Semites." Father

Sturzo, the exiled leader of the banned PPI, made sure the pope's words got published in a Belgian newspaper.[93]

Pius XI's change of heart did not ignite a collective mind shift. The Vatican did not report his words. Inside the Curia Fascist sympathizers worked alongside priests of a broader worldview. Anti-Semitism was a curse of the clerical culture that surfaced in Catholic journals in America and Europe, including *Commonweal* and *America*, in the 1930s.[94] Many bishops who backed the New Deal kept silent on Mussolini and the slurs on Jews by the popular "radio priest" from Detroit, Charles Coughlin, until his career ended.

As Mussolini closed ranks with Hitler, Nogara shifted the investments into U.S. manufacturing, bonds, and, in a $7.6 million transfer of Vatican gold out of London, the Federal Reserve.[95] Italy joined Germany's march to war. Pius XI scorned "barbaric Hitlerism" and "the myth of race and blood." When he passed away in 1939, Mussolini said, "At last, that stubborn old man is dead."[96] As the war ended in 1945, anti-Fascist partisans captured Mussolini and his mistress, executed them, and hung their corpses upside down in Milan.

Cardinal Pacelli became Pius XII. The son of a Vatican lawyer and financial adviser to Pio Nono and Leo XIII, Eugenio Pacelli had a lifelong friendship with one of Rome's distinguished Jewish physicians in whose home he had shared Sabbath dinner as a youth. In 1916, as a young monsignor, he drafted a statement for Benedict XV in support of Poland's Jews.[97] As the beleaguered pontiff in World War II, Pius XII ordered priests, nuns, and nuncios (like Angelo Roncalli in Istanbul, the future John XXIII) to help Jews avoid Nazi deportations to death camps. His refusal to publicly denounce Hitler and the Nazis was "a failure of the papal office itself and the prevailing culture of Catholicism," charged John Cornwell in the provocatively titled *Hitler's Pope*.[98] Later, in a paperback edition, Cornwell retracted some of his criticism; however, the book spotlighted deep divisions among historians and Jewish leaders over historic anti-Semitism in the Vatican and larger European church, and whether the Holocaust could have been halted. The ongoing debate has such severe implications for Catholic-Jewish relations that Pius's candidacy for sainthood seems stalled.[99] Yet he was praised by Albert Einstein in 1940 as a defender of Jews and by Golda Meir, then Israel's foreign minister, at the time of his death. In the thirteen years after the war, Pius stood on the global stage as a symbol of peace. Regardless of how the debate transpires over Pius XII's wartime reticence about Hitler and the Nazis, the two world wars turned the papal agenda toward the cause of peace, and under John Paul II the sanctity of human rights. That evolution hit a turning point in 1965, when Paul VI, speaking to the United Nations General Assembly, raised his arms and cried: "No more war! War never again."[100] How far the papacy had come since Pio Nono's complaint to a British envoy that he could not execute a single rebel in the Papal States.

In the century of that transition, the Vatican financial system shifted from a religious monarchy, scrambling to recover from the loss of Rome and the Papal States' fiefdom, to the emergent economy of the Holy See, which relied on Peter's Pence to accrue dividends by investing in the city of Rome through the decades in which the pope was a putative Vatican prisoner. Who is to say whether Italians or any other believers in the pews of American churches would object to the use of those funds had they known? None of them wanted a pope in rags. Thanks to Mussolini's payout, Bernardino Nogara forged a hybrid form of religious capitalism by investing in Roman infrastructure, gold, and foreign markets. In 1942, Pius XII established the Vatican Bank.

CHAPTER 3

SEEDS OF REVOLT

Peter Borré was no bleeding heart on the subject of poverty, but he believed in Christian duty. The low-rise projects off Mystic River were the largest concentration of public housing in New England. Borré realized that the pastor of St. Catherine of Siena, Father Bob Bowers, was about more than "reaching out" to the lowliest members of his flock. Bowers's liturgies featured Spanish songs. Rosie Piper adored Bob Bowers, the pastor with a youthful face and graying hair who welcomed the Dominicans and Puerto Ricans as he preached about dignity. Borré liked Bowers's energy for the parish, once a lost cause, now a blossoming place.

The parish named for Saint Catherine of Siena lay at the base of Bunker Hill Street. Midway up Charlestown's long incline stood St. Mary parish, a Tudor Gothic gem, just past Monument Square and the obelisk that pointed like a needle toward the sky. Several blocks farther up, St. Francis de Sales was the most insular and rock-hard Irish of the three parishes.

Bowers organized a food pantry for hungry people and English-as-a-second-language classes taught by a volunteer Jewish doctor. Many of the unskilled workers taking ESL had no citizenship papers. *He runs a good church,* Rosie Piper told herself. She felt her $10 donation on Sunday was helping Bowers steer a parish full of life. Imagining Father Bowers thirty years on, she wrote a $100 check for the spring 2003 collection for the clergy retirement fund.

Borré assumed that when the deal was struck on the settlements for the 552 clergy abuse victims, grown now and with gladiatorial attorneys, the church coffers would take a hard dent that the new archbishop would repair over time. He thought Bowers a bit of a sentimental liberal, but he liked his work and saw how hard he gave to the parish.

Warm and outgoing, with an easy wit, Bowers had been inspired by Dorothy Day's radical witness in the Catholic Worker Movement, where activists lived at homeless shelters and soup kitchens. He liked the liberation theology of Latin America and had been active in a group assisting the victims of the Chernobyl nuclear disaster in the Soviet Union. Bowers drew his values from an ideal of Jesus as a peacemaker, and peace as a living force of hope.

Born in 1960, Bob Bowers had grown up in Greater Boston, an attorney's son with three older brothers by whom he now had eight nephews. On graduating from Boston College in 1982 with a B.A. in philosophy, Bowers entered St. John, the archdiocesan seminary in Brighton. As a priest, his assignments had been in comfortable parishes where, with one exception, he had felt welcome. His previous parish had been in Milton, six miles outside of Boston.

Bowers had gotten his new assignment from Cardinal Law two days after the terrorist attacks of September 11, 2001. Exhausted from the jammed prayer services in Milton, he entered the chancery in a daze from the endless TV loop of airplanes smashing into skyscrapers, spitting back balls of fire and smoke.

Law, then sixty-nine, with white hair and a thick girth, rose from his desk with a smile. Too young to call him "Bernie" as certain older clergy did, Bowers issued a deferential "Your Eminence." Law was a Boston potentate at ease with politicians, bankers, and CEOs. But he had an emotional distance that many priests noticed, a self-centeredness that some speculated came from his background as an only child, seeing himself as the pivot point in most situations. In 1985, when Law was invested as a cardinal, several hundred Bostonians traveled to Rome. At a reception in the North American College courtyard, Law declared, "This is the strongest moment for the church since the Reformation."[1]

Strong is one way to describe Law's presence at the Congregation for

Bishops in Rome: he became the go-to prelate in choosing new men for the U.S. hierarchy. The prefect of Bishops, Cardinal Giovanni Battista Re, met with Pope John Paul II every Saturday; he saw the pope's esteem for Law and acted accordingly.[2] Law, a maker of bishops, made monthly trips to Rome. In Boston, he made late-night hospital rounds, visiting sick people, taking time to chat with his chaplains. Law was generally benevolent toward his priests, but he had a strain of cold arrogance. At a clergy conference on canon law issues, Law interrupted a lecturer to declare, "Father, while I am in this archdiocese, *I am the Law!*"[3]

Bowers's previous encounter with Law had been in 1996, when the young priest asked to be reassigned; he shared a rectory with an alcoholic pastor whose rage made daily life toxic. Law sent him to Milton, where he thrived. But the old drunk had gotten under Bowers's skin. "I want to share with you what it is like," he had written in a *National Catholic Reporter* essay:

Some do not seem to know how to pastor or why. They prefer the title and the image, which is accountable to none. I have known them. I thought we were colleagues. I thought we would collaborate. I thought we would empower. I never thought we were better than anyone else. But I never thought I would be treated as less than others.

If you are not a priest, if you have never been a priest, you cannot know what I am talking about. I barely know myself. I know I am disappointed. I thought priests followed Jesus and made mistakes. I did not know it was a mistake to think all priests follow Jesus. There are indeed some who follow power. And they are a disappointment.

Does that sound harsh? I pause in my heart to laugh about it and to cry. Priests who will not share, cannot share love. Pastors and autocrats who know their word is law. Institutions long decayed that shut people out, out of Eucharist, out of authority, out of governance, out of a shared wisdom. They do not listen, except to denial. They don't have to.

I wonder if they are afraid or hurt. But I no longer excuse it.

We are not crying about some "vocation crisis." We are not whining about the work and the task. We are not complaining

about celibacy and sexual identity and the roles men and women
play in the church. These things just add to the already burden-
some experience of being disappointed. We just want to survive.[4]

Cardinal Law wrote Bowers, demanding a letter to explain why he wrote
the article. Bowers complied; Law then summoned him. Bowers's geneal-
ogy included three cousins who had been nuns and a pair of granduncles
who were priests. He unburdened himself, telling Law how his rectory
experiences had fallen gallingly short of his seminary expectations—the
drunken priest nearly attacked him in one of his stupors. He spoke about
the chasm he felt from certain older clerics who were robed in pomposity.
Law listened. When Bowers finished, Law said, "I ordained you once and
I'd do it again." That was it: issue resolved. Law had registered *his* message:
No more troublesome articles, Father.

Bowers left the chancery on a wave of ambivalence.

Fluent in Spanish, Law was a strong advocate for dark immigrants who
came to Boston. The son of a U.S. Air Force officer, he was born in Mexico
and moved often with his parents. Elected president of his black-majority
high school class in the Virgin Islands, Bernie Law went to Harvard, and
on graduation entered the seminary. As a young priest in Mississippi during the 1960s, he championed the civil rights struggle and became a monsignor at the Jackson diocese, striding on the good side of history. After
working in Washington, D.C., for the bishops' conference, he became a
bishop and spent several years at the head of a small diocese in Missouri.
In 1984 Pope John Paul II named him archbishop of Boston, an area of
144 towns and cities, with nearly 2 million Catholics. Law announced
that the archdiocese would cover the maternity costs and handle adoption
for any unwanted pregnancy. After he became a cardinal in 1985, far fewer
people called him Bernie. He liked "Your Eminence."

His absolutism on abortion and on gay relationships did not endear
Law to liberals. But he forged ties with Jewish leaders in an ecumeni-
cal spirit, and was a visible advocate for poor people, regardless of their
citizenship. Catholic conservatives bridled when he gave Communion
to pro-choice senators Ted Kennedy and John Kerry. He backed Con-
gressman Joe Kennedy's annulment request, to remain a Catholic in
good standing after his second marriage. Kennedy's annulment took on
a ten-year odyssey through the Vatican courts, before it was stunningly

revoked, after a well-documented appeal by his former wife, Sheila Rauch Kennedy. She dissected the process in a 1997 memoir, *Shattered Faith*. After her position was vindicated, she called the process "very dishonest . . . The way it is used in American tribunals, it can be anything—a bad hair day, your goldfish died, you weren't playing with a full deck when you married twenty years ago. And people defending [the marriage], usually women, have been belittled."[5]

In sermons Law tended to elongate his vowels, a high sign of gravitas. Socially, he had silken charm. But the side of Law that had to have things his way showed in 1992, when he lashed out at media coverage of James Porter, a notorious ex-priest whose crimes caught up with him, at great cost to the Fall River diocese, as Porter went to jail. In a rare rupture of self-control, Law declared, "By all means we call down God's power on the media, particularly the *Globe*."[6] But his private side showed traces of doubt. In 1998 Law agreed to sit for an artist named Channing Thieme who was preparing an exhibition called Boston Faces. Thieme, a non-Catholic, approached him with a natural curiosity; they bantered in the two sessions as he struck a formal pose. When she returned with the finished picture, Law was delighted. What's the toughest part of your job? she asked.

"Judgment—the decisions I must make," he replied. As if peering ahead in time to some dark pit, Law added, "That is the half of it. The other half is the judgment I must one day face myself."[7]

Smoke was still rising in Manhattan from the rubble of the Twin Towers as Bob Bowers sat once more with Cardinal Law, saying that he *liked* the parish in Milton he had served for nearly six years. Law told him that St. Catherine in Charlestown was struggling to survive. Bowers's assignments had been in middle-class to upper-crust parishes; he had dreamed of working for the poor in the spirit of Dorothy Day. Law had been quietly closing several parishes a year where population shifts had left churches too empty and impoverished to survive. "Save the school," Law told him.

"Is the parish a sinking ship?"

"That parish will never close," Law declared.

Law handed him an envelope and keys. Bowers left with his new assignment. Not a word had passed between them on the parish assessment, the tax each parish pays the diocese based on its average collections. Unpaid assessments accrue interest. Law had forgiven the assessments of several poor parishes in the past. Bowers never gave the chancery taxes a thought. He was bound for the front lines—to stabilize a parish, to save a school.

St. Catherine of Siena was the poorest of the three parishes within a square mile; the other two were nearly all-white. Bowers's three-story rectory of twenty-eight rooms (with suites for five bedrooms) was an underutilized relic from an era of abundant priests. Nuns who once taught the students, drawing no salary, were gone; the school was scratching by with 120 students, most of them white. After making inquiries, Bowers learned that about seventy-five kids from the parishes up the hill went to parochial schools outside Charlestown. Dominican and Puerto Rican families who made up a third of his parish were too poor to afford school tuition, yet the parish's image hindered white recruitment for the school.

The church had gone through several pastors. "One guy had been arrested for beating up a housekeeper at a previous parish," recalled Bowers, "and the guy after him was so introverted he couldn't light a fire. I inherited a disaster." He grinned. "It was a dream assignment." The Sunday liturgies coalesced around a rainbow of people, about a third of them old Irish with local roots, another third Hispanic and mostly poor, the others upper income like Peter Borré from the storied Naval Shipyard.

The world tilted on January 6, 2002, the Feast of the Epiphany, when the *Globe* Spotlight Team, led by Walter V. Robinson, began reporting how Law and his circle of former auxiliary bishops had played musical chairs with child molester priests over the previous sixteen years. The articles rained down like lightning bolts on Bowers and pastors across the metropolitan area, jarring them and laypeople even more so with indignation about what Law and the assisting bishops had done.

Many priests were depressed; after each new report, they felt humiliated standing on the altar. The numbers at Mass began to drop; outrage in the pews was palpable. Law made public apologies. But as the plaintiff lawyers advanced and the *Globe* dug deeper, Cardinal Law in the media narrative became linked with the victims. Like an army inching up Macbeth's hill, the survivors were pushing toward a reckoning with his power, his fate.

A survivor named Arthur Austin planted himself in front of the cathedral, day after day, like a Jew at the Wailing Wall, a media sensation as the Boston story sparked questions in other newsrooms about bishops hiding other priests. Law made the *Newsweek* cover on March 4 with the subtitle "80 Priests Accused of Child Abuse in Boston—and New Soul-Searching

Across America." On those frigid days outside Holy Cross Cathedral downtown, Art Austin confided, "I felt like Sisyphus—being punished not for being bad but telling the truth."[8]

A sense of agony seeped into the marrow of Catholic Boston. At Mass, Bowers saw the anguish in people's body language, the strained faces telegraphing betrayal. He began his sermon one Sunday by stating that *he* needed to hear from *them*. Words gushed out of people who were livid at the cardinal and bishops for sending predators to new places, fresh victims. "That *bastard*, Bernard Law!" thundered one man. People said *Shush!* Bowers let him vent.

A clamor rose in the media for Law's resignation; he lumbered on.

In late April, Law flew to Rome to meet with Pope John Paul and seven other U.S. cardinals as the crisis made international headlines. Scores of reporters converged on Vatican City. Bowers followed the *Globe* and TV news.

John Paul was enfeebled by Parkinson's. His face swollen, body bent, and voice slurred, the pope once so hale and charismatic now sadly seemed to personify a power structure weak and out of touch. In a shaky voice he read a paper calling the abuse "an appalling sin in the eyes of God." But a few lines later he washed the hands of guilty bishops in saying that "a generalized lack of knowledge, and also at times the advice of the clinical experts led bishops to make [the wrong] decisions"—*blame the therapists*. As the church worked to "establish more reliable criteria," he continued, they should not forget "the power of Christian conversion . . . that radical decision to turn away from sin and back to God"—implying redemption of some kind for sex offender clerics.

The pope doesn't get it, thought Peter Borré, riveted to his TV set.

He wondered if anyone had a plan.

"People need to know that there is no place in the priesthood and religious life for those who would harm the young," declared John Paul.

But how did that square with "the power of Christian conversion"?[9] Would the pederasts be defrocked? How did Vatican courts enforce justice?

CARDINALS IN CRISIS

A world away from the daily lives of Bowers and countless priests, the cardinals and Curial members close to the pope retreated to a private caucus.

Law disappeared from the coverage. Borré shook his head. *If Law can't make his stand at the Vatican, he's finished.* The whole mess reminded him of Watergate.

The afternoon of April 23, 2002, at the closed meeting in the Apostolic Palace, beneath the ornate frescoes of Sala Bologna, Law apologized to the pope's inner circle and his brother cardinals. Prior to that, the *Los Angeles Times* had quoted an unnamed cardinal saying Law should resign. Reporter Larry Stammer's access to Cardinal Roger Mahony of Los Angeles fed speculation that the tall, lanky cardinal, who had said Frank Sinatra's funeral Mass after persuading him to make confession, viewed Law as a liability for Princes of the Church.[10]

Cardinal Darío Castrillón Hoyos had his own view. A native of Colombia, Castrillón was a remarkable linguist whose persona radiated confidence; he slept in the bed of Pope Pius XII.[11] Prefect of the Congregation for the Clergy, he had a classic Latin strain of the authoritarian, a religious version of the *caudillo*, or dictator. He bristled at the media's anti-Catholic bias. In a press conference several weeks prior to the cardinals' visit, Castrillón amazed reporters by calling the crisis a problem rooted in American society's "pan-sexuality and sexual licentiousness."[12] Besides monitoring the disposition of church property, Clergy oversaw the rights of priests, and in that sphere Castrillón had experience.

In 1992 Father Robert Trupia challenged the bishop of Tucson when he was suspended for transgressions with youths. A canonist, Trupia filed an appeal at Clergy charging that Bishop Manuel Moreno's investigation was flawed—Moreno had prejudged him. Trupia wrote to Moreno, calling himself a "loose cannon," threatening to reveal that he had had a sexual relationship with a deceased bishop, that the two of them and a third priest had had sex with a teenage drug addict. In exchange for his silence, Trupia, then forty-two, proposed to retire with a pension in good standing. Moreno asked him to enter a mental hospital. Under Castrillón's predecessor, Clergy softened the bishop's order to an administrative leave. Trupia appealed to the Apostolic Signatura, the Vatican equivalent of the Supreme Court. Moreno hired a canonist in Rome to represent his position. As Clergy's newly minted prefect, Castrillón (himself a canonist) asserted his authority in a December 13, 1996, letter to Moreno requesting that he "resolve this matter by means of a 'reasonable solution.' "[13]

We *strongly urge* Your Excellency to enter into meaningful dialogue with Monsignor Trupia regarding the terms of solution he has proposed. In so doing, Your Excellency would also be well advised . . . that the matter of damages is not outside of the purview of any subsequent decision which may be rendered.

Moreno wrote to Castrillón: "we consider [Trupia's stance] damaging to the faithful as well as to his 'victims' of the past . . . we cannot let Monsignor Trupia 'loose' if we do not know whether he is respectful and faithful to the priesthood." Castrillón replied on October 31, 1997: "Concerning damages arising from the imposition of an illegitimate decree, it is the mind of this [Congregation] that Your Excellency is liable for these from 2 June 1996 onwards. It would appear best that this matter . . . be resolved in an equitable fashion"—meaning Moreno should provide a package for Trupia to retire in good standing. Castrillón also wanted Moreno to reimburse Trupia's legal expenses and suggested using him as a canon law consultant! Bishop Moreno in his return letter to Castrillón evinces an understandable frustration:

As I informed the Congregation last week, we have now been served with a lawsuit concerning actions of Msgr. Trupia in the mid 1970s concerning a then minor altar boy. These risks are not just imaginary, but real.

I am at a loss to deal with the finding of the Congregation concerning damages. I have paid Msgr. Trupia full salary plus his medical and car insurance at all times, as the Congregation was so informed. I have been given no details so that we can even defend what other damages may have arisen.

Msgr. Trupia has resigned his office and has no right to it.

I have deep respect for the works of the Congregation for the Clergy, however, I have appealed the decision to the Signatura in this matter.

"When I saw those documents," recalls attorney Lynne Cadigan of Tucson, who had several clients abused by Trupia, "I thought, *This is a gold mine*. I know that sounds terrible, but within the confines of the clerical world, Moreno was trying hard to prevent scandal and Castrillón showed the depth of the corruption."[14] Trupia left Tucson with a tidy $1,475 monthly check and found a condo outside Washington, D.C. He landed consulting work as a canon lawyer for the Monterey, California, diocese— until the lawsuits in Arizona made him toxic. With Castrillón's letter as a proverbial smoking gun, Cadigan bargained a $14 million settlement for Trupia's victims. When, finally, the Vatican defrocked Trupia in 2004, the Tucson diocese filed for Chapter 11 bankruptcy protection in the face of claims from thirty-three other victims, most of them from a second priest. The diocese eventually settled those for $22 million.[15]

On the day of the 2002 emergency meeting in the Vatican, it is unlikely the other cardinals knew about Castrillón's fiasco with Trupia. (Michael Rezendes's *Boston Globe* report on Trupia would come four months later.) But Italians in the room knew that in America huge losses were looming. As the cardinals discussed what to say to a waiting world about the crisis, Castrillón drew a bead on the real issue: *dissent*. He and Archbishop Tarcisio Bertone of Genoa—a former Congregation for the Doctrine of the Faith canonist for Cardinal Joseph Ratzinger—insisted that "ambiguous pastoral practices" must be addressed. Priests who failed to uphold church teachings contributed to a permissive climate in the priesthood. The motivations of bishops who recycled pedophiles were not an issue to these men.

Another Curia member echoed Castrillón and Bertone: Cardinal James Francis Stafford, the former archbishop of Denver. He wanted the press communiqué on the crisis to *endorse* the 1968 papal encyclical on birth control[16]—obedience to papal teaching was paramount. But international news had shown an ailing pope with a shaky voice, unable to account for an embedded culture of sexual deviants nor up to the task of commanding an investigation. The Vatican cardinals and archbishops washed their hands by shifting blame to the lower clergy. John Paul, so brilliant a moral force against dictatorships and Soviet Communism, had stood back from the escalating priest abuse cases in the 1990s when he was healthy. He failed to ask why a celibate culture tolerated such harm to children or to ask his cardinals what to do beyond apologies.

Italians dominated the Roman Curia. Their window on the world came from the press that gave textured coverage of the Vatican: *Corriere della Sera*, *Il Giornale*, the newsweekly *L'Espresso*, *La Repubblica*, among others. But Italy's legal system had few of the surgical discovery procedures available to attorneys in America, Ireland, Canada, and Australia, which shared the taproot of British common law. As judges ordered bishops to release their files on accused priests to victims' lawyers, the depth charges from a clergy sexual underground rocked the English-language media. Italian journalists with few documents to cite found only scattered cases. The Curia and other cardinals saw "the scandal" as a product of America's odd legal system and anti-Catholic news media.

Cardinal Joseph Ratzinger did not share his thoughts about the 2002 cardinals' meeting with reporters, as others that day did. Alone among the Curial cardinals gathered there, Ratzinger had set himself on a course to confront the crisis. The American bishops had been stymied in their early efforts to contain the damage. In 1989 the U.S. bishops had canonists seek permission from the Vatican to defrock priests proven to be severe abusers. That authority lay with the pope. And John Paul said no. As a cardinal in Poland he knew the Communist police tapped phones and targeted priests for blackmail. The Polish church was the opposition party. His sense of the priesthood as a beleaguered, heroic counterforce seeded a denial, as pope, on a criminal sexual subculture in the priesthood. Vatican canonists, meanwhile, took the U.S. bishops' request as encroaching on their turf.

"In America the conference on bishops had a *machine* signing off on [marriage] dispensations," a prominent canon lawyer in Rome—interviewed on background—told me with exasperation on a sunny autumn day in 2002. "This was highly criticized in Rome by various respondents in these [annulment] cases . . . That experience of dealing with American bishops set up a resistance to special norms for pedophiles. *We see what you've done with special norms on annulments. What are you going to do with these pedophilia cases?*" To this priest, it was all so clear. "The attitude here in 1989, at the Holy See, was that you have legal provisions. *Use them!*"[17] He meant that bishops should hold secret canonical trials of predators and send the results to the Vatican for a final decision. Church defense lawyers shrank from the idea of creating a documentary record of a church court, only to wait years to get permission to defrock the perpetrator.

The bishops also wanted the five-year statute of limitations on abuse of children, as stated in canon law, expanded—again, so they could kick out perpetrators. "Only after six years of discussion—in 1994—did Rome grant the U.S. bishops a longer statute: ten years after the victim turns

eighteen," writes Nicholas P. Cafardi, a canon law scholar.[18] Had John
Paul granted the 1989 request, and *if American bishops had used it*, defrocking men rather than cycling them through treatment facilities, the
scandal's scope and titanic losses might have been contained. Instead,
for twelve years, bishops sent files on the worst offenders to an array of
offices and congregations in Rome, among them Clergy, Doctrine of the
Faith, the dicastery that oversaw religious orders, the Secretariat of State,
and the Apostolic Signatura, or high court. Most of the files came from
English-speaking countries, through the 1980s and '90s, as "bishops who
sought to penalize and dismiss abusive priests were daunted by a bewil-
dering bureaucratic and canonical legal process, with contradicting laws
and overlapping jurisdictions in Rome," Laurie Goodstein and David M.
Halbfinger later reported in the *New York Times*.[19] The system yielded gro-
tesque ironies like Castrillón helping the pedophile Trupia find canon law
work. In April 2000 bishops from the English-speaking world met with
Vatican officials, pleading for help. In 2001 John Paul signed a document
that Ratzinger all but drafted, which consolidated the responsibility on
the explosive issue in his office.[20]

None of the cardinals, it is safe to say, envied Ratzinger that task.

Ratzinger was prefect of the Congregation for the Doctrine of the Faith
(CDF)—the old Holy Office of the Inquisition. Although it had been re-
named in 1965, Sant'Uffizio (Holy Office) was still emblazoned on the
majestic rust-colored palazzo just behind the colonnade to the left of St.
Peter's. This is the building where Galileo in 1633 was convicted of heresy for claiming the earth revolved around the sun. Most of the investigations at the CDF had involved theologians accused of straying from
orthodoxy. After the 2001 order, the next nine years saw three thousand
cases of priests accused of abusing young people lodged in the office.[21] The
financial reality registered at the Congregation for the Clergy, which is
housed in a stately, pale yellow building of four stories some five hundred
yards across St. Peter's Square from the Sant'Uffizio.

In December 2001, when the papal document confirming Ratzinger's
new authority made news,[22] the ceiling for a bishop to sell church property
was $5 million. A bishop could sell property of lesser value on his own. In
June 2002, amid the worst scandal of modern Catholic history, the bishops
pulled into Dallas for their summer conference trailed by seven hundred
reporters. News coverage swung between survivors staging protests and

the bishops' parliamentary vote for a youth protection charter. In a move that drew far less notice, the bishops voted to raise the ceiling for liquidating assets to $10.3 million in large archdioceses without seeking approval from Rome. In America some two dozen priests had gone back to ministry after jail terms. The U.S. Conference of Catholic Bishops hired R. F. Binder Partners Inc., a Manhattan public relations company that specialized in damage control, to advise them amid the media onslaught after the first four months of 2002.

Back at the Vatican, on that day in 2002 as the cardinals debated other steps to remedy the crisis, Ratzinger suggested a day of prayer for the victims. It was a kind gesture, but the American cardinals faced a bleaker reality. Plaintiff lawyers in the civil suits using discovery subpoenas were gaining ever-deeper access to clergy personnel files, particularly therapists' reports on the priest offenders, in trying to show how much bishops knew. Getting such documents in an Italian or Spanish court would be most unlikely. The more damaging the evidence, the greater the money (and prestige) lost to the church.

As the cardinals' meetings ran through a second day, the Americans wanted a show of solidarity with their colleagues from other countries. But as the final session at the Apostolic Palace ended in the evening of April 23, they had no consensus on *why the crisis happened.*

As the American bishops in 1921 had resisted passing judgment on Boston's cardinal O'Connell for his nephew's secret marriage and misuse of money, so the hierarchs in 2002 avoided talk of Cardinal Law's disaster. His Eminence had apologized as the meeting began. No need of punishment there; thus they turned to more pressing matters. Encased in their small Tower of Babel, the prelates and princes ran late for a news conference. Castrillón and Bertone drafted a communiqué in Italian; three English texts circulated—so many ideas to distill. When the briefing finally began that night, Cardinal Theodore McCarrick of Washington, D.C., normally at ease with the press, faltered when asked why the document said nothing about laypeople: "I was looking for it . . . we had it in there last night." Of Catholics in the pews who had watched the church battered and stained day upon day for nearly five months, the noted author David Gibson wrote: "No reference to their sorrow, their anger, or their possible role in ensuring that such a scandal would never happen again."[23]

The worst Catholic crisis since the Reformation produced a statement that endorsed celibacy as "a gift of God." The cardinals and archbishops called on pastors to "reprimand individuals who spread dissent." The Vatican would conduct a visitation of U.S. seminaries. Bishops would hold a special day of prayer for victims and work on a process to expel "notorious" priests from the priesthood. Many of them were already going to prison.

"Where is Law?" a reporter asked. *"Is he dodging us?"* asked another. "I do not believe so," said the other official at the briefing, Archbishop Wilton Gregory, president of the USCCB. "But I could not tell you why he is not here."[24]

Law flew back to Boston, expecting to resolve the lawsuits with the John Geoghan victims, hoping to salvage some of the standing he had built up in four decades and lost in four months.

In the prosperous suburb of Wellesley, a group had formed called Voice of the Faithful (VOTF), which quickly drew several thousand members. They wanted to support the abuse survivors, affirm priests of integrity, and press the hierarchy for changes. Money was an emotion-charged issue. Joe Finn, a CPA long active on archdiocesan projects, worried about parishioners' funds going for settlements. The archdiocese had an $18 million operating budget, of which $14 million came from the annual Cardinal's Appeal. "They're in steep decline," Finn told VOTF members. "They're already cutting like crazy . . . Look around! There are five hundred cases, *five hundred*. It's nuclear winter here in Boston."[25]

Finn sought an opinion from a canon lawyer for the wealthy Bostonians who served on Law's Finance Council. These were the people who worked the phones, raising the big money when the cardinal asked. Finn sent them the canonist's opinion, which said they could veto a settlement. He added, "You guys have the power to say no." When the Finance Council did just that at a meeting with Law, the legal negotiations hit a wall. A furious Mitchell Garabedian, the plaintiff attorney, accused his counterpart Wilson Rodgers of double-crossing the survivors. Cardinal Law, meanwhile, was in a stew, unable to approve a settlement and *move on*.

The Boston agreement was in limbo when the bishops arrived in Dallas that June. The Binder spin-control team helped the USCCB planners orchestrate a drama of crisis-and-response. The bishops sat in a meeting room; journalists in a spacious reception hall watched by closed-circuit video as four abuse victims, in shaky voices, told the bishops about their lives. The bishops' grim faces joined the harrowing prelude to a vote, the

parliamentary procedure by which they adopted a youth protection charter. They pledged to remove any priest with a single past transgression, a
"zero tolerance" policy that made international headlines and assured a
bottleneck of dismissal cases for Ratzinger's staff in the Sant'Uffizio. The
bishops agreed to empanel advisory boards to field complaints against
priests. The Vatican had already insisted that bishops and cardinals be excluded from the jurisdiction of the lay review boards. One justice standard
for priests, a much softer one for bishops.

A National Review Board for the Protection of Children and Young
People, composed of twelve prominent laypersons led by outgoing Oklahoma governor Frank Keating (a former prosecutor), would conduct
hearings and produce a report. The bishops hired the John Jay College of
Criminal Justice to gather the data on the perpetrators, victims, and costs
to the church. The bishops were still under a harsh media spotlight, but to
their credit, they had responded with apologies, a vote, and a plan.

Back in Boston, assets were under scrutiny. The *Boston Herald* found a
value of "nearly $160 million in land and buildings that are not being used
by the church." Jack Sullivan and Eric Convey reported that the assets
were "a fraction of the archdiocese's total property holdings, estimated at
$14 billion." The archdiocese, "land rich and cash poor," had the advan-
tage of a hot market in real estate for residential developments.

> In nearby Brookline, the archdiocese has closed two churches,
> including St. Aidan's, where slain President John F. Kennedy
> was baptized and served as an altar boy. The church and rectory,
> valued at $2,880,200, has been targeted by the archdiocese to be
> rehabbed for condominiums including nine high-end units mixed
> with affordable housing.
>
> On West Roxbury Parkway in Brookline, the former Infant
> Jesus church, which was consolidated with St. Lawrence, sits
> empty as does its well-kept four-bedroom rectory in the upscale
> neighborhood. The buildings are valued at $1,512,400 . . . In
> Newbury, developers have been clamoring to buy a former church
> assessed at $3.34 million.[26]

Mindful of Law's warning to write no articles, an angry Father Bowers
told a *Globe* reporter of "this feeling of disgust and betrayal . . . I don't think

any of us understood the role of the church—whether it was denial or in-competence. I think the jury is still out on that."[27] The *Globe* Spotlight Team had spent weeks reading the clergy files before publishing the first report. As the news rolled out in episodes, public response rose against the church. Bowers accepted the hierarchy's old-boy network as politics: friends helped their pals. And priests had flaws. But recycling sex criminals like Paul Shanley (whose superiors knew he had endorsed "man-boy" love) stag-gered Bowers's imagination.

Sitting in the pew with his mother-in-law, Peter Borré watched Bowers struggle in response to people's outrage. Borré's curiosity was growing, too. How did a "land rich" church manage its assets?

Bowers knew many priests demoralized by the scandal's impact on the church they helped make. But his overtures to his neighboring pastor, Fa-ther Dan Mahoney at St. Francis de Sales, to steer school-age youngsters to St. Catherine, had failed. Mahoney, a generation older, was focused on his own parish. Bowers had pulled together a cadre of serious volunteers, mostly women. A Townie who had done time for drugs and been clean for seventeen years ran the daily AA meetings. Despite his parishioners' anger, Bowers had stabilized the finances, though he had paid no assess-ment to the archdiocese.

Law was in his own scramble. The archdiocese typically covered op-erating shortfalls by tapping a line of credit at Fleet Bank, borrowing in summer and fall, repaying in winter or spring. Cash flow rose between Christmas and Easter, when the parishes took in more. "Donations to the annual Cardinal's Appeal usually arrive in two bursts," the *Globe* reported. "In late May and early June after the Appeal is launched, and in late No-vember and December when many donors are looking for tax deductions." With cash flow deeply down, the archdiocese in late September mort-gaged the cardinal's estate with the Knights of Columbus, the Catholic insurance group, for $38 million.

> Much of the initial advance will be used to retire a short-term $9 million debt to Fleet Bank, part of a $17.5 million unsecured line of credit that was shut off by the bank earlier this year. Another portion of the Knights of Columbus loan will be used to complete the new Shaughnessy Family Center, a social service center serv-ing low-income families in South Boston.

Church officials say the sluggish economy slowed donations in recent years and that the trend has been exacerbated by a downturn in the stock market and the sexual abuse scandal that erupted in January.[28]

The Boston Priests' Forum was in its own crisis. Formed in 2001 by three clergymen concerned about issues of isolation and overwork, the forum had become an ad hoc support group; its membership surged to about 200 out of 1,250 priests in active service, as the scandal intensified. The forum discussions got past commiseration: the priests were incensed about the betrayal *they* felt. Bowers felt an aching irony. Like a benevolent lord, Law had put him under no pressure for the unpaid church taxes. But the cardinal who had given him the best job of his life had sold all the priests down the river.

The weight of the scandal bore down on Bowers just as he was discovering the ideal of peace. Peace was measured by the presence of justice— what Dr. Martin Luther King Jr. called "love in calculation." To follow Christ in service of the poor was giving love its calculation. Bowers, at age forty-two, was learning the pursuit of that love in the marginal parish where pockets of people who had money made spiritual community with the Other. *The chance to live it,* he would reflect, *with people who were hungry, were aliens, did drugs, lived in violence and fear. It was far from the image of church we so often lived, but it called out the best in the people and in me.* His own cardinal and several assistant bishops had squandered innocence, the seeds of peace. *Twisted lies from men: power and control. Submerged in the muck of covering it up and protecting what was unspeakable. God, how they turned it all so sour and sick!*[29]

On December 9, 2002, Bowers joined fifty-seven others in the Boston Priests' Forum by signing a public letter, telling Law he was "so compromised that it is no longer possible for you to exercise the spiritual leadership required for the church in Boston."[30] News coverage of the letter was like a shot across the bow. Four days later, at a private audience with John Paul, Law resigned as archbishop of Boston.

For the Vatican, the resignation of America's most powerful archbishop, who nevertheless remained a cardinal, meant that whoever followed Law *had* to be a superb pastor and a good manager. To fill the breach until the new man was named, Rome installed a fifty-five-year-old auxiliary bishop named Richard Lennon with the title of Apostolic Administrator. Untarnished by the scandal, Lennon was loyal to Law, who had basically made him a bishop. Dick Lennon had a prickly personality and among priests was not exactly beloved. But he worked hard and had a commanding sense of his role in achieving whatever needs to be done. As he monitored the negotiations with the plaintiff attorneys, Lennon was drafting a plan for widespread parish closures.

Three days before Christmas, in words aimed at the 552 victims and their attorneys, Lennon announced he was surveying church properties to put on the market "as soon as possible, so we can show our commitment" to resolve the lawsuits; liability coverage by insurers Kemper and Travelers would cover a substantial portion, according to the *Globe*.[31]

With all that liability coverage, wondered Peter Borré, *why sell property?*

Bowers wondered how the struggling parish he had come to love would fare in Lennon's plan. He asked for a meeting with Lennon, to no avail.

RECONFIGURATION DAYS

The son of a suburban deputy fire chief, Dick Lennon was six foot two; he had grown up a sports-loving kid but with a stutter so severe he rarely spoke in class, fearing humiliation. He entered Boston College, majoring in math. In 1967, after his sophomore year, he entered St. John, the diocesan seminary next door to BC in Brighton. Social protests that jolted campuses in 1968 hit St. John, too. Some seminarians clamored for direct involvement with the ghetto in Roxbury; others wanted the traditional path of enclosed study. Liberals clashed with Cardinal Cushing; half the seminarians soon left. Coming out of those years, Dick Lennon fell in love with canon law. He pursued it the hard way, teaching himself avocationally, from his studies in theology and the master's he would earn in church history. He read voluminously in church law, amassing a library of three hundred books. Dick Lennon lacked the stylized polish of clerics educated in Rome, but having conquered his stutter, he could take whatever life threw in his way. In 1998, after a decade of parish work, the autodidactic canonist was plucked by Cardinal Law to be his canonical adviser. In 1999 Law named him seminary rector. In 2001 he became an auxiliary bishop. Within the priestly society he was known for his cold candor.[32]

Determined to salvage his parish, Bowers put out feelers to rent some of the unused space in the large rectory. A law firm said yes. A cell phone company approached him about installing a tower behind the steeple. Bowers was thrilled! Let the private sector subsidize the school! Build an endowment, offer scholarships to worthy children. But then he hit a wall. The chancery told pastors to make no new contractual agreements until Bishop Lennon's parish Reconfiguration was done. No law firm rental, no cell tower revenue.

Faced with the hard demographic realities of Charlestown—three parishes with reduced populations, school-age children at parishes up the hill eschewing the neighborhood school—Bowers and the principal reluctantly made spring 2003 the last semester for Charlestown Catholic Elementary School, the one Cardinal Law had told him to save.

During Law's seventeen years in Boston, he had reduced the archdiocese from 402 to 357 parishes, without great protest. But Bishop Lennon entered a minefield. The Cardinal's Appeal had raised only $8 million of the needed $17 million for archdiocesan operating expenses. Through the winter of 2003, as lawyers wrangled over the victims' settlement, Lennon surveyed the topography of Catholic Boston—a church infrastructure in the city and outlying towns crisscrossed with map lines of money. What could be closed could be sold. The proceeds from sales would allow the church to regain its financial footing.

In a city with neighborhoods steeped in tribal loyalties, closing a given church cut deep into social cloth. In "Southie," as South Boston is called, St. Augustine Elementary School was a bedrock for families of cops, firemen, and blue-collar and city workers. St. Augustine's Cemetery, with a Greek Revival chapel, was the city's oldest Catholic graveyard. A Southie pol once quipped he would be buried there because "I want to remain politically active."[33]

But as older people who had raised large families died off, many of their children moved away, and Southie, like Charlestown, had a shrinking core of old Irish mixed with poor people in projects and the incursion of upscale couples, some without children, who were renovating buildings, laying on a patina of gentrification. "Sixty-one percent of South Boston residents have lived here less than five years," reflected Brian Wallace, Southie's representative in the statehouse. "The majority of them have no children . . . and the number of students going to Catholic schools is rapidly declining."[34] St. Augustine's, with 158 students in grades K through 8, relied on a $100,000 subsidy from the archdiocese. The pastor, Monsignor Tom McDonnell, was a Southie institution, and he had good ties with the cardinal. Law had forgiven a $328,000 parish debt on its unpaid assessments in 2000.

Three years later, in May, as Bishop Lennon remapped the infrastructure, students went home with notes to their parents: St. Augustine Elementary was closing. "This was a decision that came out of the parish," a priest-spokesman for the archdiocese stated. Because of declining enrollment and rising repair costs, "the parish didn't believe it could go on any further."

Not so, said one of the parents, Anne Spence. The archdiocese "kept vehemently denying that the school was closing. Then, all of a sudden, here's a letter—the school's closed, goodbye, don't bother coming back next year."[35]

In the bitter protests that followed, parishioners screamed at the aging pastor, Monsignor McDonnell, for selling them out. Parish leaders plunged into emergency fund-raising; two city council members and a state senator met with a poker-faced Lennon to pitch a turnaround plan. Brian Wallace went separately to the chancery with a colleague to meet Lennon. Wallace knew the church had a money crisis, but Lennon's closure on an unsuspecting pastor had hung McDonnell out to dry. In the chancery Wallace took his seat opposite the Apostolic Administrator. Lennon glanced at his watch. "You have five minutes."

"*Five minutes?*" snapped Wallace. "Here's *five seconds!*" And with that the state representative walked out.

Whatever honeymoon Lennon had had with Catholic Boston soured in the media coverage over the St. Augustine closure. Bitterness over Law's betrayal spilled out in cascades at Lennon.

When Seán O'Malley settled in as archbishop in the summer of 2003, Bishop Lennon retreated from the spotlight. O'Malley, with his white beard, serene demeanor, and soothing tones, had the persona of a peacemaker. He met with abuse survivors to advance the healing. The archdiocese agreed to the $85 million legal settlement for the 542 abuse survivors; the threat of bankruptcy receded as the archdiocese and Boston College moved toward the sale of the cardinal's estate. But O'Malley minced few words of his own on the depth of the financial crisis. On February 13, 2004, Lennon wrote to Boston priests explaining that Archbishop

O'Malley "has deliberately chosen the canonical procedure of suppression, rather than merger." A suppressed church would close, its assets going to the archdiocese. The assets of a church that merged with another parish would follow parishioners to the new church. Lennon's letter asserting that the archbishop had "deliberately chosen . . . suppression" suggested that O'Malley was a joint designer of the Reconfiguration blueprint. The archbishop set a March 8 deadline for leaders from eighty regional clusters to recommend which churches in their groupings should close.

Peter Borré, who had seen his share of layoffs in the corporate world, was struck by the icy logic of Reconfiguration. The order bore the archbishop's signature, but everyone knew it was Lennon telling parish groups to vote on whose church took the bullet. In corporate downsizing, you never asked people to vote on who kept their job. "Suppression"—a canon law term evocative of the Inquisition—meant you were evicted from your spiritual home, and all the money you and your people had put into that sacred space back through time went down to prop up a debt-ridden chancery. *This is going to blow up on them,* Borré told himself.

Bowers secured an appointment with Archbishop O'Malley.

The new prelate in his friar's robe sat at the end of a long table. Seán O'Malley was visibly subdued. He spoke slowly, in a voice so low Bowers sat forward to hear, explaining that the church faced hard decisions about consolidating parishes. Bowers delivered an upbeat account of his parish, the diversity of people, rich allied with poor, a financial curve bending their way. O'Malley as a young deacon had done missionary work with Indians on Easter Island, far off the coast of Chile. The prelate who had read Spanish literature in graduate school would surely warm to the picture of brown folk from Puerto Rico making a spiritual home at St. Catherine of Siena. Or so thought Father Bowers. But as he spoke of his parish's resilience, O'Malley seemed drained. "We are facing tough decisions," he reiterated. Bowers wanted O'Malley to see the parish. Would he come to St. Catherine of Siena and say Mass? *Yes,* replied O'Malley stiffly.

O'Malley seemed sad and listless as Bowers left.

As Peter Borré suspected, the cluster meetings threw many people into bitter standoffs with neighboring parishes over whose should close. On March 12, 2004, the study group Bowers had worked with sent a "Minority Report" by lead author Val Mulcahy to Bishop Lennon. In a dispassionate economic analysis, the document provided Lennon the blueprint to reverse the financial decay and revitalize the area. Politically speaking, it gave Lennon cover.

Where Mass attendance in generations past had been 45,000 a week, Charlestown had only 1,500 people per Sunday at the three churches. Charlestown could do with one church. Two parishes would cost $250,000 yearly in extra debt-servicing costs. "The luxury of retaining two parishes means that the community forgoes an annual surplus of $155,000," the report stated.

> The three struggling parishes could not maintain a school that gave parents confidence, because it was poorly funded. The cycle fed upon itself, poor funding begot low enrollment, which drained the funding, worsening the facilities even more. A prosperous parish might possibly reprime that pump and support a successful school. There is the demand for a good school but not a hand-to-mouth school.[36]

As parishioners from rooted families died or moved away, the demographics posed tough choices. "Newcomers see more value in a financially secure and culturally vibrant parish rather than in the preservation of historic buildings," the document stated. And then, the report hit dead-on what the Boston archdiocese—and the American church writ large—now faced:

> The trend is away from large households of Catholic families and is towards a lower density, diverse population. There will be an accelerating trend towards both poorer families in the projects and a transitory population of single and young married folks passing through [Charlestown] on their way to middle-aged suburban homes and families. If there is an upsurge in Catholic participation it will be at this new end of the spectrum. That end of the spectrum is not traditionally the source of generous offertory giving. They cannot be because they do not have as much to give. There will be no future wave of financial bounty that will buoy up two struggling parishes.
>
> We don't need to get sad about this. These groups are full of new energy, the young will get older (for sure), the poor will get

richer (God willing) and contribute elsewhere. While in Charlestown they will keep the faith alive and creative.

Closing one parish in Charlestown does not achieve guaranteed financial security. Closing two parishes would almost certainly provide that security. One Catholic community would be a stronger pastoral presence in the town.[37]

The report left open just how the phaseout would be handled, though a transition via facilitators was written between the lines.

Lennon never replied to the plan.

Two months later, on May 25, the chancery sent letters to eighty-three pastors by Federal Express, a rather lavish expenditure in light of the financial crisis and availability of e-mail. But with reporters and TV cameras huddled in the rectory, waiting to gauge how Bowers and his small staff and volunteers, mostly women, would react to the news, the coming of the FedEx trucks was a moment of high drama. Bowers's voice choked as he read the letter from O'Malley— the parish must close. Each parish had the option of appealing the decision to Archbishop O'Malley, and if he said no, to the Vatican. But the chances of the Congregation for the Clergy reversing an archbishop were remote, as Bowers knew. The priest was crying on TV news. The next morning's Globe carried parallel photographs on page one: O'Malley reading a statement, Bowers in anguish.

The archdiocese had spared the other two parishes in Charlestown. Lennon and O'Malley had ignored the research by the study group that had pinpointed $1.73 million in deferred maintenance. Closing one parish would not reduce the debt building at the other two. The smartest remedy was a single consolidated parish. In selecting two parishes at the expense of one, reconfiguration had flouted the hard research of the Charlestown group's report.

"Numerous parishes targeted for closing held prayer vigils last night," reported Michael Paulson, the Globe's astute religion correspondent. Paulson sized up the territory:

> O'Malley said the closings are necessary because the Catholic population has been moving to the suburbs and because attendance at Mass is declining. Other reasons, he said, include financial problems, the poor state of repair of many parish buildings,

and a dwindling number of priests. He said that more than one-third of all parishes are operating at a deficit and that 130 of the archdiocese's pastors are over 70.

The archdiocese has hired a real estate specialist to help sell off the property associated with the closing parishes, many of which own churches, rectories, convents, schools, other buildings, and, in some cases, open space. The archdiocese has not said how many properties it plans to sell, but it is sure to be significant.[38]

The next day, May 27, came the news that Pope John Paul II had appointed Cardinal Law pastor—or "archpriest," in Vatican parlance—of Santa Maria Maggiore, one of the great basilicas in Rome. Peter Borré understood gilded parachutes as a reality of corporate life; but *redeeming* Law, with an elevation from the convent in Maryland to a perch in Rome, showed a huge disregard for the suffering he had caused. Abuse survivors and Voice of the Faithful activists raised an outcry. John L. Allen Jr., Vatican correspondent for *National Catholic Reporter,* explained the Curia's view to the *Globe:* "The idea was to find a position in which his baggage would not bog things down, but give him a job which allows him to set up shop here, where he's still treated with deference and respect, in part because he's a cardinal and in part because some people think he got a raw deal."[39]

For Lennon—but more so for O'Malley—the timing was awful.

Angry parishioners saw their churches on a chopping block while Law, who had betrayed them, found redemption with a cushy job in Rome. Archbishop O'Malley had a meeting the following day with pastors from across the archdiocese. Media trucks waited outside the church in Weston. Law's new job "is adding fuel to fire that is already burning in people," Bowers told a reporter. "It's an utter disgrace."[40] His words were sure to incense the archbishop, a Franciscan who believed in vows of obedience; nor was the language a tool for negotiating. But hostility was rumbling among certain priests toward Lennon, as Law's handpicked successor, and whether he knew how Law had managed the money.

Father Stephen Josoma had come to the meeting with his own misgivings. Josoma's St. Susanna parish was in Dedham, an island of the Charles, and it had made the suppression list for no reason he could see other than its eight prime acres with plenty of shade. The letter ordering the

suppression gave no adequate reason. Josoma wanted answers for his people. O'Malley's responses at the closed meeting stressed that Bishop Lennon's clustering was carefully planned; Reconfiguration would be painful,
parishes could file a request for a review, but the priests must support the
plan.

In the five-hour meeting, Archbishop O'Malley quieted some fears by
assuring the priests that none of the fifty-eight who signed the letter asking Law to resign would be punished. The closures were not about repri-
sals, he insisted.

Church officials disseminated a 168-page manual on how to terminate
employees, remove sacred objects, and deal with journalists. Sacred items
must be removed to a specified place. "Shortly after the doors are closed,
Archbishop Séan will deconsecrate the Church so that we can sell it," the
manual continued. "Sacred items will be removed . . . After this is done,
the Church may be sold for any use except one that would be deemed
sordid."[41]

During a break, Josoma introduced himself to the archbishop as one of
the fifty-eight priests who had demanded that Law resign. "You're asking
me to do something I cannot in conscience do," he said. "Is this because of
me or our real estate?" "Neither," insisted O'Malley. The *Globe* had published a list of the parishes and their assessed values, with a fair market
value in the $100 million range. "We'd be lucky if we got even the assessed
value," O'Malley added. "Well, let's make a deal," said Father Josoma.
"We're assessed at $320,000. What if I give you a check for $600,000?
You'll get double your amount." The priest extended his hand to shake
on it. O'Malley laughed, but would not shake hands. Josoma replied, "You
know and I know that the parish is worth a lot more." O'Malley's lips
parted in an enigmatic smile.

On the last Sunday in May, Peter Borré and his mother-in-law went
to St. Catherine of Siena for a Mass that was packed with people wanting to know what Father Bowers would say. Reporters were following the
story of a parish struggling to stay alive. Bowers was so upset he barely got
through the liturgy. He was also afraid. Pitting himself against the archbishop would do his career no good. After the service, he opened the floor
for discussion. "Let's pray the rosary," a woman offered. But people were
crying and angry; they needed to talk.

Rose Mary Piper gave her son-in-law a prod of the elbow: "You shoot off your mouth about everything under the sun. So say something about this." Peter Borré rose and suggested they send a petition to the archbishop, asking him to meet with them. People applauded. A haggard Father Bowers said, "You're volunteering to help?"

"I just did," said Borré, a little unsure just why.

With help from Mary Beth Borré, the lapsed Catholic, Peter and several members of the parish gathered 3,500 signatures. On a warm June day, Peter and two ladies from the parish entered the chancery in Brighton, opposite Boston College. A receptionist sat behind Plexiglas. The tension in the place was palpable. Borré imagined the stress on people here, coming to work over the grueling eighteen months to date. He told the lady they had a petition for the archbishop. She eyed him nervously. Just then a priest entered the foyer. In his mannered way Borré explained the purpose of their visit. "We're not interested in petitions," the priest uttered.

Borré asked what they should do with the petitions. The cleric, whom he recognized as a chancery official, retorted, "You should go fuck yourself."

As the priest withdrew, leaving two startled ladies and Borré to swallow his anger, they went out into the summer day. He got behind the wheel of the car, his rage rising like a volcano. He considered Romans the most anticlerical people on earth, a facet of long memory from Pio Nono and the Vatican's history as an overlord. Borré's trust in a modern hierarchy buckled. Mary Beth heard the fury in his voice when he called from the car, saying he'd just been f-bombed by a jerk in a Roman collar. In the days that followed he distilled his anger into a plan of attack that would send him back to Rome to confront a power structure he had once held in awe.

CHAPTER 4

THE VATICAN, the VIGILS, AND THE REAL ESTATE

When Seán O'Malley reached Boston he was an emergency politician for the church, a specialist in damaged dioceses. As a young priest he had never envisioned such a role for himself: the clerical culture was intact. Born in 1944 in Lakewood, Ohio, and raised in western Pennsylvania, O'Malley entered the Order of Friars Minor Capuchin, a branch of the Franciscans who work with the poor. He earned a Ph.D. in Spanish and Portuguese literature at Catholic University of America, and stayed on in Washington, D.C., as founder of Centro Católico Hispano to give immigrants educational and legal help. In 1984 John Paul II made him a bishop and appointed him to the diocese of St. Thomas, Virgin Islands.

In 1993 the Vatican sent O'Malley to the diocese of Fall River, Massachusetts, which had a large Portuguese community and was reeling from the aftershocks of the notorious James Porter. Legal settlements for 131 survivors of the imprisoned ex-priest cost $13.2 million, about half of it paid by insurance policies. O'Malley ordered a sale of nonparish properties;[1] but to secure the necessary funds, he turned to Knights of Malta, an elite fraternal society which contributed several million dollars to the settlement, according to Tom Doyle, a former priest who served as a Vatican embassy canon lawyer in the 1980s and warned the bishops of the forthcoming crisis.[2] The Sovereign Military Order of Malta began in the Crusades and evolved into a lay society with the trappings of chivalry. The Knights of Malta had a history of Fascist sympathies before World War II and fervent anti-Communism thereafter. Three CIA directors—John McCone, William Colby, and William J. Casey—and former secretary of state Al Haig were Knights of Malta.[3] "Wealth is a de facto prerequisite for a knightly candidate, and each must pass through a rigorous screening," wrote journalist Martin Lee in 1983. The group issued its own passports and was known for international relief efforts.[4] Peter Borré's father was inducted at St. Peter's Basilica in a ceremony officiated by Pope John XXIII.

As the Boston scandal sent out shock waves in 2002, the Vatican dispatched Seán O'Malley to the diocese of Palm Beach, Florida, after Bishop Anthony O'Connell calmly admitted at a news conference that, yes, he did have inappropriate contact, years ago, with a seminarian who had just publicly accused him, and by the way a second accuser might be in the offing. Three men ended up suing O'Connell.[5] In Palm Beach, one of the wealthiest dioceses, O'Malley had the unenviable task of replacing a corrupt bishop who had replaced a corrupt bishop. Before the Irish-born O'Connell, Bishop J. Keith Symons resigned in 1998 upon disclosure that *he* had molested altar boys years before.[6] Symons moved to a Michigan retreat house, O'Connell to a South Carolina monastery. But in the Vatican idea of apostolic succession, both men remained titular bishops. Cardinal Ratzinger's tribunal at the Congregation for the Doctrine of the Faith laicized priests, not hierarchs.

In Palm Beach, O'Malley formed a lay panel to monitor accusations against clergy. He told victims, "I want to do what I can to promote healing for you and for all those affected by this abuse."[7] Before the year was out, the Vatican sent him to his third scandal-battered post. Boston's historic status also put O'Malley in line to become a cardinal. His modesty was refreshing. Unlike the imperial Law, he encouraged people to call him "Archbishop Seán."

In the summer of 2003, the newly appointed Archbishop O'Malley went to Rome. He had issues to review with men in high places. O'Malley's meeting at the Vatican is key to our grasp of the larger financial issues in the American church that would engulf him and other bishops who slogged through property disputes that pitted people in the pews against the Vatican.

Cardinal Darío Castrillón Hoyos at the Congregation for the Clergy was a pivotal figure for O'Malley's presentation on the impact of the proposed settlement for the 552 victims. Discussions of a possible bankruptcy pleading had leaked to the press.[8] A Chapter 11 filing, if the court approved it, would freeze debts as the church reorganized its finances and its lawyers tried to bargain down the survivors' attorneys. The gamble was the backfire potential. The law required disclosure of *all* assets, swatches of which the media were already scrutinizing: spreading everything on the table could make the cash-strapped archdiocese seem rich. It also meant that O'Malley would begin his most important job having to explain to the many victims expecting compensation that his predecessor had, in effect, broken the bank. For as Peter Borré would learn, months later, on ferreting out copies of the archdiocese's past financial statements from a privileged source, the archdiocese had lost $10 million in fiscal year 2000, $8.3 million in FY 2001 (before the *Globe* series on the abuse scandal), and $12 million in FY 2002 that forced a sale of assets from its investment portfolio. When O'Malley reached Rome that day in 2003, the archdiocese he had come to govern had lost $30.3 million in the preceding three years. Besides a horrific sexual scandal, Bernie Law had bequeathed a financial sinkhole to Seán O'Malley. Where had all the money gone?[9]

When he sat down with Castrillón, the Franciscan prelate with a vow of poverty needed a huge pump of money. He also faced "the alienation of church property," the canonical term by which the Third Office in the Congregation for the Clergy processed bishops' appeals to liquidate assets.

The American bishops at their June 2002 conference in Dallas voted to request approval from Clergy to raise the threshold for permission to sell property from $5 million to $10.3 million. For property or assets below that level, a bishop could sell as he saw fit. (For dioceses with 500,000 people or fewer, the threshold rose to $5 million.) The Vatican approved the measure, and also agreed to adjust the threshold to inflation, such that in 2009 for large dioceses, it was $11.4 million.[10]

According to a former Congregation for the Clergy staffer who spoke on background, the procedure for selling expensive property calls for the bishop to evaulate the assets with his Finance Council, then ask Clergy for the authority to sell, explaining the use for the proceeds. O'Malley knew he had to win trust of the Finance Council that had rejected Law's request for the victims' settlement.

Cardinal Castrillón and his staff faced three issues. For them, the first question was whether selling assets would harm the Boston archdiocese's ability to function. A question arises: how does the Vatican know what might disrupt any archdiocese if it sells property? Barring a flood of information from people, reports or documents from a diocese, Clergy staffers rely on what the bishop tells them. In O'Malley's case, the Boston crisis had generated press attention even in Italy. Lennon was deep into research on available property.

The second concern in the Congregation for the Clergy was that the bishop have a valid plan for use of the funds from the property sale. In Boston, the plan seemed clear: to compensate victims. The last issue was in this case the toughest: if the Boston archdiocese needed substantially *more* than $10.3 million, was it just and prudent for the Vatican to grant approval?

Priests who work at rarefied levels of the Roman Curia know that they are acting for the Holy Father. They take seriously the idea of apostolic succession—that the bishops they meet are spiritual descendants of Jesus's apostles. In the milieu of a religious monarchy, the priests in those offices use ornamental courtesies in calling a bishop "Excellency," a cardinal "Your Eminence," even employing elegant terms in the third person, as I learned in July 2009 on seeking an interview in Rome with the former St. Louis archbishop Raymond Burke, the prefect of the Apostolic Signatura. "This is not possible," explained a cleric in cool, soft cadences at the other end of the phone. "His Grace is away." Ah. Did they call him "Your Grace" back in Missouri?

For all of the fawning attention Curial staffers give bishops, the Third Office priests in the Congregation for the Clergy understood "the alienation of church property." Their duties included safeguarding the rights of the dead.

Generations of Catholics who had donated money, land, art, buildings, or made provisions in their estates to benefit a parish or diocese, slept now in sacred soil. Many were buried in cemeteries behind their family churches. Canon law honored their intentions as souls. Clergy's Third Office had to ensure that their property and gifts would not be wrongfully liquidated.

O'Malley refused interview requests for this book. So did Bishop Lennon. So did Cardinal Castrillón, who left Clergy in 2006 for another Vatican office (and has since retired). Monsignor James McDaid of Clergy, who was an assistant to Castrillón and his successor, Cardinal Cláudio Hummes, rebuffed my requests in Rome for interviews with himself and Hummes.* Nevertheless, two other men knowledgeable of Clergy provided insight on O'Malley's meeting in 2003. This information is also buttressed by a Vatican canon law proceeding. The Congregation for the Clergy occupies an upper floor on Piazza Pius XII just off St. Peter's Square. In Cardinal Darío del Niño Jesús Castrillón Hoyos, O'Malley found a welcoming ally, a man wrapped in the elite assumptions of apostolic succession.

CARDINALS AND POLITICS

Born in 1929 in Medellín, before the provincial city became synonymous with drug cartels, Castrillón was a young priest with a great talent for languages. He earned a doctorate in canon law at the Pontifical Gregorian University in Rome, another in religious sociology at the University of Louvain, in Belgium, and at age thirty-six became a bishop back in Colombia. A champion of the homeless in the diocese of Pereira, he walked the streets to feed abandoned children. The boom in cocaine commerce gave Castrillón a Machiavellian slant on power. The media showed him blessing a restaurant owned by a drug mobster. "In fact, his relationship with the traffickers was complex," writes Elena Curti of *The Tablet*. Castrillón materialized in a milkman's outfit at the home of Pablo Escobar, the most wanted man in Colombia, "and persuaded him to confess his sins." At a 1984 meeting of Latin American bishops, she writes, Castrillón

> said he had accepted cash from Escobar's drug cartel for charitable purposes. He justified his action by saying that by taking the money he stopped it being used in illegal activities such as prostitution, and said he had warned the donors that giving money "would not save their souls." But, later, as Archbishop of Bucaramanga (1992–1996), he made several public statements against corruption in Colombia, unafraid to embarrass local and national officials and politicians.[11]

---

*In October 2010 Hummes was succeeded by Mauro Piacenza, who soon became a cardinal.

Accepting dirty money for higher good meshed with Castrillón's idea of the Catholic hierarchy abiding by its own supreme law. In 2001, when a French prelate received a three-month sentence for having sheltered a pedophile, Castrillón posted on Clergy's website a letter in which he praised Bishop Pierre Pican of Bayeux-Lisieux: "I rejoice to have a colleague in the episcopate who, in the eyes of history and all the other bishops of the world, preferred prison rather than denouncing one of his sons, a priest."[12]

When he met with O'Malley in 2003, Cardinal Castrillón greeted a younger bishop who faced a taxing crisis of so many victims, foretelling huge losses. His natural instinct in the fraternal culture was to help. The Holy See would not provide financial help to the archdiocese—that was unthinkable. The Vatican in 2003 was running a deficit of $11.8 million on a $250 million operating budget. Peter's Pence donations of $55.8 million helped defray the loss.[13] So did whatever funds the Vatican Bank delivered in its secret subsidy to the pope. For O'Malley, the situation was vastly more severe than that in Fall River a decade earlier, when the Knights of Malta had deep pockets. Law's arrogance left a fund-raising nightmare. The size of the settlement figures being bargained, well north of $50 million, explains why two Italian cardinals joined O'Malley and Castrillón later: Angelo Sodano, the secretary of state, and Giovanni Battista Re, the prefect of the Congregation for Bishops.

Cardinal Re, a renowned workaholic with a toothy grin and booming voice, had done eleven years as *sostituto* in the Secretariat of State. In that job overseeing daily operations, Re had enjoyed access to John Paul without need of appointments. Now, in his post overseeing the world's bishops, Re no longer had the turnstile to John Paul. He worked through the Curia's channels.[14]

Sodano, at age seventy-five, was the more imposing presence. With square-set shoulders, sagging jowls, and thick glasses, Sodano as secretary of state functioned as the Holy See's prime minister and, internally, as a de facto chief of staff. In the nine congregations, or dicasteries, that are roughly akin to cabinet departments, each prefect had autonomy; the foreign minister fell under Sodano. In the dozen years he had overseen the Curia, Sodano was a bullish alter ego to John Paul on foreign policy, which the pope had guided via his own close hand until his final illness.

Born in 1927 in Isola d'Asti, Piedmont, Sodano was one of six children. His father had been a Christian Democrat elected to Parliament

in the 1948 elections, serving until 1963. After attending the local seminary, Sodano earned doctorates in canon law and theology from Pontifical
universities in Rome. At age thirty-two he joined the Vatican diplomatic
corps. In 1978, after several Latin American postings, he was named papal
nuncio in Chile amid one of South America's worst dictatorships.

Chile had a history of economic stability and democratic governance
when President Richard Nixon, in 1970, reacting to the election of Dr.
Salvador Allende, a Marxist, told CIA director Richard Helms, *Make the
economy scream,* in order to upend Allende.[15] The CIA had entreated
Christian Democrat leaders in Western Europe to pull out the stops in
helping the Chilean counterparts defeat Allende. A CIA report says that
a leading Italian Christian Democrat (his name redacted) "saw no point in
risking his reputation in a lost cause."[16] Allende won in a plurality. Nixon
authorized $10 million for the CIA to disrupt the economy.[17] Three years
later, a CIA-supported coup by General Augusto Pinochet drove Allende
to shoot himself as troops stormed the presidential palace. Pinochet authorized kidnapping, torture, and murder of Allende supporters to solidify
power. Military men took over universities and censored the press. Several
prominent Chileans critical of the regime who were living abroad were
murdered. Pinochet sold off public services in a free-market strategy inspired by University of Chicago economist Milton Friedman. The regime
moved 28,000 poor people from scattered areas into slums that ballooned
to 1.3 million people.[18]

In 1978, when Archbishop Sodano arrived as nuncio, the labor
unions were surviving with the help of Cardinal Raúl Silva Henriquez.[19]
Center-right bishops were relieved Allende was gone; Silva and a few others pressed for human rights.[20] Chile's agony put in high relief Latin America's chasm between traditional bishops, focused on personal piety, and the
more activist bishops influenced by liberation theology's idea of structural
sin. The 1968 continental bishops' conference in Medellín endorsed "a
preferential option for the poor." Castrillón was hostile to liberation theology; Sodano was in the same camp. John Paul II and Ratzinger, reacting
to Communism as a monolithic evil, equated Soviet bloc dictatorships
with the liberationists' Marxist analysis of plantation-based poverty. But
as journalist John Allen has learnedly written, older European currents
shaped the Latin American theology, too.[21] Scripture discussions perme-
ated the Christian base communities, small groups of priests, nuns, and

lay folk active in South America's slums. Ratzinger investigated Father Leonardo Boff of Brazil in his tribunal and in 1985 imposed a yearlong "silence." Six years later he banned Boff as a theologian. "Ecclesiastical power is cruel and merciless," Boff bristled after quitting the priesthood.[22]

"It is in the poverty and exploitation of the Third World," writes Paul Collins in The Modern Inquisition, a study of the CDF under Ratzinger,

> where Boff finds the Church to be most truly itself. For him . . . it is only through reflection on living experience, on the "stuff" of history, that the Church can discover God's will for itself.
>
> For Ratzinger, the Church transcends history. It is not the Jesus of history who provides the CDF's prefect primary theological focus. It is the risen and ascended Christ who stands in splendour outside the world-process, both as saviour and judge, who is the fundamental focus of Ratzinger.[23]

By 1980 more than eight hundred priests and nuns had been murdered by Latin American death squads. As Ratzinger punished more theologians like Boff, Sodano befriended the Pinochet family; he appeared at a televised rally where Chile's dictator denounced the church in his speech. In vetting bishops, Sodano promoted men supportive of the regime.[24] In 1986 a group called the Vicariate of Solidarity asked the Chilean bishops' conference to have Sodano recalled to Rome: "For a long time now, numerous communities have been demanding this. Hundreds of priests and nuns have also asked for this. The people know of his 'reports' to Rome and of his excessive attachment to the military regime . . . We do not see in him diplomacy, but rather complicity."[25] Sodano stayed on the job. The quality of John Paul's intelligence on Chile from Sodano will be one of history's black holes until the Vatican releases the information he sent.

When John Paul embarked on his historic 1987 trip to Chile, Pinochet faced rising international pressure. A Vatican priest, Roberto Tucci, coordinated the trip. En route, John Paul told journalists, "To the Gospel message belongs all the problems of human rights, and if democracy means human rights then it also belongs to the message of the Church."[26] The pope added, "We will find a system that is dictatorial, but one that is transitory by definition."[27]

As the motorcade entered Santiago, huge crowds chanted, "Our brother,

Pope, take the tyrant with you!" People held signs naming loved ones who had disappeared. John Paul met with opposition leaders and members of all parties in a gathering that Sodano organized.[28] Sodano also helped Pinochet maneuver the pope onto the presidential balcony for a photo op that sent a chilling message to people traumatized by the dictator. But a countermessage rose when crowds flooded into a Mass in the same stadium where fifteen years earlier troops had rounded up and slaughtered Allende supporters. The pope heard "speaker after speaker who complained of censorship, torture, and political murder," wrote Jonathan Kwitny. "Crowds burned barricades, threw rocks, and taunted police." John Paul praised Chilean priests seeking justice, denounced the brutality, and called "suffering for the sake of love, truth and justice . . . a sign of fidelity to God." His voice rang out as the police used roaring water cannons to drive people back: "Love is stronger . . . love is stronger."[29]

Chile was close to restoring democracy, in 1988, when Pinochet gave Sodano a medal as the nuncio returned to Rome. His ease with Latin strongmen helped the United States in the invasion of Panama. President Manuel Noriega, estranged from the CIA for his ties to drug cartels, took sanctuary in the Vatican embassy. Sodano persuaded him to surrender. U.S. authorities flew Noriega to Florida, where he was tried, convicted, and put in a federal penitentiary.[30]

In 1991 Sodano became secretary of state. Of all the cardinals in the Curia, why did John Paul choose one so close to a dictator with bloody hands, a surreal contrast to the papal stance of peaceful nonviolence? The pope bypassed Cardinal Achille Silvestrini, an adroit diplomat on arms control, human rights, and a protégé of Cardinal Agostino Casaroli, the outgoing secretary of state. Casaroli had spent decades negotiating with Eastern bloc officials to ease the persecution of Catholics behind the iron curtain.[31] For his part, Sodano called diplomacy "an instrument of dialogue, aimed at defending and promoting the rights of Catholics and favoring international relations."[32]

Behind those vanilla words lay a strange reality, according to Giovanni Avena, a priest-turned-editor of Adista, a liberal Catholic news service. "Casaroli had great diplomatic skills; he presented the church in a sober, businesslike way," Avena told me in Rome. "Casaroli thought Sodano was dumb. They sent Sodano to Latin America and he muscled his way, making friends with the worst right-wingers. John Paul clashed with Casaroli over how to deal with Communism. The pope wanted more hard-line re-sistance. Silvestrini was an heir to Casaroli. Sodano is a foot soldier, not a thinker. He was put there [as secretary of state] as manager of the Curia. He is perfectly gray."[33]

By "gray," Avena meant a calculated neutrality capable of turning colors on a given issue. John Paul, famously bored by Curial politics, had in Sodano a firewall from the inner wrangles *and* a militant anti-leftist for conservative governments and donors. John Paul was famously bored by finances, too. The Vatican Bank scandal erupted in 1982, when Italy's largest bank, Banco Ambrosiano, collapsed under $1.2 billion in bad debts brought on by a Cosa Nostra money-laundering scheme that utilized the IOR under Archbishop Paul Marcinkus. John Paul allowed Marcinkus to use diplomatic immunity as a latter-day prisoner of the Vatican. It fell to Secretary of State Casaroli to admit an "abuse of trust" to Italian state investigators; he negotiated a $242 million payment in 1984 to resolve the IOR fine.[34]

In 1990 John Paul summoned Cardinal Edmund Szoka of Detroit to manage the city-state. "When the budget's finished in November we go over it for about an hour," Szoka told the biographer Kwitny. "He can't look at all these details. I keep him aware of what's going on and how we're doing."[35]

A pragmatist, Szoka called more than one hundred presidents of the national bishops' conferences to a first-ever meeting on April 8, 1991. As they sat in red velvet chairs, Cardinal Szoka explained that two decades of Vatican deficits had hit a record $87 million. Without assigning quotas, he asked them to help. In one of those cameos of democracy that lend irony as icing to church politics, the bishops took a vote, and of course agreed to send more. An extra $8 million arrived in 1992. In 1993 the Holy See actually ended with a surplus; Peter's Pence also hit $67 million that year.

Vatican Bank "funds are primarily used by John Paul to bolster the Church in poor countries," papal biographer George Weigel wrote. "It is not unusual for the IOR to get a call from the papal apartment in the morning, saying that the Pope needs a certain number of envelopes con-taining $20,000 or $50,000 by noon—gifts to bishops from Africa, Latin America and Asia."[36] The bank that did not exist on the Holy See annual report produced cash on demand for the pope.

After Cardinal Sodano became secretary of state, he assumed the lead role in an IOR oversight commission of five cardinals; he also managed the Curia's heavily Italian bureaucracy. "There has been created a certain mystery about the Roman Curia," Sodano observed in 1992, "but those who are inside it see it as a brotherhood."[37]

When the brotherhood embraced Archbishop O'Malley in the summer of 2003, John Paul was in a deepening decline from Parkinson's disease. Cardinal Castrillón presumably wanted Sodano's approval for a major transfer of wealth. The Vatican cardinals gave O'Malley the nod to exceed the $10.3 million threshold in the "alienation of church property." This decision was borne out in a Vatican document that emerged many months later, after Peter Borré spearheaded canon law appeals by nine Boston parishes seeking to halt their closures. The Congregation for the Clergy rejected those requests. The parishes appealed to the Signatura. In that proceeding, one Martha Wegan, a veteran practitioner in Vatican tribunals, filed a brief as the advocate for the Archdiocese of Boston. She wrote:

> In this truly very painful case, maximum discretion was given to the Excellent Archbishop of Boston [sic] so that he might save the archdiocese from monetary ruin provoked . . . by the sexual abuse crisis. It is in this context that all actions of this process of reconfiguration and "closing of parishes" are to be understood, not excluding the suppression of wealthy parishes, not excluding the suppression of parishes of maximum vitality.
>
> Viability must be not at the parish level but at the level of the whole archdiocese, not excluding the giving of goods of extinct parishes to the archdiocese.[38]

"Maximum discretion" here translates as carte blanche to close and to sell. When O'Malley, the new archbishop, returned to Boston in 2003, Bishop Lennon had the authority to "alienate property."

Nothing of its scope had ever been done in an American diocese.

That realization left a marked impression on Cardinal Sodano.

SUPPRESSION

Under canon law, when a parish merges with another, the funds of the closed church follow its members to the new one. But a parish that is "suppressed" by the bishop loses its building, land, bank deposits, all assets to the bishop-as-banker. Lennon wanted parishes with good land value, and surplus funds, for a strategic outcome: plug the deficit. Lennon was using suppression as foreclosure, a kind of Peter's Pence enforced. The dead people whose gifts had built the parishes posed no opposition unless the living learned to penetrate thickets of canon law.

Among the suppressed parishes, Infant Jesus in affluent Brookline had $4 million in the bank. An hour's drive east of Boston in Scituate, the suppressed St. Frances Cabrini sat on thirty lush acres near the Atlantic, a real estate developer's dream. Our Lady Help of Christians in the town of Concord had $800,000 in the bank, and the year before had opened a $1.3 million parish center.[39] Lennon's letter to the faithful said that O'Malley had ordered the suppressions, but on that issue the two bishops were joined at the hip.

By Peter Borré's reckoning, of the eighty-three parishes on Lennon's list, twenty-four were financially solid with active parishioners. Borré, a hardened realist on assets that failed to deliver, was not alone in being offended at Lennon's sloppiness: soak the rich, screw the poor, trample hard-toiling folk in the middle to raise funds for a debt-riddden chancery. Mayor Thomas M. Menino was upset. "This is the first I've heard of where the money is going," he told the *Globe*. "Families have been going to these churches for years." Massachusetts secretary of state William F. Galvin bristled at "a deceit to the people in the pews if the money is going to unknown purposes of the central fund," which, indeed, it was.[40] Borré concluded that two dozen parishes needed to close. Many parishes in the middle had issues that seemed soluble with enlightened leadership.

From canon lawyers, Borré learned that an appeal had to be filed in the Vatican soon after a bishop's rejection of the parish's request that it be allowed to survive. With help from a kitchen cabinet, he began working on a document.

For Father Bob Bowers, reality hit when the archdiocese sent a team to take inventory of St. Catherine of Siena parish property. They opened cabinets, took photographs, and made lists of furniture, other tangibles, icons, benches, and sacred items of the church. Meanwhile, a summons came from the chancery: Archbishop O'Malley wanted to meet with Father Bowers.

In a series of trips to the chancery office in Brighton, across Common-

wealth Avenue from Bowers's alma mater, Boston College, he took comfort from his driver, Peter Borré, who offered moral support as the priest's
stomach churned like a fuel pump. Borré had no desire to sit in the foyer
where the chancery priest had told him to go fuck himself, and so he
waited outside.

Father Bowers sat across a long table from the taciturn archbishop.

"We have a problem," said O'Malley.

"We do, Archbishop. You need to come see the people in the parish."

No, came the reply. O'Malley had advisers guiding him through this
difficult process, he explained. And he had to follow their advice.

Silence fell between prelate and priest, a lengthening emotional distance: silence begetting silence. *He wants me to obey*, realized Bowers. *He
is a Franciscan. Obedience to superiors is their norm, an expectation of the
communal life. We diocesan clergy can be more unruly. I am resisting something
that is unjust, trying to persuade him to see what I see.*

The two men stared at each other. Bob Bowers, with his strain of
flamboyance and supercharged enthusiasm, sat quiet now, as unmovable
as his archbishop. The meeting ended as the next one began, some days
later, layered in tension and thick with silence. O'Malley wanted Bowers
to resign, take a new assignment, let Reconfiguration move forward. But
O'Malley could not evict a pastor unless he committed a grave violation of
church law. Fighting to keep his parish open, making an issue of it in the
media, Bowers was attacking *the plan*—Richard Lennon's work product.
Still, that put him in O'Malley's face.

Bowers realized that Seán O'Malley was depressed.

Other priests saw it, too. The leaden expressions and slow speech
sparked speculation that O'Malley was taking antidepressant medication.
O'Malley lived in a spartan room in the Holy Cross Cathedral rectory. His
kindness and politeness were offset by reserve, a holding back of emotions.
He had come to Boston as a healer and Reconfiguration had blown up in
his face. *He cannot understand why one of his priests will not agree with him*, reflected Bowers. When he gave O'Malley the Charlestown consolidation report that his parishioner Val Mulcahy had sent to Lennon, the archbishop
rebuffed the gesture.

He said: "I want you to do what I'm telling you"—resign, take a new
assignment. But that meant a death warrant for the parish where Bowers

had planted heart and soul. Lennon's plan ignored the research group's advice on a long phaseout, fusing three parishes into one. The meeting ended in a stalemate.

Bowers turned to Father William Leahy, the Jesuit president of Boston College, who assured him that he had sent the report to Archbishop O'Malley.

PARISHES AS REAL ESTATE

Priests in the fourscore parishes on the closure list confronted a maze of issues. Some pastors in neighborhoods with few parishioners and unmanageable debt accepted reality. The clustering process put stress on other clerics whose followers wanted to keep their parishes intact.

Among the priests at parishes targeted for suppression, Father Stephen Josoma in Dedham had followed Bowers's travails and decided on a different approach. Born in 1955 into a close-knit family, his father a technician at MIT, Steve passed boyhood summers mowing lawns with his Irish-born grandfather. The old man had done time in Galway Prison as a Sinn Féin rebel before shipping out to America in 1920. Josoma saw him as a landscape artisan. Each night the old man knelt in prayer, "not an in-your-face piety, just a peaceful guy with trust in the Lord," Josoma recalled. "That stayed with me." Of the twenty men with whom he began seminary, only Josoma became a priest.

In 1997, at a church in Dorchester, he succeeded a popular priest "who had lived in a condo half the time while the parish ran up millions in deferred maintenance," he recalled. Josoma and an associate priest "turned the finances around. The accountant warned us we had to cover the school deficit out of parish funds—$70,000. We achieved that. Next, we put in a cafeteria, a science lab, a library. We had an army of kids selling wrapping paper door-to-door. People saw that, they gave more on Sunday. We got the teachers raises. You can do a lot when the people are behind you."

Josoma put his popularity on the line when he clashed with real estate agents he accused of redlining sales to keep blacks out of Dorchester. The experience was so searing he took a one-year leave from ministry and lived with his folks. In 2001 Cardinal Law asked him to become pastor at St. Susanna in Dedham, a cohesive flock, largely white, that was absorbing

Filipino families. Dedham sits on an island in the Charles River with a population of twenty-four thousand.

"This parish was created by Cardinal Cushing in 1961 for his friend Father Michael Durant," Josoma said, smiling in the fading light of a winter afternoon. "In those days, churches were like fiefdoms. The other parish, St. Mary of the Assumption, is 125 years old and three times our size. They called it 'the cathedral in the wilderness.' Twenty-five hundred families stayed at St. Mary when this one opened. St. Susanna had 300 families and a rectory with three priests, a housekeeper, and a cook. Today, it's me and Felix [the dog] for 850 families. At least half of our families come from outside of the town, mostly from neighboring Needham. We're a bit staid, perhaps, but more family-friendly."

A wave of foreclosures hit Dedham in 2008. The parish food pantry fed rising numbers in an area where the idea of hunger belied the image of leafy New England lanes. Josoma's popularity in drawing parishioners from a nearby town tracked a national phenomenon of Catholics seeking a spiritual allegiance beyond the neighborhood.

Lennon's plan called for St. Susanna members to join St. Mary while the archdiocese took St. Susanna's money. How would that go down with people who had already bypassed the "cathedral in the wilderness"? Just off Highway 128, Josoma's parish sat on eight sylvan acres adjoining an animal rescue preserve, buffered by wetlands of the Charles River. The road past the church curled into a wooded cluster of homes. Like the Scituate parish on thirty prime acres near the sea, St. Susanna's acreage held proverbial rubies in its loam. The parish sent $10,000 a month in assessments to the archdiocese.

"The bishops' pedophilia cover-ups appalled me," explained Josoma. "After Law left, Bishop Lennon as Apostolic Administrator met with the priests and said we were $10 million in debt for lay employees' pensions because pastors had not sent funds to the chancery. I was thinking, *Ten million dollars?* How could the chancery have let this happen? Within a year, the first time Archbishop O'Malley spoke, [the debt] was $25 million. What is going on here?"

St. Susanna, with neither debt nor a school, was growing. St. Mary, the much larger parish, had a $1.6 million debt for renovation costs, which it had been paying down with help from the $25,000-a-month rental of its school building to a private academy. When the 2004 clustering order came down, the two parishes sent a joint statement outlining their services and finances. The larger church had 1,930 people attending five Sunday Masses; St. Susanna had 640 people at three Masses. But the smaller church, debt free, was on a surge of growth, with 20 percent more members than in the last year.[41]

Josoma and the other pastor, the Reverend John A. Dooher, prepared the March 8, 2004, joint statement on clustering. They recommended that neither parish close, even though as Josoma explained, "That was not an option given us." He clashed with Dooher until the day the report was due because "it omitted mention of St. Mary's million-plus debt. Dooher told me, 'The diocese knows what we owe.' I told him the Reconfiguration committee didn't know that."

But Dooher was being considered for the hierarchy. Josoma made a political calculation not to spotlight what he knew of Dooher's track record with financial management lest it seem an attempt to thwart him from becoming a bishop and backfire on Josoma's efforts to save his parish. Dooher's church had a $101,129 annual deficit. The school had lost its tenant. The lower level of the church had cut off heating to save money—and developed mold. In 2007 the new pastor reported that the $1.2 million debt to the archdiocese would be more than halved with a $675,000 sale of land to the town of Dedham.[42] By then, the pastor who left the debt behind had become Auxiliary Bishop Dooher.

"Politics of the club," said Josoma drily. "And why are we in a mess?"

Amid the clustering debate, one of St. Susanna's deacons, a Harvard-educated attorney, told Josoma the suppression order was "a cash-grab."

Josoma secured an appointment for himself and ten parish leaders with Archbishop O'Malley and Bishop Lennon.

They had done background research on the Santa Fe, New Mexico, archdiocese, which raised about $8 million to pay its share of a $25 million abuse settlement in the early 1990s. Archbishop Michael Sheehan asked parish leaders to help. Through heightened donations and parish property sales, the group provided close to $2 million, while avoiding widespread closures.[43] Sheehan's predecessors had allowed predators in treatment at the Servants of the Paraclete facility in Jemez Springs, New Mexico, to do weekend parish work, where they found fresh victims. The Paracletes' standards were so shoddy that litigation drove them out of the treatment business in New Mexico. Archbishop Robert Sanchez resigned in 1993 when his sexual relationships with young women and teenage girls made news. His replacement, Sheehan, had come with his own baggage from the Dallas diocese, where as seminary rector he ignored warning flags on one Rudy Kos, whose ex-wife had warned church officials of his psychosexual problems. Kos, as a seminarian, had guardianship of a teenage boy who stayed some nights at the seminary, where Kos abused him. Sheehan testified that he had not met the boy. "I just considered that a personal matter, that Rudy was an adult and could take care of it."[44] Kos was ordained. Eight youths in well-to-do parishes and Kos's ward later sued him and the diocese for abuse. The 1997 jury verdict of $119 million was a stunning rebuke of Bishop Charles Grahmann, whom jurors singled out by name for his oversight failures. As often happens in large verdicts, the plaintiff attorneys agreed to a lower settlement—$31 million—to avoid a lengthy appeal.[45] Perhaps the Dallas debacle made Sheehan wiser. In Santa Fe, he worked with pastors and lay leaders in choosing property to sell and fund-raising to pay for settlements.

In the Boston chancery, Josoma and ten parishioners cited Santa Fe as an enlightened response to financial crisis. O'Malley and Lennon listened. St. Susanna's group argued the benefits of transparency. Josoma said the jump from $10 million to $40 million in archdiocesan debt was hard to fathom. Where had the money gone? O'Malley was quiet. Lennon cited greater deferred maintenance of church properties, a sharp downturn in donations, rising pension costs. The group gave the bishops a packet of information with charts and graphs to bolster their stance that a vibrant parish need not be closed.

Josoma asked O'Malley if he would come celebrate Mass at the parish.

"I don't want a media circus. I thought this meeting would suffice," the archbishop demurred.

"These are two different realities," replied Josoma.

And then, as agreed upon with his parish council, Father Josoma offered Archbishop O'Malley four acres of the church land—prime real estate—at a value which they calculated at nearly $2 million.

"*It's not about the money, Steve!*" yelled Bishop Lennon, slamming his hand on the table. The group of parishioners stared.

"Nice to know it's not personal," replied Josoma.

For it was *exactly* about the money, as everyone in the room knew. But in the fog of diplomacy, no one wanted to embarrass Lennon. O'Malley, having said little, closed the meeting on a promise to consider their views.

Josoma believed in the church teaching that a diocese existed to serve the parishes. Now it seemed the archdiocese was trying to suck money from its churches. When an archdiocesan inventory team arrived to catalog objects in his church and rectory, Josoma saw his volunteers go numb; he said to the men with clipboards and cameras, "If you want to loot us you'll have to come later. You must leave now."

DEPTH CHARGES FROM THE HINTERLANDS

On July 6, 2004, the Portland, Oregon, archdiocese, facing new lawsuits after a $53 million settlement for a hundred abuse claims, filed for Chapter 11 protection under the U.S. Bankruptcy Code. "Parish assets belong to the parish," stated Archbishop John Vlazny. "I have no authority to seize parish property."[46] Several weeks later, the Tucson, Arizona, diocese filed for Chapter 11 protection, but did not echo Vlazny's position. The Spokane, Washington, diocese followed suit that December, after spending $400,000 on public relations.[47] In that case, Nicholas P. Cafardi, a canon lawyer and the dean of the Duquesne University Law School, gave an affidavit that sent a booming echo to suppressed parishes in Boston. "Neither the bishop nor the diocese is the owner of parish property under the Canon Law," stated Cafardi. "The bishop can only dispose of parish property with the consent of the pastor."[48]

By opening the "estate" of dioceses to these courts, defense attorneys hoped to remove parish property from the base of assets. Yet in Portland and Boston, as in Chicago and many smaller sees, such as New Orleans, the bishop was a corporation sole, a juridic person who owned all parish and church properties (excluding schools and universities). Portland defense lawyers argued that Vlazny held "bare legal title," meaning canon law restricted his selling rights, and religious freedom in the U.S. Constitution barred tampering with a bishop's authority. In Spokane plaintiff attorneys argued that as a corporation sole, the bishop held all the assets that were fair target for victims' compensation.

An editorial in the *National Catholic Reporter*, an independent weekly, scoffed at the bishops' legal gambits:

The arguments made by the diocese of Spokane and Portland bring to mind Marx's (Groucho's not Karl's) famous question: Are you going to believe me or your own eyes? The niceties of canon law aside, power in the U.S. church, ownership, if you will, clearly resides with individual bishops in their dioceses. That power is wielded benignly by some, less so by many, but it is disingenuous to say that it doesn't exist. Bishops answer to Rome, and, presumably, to God, but not to their pastors and certainly not to the people in the pews.

It is a bankrupt church in more ways than one.[49]

THE VIGIL MOVEMENT BEGINS

A public Mass on August 15, 2004, at the greenery of Boston Commons, organized by Voice of the Faithful, drew a thousand people under a chilly, rain-darkened sky. Josoma and Bowers were among the five priests who celebrated the liturgy. "The Archdiocese of Boston has confused the mission of the church with the money of the church," declared Bowers in his homily, pulling applause. "What we don't have are bishops who have the courage to say *why?*"[50] Bowers's barb gave voice to the frustrations of people holding signs that said "Keep St. Albert's Open"—referring to a Weymouth parish with 1,600 families that was debt free and had nearly $200,000 more in income than expenses.[51]

Like the churches in Charlestown and Dedham, St. Albert the Great had in its pastor, the Reverend Ron Coyne, one of the fifty-eight signatories to the letter that called for Cardinal Law's resignation. Like Bowers and Josoma, Ron Coyne had revitalized a parish that had been losing membership. The three priests oddly mirrored the role that the Vatican imposed on Archbishop O'Malley as turnaround specialists, albeit of parishes rather than a diocese. Coyne had the smallest building among five parishes in Weymouth; it also had no school. As outrage crackled among parishioners opposed to Reconfiguration, ten people in Weymouth announced on closure day, August 29, that they would not leave. They came with pillows and blankets and slept in the pews. "I feel very sad about it," Coyne told the Associated Press. "It's very unjust. [The archdiocese] saw new life coming into this parish and yet didn't even take that into consideration."[52]

Within two days two hundred people had joined a list to maintain the vigil in rotating shifts. The parish filed a canonical appeal to the archdiocese.

"We're not going to drag people out of church," the chancery spokesman said in the quickening media coverage. "The archbishop says let's just be patient and work this out as Christians." But Christians from the pews of St. Albert the Great raised $100,000 for legal fees and sued the archdiocese, claiming *they owned the parish*. "We now understand that we are the church and we are followers of Christ and not the archdiocese of Boston," read a parish council statement, all but declaring a religious secession, or schism.[53]

Archbishop O'Malley let the rebels stay in Weymouth's priestless church.

At St. Catherine of Siena, Peter Borré watched people groping for a strategy. They wanted to meet with the archbishop. Borré wondered how to expose the financial duplicity and use that information to force the archdiocese into reversing course. Bowers held more meetings with O'Malley, to no avail. As much as he liked Bob Bowers, Borré, with his corporate background, was a gritty realist on the dynamics of large organizations; he was skeptical that the idealistic pastor whom his mother-in-law adored had a real strategy. Bowers was a go-to figure for reporters, speaking truth to power in the media narrative. Borré saw the coverage affording leverage for dealing with O'Malley (or Lennon, as the power behind the throne) but only if a strategy pushed beyond the headlines.

As autumn settled over Boston, Borré drove out to St. Thomas the Apostle parish in the town of Peabody where he had been tipped off that Lennon would make a rare appearance. People in pews, incredulous at the suppression order for their prosperous parish, were silent as the bishop rose to speak. With thinning black hair, a lean face, and a paunch traversed by the prelate's gold chain, Lennon gave a cold recitation on the crisis. The deepening shortage of priests meant too few pastors to go around. Twenty-five percent of the parishes were not paying their assessments. *But he's closing some of the wealthiest parishes that paid proportionally more*, Borré brooded. The archdiocese was having to cover extra costs of priests' medical insurance, Lennon continued.

A parishioner asked if they had a canonical right to appeal. Lennon stared, letting his silence seep in for effect. Finally, he said, "Don't waste your time."

He does not want a canonical fight, Borré reported to himself.

St. Thomas was spared after a wealthy supporter of the parish made a large donation. Meanwhile, parishioners at seven other churches refused to leave when the doors closed. Cynthia Deysher, the forty-seven-year-old president of an investment consulting firm, was sitting in a pew of St. Anselm in Sudbury, wondering where this vigil would go, when a man sat down by her, introduced himself as Peter Borré, and asked if she would be cochair of a parishes council. Borré wanted to harness the vigils' passive resistance into an energy the archdiocese could not avoid. Deysher, who had worked as a chief financial officer for three companies she helped steer to public stock offerings, was as unlikely as Borré to join a breakaway group. For years she had recorded the collections on software and made the weekly deposits.[54] Joining St. Anselm's 24/7 vigil rotation, Deysher thought Reconfiguration was a sham. "Catholics can be generous when properly inspired," she told me later. St. Anselm, sitting on land worth a couple of million, had no debt and $600,000 in the bank. St. Bernard in Newton was worth $12 million, she reckoned.

Deysher had a more short-range goal than Borré: to keep her parish open. Married, with daughters in high school and college, she wanted the archdiocese to recover. Voice of the Faithful (VOTF) had allied itself with abuse survivors, many of whom didn't care if churches closed, while its leaders tried to engage bishops in dialogue. Borré wanted a more radical strategy of building pressure against the archdiocese with vigil protests, pushing in the civil courts over parish ownership, and taking their case to Vatican tribunals.

As the pressure bore down on St. Susanna, a lady parishioner died with no provisions for burial. The family decided on a cremation. A few steps outside Steve Josoma's rectory lay a garden; the family was delighted when he offered to inter the ashes in parish earth. With that burial, Father Josoma consecrated sacred soil. Now, St. Susanna parish had a cemetery. Soon after, parishioners gathered for two more funerals. Evicting people from a parish with a cemetery would cause more headaches for O'Malley, creating new issues under canon law. Josoma kept the information as a hidden ace should the closure order come.

He wanted the living to have the same canonical rights as the dead.

The St. Susanna parishioners' presentation to O'Malley led to the granting of a three-year reprieve. The archbishop could rescind the order at any time. But a reprieve, supplanting the suppression order, eased Jo-soma's stress.

O'Malley signaled a bigger shift on October 3, 2004, by announcing a committee of eight prominent Catholics to review the closures and report back to him. The cochairs were Sister Janet Eisner, president of Emmanuel College, and Peter Meade, the board chairman of Catholic Charities and executive vice president of Blue Cross and Blue Shield of Massachusetts. With a "review" of Reconfiguration, O'Malley was cutting bait on Len-non. "I would be surprised if the archbishop didn't reconsider some [of the closures]," Meade told the *Globe*.[55]

Peter Borré and Cynthia Deysher formed the Council of Parishes on October 14, 2004, with seven churches in vigil, asking "the process of closing parishes to be suspended; for closing decrees to be revoked; and to cooperate with Archbishop O'Malley in addressing archdiocesan con-cerns." Doris Giardiello, who had spent sixty of her seventy-five years at St. Therese church, slept on the altar in her beige winter coat.[56] Harking back to sit-in protests of the Southern civil rights era, Boston's vigil mem-bers, with their pillows, sleeping bags, and cell phones, put their sacred spaces in conflict with the archbishop.

AGONY OF AN ARCHBISHOP

"I have a plan," Archbishop O'Malley had told Bowers on the phone.

As before, Borré drove his pastor to the chancery and waited outside, unwilling to sit in the foyer. Now, on a luminous autumn day, Mary Beth Borré's beloved Red Sox were battling into the World Series and her candidate, Senator Kerry, was in a close race with President Bush. If the hard-luck Red Sox could do it, anything was possible. Borré was pleased when O'Malley appointed David Castaldi, a former chancellor of the archdiocese (and Harvard Business School classmate of Peter's), to chair a Reconfiguration oversight committee. Lennon now faced two groups au-thorized by O'Malley.

Father Bowers sat opposite Archbishop O'Malley, who explained that he had decided to close all three churches in Charlestown and consoli-date them into a single parish. "A fresh start," said the prelate; however, it would require all three pastors to resign. Bowers did not want to re-sign, but he was wiped out emotionally and physically; he took heart that the archbishop had embraced his advisory group's recommendation of a planned phaseout. "Did you get the other two pastors to resign?" Bowers wanted to know.

They had indeed agreed, O'Malley assured him.

The long process of trying to save the parish had left Bowers feeling like a piece of wood into which a screw has been driven so deeply as to make it split. His group had advocated a long transition guided by three pastors; this was the opposite. *If I don't resign, my parish closes,* he brooded. *If I do resign, all three pastors leave and one church will stay open. At least it creates a level field.*

O'Malley promised that the parish would not close for at least a year, that whatever melding of congregations into a chosen church would be handled by the new pastor. Exhausted and dispirited, Bowers took it as the best deal he could get. The archbishop wanted him to leave within a week. Bowers needed more time, both to pack and to prepare his flock for a hard transition. O'Malley agreed.

Bowers approached the car, deep in thought. "How'd it go?" asked Borré.

"I think it went pretty well. Seán hugged me at the end of the meeting."

Resisting the urge to bellow *What the hell happened?* Borré started the car, gently prodding for details. He felt a sinking disappointment at what he heard. Borré wanted St. Catherine of Siena to join the vigil protest. Bowers said the parishioners would have to decide for themselves. Borré's disgruntlement rose on realizing that the force of fifty-eight priests who had signed a letter denouncing Law for concealing abusers would not carry into the realm of parishioners losing parishes. Law, after all, was gone. Bowers got the deeper message when he returned to sign the papers affirming the agreement. He asked O'Malley where he would go next as pastor. "You will not be a pastor for a very long time," the prelate said gravely. "Many priests are angry with you." *It's he who is angry with me,* thought Bowers. He asked for a sabbatical and received it on the spot.

Lennon refused to answer questions for David Castaldi's group and stood aloof from the Meade-Eisner inquiry. With people bedding down in pews of eight parishes, O'Malley's reform status was at risk.

Then a hole broke in the dike. O'Malley released a letter on November 13, 2004, which carried an amazing tone of misery. "Closing parishes is the hardest thing I have ever had to do in forty years of religious life," he wrote.

I joined the monastery knowing that I would have to do difficult things for the rest of my life, but I never imagined I would have to be involved in anything so painful or so personally repulsive to me as this. At times I ask God to call me home and let someone else finish this job, but I keep waking up in the morning to face another day of reconfiguration.[57]

A prelate calling reconfiguration "so personally repulsive" as to wish God to end his life made Peter Borré sit up. What an indictment of Lennon's plan! A priest told Borré that Lennon learned of the letter when he read it in the *Globe*. If true, that signaled an even deeper breach between archbishop and bishop.

O'Malley's letter did not mention Lennon as it reiterated details of the crisis: an operating budget chopped $14 million in three years; a deficit of $10 million; a troubled stock market causing "an unfunded pension liability of $80 million"—lay employee and clergy retirement, both endangered.

Many communities who meet their expenses do so by selling land and buildings and spending down savings. (In the last nine years parishes have sold 150 pieces of property mostly to pay bills.) Some people think that reconfiguration will mean a great surplus of money for the Archdiocese. Unfortunately, this is not true. I have asked the Finance Council to work on a strategic plan for the Archdiocese which I shall share with you. I am committed to financial transparency and to using our human and financial resources for the mission of the Church.

Borré told the *Washington Post* he was "astounded by the depth of emotion." Borré conceded that demographic changes meant some parishes had to go. "The question is what is happening to the archdiocese's finances, and the answer is we don't know."[58]

In search of a seasoned canonist in Rome, Borré obtained *Annuario Pontificio*, a thick book that lists dioceses alphabetically and Vatican offices with names, postal addresses, and phone numbers. It helped to know Italian. Unbeknownst to Borré, as he assembled names of practitioners in the Vatican tribunals, Cardinal Sodano and his nephew had a plan for shuttered American churches.

CHAPTER 5

ITALIAN INTERVENTIONS

By the fall of 2003, with John Paul II fatigued and bloated from his treatments for Parkinson's disease, Cardinal Sodano exerted greater power than ever in overseeing the Roman Curia. "The scandals in the United States received disproportionate attention from the media," Sodano announced. "There are thieves in every country but it is hard to say that everyone is a thief."[1]

Earlier in the year, as America prepared for war with Iraq, papal representatives sent warnings about an invasion. Condoleezza Rice, the Bush administration's national security adviser, stated that she didn't understand the Vatican position. As the standoff mounted between President George W. Bush and Saddam Hussein, Sodano told Italian journalists, "The Holy See is against the war; it's a moral position. It's certainly not a defensive war." He added a dose of pragmatism: "We're trying to provoke reflection not so much on whether it's just or unjust, moral or immoral, but whether it's worth it. From the outside we can appear idealists, and we are, but we are also realists. Is it really a good idea to irritate a billion Muslims? Not even in Afghanistan are things going well. For this reason we have to insist on asking the question if it's a good idea to go to war."[2]

Hours after the first missiles smashed down on Baghdad, John Paul denounced the war as "a defeat for reason and the gospel."[3]

Rice visited the Vatican on February 8, 2005, in her new position as
secretary of state and met with her counterpart, Cardinal Sodano. The
Boston church closings and the bankruptcy cases of five other dioceses
had become a greater issue for the Curia since Archbishop O'Malley's
2003 meetings at the Vatican. After discussing Iraq and the Middle East,
Sodano surprised Rice with a bald request: that the Bush administration
intervene against a class action lawsuit that Louisville attorney William
F. McMurry had filed against the Holy See in federal court in Kentucky,
seeking damages for all victims of clergy sex abuse. Rice told him the Constitution prevented such a move by any administration.

Several attempts to sue the Vatican on other issues had failed under the
1976 Foreign Sovereign Immunities Act. "Sodano's decision to raise the
matter with Rice suggests concern in Rome that sooner or later its immunity may give way, exposing the Vatican to potentially crippling verdicts,"
wrote John L. Allen Jr. for *National Catholic Reporter*.[4]

Sodano's ham-fisted design on diplomacy was all of a piece with his
response to the abuse crisis. Realizing that dioceses were unloading assets, in many cases to pay their share of litigation, Sodano persuaded the
silver-haired Cardinal Castrillón to appoint Monsignor Giovanni Carrù
as undersecretary of the Congregation for the Clergy. Carrù, who began
work on November 1, 2003, had specialized in catechism in the Turin diocese, in Sodano's native Piedmont, in northern Italy. A man of warm and
genial ways, Carrù was physical, putting hands on people's cheeks, giving
the affectionate hug, an effusive Italian friendliness, explains a priest well
versed in Clergy's inner workings.

Cardinal Castrillón was not pleased, this cleric explains. Castrillón felt
Carrù was inflicted on him. Carrù, this source surmises, would have been
happy as a bishop in his small diocese, but in his affable, simple way Carrù
did what he was told. He liked to be important. The cleric describes Carrù
in meetings, impatiently waiting for them to end, saying, *And now we are
done?*—when often, no, they weren't done, and discussions stretched on:
after all, it *was* the Vatican. Monsignor Carrù as undersecretary led the
closing prayer before they scattered for lunch.

As third in command, Carrù was a traffic manager for Clergy's mail,
faxes, and documents from the world's dioceses, bishops, and priests who

had business with the congregation. Clergy's internal offices dealt with priestly discipline, catechetics, and patrimony, meaning property. Carrù took a special interest in the Third Office's alienation of church property. His patron, Cardinal Sodano, took special interest in his nephew, Andrea Sodano, whose company Carrù helped with leads on church property as it came on the market.

In the long history of American Catholics bailing out the Vatican, it was perhaps inevitable that some shrewd Italian would see profit escalators in shuttered New World churches. To that end, Andrea Sodano, a structural engineer from his uncle Angelo's hometown, Asti, had a front man who could have come out of central casting.

Enter Raffaello Follieri, with cheeks like a cherub, a tousle of brown hair, and deep, dark eyes. In November 2005, the twenty-seven-year-old Follieri was leasing a two-story $37,000-a-month apartment in Manhattan's Olympic Tower; his foundation touted vaccinations for poor children in Latin America. Raffaello thrilled to the halo of celebrity circling his airplanes-to-everywhere romance with the movie star Anne Hathaway. Since her breakout role in *The Princess Diaries*, dark-haired Annie (as Raffaello called her) had made Follieri famous. The paparazzi and tabloids seized on their episodes in society. They were part of a New Year's Eve soiree at a Dominican Republic resort with Bill and Hillary Clinton among the guests.

Every time his photograph appeared with Anne and her magic smile, Follieri knew it was good for business. The decidedly less glamorous Andrea Sodano was Follieri Group's vice president. To call Sodano the brains of the operation would be unfair, since Follieri had the raw materials of a master salesman. But Raffaello was an amateur compared with the worldly-wise Andrea, who had the Vatican connections through his uncle.

The faxes generated from Follieri Group in New York that landed on Giovanni Carrù's desk in the Congregation for the Clergy did not go unnoticed among other priests in the office. Gossip is the mother's milk of bureaucracy. For Andrea and Raffaello, the information on American church properties that Carrù sent was worth the investment.

The Follieri Group website listed Raffaello as chairman-CEO and his father, Pasquale, as president. A native of Foggia, in the southern region of Puglia, Pasquale Follieri had done real estate work in Italy. His bio said he was a lawyer for two Italian banks; an expert in arbitration; a member of "the Court of Cassation" (comparable to the United States Supreme Court); an experienced journalist and a newspaper editor—but no mention of his conviction "in an Italian court [for] misappropriating more than $300,000 from a failed resort company whose assets he had been charged with overseeing," as the *Wall Street Journal* would report. He appealed the conviction.[5]

Born in 1978 in Foggia, Raffaello had gone north, to Rome, to study at university. He lived for a time with the actress Isabella Orsini. Pasquale was having legal problems when his son dropped out of college. Raffaello founded Beauty Planet, a cosmetic supplies business with "the prestige hair and body care line Shatoosh." The Follieri Group website said he sold the company in 2002 and joined a "London-based holding company" for oil trading and diamond mines. No mention that Beauty Planet lost money or the London company tanked.[6]

. Raffaello made his first trip to New York at nineteen. Back in Italy, he hungered for Manhattan, to make his name in the city of cities. He met Andrea Sodano at a party in Rome. He barely had pocket change when he returned to New York in 2003, but Raffaello was fueled by rockets of ambition. Pasquale helped him establish the company. Andrea Sodano played surrogate for "the Vatican" in pitching potential investors and clients. The plan was to buy church properties below market value and develop them for lucrative resales.

When Raffaello and Andrea pulled into Washington, D.C., for the American bishops' autumn 2005 convention, a beaming Cardinal Francis George of Chicago greeted them in the lobby of the Capitol Hill Hyatt Regency. George's radiant delight made an impression on Joe Feuerherd, the Washington correspondent for *National Catholic Reporter.* Feuerherd took note of Cardinal Sodano's nephew. Slight of build, bespectacled, about five foot ten, with salt-and-pepper hair, Andrea had a patina of worldly experience that stood out in high relief from Follieri's effusive, youthful charm.

As it happened, Joe Feuerherd had worked in the affordable housing field earlier in his career; he knew how lenders and public agencies come together on big-ticket projects to secure funding. Many bishops have staff to manage their dioceses' real estate holdings; some help develop housing for the elderly and low-income, sometimes under church auspices. The Conference for Catholic Facility Management is a professional association in its own right. As Follieri headed off to a Hyatt hospitality suite to welcome bishops, priests, and lay staffers, Feuerherd wondered how he got his money. Andrea Sodano, with a flip of the cell phone, had digital photographs to show of Uncle Angelo in the Vatican.[7] "When Raffaello wants to meet with the bishop, they put the touch on from the Vatican and they get the meeting," a church source told Feuerherd. "They're about as connected as it gets."

The Follieri Group's website announced "contracts for the acquisition of over $100 million of church property in three U.S. cities." Follieri's business director wrote to a religious order:

> Our intention is to purchase properties from dioceses and religious organizations, to renovate them, and if necessary, convert them to new uses, such as housing (lower, middle and upper income, depending on the area) and commercial use . . .
>
> Because of the Follieri family's deep commitment to the Catholic church and its long-standing relationship with senior members of the Vatican hierarchy, the Follieri Group understands very well the imperatives of the church and is sensitive to its needs.[8]

So, Feuerherd asked Follieri, do you plan to use the low-income housing tax credit at 4 percent or 9 percent? Raffaello had no idea, but cheerfully waved off his inexperience—he had staff to handle that. *He's a huckster,* thought Joe Feuerherd.[9] Nevertheless, his article showed restraint.

> There were two initial factors motivating the company's interest in U.S. church real estate, Raffaello Follieri told NCR. First, he said, "The [sex abuse] scandal in America [where] dioceses were paying a lot of money to pay [off] the lawsuits" would necessitate the sale of church property. Next, he said, the changing demographics of the church—from North and East to West and South and from city to suburb—mean that "a lot of the schools and churches that were full of people in the beginning" are now largely unused . . .
>
> For competitive reasons the real estate industry is hyperdiscreet. Only when a deal is consummated—a process that can take months as prospective purchasers arrange financing and conduct

environmental and other land and structural analysis—do sales
records become public.

Even then, in some jurisdictions, religious institutions are ex-
empt from some disclosure requirements. Dioceses and religious
orders, meanwhile, are notoriously reluctant to discuss their
business dealings, especially when senior Vatican officials are
involved.[10]

"This thing smells in my opinion," a religious order official told Feuerherd, his name withheld. "I wouldn't get close to these people." Translation: in the small tent of church politics, you don't want your boss knowing
you've scoffed at a pitchman in the person of Cardinal Sodano's nephew.

"I have worked for the Follieri family for the past fifteen years as an
engineering consultant," Andrea Sodano told Feuerherd by e-mail. "My
involvement long predates the Follieri Group's interest in the States. The
Follieri Group's long and successful track record in real estate speaks for
itself."[11]

Melanie Bonvicino, a former *Vogue* model and a New York publicist
with many celebrity clients, helped Raffaello in the start-up phase. She
calls Andrea Sodano "very calculating, restrained, and absolutely gay. He
looked upper class. He sits there, the nephew of the cardinal—what do
you think Americans are going to think? It's the image. Raffaello was like
an actor cast in the lead of a movie. He was not particularly intellectual.
He was a provincial young man from southern Italy, humble beginnings,
but the accent, his good looks, and the clothes helped. He had very good
manners, which goes a long way for most people. The entire business was
predicated on associations, a veneer of something. He was charming, charismatic. He made people feel *good* . . . [Anne Hathaway] was reading blogs
all the time. He made *her* dazzling, he made *her* interesting."[12]

Richard Ortoli, a Manhattan attorney who drew up the incorporation
papers, was so impressed with Raffaello Follieri that he invested close to
$100,000; he let Raffaello sleep for a time in his spare room and hosted a
party to launch the Follieri Group at the elite, wood-paneled University
Club. As Michael Shnayerson reported in *Vanity Fair*, Cardinal Sodano
circulated, shaking hands, smiling, his mere presence a Vatican show of
support. Through Andrea Sodano, Follieri met princes of the American

church to help gloss his image. Vincent Ponte, a restaurateur and TriBeCa developer took note when New York Cardinal Edward Egan gave Raffaello the grand hello in Filli Ponte restaurant. After conversations with Raffaello, Ponte invested $300,000 in the Follieri Group and lent Raffaello a white Mercedes with a driver.[13]

In 2004 Raffaello fell in love with the twenty-two-year-old Hathaway. She would become a bigger star as the ingenue magazine secretary in *The Devil Wears Prada*. Her celebrity status boosted his as he opened doors. Philanthropy was a calculated part of his plan. Although the Follieri Foundation did pay for vaccinations for children in Honduras, Raffaello in early 2005 sent a more important gift of 20,000 euros (roughly $34,000 at prevailing exchange rates) to the Congregation for the Clergy via Carrù. On March 8, 2005, Cardinal Castrillón sent a letter of thanks "for those priests who are most in need . . . Mons. Giovanni Carrù has spoken with me about your very successful professional activities in the building industry which you carry out with seriousness and devotion. I wish you every heartfelt success."[14]

Priests who bring in donations rise in the eyes of their superiors. As Monsignor Carrù pleased Cardinal Castrillón, Raffaello Follieri had in Carrù the third-ranking undersecretary in the office with files on church properties to be sold. Carrù, a priceless insider for information on real estate that bishops and cardinals had to sell, would have his needs.

"My boyfriend is incredible in a lot of ways," Hathaway gushed to a fashion writer. "One of the most untouched aphrodisiacs in the world is charity work. Seriously, you want a girl to be impressed, vaccinate some kids, build a house."[15] Although Raffaello and Anne did go to Honduras to inoculate poor children against hepatitis, Follieri's public relations firm made sure the wire services got access to the right photographs. Follieri cast lines to Doug Band, the gatekeeper to Bill Clinton, suggesting he was poised to make a big donation to the Clinton Global Initiative. Soon he had a meeting with Clinton and his pal Ron Burkle, a billionaire real estate developer. Cardinal Sodano vouched for Follieri to Clinton's office. When reached by the *Wall Street Journal*, Sodano's "personal secretary [said] the cardinal declines to comment."[16]

Burkle was so impressed that his private equity fund, Yucaipa Companies (board members included Clinton and Jesse Jackson), which funded inner-city supermarkets among other projects, agreed to a $100 million stake in Follieri Group LLC, to be paid in installments pegged to specific deals.

Follieri's early purchases included an abandoned school-and-parish complex in the Camden, New Jersey, diocese. An Atlantic City pastor, Monsignor William Hodge, was "absolutely thrilled" with Follieri and soon went to work for him. The company bought a vacant lot from the Chicago archdiocese and two closed parish facilities in North Philadelphia for more than $1 million.[17]

In Boston, Follieri did not succeed. "He kept saying, 'I want to *buy*,' " recalled Bill McCall, the chairman of the archdiocese's real estate office. "To me, there was a naïveté there—I'm not sure he ever would have achieved the rezoning that he needed."[18]

In the summer of 2005, flush with money from Yucaipa, Raffaello Follieri had a $480,000 salary, yet his spending was off the charts. Beyond the $37,000 monthly rent at the Olympic Tower apartment, he had an executive chef, a Trump Tower flat for his parents, his father Pasquale's orthodontist bills, the dog-walking service, and lavish trips with Anne Hathaway. Among the celebrity-glommers to visit their rented yacht in the Mediterranean was Senator John McCain, a maverick in his own mind. Follieri siphoned off Yucaipa funds for a nonexistent office in Rome. At Follieri Group's Park Avenue office, the receptionists were Filipina nuns. Raffaello put an altar in one room and stocked black clericals in a closet for Hodge and another monsignor on staff, George Tomashek, to wear for image enhancement on property calls.

In the weekly conference calls with Burkle's company, Follieri escalated the requests to pay Andrea Sodano, stressing that the Vatican needed the engineering reports in order to approve the sales of church property. The Follieri-Yucaipa partnership paid more than $800,000 to that end. The Follieri office sent payments to Andrea Sodano's office in Italy (and in some cases directly to the Vatican) by bank wire transfer. The invoices disclose a two-month flurry of payments in 2005 (the money came from Yucaipa's investors). The Follieri-to-Sodano outlays included $75,000 on August 22, for "Engineering Services"; a September 12 invoice for $15,000 for work in Atlantic City, New Jersey, and $80,000 for Orland Park in the Chicago archdiocese; and on October 21, $70,000 for Canyon City (no state given in the invoice), another $50,000 for

Orland Park, and $75,000 for unspecified "Engineering Services," making a tidy $195,000 net on that single day. None of the invoices included a paragraph on work done.[19]

An FBI investigation later determined that Follieri wired $387,300 to a layman who worked as an administrator in the Vatican, one Antonio Mainiero. Mainiero's day job was on the staff of the Congregation for the Causes of Saints. His role, as the FBI determined, was to help cultivate church officials, "show the gardens of the Vatican to Follieri and his guests, and arrange for guided tours of a museum at the Vatican to make it falsely appear that Follieri's ties to the Vatican provided him with the right of first refusal" on church properties.[20] But to appear as if Follieri had a right of first refusal was an image of mutual design. Follieri's bank wire transfers to Mainiero in the Vatican spotlight an enterprise whereby Vatican-connected operators profit off U.S. church sales. On November 2, 2005, Follieri wired Mainiero $25,000; on March 1, 2006, a wire for $140,000; on May 16, 2006, a wire for $70,000; on June 30, 2006, a wire for $52,300; and on November 17, 2006, a wire for $100,000.

On March 8, 2006—one week after the largest payment sent to Mainiero in the Vatican, $140,000—Cardinal Sodano sent a letter of complaint to Follieri. "I feel it is my duty to tell you how perturbed I am," he wrote,

> to hear that your company continues to present itself as having ties to "the Vatican," due to the fact that my nephew, Andrea, has agreed on some occasion to provide you with professional consulting services.
>
> I do not know how this distressing misunderstanding could have occurred, but it is <u>necessary</u> now to avoid such confusion in the future.
>
> I do, therefore, appeal to your sensibility to be careful with respect to this matter. I shall accordingly inform my nephew Andrea as well as anyone else who has asked me for information regarding your firm.
>
> I take this opportunity to send you my regards.[21]

The letter is clearly in response to Feuerherd's long article of March 3 in *National Catholic Reporter*. In the course of sending intelligence to its government, the Vatican embassy in Washington undoubtedly alerted the secretary of state of the Holy See to unflattering news references to himself, his nephew, and the "this thing smells" quote from a religious order official. Cardinal Sodano's natural instinct was to cover his tracks. Although Andrea was milking the business, Cardinal Sodano—having lent his sacred office to greeting the potential backers and clients at Follieri Group's Manhattan launch—feigned ignorance. Ties to the Vatican? A "distressing misunderstanding." How much clearer could the Follieri brochures have been on the Vatican ties, or the sales calls with Andrea in his role? But as Iago prodded Othello to his fate and then withdrew, Andrea, who lived in Italy, could readily cut bait on Raffaello.

Behind the cardinal's underlining of "<u>necessary</u> . . . to avoid such confusion" looms the cold mien of power, warning the flamboyant Follieri sotto voce, "Be careful." One could infer he also meant, "We won't guard your back." For as Raffaello Follieri trumpeted his ecclesial connections to potential investors and church sellers, his braggadocio extended to telling people he was the *chief financial officer* of the Vatican! As the tailwinds of Follieri's hubris wafted back to the Apostolic Palace, Cardinal Sodano sensed trouble. Still, his letter's ambiguous language of chastisement begs a question: why didn't the cardinal send Follieri a cease-and-desist message? But to do that would have gored the golden calf servicing sweet meat for Andrea, Antonio Mainiero, Monsignor Carrù, if not the cardinal himself.

Four months after the cardinal's letter, with Burkle and company feeding money into Yucaipa Follieri Investments LLC, Raffaello and Andrea flew to Brazil on a property-scouting trip. As he had done with the 20,000 euro donation to the Congregation for the Clergy, Follieri had a check for $25,000 for the archbishop of Salvador da Bahia, and a check for $85,000 for the archbishop of Rio de Janeiro. "The recipients of these donations did not know that Follieri had stolen the money to give to them," cautions the FBI.[22] Follieri and Andrea Sodano had a strategy that was impossible without Vatican help: take the American money, give some to the right bishops, get an inside track on the available real estate, buy low, sell high.

In the spring of 2007, Ron Burkle suspected he was being fleeced. He wanted to see the engineering reports. Follieri stalled. The billionaire who flew in his private jet and partied with his pal Bill Clinton *demanded* the documents. Follieri made a secretary stay up all night writing the reports, which he backdated and disgorged to Burkle's people. "The reports were in Italian," Theodore Cacioppi, an FBI agent, told me later. "Each one was about two to five pages long. None of them contained any schematics, technical drawings, diagrams, or anything that appeared to relate to engineering." The reports putatively from Sodano "were almost worthless, did not reflect any engineering work, and were certainly not worth over $800,000."[23]

Burkle's Yucaipa Companies had their own investors, notably the New York State Common Retirement Fund, the California Teachers' Retirement System, and the California Public Employees' Retirement System. In June 2007, when Yucaipa sued Follieri for $1.3 million, the needle hit the balloon. Raffaello was closing in on a deal with Helios, a London-based company, to buy church properties in Europe. First he had to blunt Burkle's legal strike. He managed to repay Yucaipa, but a June 15, 2007, *Wall Street Journal* piece by John R. Emshwiller on the lawsuit "got us interested in Follieri," says FBI agent Cacioppi.

As the FBI probe began, Raffaello was bouncing checks. Hathaway paid the last four months' rent ($148,000, excluding the chef's salary) on the Olympic Tower lease, according to Melanie Bonvicino. Raffaello moved in with his mother at Trump Tower. He and Anne were quarreling when he flew to Rome in June 2008. He called Bonvicino, the publicist who had helped him in the start-up months and returned in the pinch. "I was doing crisis management," she says. "The Helios deal would have put him in a situation where he'd have an opportunity to cover his debts and redeem himself professionally . . . When the relationship with Yucaipa blew up, Raffaello gave Burkle a pick of his properties. Burkle took the crown jewels of the portfolio. He made a very handsome profit."

The Catholic Church has extensive property holdings in Ireland and the United Kingdom. Follieri's development plan with Helios would add new gems to his crown. He was getting information from Antonio Mainiero in the Vatican, whom he promised to set up as an officer of his branch company in Rome. And Monsignor Carrù from Clergy was feeding the fax requests. According to Melanie Bonvicino, "I told the Helios people, '*Put him on an allowance, cover his approvable expenses so he does not go out of pocket.*' Like you do with actors who have drug problems. There's no magic to what Raffaello did. He worked all the time, very hard. When he traveled he was always meeting people. People are money. Sit with the right person, get your picture taken, find the next person. It was like [the movie]

American Gigolo, dating a starlet, meeting people, but Raffaello was picking up tabs . . . He was always looking for business."

When Bonvicino reached Rome, Raffaello Follieri was short of cash. Monsignor Carrù was hectoring him for money. *We need their support,* Raffaello told her. A cradle Catholic with her own issues about the church, Bonvicino wondered why church officials had tolerated Raffaello's extravagant promotion of himself in alliance with the Vatican. The reality she found was the Vatican's involvement in the selling of U.S. church properties. Business is business. People are money. Into her purview that day in Rome came Monsignor Carrù, a small man in his early sixties whose effeminate mannerisms seemed out of sync with his deep, low voice of *furbo,* meaning clever, calculating, a legendary trait. Carrù seemed to her *furbo* personified.

Raffaello told her they needed Carrù's information to succeed with Helios.

Monsignor Carrù explained he was about to leave on holiday. The trio went to a restaurant, La Rosetta. "Carrù knew a lot," continues Bonvicino. "I think Carrù was tipped off. It was one last milking of the cow. The priest had wine. I paid for the lunch. He gave me a blessing after the meal." The next day they met him in Vatican City. She withdrew $1,000 worth of euros on her ATM card and gave it to Monsignor Carrù along with her personal check for $9,000 (on which she wrote *donation*), which he cashed an hour later at the Vatican Bank.

Bonvicino and Follieri flew back to New York, then to London, where Helios was intent on raising 100 million euros for developing church properties in Ireland and the UK. Melanie told Raffaello to stay in London, duck the celebrity lights until he could repay his debts, hire a lawyer, negotiate with the federal authorities in Manhattan, and try to avoid being arrested.

But the heart is a merciless magnet. In the meltdown with Hathaway, the cell calls and text messages flying across continents and time zones pulled Raffaello back without a defense attorney to prepare the way. He wanted his Annie. She was on tour for the movie *Get Smart* as their fraught dialogue played out. Caring for her dog at the Trump Tower apartment, he had no clue his lover was cooperating with the FBI. So were the two American monsignors, Hodge and Tomashek, among others in his employ. On June 24, 2008, Raffaello was asleep in his boxer shorts at his mother's flat when the FBI rang at 6:00 a.m. They arrested him for fraud and money laundering. His father, Pasquale, was back in Italy. In Raffaello's safe, the FBI agents found the letter from Cardinal Castrillón and "the smoking gun" letter from Sodano, as Agent Cacioppi calls it.

"The investigation started because he was in the press constantly and he made a great catch," opines Melanie Bonvicino. Indeed, the Vatican's true role was obscured in the media's juicy coverage of Follieri's spectacular meltdown with his movie star sweetheart. As he sat behind bars, with a $21 million bail he could not meet because the U.S. Attorney's office deemed him a flight risk, Follieri had no U.S. passport nor the stroke in Rome to negotiate an extradition so that he might serve time in Italy. He pleaded guilty to fourteen counts of wire fraud, money laundering, and conspiracy on October 23, 2008. He forfeited $2.4 million, jewelry, and twelve watches.

"We believe Studio Sodano [Andrea's corporate name] took in fraudulently earned money," Cacioppi told me. And Antonio Mainiero and Carrù? "We considered these people unindicted coconspirators. The relevant part from Italy is that we presumed this was bribe money paid to the little functionary [Mainiero] and to this secretary Carrù. We did not need to put those people on the stand. We did get intimations from the State Department that they were not inclined to talk with us. As a matter of resource allocation it was not worth trying to get them." Cacioppi went on to investigate Bernard Madoff.

With Follieri sentenced to fifty-four months, questions hover. What did Mainiero do with the $387,300? Did Cardinal Sodano share in the proceeds? Were the incoming funds allocated to the Congregation for the Clergy, or any other Vatican departments? Did the Vatican Bank play a role? How does the Congregation for the Clergy safeguard information when the number-three man—Monsignor Carrù—was put in his job by Sodano and serviced an operator like Follieri? Do Vatican officials profit from property sales in many dioceses? Does the Vatican profit from church sales in other countries? Did the Vatican Bank engage in money laundering?

Despite the bad publicity Carrù took from the press coverage, on July 20, 2009, Pope Benedict installed him as archaeological superintendent of the catacombs, "an important task entrusted to a scholar with great experience," according to an archbishop at the Pontifical Council for Culture.[24] Perhaps the new post was an elevation of duties, though the image of Giovanni Carrù prowling the ancient tunnels where Christians hid from Roman authority suggests a soft-glove demotion to make Cardinal Sodano nod with *furbo* of his own. Carrù was not the safest man in Vatican City to handle sensitive real estate information. Still, it took a year after Follieri's arrest before Carrù was removed from the Congregation for the Clergy.

Follieri was indeed a big catch for the Justice Department in the national media, but the greater corruption was at the Vatican. Burkle's people realized Raffaello was off the charts when he leased a private jet for $62,000 to make the quick hop from Los Angeles to Las Vegas instead of taking a commercial flight for a few hundred dollars. Why did the Sodanos get involved with him in the first place? Any number of real estate agents would have profited from unique access to Clergy property files, though Andrea's greed would have become an issue. The Sodano scheme went sour because Follieri lost his grip on reality. When he crashed, at least $800,000 was tucked away in Italy.

*

CODA

"What Raffaello did in four and a half years takes a lifetime for some people," asserts Melanie Bonvicino. "He put together a business that ended up making money for Burkle, and would have made serious money for Helios. In the end everybody ditched him. But the Vatican let this man run wild. Why?"

As Raffaello sat in a federal prison, abandoned by Anne, his parents back in Italy, Melanie Bonvicino made occasional visits. He owed her $131,000 for a blizzard of work at the back end, she says. They were never romantically involved. "But," she adds with a trace of sympathy, "I actually do care about him."

CHAPTER 6

THE CASE OF THE MISSING MILLIONS

As the Boston vigil protesters dug in, Peter Borré culled advice from sympathetic canon lawyers and drafted an appeal that he sent in early 2005 to the Congregation for the Clergy. His goal was to halt the suppression order, to undo Bishop Lennon's handiwork. Archbishop O'Malley wanted the protesters to vacate the parishes, but for the prelate who had publicly confessed his agony over the parish closings—asking God to take him on the worst days—calling the cops seemed out of character. His religious order was founded by Francis of Assisi. Having cops arrest people for occupying pews could be a body blow to area Catholics already steeped in bad news about the church.

As solidarity grew among people in those empty churches, the culture of resistance drew on Catholicism as a tissue of values. The sacred spaces became arenas of family and community reimagined. On Friday nights at St. Frances Cabrini in Scituate, the parish near the sea, the seven-year-old Arnold triplets—Christian, Scott, and Sean—scampered down the aisle in their slippers, knelt before the altar, and lay down in their sleeping bags.[1] Jon and Maryellen Rodgers, leaders of the vigil in Scituate, were mapping plans for a civil lawsuit to wrest ownership of St. Frances Cabrini from the archdiocese.

"We believe that we control the assets and the liabilities of the parish property," an archdiocesan spokesman explained to the town newspaper. "The Archbishop understands the anger and pain people are feeling."[2]

The civil lawsuit failed. The vigil continued.

At St. James in Wellesley, which sat on eight acres worth $14 million, vigil leader Suzanne Hurley evinced a rough pragmatism: "Once churches close, the towns can send tax bills to the archdiocese." Hurley had children aged eleven and seven when the 2004 vigil began. She was well paid as an assistant to a corporate CEO. Four years later, sitting in a quiet pew of the once-bustling church, with a handful of women preparing for a Council of Parishes gathering, Hurley cited an independent contractor's study which concluded that St. James was the parish best suited for growth in its geographic cluster. "We determined that no church in the cluster should close. It's like being voted off the island in *Survivor*," she said. "This parish sits on land donated by the Maffei family. They paid $25,000 for the marble altar. Kay Maffei, ninety-two, went to court. She wanted to keep the church open."

The state's Supreme Judicial Court denied standing for the case.

For O'Malley, the cost of defending the archdiocese in legal challenges was another expense layered into the protracted dispute. The chancery had to keep utilities working to maintain insurance; drawing down the cash reserves in a given parish, while the parish no longer paid an assessment, meant losing money at both ends.

In lieu of Sunday Mass, the parish had Communion services for which sympathetic priests in open parishes provided them consecrated wafers. "I am a lapsed Catholic," Hurley reflected one chilly night with Christmas three weeks off. "I feel attached to this *place*"—she gestured toward the stained-glass windows. "I had been a lector at Mass, but it wasn't until this parish that I heard the words differently, and it gave me a sense of ownership about faith. I've become jaded. My kids are well past their First Communion. I listened to my son ask, 'What's a pedophile?' I'm not concerned about something happening to my children, but I could not ask them to look up to me if I ran from this church. My father-in-law goes to Mass at his church, then comes to our vigil. I consider these services as legitimate as the Mass. I was hurt by the injustice of the Reconfiguration process. I remember sleeping in the choir loft, the first time. My husband said, 'I've had enough. I will never walk my daughter down this aisle.' . . . It takes a toll." The moral premise of the vigil, the human investment in sacred space, had its own logic. "I feel I can raise my children as good Catholics or good Christians."[3]

As the vigil movement gained momentum in 2005, Peter Borré's strategy with Cynthia Deysher on the Council of Parishes was to play for time, expect a loss at Clergy, and plan an appeal at the Apostolic Signatura, the Vatican high court; in the meantime, the parishioners occupying churches would keep the issue in the news. Sympathetic lawyers were exploring other strategies, but Borré knew that even in liberal Massachusetts an intrachurch dispute was a legal long shot, given the Constitution's guarantee for freedom of religion.

Borré was prepared at his own expense to spend time in Rome to see if just a few high church officials could grasp that each week in which a given group of parishioners kept their vigil meant lost Sunday collections, no taxes to the archbishop, continued expenses for the archdiocese, and the potential of losing good Catholics who wanted the sacraments *in their home churches*. O'Malley was losing money on each occupied parish. But Borré and the vigil members were clear-eyed about Vatican tribunals. The church legal system was not democratic. Bishops governed as princes. The pope as supreme arbiter of canon law could intervene in any proceeding; however, that rarely happened. Making the system work for protesting laypeople was one tall order.

For Mary Beth Borré, the biggest surprise was watching her husband "take on the role of a Don Quixote," as he headed out on an exotic journey against the odds. "It seemed a natural progression of the fight he chose to wage," she said later. "Peter is a natural entrepreneur. His greatest strength lies in seeing opportunity where others do not and being able to take advantage of the vacuum." Those traits ill fit the character of Cervantes's chivalrous madman on horseback. Still, Peter Borré, toughened by years in the oil industry, had never embarked on anything so remotely idealistic. The search for a point where faith and justice might meet had become a quest that, somehow, appealed to him.

He drew encouragement from the 2004 bankruptcy filings by the dioceses of Portland, Spokane, and Tucson. Canon lawyers were divided on the proprietary rights of bishops, but everyone realized that the bishops wanted to keep those diocesan parishes from being lumped into the assets that plaintiff lawyers were trying to recover in the mass-settlement cases for victim survivors. If parishes were off-limits in a diocese grappling with bankruptcy, how could the Suppression decrees in Boston—the bishop seizing parish assets—be valid?

As the Congregation for the Clergy's Third Office reviewed the appeals from the vigil parishes, the priests in Greater Boston were jolted by the news that the archdiocese was cutting back on benefits from the clergy pension fund. A priest leaked to *New York Times* reporter Mary Williams Walsh an internal report from the archdiocese's financial consultant, Towers Perrin. Between 1986 and 2002, "the archdiocese made no contributions" to the clergy pension fund, wrote Walsh. "Twice a year, at Christmas and at Easter, the archdiocese has held fund-raising drives in the parishes for priests' retirements, raising about $4.5 million a year. But for many years the archdiocese has used that money to fill other needs." The archdiocese was freezing pensions at $1,889 a month and "has sold church-owned real estate to the priests' pension fund to raise cash."[4]

The pension fund had money before the decade plus six years in which the annual donations were channeled elsewhere—enough, at the front end, such that it earned $1.5 million in interest on a $15 million loan to the archdiocese for the $85 million victims' settlement in 2003. But with $134.4 million in assets on hand at the close of the 2003 fiscal year, the retirement fund needed $204.7 million to meet its projected commitments, a $60.3 million shortfall. "I think we are all very perplexed as to how the archdiocese accumulated such a large unfunded pension liability, because parishioners have been giving for years," Cynthia Deysher told the *Globe*. "Now it has come out that they never put the money in for sixteen years. That is fraudulent."[5]

Peter Borré calculated that if the $4.5 million yearly inflow for the Clergy Retirement Trust, starting in 1986, had been invested conservatively in a balanced portfolio of stocks and bonds, at an assumed annual return of 5 percent, more than $140 million would have accumulated by the close of fiscal year 2002. In whatever fashion Cardinal Law had used the $4.5 million yearly donations, Borré considered the diversion a gross violation of trust.

The archdiocesan *Pilot* then reported that the Christmas and Easter donations went to the Clergy Benefit Trust, "which provides for the needs of priests including . . . the Clergy Retirement and Disability [Trust] and the Clergy Medical/Hospitalization [Trust]." The chancellor, or chief financial

officer, was a layman named David Smith. Smith explained that most of
the funds went for yearly medical costs. He put the onus on parishes for
not sending enough money downtown, a subtle gambit of shifting blame
to pastors for not collecting more from the pews: "The billing [to the par-
ishes] has never caught up with the cost, because the cost keeps going up.
There is a reluctance to put a burden on the parishes, so premiums have
been raised slower than the cost." *The Pilot* offered more explanation:

> Smith explained that the collections were never intended to be
> used exclusively for retirement benefits. "I have gone back to
> check what we said and could not find a single [communication]
> that said 'only for retired priests,' " he said. Smith maintained that
> the collections were used appropriately. "Every dollar that was
> collected was used exclusively for the needs of priests, and a great
> deal of it went to the needs of retired priests," he said . . .
>
> The collections were not needed for the retirement fund be-
> cause returns from investments in the booming stock market pro-
> vided the plan with sufficient funds.[6]

Smith was more forthcoming while under oath in a June 2002 civil
deposition, after the archdiocese pulled back from agreeing to a settlement
with the first wave of eighty-six victims of John Geoghan. (The cases
settled that fall before the much larger victims' group.) Plaintiff lawyers
Mitchell Garabedian and William H. Gordon were focused on Cardinal
Law and his Finance Council. Bill Gordon asked the questions; he zeroed
in on funding streams. "I'm not a trustee," Smith stated, "but essentially
the Clergy Benefit Trust is for medical and ultimately retirement benefits
for clergy."

> *Is there a separate trust called the Clergy Medical Trust, then?*
> Clergy Medical and Hospitalization Trust is essentially, it is
> another trust, it is a separate legal vehicle. It is essentially the
> checkbook that pays those medical bills.
>
> *And the Clergy Benefit Trust in contrast to that is for—*
> Well, the Christmas and Easter collection monies flow into the
> Clergy Benefit Trust. They flow out of that trust either to the Clergy

Medical Hospitalization or to the Clergy Retirement Disability
Trust, and occasionally for special needs of priests for medical that
wouldn't normally be covered under the plan, the Clergy Benefit
Trust would cover that.

The Medical Hospitalization Trust is essentially a checkbook. It's
the device that literally pays the bills.

Another part of the organizational structure, the Clergy Fund Advisory
Committee, had its own priest-secretary. Gordon bore down on Smith.

*Is there a dollar limit when the committee must be consulted before
any expense is made?*
I'm not aware of any dollar limit . . .

*Has the Clergy Benefit Trust been used to pay loans to priests to
retain counsel when they've been involved in legal matters?*
Not to my knowledge.

*Which trust would produce loans to priests to retain counsel when
they're involved in legal matters?*
As far as I know, there's only one trust that has ever made any
loans to any priests, and there isn't a specific trust for legal matters.
The Clergy Assistance Trust makes loans to priests who need them,
and they are Boston priests only . . . It could be somebody's mother
died and needed to be buried. It could be, you know, any kind of
family-related, personal issue. There isn't any restriction that I know
of that describes what kind of assistance they can get.[7]

Smith was describing a shell game: the money starts out beneath one
shell, the Clergy Benefit Trust, after the two big dollops of contributions
from the pews at Christmas and at Easter. From the Benefit Trust, a line of
money slides over to the shell called Medical/Hospitalization Trust, which
"is essentially a checkbook" used to pay for, among other bills, the psychiatric facilities where the child molesters were sent, at least the portion
of charges not covered by ordinary health insurance. A separate Medical/
Hospitalization Trust suggests a need beyond standard coverage. When
legal expenses arose, the Clergy Benefit Trust shifted the funds to another

shell, the Clergy Assistance Trust, for "any kind of . . . personal issue," Smith testified. "There isn't any restriction."

Unaware of Smith's deposition, Peter Borré pounced on the chancellor's line from the *Pilot* article: "Every dollar . . . used exclusively for the needs of priests."

How exclusive, he wondered, *did those needs get? And at what cost?*

The case of Paul Shanley was vexing. Father Shanley moved to California in 1988, in good standing courtesy of his seminary friend Father John McCormack, who was destined to become a bishop for his chancery work. Shanley had a *seventeen-hundred-page* personnel file with sexual allegations to boggle the mind. After a stint at a mental hospital, he left the archdiocese early on a $1,000-a-month pension to become a weekend priest for the San Bernardino diocese. Shanley also bought a half interest in a Palm Springs hotel known for gay sex parties. He lived there part-time; his co-owner was another exiled Boston cleric, a recovering cocaine addict. Arrested in 2002 and extradicted to Massachusetts, Shanley was tried and imprisoned for crimes from years gone by.

"It is horrifying to see up close the psychic damage allegedly inflicted by Paul Shanley," Maureen Orth wrote in a *Vanity Fair* article before the trial.

> I have spoken to nine accusers, whose ages at the time they claim they were abused ranged from 6 to 21. A number have become alcoholics, some have developed suicidal tendencies and post-traumatic stress, and one has undergone electroshock treatments . . . What is truly alarming is how closely their stories resemble one another, according to their ages when they were abused. Shanley allegedly lured the youngest children with games such as strip poker, the younger teens with the pretext of examinations of their penises during puberty, the older youths with an invitation to use his body to get over their fears of homosexuality. He apparently was a master of manipulation and cunning.[8]

Cardinal Law, Bishop McCormack, and the church bureaucracy concealed Shanley's sexual career, one cover-up begetting another, until they sent him as a "supply" priest, a part-timer, to San Bernardino. In 1989 Shanley's friend McCormack flew out to discuss things. No way did they want him back in Boston. "Thank you for your kindness during your brief visit to the wild west," Shanley said in a letter that nearly grinned. McCormack acceded to his request for a boost to $1,890 a month. The archdiocese eventually put $2,500 down on Shanley's legal fees before the endgame trial.

In 1990 Father Richard Lennon was advancing up the chain of command as Vicar for Administration when he certified Shanley as a "priest in good standing" for San Bernardino. Cardinal Law placed Lennon and McCormack as facilitators for the in-house response by which administrative clergy, called "delegates," monitored priests who got in trouble.

MEMORANDUM

TO: Father Lennon
FROM: Father McCormack
DATE: February 14, 1994
RE: Reverend Paul Shanley

Recently, Paul Shanley changed his address from San Diego to Palm Springs. Would you please inform the appropriate offices of this change of address:

Reverend Paul Shanley
970 Parocela Place
Palm Springs, California 92264

The knowledge of this address is for internal use only. It is not to be made public.[9]

The thousands of pages from Boston church files that became available through the grind of legal discovery were scanned and organized for ready retrieval on the Internet by Anne Barrett Doyle and Terence McKiernan as they gathered documents from many dioceses at BishopAccountability .org in the town of Waltham. Barrett Doyle and McKiernan were stocking the raw materials for journalists, historians, and anyone else on the inner workings of the hierarchy. When Lennon began as Apostolic Administrator, the acting bishop of Boston after Law, he told reporters in a press

conference the week before Christmas 2002 that he had "no involvement" in the case of a recently accused priest, although, as the *Boston Herald* soon reported, he had attended a long meeting about the cleric.[10] The
Globe unearthed Lennon's role in handling a pathological priest named
John Picardi, in which he showed exquisite concern for ecclesiastical life
as a law unto itself:

> [Father John] McCormack recommended that Picardi be allowed
> to serve temporarily in the Paterson, N.J. diocese after treatment
> at a counseling center. McCormack told the Paterson diocese
> only that Picardi "admits to a sexual incident with an adult male
> in Florida."
>
> In New Jersey, Picardi faced another accusation in 1995, in
> which he was alleged to have inappropriately touched a fifth-grade
> girl. It was then Lennon became involved, urging that Boston,
> and not Paterson, take up the charge against him.
>
> In the September 1995 memo, Lennon appeared to express
> concern that allowing the Paterson diocese to investigate might
> cause a scandal. "Opening such an investigation runs the real risk
> of negative fall-out both for Father Picardi and for the Church,"
> Lennon wrote.
>
> On October 6, 1995, Law received a memo from another aide,
> the Rev. Brian Flatley, noting that Picardi had admitted to the
> 1992 rape. "However, we allowed him to return to ministry in Pa-
> terson after that incident . . . Because of this, according to Father
> Lennon, canon law does not allow us to use this incident to keep
> Father Picardi out of ministry now."[11]

The review board Law impaneled to scrutinize men like Picardi advised
against a job in ministry and suggested the priest ask the Vatican to be
laicized. Picardi balked. And why not? No policeman or prosecutor had
gone after him. Law and Lennon sought a compromise by which Picardi
went to the Phoenix diocese. But as news of his past overtook him, Picardi
was suspended from the priesthood in 2003.

Lennon under Law shouldered two functions that gave him an exceptional lens on money and the church's response to clergy sex offenders.

As Anne Barrett Doyle and Terry McKiernan later wrote on Bishop Accountability.org:

- In the mid-1990s, he was the facilitator for the [so-called] Clergy Fund. In this role, he worked closely with Cardinal Law's abuse delegates and paid out reimbursements for psychiatric treatment of accused priests, travel expenses for priests going to treatment centers for assessments and in-patient care, and travel costs for the abuse delegates, when they traveled to St. Luke Institute and Southdown to participate in assessments.

- During the 1990s Lennon received Status/Address changes for every diocesan priest, so that he could maintain the "clergy cards" that contain priests' assignment histories. He also maintained cards listing the assignments of order priests who worked in the archdiocese. As a result, Lennon knew every instance of promotion and demotion, what priests were unassigned and on administrative leave, and what priests had been "lend-leased" to other dioceses. This information, combined with the abuse payment information that he also handled, provided Lennon with unique and extensive administrative perspective on the abuse crisis in Boston.[12]

In spring of 2005, as Peter Borré became a person in the news, Lennon's background was far from fully surfaced. Borré got a call from Father David Burke. Well into his eighties, sixty-three years a priest, and the pastor of the high-end St. Pius X parish in Milton, Burke was piping hot upon learning that *his* parish was slated for suppression. Father David Burke lived in a fourteen-room rectory. Borré took his seat in the wood-paneled study at a conference table sufficient in size for twenty-four people. Seated across from him, Father David Burke said, "I'd like to go downtown and punch O'Malley in the nose."

"Ah, Father, you don't really mean that."

"You wouldn't understand. You're not Irish."

But it was Lennon, Borré pointed out, who had designed Reconfiguration. "*Seán* is the archbishop," snorted Burke. "He can't hide behind Dick."

Burke went to the chancery and threatened to lead his parishioners in a vigil. They lobbied with petitions, bumper stickers, and letters, the sum of which had some impact. St. Pius X was taken off the Suppression list before its vigil coiled into action. Two years later Burke suffered a stroke. He was in a coma when Borré visited the hospital, and he never regained consciousness.

When they first met, Burke had given Borré a copy of Lennon's letter to the priests on the status of clergy finances. The five-page letter, written in December 2003, is addressed "Dear Clergy Fund Member."[13] Three pages of figures and a copy of what Lennon called the Clergy Fund report were attached. (The individual priest was a beneficiary of the various trusts. Lennon used a generic term: Clergy Fund Member.) Intrigued by the date, Borré created a spreadsheet, realizing that Lennon, who reported to O'Malley, knew where dubious numbers were buried.

In the letter, Lennon explains how the various funds that benefit Boston's clergy function. He makes clear that the Clergy Benefit Trust "pays for those clergy who are in special circumstances . . . or *who are in between assignments and so do not have a stable source of income*" (my emphasis)— an oblique reference to the predators put out of commission, some few of whom, like Geoghan and Shanley, ended up behind bars. Borré read the letter hungrily, realizing that in those last days of 2003 Lennon was immersed in researching property values for the parishes to be suppressed come spring.

Lennon's letter deals at length with new procedures for co-payments and matters on health insurance. A passing reference to the $600,000 decline in donations amid the scandal chalks it up to "quite simply two bad years."

The letter avoids any discussion of how the parishioners' donations to the annual fund for the clergy retirement needs were actually spent. Instead, Lennon cites an earlier letter by Father Mark O'Connell, facilitator of "Clergy Fund"—a generic, umbrella term. O'Connell had soberly reported

> the same issues that have plagued every financial entity of the Archdiocese; namely, the effects of the poor economy, the huge increases in health care cost (most especially prescription costs), and the financial effects of the Clergy sex abuse scandal. I can assure you that these funds are a high priority with Bishop Lennon,

but all of us need to be prepared to face this difficult issue in the near future.

"Not all is bad news," resumed Bishop Lennon, with property and liquidity high in mind. "In fact, I believe I can give you good news concerning some of our past investments in Real Estate."

> Clergy Funds purchased [an unnamed] home in Pocasset, Massachusetts for $1,750,000.00 in June of 1999. Also in May of 2001, the Clergy Funds purchased Our Lady's Hall in Milton, Massachusetts for $1,900,000.00. Finally, the Clergy Funds made a loan of $4,150,000.00 as part of the re-development of the St. John of God Hospital in 2001. It was thought at the time that this project would house Senior Priests, however, upon further reflection the Advisory Committee have [sic] decided to go in a different direction.

In David Smith's deposition he stated that his power as chancellor, or chief financial officer, had a limit of $1 million on which he could sign a check involving property. Any disbursal above that—and final approval on big-ticket issues—resided with Cardinal Law. As Lennon composed his 2003 letter, Law had been gone a year, not yet promoted to Rome. Six months earlier Lennon had stepped down as Law's interim successor. The time frame is important, for the aforecited paragraph implies that Lennon had a major hand in real estate transactions. In his letter, Lennon then turns to the seven-month period in which he had interim control, after Law's resignation, in December 2002:

> As Apostolic Administrator, I authorized the sale of two properties that had been bought, and I concurred with the Advisory Board to end our involvement in the St. John of God project. As a result of these actions, the Clergy Funds have recovered all of its original investments and have made a profit as well. The home in Pocasset sold for over $2,550,000.00 and after expenses the Clergy Funds realized $2,433,073.00 for a profit of $683,073.00. Our Lady's Hall was sold for $3,300,000.00 and after expenses realized $3,135,000.00, for a profit of $1,235,000.00 Finally, we

received all of the $4,150,000.00 back from the St. John of God investment, plus interest totaling $521,054.30. *All of this money, totaling $10,239,127.30, has been returned to the original Trusts they came from.* (emphasis added)

With his powers before the advent of O'Malley, Lennon pulled in a profit just under $2.44 million in real estate transactions for the interlocked "Clergy Funds," which suggests another name for the controlling account, Clergy Benefit Trust. Not a bad profit. But the "good news concerning some of our past investments in Real Estate" obscured the *bad* news: the missing millions given by parishioners on those designated Sundays from 1986 until 2002. Substantial though they are, the real estate profits in Lennon's seven-month tenure come to roughly six months' donations by parishioners for the priests' retirement, which averaged $4.5 million per year. Where had all the parishioners' money gone?

"By 2001, the Boston archdiocese knew of allegations against at least 190 priests," states Anne Barrett Doyle of BishopAccountability.org. "Only about 25 of those cases had appeared in news reports before the *Globe* series in 2002." By March 2002 the personnel documents that the newspaper and plaintiff lawyers made public listed some 80 clergy sex offenders, most of whom had evaded prosecution by going to treatment facilities before reassignment or departure from active ministry, with pension. That still left 110 priests, each one of whom was an expensive mess.

Against the temptation to see Law as a high prince obsessed with secrecy, we must weigh the burden imposed on him and countless bishops by John Paul II on what to do with clergy sex offenders. Having spurned the U.S. hierarchy's 1989 request for canonical power to dismiss those men, John Paul stuck the bishops with them. The laicization cases—which priests could and often did oppose—moved at a glacial pace through one or another of Rome's congregations, until 2001, when Ratzinger consolidated the authority over them. Not only were the bishops handcuffed in defrocking the abusers, they also had to subsidize their living, medical, and legal expenses.

The missing millions from the Clergy Benefit Trust in 2005 was a bitter pill to the nearly eight hundred priests across the archdiocese who had served the church and pondered how they would retire in the coming years. Law had landed a basilica pastorship in Rome that paid $12,000 a month while the clergy troops endured the aftershocks of the abuse scandal, only to see good parishes close. Had Bernie Law sold out their retirements, too?

A BISHOP'S WARNING

For Bruce Teague, who was a chaplain at Beth Israel Deaconess Medical Center in Boston when the news broke, the memories rolled back of his surreal epiphany about church finances.

In the summer of 1994, Father Teague had a parish in Springfield, Massachusetts, when he paid a valedictory call on his bishop. John Marshall was sixty-six and dying of bone cancer. Teague wanted to express his gratitude for the older man's stance on a threshold issue. The monolithic Catholicism of Teague's youth had splintered over the Vatican's stance on birth control, homosexuality, and priests who abused youngsters. Teague found an ironic touchstone in Flannery O'Connor's stories of backwoods Southerners bewildered by faith, spiritual outcasts holding a mirror to his own troubled church.

When Teague was nine years old in Dorchester, a working-class parish of Boston, a priest molested him. It was 1956; his father was off in the navy, his grandfather had just died, his mother was pregnant, and the close attention from that priest at first made him feel special. For years he stuffed the sensations of guilt and anger; when the first wave of clergy abuse lawsuits hit in the early 1990s, Teague befriended abuse survivors. One day he went to the grave of the priest who had abused him, and said prayers of forgiveness.[14] In those painful words to God he felt a cleansing. Bruce Teague enjoyed being a priest.

As the bishop of Burlington, Vermont, in the 1970s, Marshall put a child molester back in ministry. When he abused again, Marshall yanked him; he persuaded the prosecutor not to take action; he approved the church lawyers' grueling tactics to wear down the survivors who sued the diocese.[15] The cases eventually settled with out-of-court payments. In the late 1980s Marshall went through a turn of mind. He lost trust in therapeutic facilities to treat clergy predators. He petitioned the Vatican to defrock one priest.[16] In 1992 Marshall became bishop of Springfield. He confronted another scandal, another priest. This time he eschewed a litigation-by-ordeal strategy, which many bishops deemed a necessary evil to protect church assets. Marshall pushed for timely settlements; he met with survivors. "We have to do this out of justice and charity," he had told Teague at the time.

At the bishop's mansion a nun ushered Teague into the parlor.

Pallid and gaunt, Marshall sat in a commodious chair, propped up with cushions, an IV tube planted in one arm. Teague took a seat. Light came to the bishop's eyes. After small talk, the priest thanked him for his sensitivity toward the survivors. Marshall nodded. There was a bigger problem, he rasped. Teague listened. Stirring in the pillows, the bishop leaned forward and growled, *"Wait until the Internal Revenue Service gets ahold of us!"*

Teague had never heard a bishop speak so baldly about church finances.

Money was a source of gossip and folklore among clergy, most of it not good. Priests in religious orders, like Jesuits and Dominicans, take vows of poverty. Diocesan clergy take no such vows, but with modest salaries, a car, housing, health insurance, and presumed pensions, they lived with comforts. Teague knew clerics who traveled well, with money presumably from family or generous friends. Priests were expected to be prudent in handling a parish's money. Pastors with large parishes had laypeople to handle bookkeeping, paying bills, and other jobs. But with all the cash washing through collection plates, money required vigilance. Teague knew a pastor who had been responsible for two parishes; he borrowed from the first to pay bills at the second, creating a mess at both ends. In Springfield, Bishop Marshall faced other thorny problems. An accountant pilfered from a parish's fund for staff Social Security taxes. Another pastor renovated his rectory with funds reserved for cemetery maintenance. Marshall intervened in both situations; he saw that the taxes were paid.

Financial deceptions to race the blood of a dying bishop have come out in the open. Reform groups like Voice of the Faithful clamor for financial transparency; many bishops treat VOTF as enemies, alienating the kind of diligent Catholics that a diocese needs.

Bishop Marshall's admonition about money took on heightened meaning after the next bishop sent Father Teague to St. Brigid in Amherst. "The parish was bleeding money," Teague told me. "A lot of renovation had been done to the interior of the church. Our income was about three thousand a week. I had been a college chaplain and knew nothing about running budgets. This was in 1996. We suddenly had a termite problem that needed attention—you'd be surprised, Amherst has a large termite population. Then the boilers started to go out, and right before Christmas a *new* boiler broke. My predecessor had raised a lot of money and left $100,000 in a surplus fund. But we had an old accounting system: there was no debt listed on the books. The window washer came to me at Christmas, he hadn't been paid. A guy doing repairs on the organ was owed $1,000. All of a sudden a lot of bills were coming due . . . I thought my treasurer was handling everything. When I went through St. John Seminary in Boston, we never had an accounting course."

Catholic cemeteries sell a service called perpetual care, which guarantees the tending of a plot beyond the life of a family. Teague said that in his parish, which had a cemetery, "We couldn't say for sure where everyone was buried. The caretaker dropped dead at fifty and left no records of who was where. So a former schoolteacher came in and did dogged research with funeral directors."

He paused. "You know, at one time being a pastor was like a sinecure. Older priests talk of the pastor taking the Christmas and Easter collections and dividing it five ways with the assistant priests. My home parish was built and paid off during the Depression. Cardinal Cushing wanted to take excess money from the parish to build new ones in the suburbs. My grandfather and a few others went to Cushing and said, *Over our dead bodies*. It's so different today, with not enough priests to staff the parishes. Fund-raising is hard."

As the bills mounted against the chaotic record keeping he had inherited, Teague installed a software accounting system. "Only then did we realize what trouble we were in." The parish owed the diocese $100,000 in assessments to the chancery office, which is not quite like dodging the IRS. For Teague, the unpaid assessments masked a larger problem. St. Brigid was not a poor parish. "But it reached the point where we couldn't meet payroll. I had to let go of some people. I made a lot of enemies."

"But you walked into a quagmire," I countered. Teague nodded. "My predecessor's sin was a politician's sin: taking care of his friends. He was a good guy to the poor, the sick, the elderly. He also spent $2,000 a month on food. He had lavish dinner parties in the rectory for priest friends." Slowly, Teague stabilized the finances and linked the weekly donations to the parish operating expenses, using excess funds to pay down debt and keep anything extra on reserve. Resolving the bill to the diocese over long-deferred assessments was a problem Teague did not solve in his tenure.

He was glad to take a chaplain's job back in Boston for other reasons. In Springfield, the new bishop, Thomas Dupré, returned to ministry several priest-abusers Marshall had yanked. New scandals erupted.[17] Then, in 2004, Bishop Dupré abruptly resigned and fled to Suitland, Maryland, where he checked himself into St. Luke Institute, a clergy psychiatric hospital that specializes in treating pedophiles. Two men accused the bishop of abusing them years before; their cases against the diocese eventually settled. After a long investigation the Springfield prosecutor decided against indicting Dupré: the statute of limitations had lapsed. Dupré lived at the clergy hospital in Maryland for five and a half years, until 2010, still a priest, still a bishop without a portfolio.

Bishop Marshall's deathbed warnings seemed prophetic as Teague reflected on the church's struggles over breakfast in a café near Beth Israel Deaconess Medical Center where he had worked for several years post-Springfield. The IRS had not gone after the church, but the financial problems had reached a crisis stage for the Boston archdiocese, which had deepening deficits and rising pension costs that were not covered.

"It's not just the abuse settlements," Teague said, sighing. "The mismanagement shouts out. They can't guarantee us a decent life after we retire." Teague, who was sixty-two in 2008, gazed out at the chilly wind-swept morning with a stoic's resolve. "Dupré gutted the system that had a social worker in charge of the lay review board. He put two pedophiles in positions of authority. One working with annulment cases, the other in charge of the diocesan archives. An eighty-year-old priest came to live with me. He moved into the rectory, which guaranteed five meals a week and laundry cleaning. This guy left the previous rectory because he couldn't get heat in the room, and the five meals were TV dinners. The reality is, if you're betraying people on one level, you're betraying them on another. In Boston the retirement program has gone belly-up."

Where did the money go?

Teague shrugged. "Law divided the clergy pension fund for payouts on the abuse costs before the scandal broke in 2002."

Teague's conjecture matched what many other people believed, though the release of new financial documents put more riddles over an easy answer.

THE NEWS FROM ROME

"The *Globe* made repeated efforts in Rome to get an explanation of the appeals process from the Vatican's Congregation for the Clergy," Michael Paulson reported in early May 2005.

> An undersecretary at the office at first denied that the agency was involved with the parish closings; after the *Globe* pointed out that the agency's secretary had signed letters to many of the closed parishes, the undersecretary referred calls to the secretary, who then referred calls to the prefect, Cardinal Darío Castrillón Hoyos. The cardinal did not respond to repeated requests for an interview made both by phone and in writing.[18]

But in August, the Congregation for the Clergy ruled that the Boston archdiocese had erred in its canonical claim to the assets of eight parishes it had suppressed. Borré was delighted. "Within this archdiocese," he told the *Globe*, in a jab at Lennon, the self-taught canonist, "they are improvising in the area of canon law, and they are doing as poor a job under canon law as they have done under Reconfiguration." But under the Vatican's royalist system of justice, even as Clergy ruled against Boston's suppression, Cardinal Castrillón's staff was helping O'Malley confect a way for pastors to voluntarily turn over parish funds to the archdiocese, putting everyone in compliance with canon law to ensure that the chancery got what it needed. O'Malley told Paulson of the *Globe*, "We're glad that the Holy See seems to be supporting our situation and needs and is trying to suggest to us ways that we can achieve those needs."[19]

"Supporting our situation" was a genteel way to describe a tribunal system that swung behind a bishop to help him overcome its own decision against his property seizure. As those negotiations cleared a path of sorts for the plan to proceed, its author Bishop Lennon was feeling pressure from David Castaldi, chair of the Parish Reconfiguration Fund Oversight Committee. In choosing Castaldi for that task, Seán O'Malley had turned to a reformer with loyalist trappings. Castaldi was a member of Voice of the Faithful, the lay group many bishops loathed, but he had a long background with the church.

Raised in small-town Indiana and a graduate of Notre Dame and Harvard Business School, Castaldi had founded, directed, and sold two biotechnology companies. He was "comfortably secure" when a priest in late 2000 suggested he interview for the job of chancellor of the archdiocese. Slender and bespectacled, Castaldi, then in his early sixties, had never met a bishop. Law impressed him; he took the job at a salary well below what he could have commanded: a way of giving back. He lasted eleven months. "Dave, this just wasn't a good fit," Law said in parting.

A decade later, sitting in the airy lounge of a Beacon Street hotel, Castaldi spoke in measured tones. "It wasn't a good fit, I suppose. I tried to be diplomatic but I offended people. For the cardinal's residence, I insisted that petty cash follow good procedures; the nuns were used to *no* procedures. I wanted documentation and receipts as a basis for replenishing petty cash. They didn't like that at all." Castaldi evinced a wry smile and took a sip of Diet Coke. "We needed more space in the chancery. Good operating practices suggested that we use that scarce resource more wisely. You had to make decisions, but you're in a clerical culture. I wanted a priest to have a smaller office. He insisted he needed a larger office. His space changed: he was offended."

Although Castaldi offered no defense of Law's behavior in the abuse crisis, he spoke admiringly of Law's response, after a zealot murdered someone at an abortion clinic, getting pro-life and pro-choice advocates to sit down and defuse tensions. "Law showed leadership," resumed Castaldi, in his careful cadences. "And I wanted to instill better financial procedures. Compared to industry, procedures were not at an appropriate level. Maybe I didn't have the right touch." I asked, "What kind of procedures bothered you?" Castaldi raised his eyebrows, then said, "No one can approve their own expense reports. That doesn't happen in private industry. I felt it had to change. The church had been run by priests, not laypeople with accounting degrees and business education. I didn't fit into the clerical culture. More than the procedures I wanted to implement, I was abrasive to the culture in some respects."

He paused. "It has changed considerably under Cardinal O'Malley. O'Malley has an endearing personality, but he's not charming, like Law was. The last thing Law would have done was sell the cardinal's estate.

Cardinal O'Malley gets criticized by VOTF, SNAP [Survivors Network of Those Abused by Priests], and BishopAccountability, but he does things other bishops have been unable to do. They're posting financial statements on the archdiocesan website. I think it relates to his ability to part with *things*."

David Castaldi's parish had deferred maintenance issues, including asbestos, which prompted his support for the decision to close the parish. But the process of meetings to reach that end had been poorly handled. Although he liked Lennon from their past dealings, when he approached him for information on the Reconfiguration oversight work, Lennon resisted. "He interpreted the charter I negotiated with him very narrowly," explained Castaldi. "Lennon stopped trusting us . . . All hell was breaking loose with the vigils. He told me, 'There is no good way to close someone's church. Do it quickly, get it over with, and things will go back to normal.' "

Castaldi's committee found a $12 million shift from Reconfiguration money to the Central Fund; they objected to the use of the proceeds from church sales to fund operating costs.[20] Outgoing chancellor David Smith's comment on the 2005 financial statement had been somber:

> The Central Administration of the Archdiocese is not sustainable in its current form. While we do have liquidity, we have little left to sell, and we are faced with substantial obligations. In spite of reductions in force of nineteen percent since the beginning of the abuse crisis, our Central Administration, in an effort to maintain services at pre crisis levels, has operated with deficits each year. As you will see, those deficits were funded with borrowings, property sales and, in the last two years, with parish reconfiguration assets.

O'Malley was boxed into a corner. An unwritten law of the apostolic succession holds that one bishop does not overtly criticize another, and an archbishop should preserve the reputation of his predecessor, particularly a cardinal. O'Malley could not bring himself to state publicly that Law had mismanaged the money, stuffing money into written-off loans for clerics' legal fees and writing checks for the expensive psychiatric facilities. *One hundred and ninety priests* put out to pasture had cost the archdiocese for their legal, medical, and stipend costs, while proportionally fewer priests performed the banal but crucial job of raising a parish's money. As much as Seán O'Malley found Reconfiguration a nightmare, he would not violate an unwritten law of the apostolic succession and open the relevant documents of those accounts to public accounting, lest it invite scrutiny of his predecessor Law. Even if he disliked Lennon, as many believed, O'Malley needed to know what Lennon knew. And part of O'Malley's unwritten job description was *protect Bernie Law.*

O'Malley had become a cardinal as he opened a realm of transparency in the late winter of 2006, releasing substantial data and annual reports that revealed $330 million in assets, against debt of $346 million. "We're not trying to keep secrets from people," he told a press conference. "We're trying to use the limited resources we have for the mission of the church." He won praise from Cynthia Deysher: "We've never seen this level of financial disclosure from the archdiocese before."[21] O'Malley had restored the trust with certain of Boston's heavy hitters, like Jack Connors, a public relations executive who was raising money for the parochial schools.

Castaldi had a more benign view of the pension crisis than Borré. By his lights, the Clergy Retirement/Disability Trust was fully funded in the late 1990s. "The money could go for other uses," he explained. "The stock market started going down in 1999 and continued through 2005. At the same time, clergy health and housing benefit costs were going up . . . When I was there, laypeople were not involved in decisions about priests. We were not consulted. That needed to change. I participated in lay trust funds and health issues, but not oversight of clergy trust funds."

The failure to invest the annual donations was a serious mistake. Still, Castaldi concluded, "I see no sign of misappropriation of assets."

But the documents on how clergy funds were spent from 1986 to 2000 were not available, according to the archdiocese. I asked: "So how do we know what happened?" Castaldi nodded at the question, and said, "Those are the detailed transactional documents. That's not a big surprise. You don't keep those documents forever." On the mystery of what those documents held—how much to the legal, therapy, housing, and early retirement costs of the several score child abusers Law had eased out—Castaldi had no answer. The problem, he averred, was more complex than absorbing costs of bad priests. "The culture in the club indicated lots of good things to help people. It's instinctive in priests. The money will come from somewhere. That mentality builds in structural deficits, and it's hard to get them under control. The abuse crisis put the club at the tipping point."

LOCATION, LOCATION, LOCATION

The Reconfiguration saga took a new turn on November 16, 2006, when the archdiocese sold an East Boston parish, St. Mary Star of the Sea, for $850,000 to Michael Indresano, a commercial photographer. Twenty days later he resold the property for $2.65 million to a Brazilian-led evangelical sect, Universal Church of the Kingdom of God. Indresano had presented a plan to the archdiocese's real estate office to develop a photography studio, six condos, and a parking lot, but the sale contract did not preclude him from changing his mind, which he did quite soon, pulling in a $1.8 million profit for the flip.[22]

The new church owner had sparked a huge controversy in Brazil in 1995, when a pastor "repeatedly kicked a statue of the country's patron saint on national television, prompting condemnation of the UCKG by the Roman Catholic Church," reported Laura Crimaldi of the *Boston Herald*. The church's founding bishop "owns one of Brazil's largest television stations, as well as radio stations, newspapers and a soccer team."[23]

Peter Borré sent a letter of protest to the papal nuncio in Washington, D.C. David Castaldi promised further inquiry by the Reconfiguration oversight committee. Cardinal O'Malley, in a deft move, appointed a retired judge to conduct an investigation and write a report on what went wrong.

The archdiocese had turned down an earlier offer of $2 million from a different church. "A discussion with former [archdiocesan] chancellor David W. Smith lends credence to the notion that [the Boston archdiocese] was reluctant to get the word out that it was unwilling to convey the property to another religious institution, no matter what the nature of the denomination," wrote Kevin J. Herlihy, the retired judge. "Mr. Smith also left no doubt that the Vicar General, Bishop Richard G. Lennon, D.D., saw, read and presented the memo dated January 19, 2006 to the [archdiocesan] Board of Consultors recommending no restriction in the deed to Indresano. Although the memo purports to be from Smith to the Vicar General,

Smith could not rule out with certainty the possibility that Bishop Lennon actually prepared the recommendation."[24]

By the time Judge Herlihy's report was released, in October 2007, Lennon's disastrous handling of Reconfiguration in Boston had catalyzed nine parishes into vigil and another round of canonical appeals in Rome. Cardinal O'Malley resisted sending in the police. He was relieved, however, to wash his hands of Lennon. In the culture of ecclesiastical princes, where mistakes are often rewarded, Richard Lennon would soon be moving on, and up, to assume a diocese of his own.

CHAPTER 7

FATHER MACIEL, LORD
OF PROSPERITY

Father Christopher Kunze was thirty-six when he began work at the Congregation for the Clergy in December 1997. His admiration for Cardinal Darío Castrillón Hoyos grew quickly. The Colombian prefect with a silver mane and patrician bearing "spoke all the modern languages and knew Arabic, Hungarian, and Russian," Kunze recalls. Journalists covering the Vatican considered Castrillón *papabile*, a cardinal on the short list to become pope.

Chris Kunze was an American. At six foot two, with receding blond hair and an easy smile, he was pursuing a master's in theology at the university his religious order, the Legion of Christ, was building in Rome. His Vatican salary was about $28,000, which he signed over to the Legion. Kunze spoke German and therein lay his value. Cardinal Castrillón needed an undersecretary for case work from Germany and Austria. Kunze had spent several years in the Cologne archdiocese as a university chaplain, working to secure a presence for the Legion's network of schools. The Jesuits and the Dominicans were centuries-old teaching orders, but the Legionaries had begun their mission only a half century earlier, during World War II. The founder with an extravagant name, Marcial Maciel Degollado, was a Mexican who fostered a militant spirituality and rock-ribbed loyalty to the pope.

Father Maciel had befriended Castrillón, then president of the Latin American bishops' council, in the late 1980s. Praised by Gabriel García Márquez as "this rustic man with the profile of an eagle," Castrillón was a scourge of liberation theology, the Latin American movement of "a Church being born from the faith of the poor," in the words of the Brazilian theologian Leonardo Boff.[1] Castrillón believed in helping the poor, but he looked to the prevailing winds from Rome. In 1985 Cardinal Ratzinger jolted the Brazilian bishops by imposing a yearlong "silence" on Boff, which turned the prolific Franciscan into a national hero. A student of Ratzinger's in Germany years before, Boff had likened the Vatican tribunal that judged theologians to "a Kafkaesque process wherein the accuser, the defender, the lawyer and the judge are one and the same."[2] Boff wanted open theological inquiry. Ratzinger attacked him for an "uncritical use of Marxist mode of analysis."[3] In a dispassionate account of the conflict, Harvard Divinity professor Harvey Cox observed:

> In their famous meeting at Medellín, Colombia, in 1968, the Latin American bishops proclaimed that the church should exercise a preferential option for the poor. Liberation theology is an expression of this preference. It is the attempt to interpret the Bible and Christianity from the perspective of the poor. It is in no sense a liberal or modernist theological deviation. Rather, it is a *method*, an effort to look at the life and message of Jesus through the eyes of those who have normally been excluded or ignored . . . [Liberation theologians] work closely with the burgeoning "Christian base communities" of Latin America. These are local groups of Catholics, most of whom are from the lowest tiers of society, whose study of the Bible has led them to become active in grassroots political movements. Thus liberation theology provides both an alternative to the topdown method of conventional academic and ecclesial theology as well as a source of guidance to the long-neglected people at the bottom.[4]

"Boff will have to ask God to forgive him," huffed Castrillón, "and when God answers, then the pope and I will know whether to forgive him or not."[5]

When John Paul II summoned Castrillón to the Curia in 1996, the

Colombian had an ally in Father Maciel, who sent young Legionaries to move his boxes into the Vatican apartment. Castrillón was grateful, although they smashed a leg of his grand piano which had to be fixed. Sending seminarians to do heavy lifting folded into Father Maciel's way of cultivating Vatican officials.

Chris Kunze had barely seen the surface of Maciel's politesse.

Rome was in a postwar shambles when Maciel, an obscure young priest, arrived in 1946 in hopes of meeting Pope Pius XII. He had been ordained only two years, but at that ceremony in Mexico City a cameraman filmed the twenty-four-year-old at the altar, with steepled fingers and a deep sigh as in the opening scene of a cinematic life. The footage would be used for the Legion's lucrative marketing in later years.[6] Maciel founded his order while in private tutelage for the priesthood under Francisco González Arias, one of his four uncles who were bishops, and the one who ordained him. Maciel, twenty-six, had gone to Rome via Madrid, seeking scholarships the Franco government had announced for Latin American seminarians to study in Spain. The Spanish foreign minister, Alberto Martín-Artajo, told Maciel he needed Vatican approval if his Mexican "apostolic schoolboys" were to qualify for the Spanish benefits.[7]

With the backing of several of Mexico's wealthiest families, including that of its president, Miguel Alemán Valdés, Maciel wangled a meeting with Clemente Micara, a newly named cardinal. Maciel, tall, lean, with fair brown hair and searchlight eyes, spoke no Italian; Micara, a portly sixty-seven-year-old diplomat, spoke Spanish. Maciel gave Micara $10,000, "a huge sum in a city reeling from the war," says a priest with seasoned knowledge of Legion finances.[8] *The Legion of Christ: A History* (all but dictated by Maciel and published by a Legion imprint) makes no mention of Maciel giving funds to Micara; however, it says that Maciel traveled with "a confidential document and a sum of money" from Mexico's apostolic delegate (nuncio) for Cardinal Nicola Canali, the governor of the Vatican city-state.[9] Canali, a leading Fascist sympathizer during the war, got along well with Maciel, who was a devotee of General Franco.[10] The two cardinals helped Maciel gain an audience with Pope Pius XII. Maciel returned to Madrid with letters of approval that allowed the apostolic schoolboys from Mexico to study in Spain. But why would the Holy See, with established channels to transmit documents, entrust sensitive material to a priest without a diplomatic passport?

The other part of the story, "a sum of money," was the shape of things to come.

The Midas touch of Father Maciel opens into a saga of how one man financially seduced influential members of the Roman Curia, compromising their values as he cultivated powerful conservatives from Carlos Slim, the Mexican billionaire (and by some accounts the world's richest man), to Thomas Monaghan, the founder of Domino's Pizza and Ave Maria University in Florida. Harvard law professor Mary Ann Glendon, who praised Maciel's "radiant holiness," became President George W. Bush's ambassador to the Holy See. Maciel cultivated a who's who of Catholic conservatives to support the Legion or himself. The list includes former CIA director William Casey; Father Richard John Neuhaus, editor of *First Things* and a tireless propagandist for Maciel; George Weigel, the conservative activist and a biographer of John Paul II; William Bennett, the Reagan drug czar and subsequent CNN commentator; William Donohue of the Catholic League; Steve McEveety, the producer of Mel Gibson's *The Passion of the Christ*; former Florida governor Jeb Bush; and former Pennsylvania senator Rick Santorum, who spoke at Legion gatherings, as did former CNN correspondent Delia Gallagher. The list runs on.

But it was John Paul II and Vatican officials who put the imprimatur on Maciel by willfully ignoring the signs of rot in a man the Legionaries called Nuestro Padre, "Our Father." Maciel was the master salesman of resurgent orthodoxy, an ethos of wealth-as-virtue that triumphed over liberation theology's idealism in the Vatican mind-set. This religious mercantilism crystallized on John Paul's 1999 trip to Mexico with Vatican-franchised street sales of papal trinkets and potato chip bags sporting the papal coat of arms. The scholar Elio Masferrer Kan has criticized this theology of prosperity,[11] a gilded cousin to the prosperity gospel of commercially minded Pentecostal sects. Maciel *embodied* the theology of prosperity. The greatest fund-raiser of the modern church, Maciel used religion to make money, buying protection at the Vatican lest his secret life be exposed. For most of his life, it worked.

MILWAUKEE TO ROME

Chris Kunze witnessed the crossroads of faith and money on a 1990 trip to the Netherlands. He accompanied Father Maciel to Eindhoven and the home of Piet Derksen, a Catholic philanthropist. Maciel, who was thoroughly Mexican despite his French surname, spoke only Spanish. The mannered Latin persona held a piercing gaze behind his glasses. Maciel, seventy and nearly bald, took daily walks to keep trim despite a history of illness. He spoke in firm cadences, pausing for Kunze to translate into English for their Dutch host, stressing that the Legion was building the first university in Rome in generations. Kunze was supremely aware of his role in the presentation: a future priest in Maciel's movement of neo-orthodoxy. Seminarians accompanied Legion priests to call on donors. "Derksen gave $1.5 million," says Kunze, "which helped pay our debts in Germany and helped build Regina Apostolorum"—the university in Rome.

Born in 1961, Christopher Kunze grew up in Milwaukee with a younger brother and twin sisters. His mother was a hospital administrator, his father a real estate agent who had fled Communist East Germany at fourteen. Kunze spent a year in the high school seminary, but it closed for lack of numbers. A fullback on his football team, he went on to Marquette University, majoring in philosophy. As a sophomore, he moved into Milwaukee's major seminary, continuing classes at Marquette. Most of the seminarians were gay. After two faculty priests made sexual advances on him Kunze left in disgust. A Phi Beta Kappa, he graduated from Marquette in 1984, yearning to become a priest. A pastor suggested the Legion of Christ. Drawn to a "spiritual warrior mystique about the priesthood," Kunze entered the Legion novitiate on an elegant estate in Cheshire, Connecticut.

In addition to Latin, Greek, and Spanish, he learned the history of Father Maciel's odyssey from war-torn Mexico, how he gained support in Rome and built an educational network that spread to other countries. America had two dozen Legion prep schools and two seminaries.[12] Maciel's photograph hung in Legion schools, where students absorbed a mantra: *Nuestro Padre is a living saint.*

Kunze had never encountered such demanding discipline. Every Legionary took private vows, unique to the order, laying a hand on the Bible, swearing to never speak ill of Nuestro Padre nor any Legion superior, and to report any member who might be critical to the superiors. Speaking well of others was a virtue. The private vows rewarded spying as an act of faith. Sacrificing one's own ambition in love for Christ and not criticizing others were hallmarks of a good Legionary. They had three hours of daily prayer and long periods of monastic silence. Superiors screened the letters they wrote home once a month and read their incoming mail. The men saw their families once a year. Cutting away from the family signaled one's closeness to Christ.

That first year in Cheshire, Kunze made a forty-five-minute "general confession" to Father Owen Kearns, an Irishman. To prepare, Kunze reviewed "pages and pages I had written, recounting all the sins of my life, sins I had already confessed. It was embarrassing, and a little frightening, too."

Out of the fear came a fierce cleansing, a purity in paring himself down, melding his will with an elite corps of men chosen by God to reevangelize the Catholic Church. They embraced Maciel's vision of saving the church from post–Vatican II decay as in liberation theology. Kunze and other young Legionaries wrote letters to Nuestro Padre, detailing their sins and shortcomings, hopes and aspirations. Forging a new life, Kunze felt a powerful surge of righteousness.

They spent hours discussing the constitution of the Legion of Christ.[13] Of the many bylaws, the seminarians memorized important ones that dealt with life in the Congregation, as the religious order was called:

> 268.1 Abhor slander as the worst of all evils and the greatest enemy of the union and charity among ourselves.
>
> 2. If someone, through gossip or any other means, seeks internal division among ourselves, he shall be removed immediately from the center where he is to be found and stripped of all responsibilities . . .
>
> 3. Superiors shall learn to amputate with a firm and steady hand any member infected with the mortal cancer of slander and intrigue, if they do not want to make themselves responsible for the ruin of the Congregation.

They studied Nuestro Padre's letters written over many years, particularly his ruminations for the affiliate group, of predominantly laypeople, called Regnum Christi, Kingdom of Christ. Regnum Christi began in the 1970s. This passage bears a "Madrid, 1944" dateline, but was written a generation later:[14]

Worst of all is the terrible threat of Communism and the Protestant sects which try to tear away from [the church's] bosom all
the children she has made with her blood and whom she sustains
through abundant and prolonged sacrifices . . .

[W]hen I meet up with the strength of youth withered and torn
apart in the very springtime of life for lack of Christ, I cannot hold
back the cries of my heart. I want to multiply myself so as to write,
teach, and preach Christ. And from the very depths of my being,
from the very spirit of my spirit, bursts forth this single resounding
cry: My life for Christ! Re-Christianize mankind. This is our mission, this is our goal, this is the reason for our Movement.

Kunze lived in a community of sixty priests in the Center for Higher
Studies at the Legion's tree-lined campus on a plateau of western Rome.
Kunze was among a dozen younger priests, all forbidden to speak to older
clerics. The 320 seminarians, about evenly divided between students of
philosophy and theology, were also forbidden to speak across lines of academic formation. Superiors screened their e-mails and approved website
viewing. Across the lawn Kunze watched the construction of Pontifical
Athenaeum Regina Apostolorum, which Piet Derksen's $1.5 million was
helping to build.[15] Weekday mornings Kunze sat in a Peugeot with two
other Legion priests who worked in the Curia as they took turns driving
down Via Aurelia, turning onto Via della Conciliazione, the grand bou-
levard cleared by Mussolini that ran from the Tiber River to St. Peter's
Square. The Congregation for the Clergy was in a pale yellow four-story
building of neoclassical design. The elevator opened into a marble foyer a
floor above a religious souvenir shop looking out on Bernini's columns in
the square.

When Kunze began work on December 8, 1997, he found an office still
agog over the $119 million jury verdict in Dallas awarded to eight victims
of the ex-priest Rudy Kos. The verdict that July had made international
news. Castrillón fumed about money-grubbing lawyers. Clergy staffers
wondered why American courts were so hostile to the church. The Dallas
case, after six years of litigation, ended in 1998 with a negotiated settlement of $31 million for the plaintiffs.[16]

Monsignor James Anthony McDaid ran the English-language desk.
A short, stocky, Irish-born canonist who had also served as a priest in

the Denver archdiocese, Tony McDaid bristled about bishops giving ped-erasts a second chance. He had a law-and-order approach: defrock 'em. McDaid viewed St. Luke Institute in Suitland, Maryland—the foremost church-owned hospital that treated pedophiles—as a scandal in itself. The treatment included sex education films. McDaid brooded that they induced priests to masturbate.[17]

Although he did not work in the Third Office, Kunze picked up on his colleagues' concerns when certain bishops sold assets. "Weakland's at it again," Tony McDaid groused one day, referring to canonical protests of the Milwaukee archbishop's parish closures (see page 4). But Clergy backed Weakland, inevitably.

The workaday world at the Congregation for the Clergy exposed Chris Kunze to personalities who mirrored a greater diversity than he found in the Legion. The secretary and second in command, Archbishop Csaba Ternyak, was Hungarian. He believed priests should be allowed to marry. In his aloofness from Kunze, Ternyak telegraphed that he was no fan of the Legion.

Kunze read reports from the German-speaking bishops, often a hundred pages or longer, covering all dimensions of a diocese from finances to bap-tisms, and distilled the information for Cardinal Castrillón. He summa-rized the notes he took on the phone or in conversation for the files. No document could ever be taken home. Kunze followed the furor in Austria since Vienna's cardinal-archbishop, Hans Hermann Groër, retired in 1995 amid accusations that he had coerced sex with young men in a monastery years before. Behind the scenes, Sodano and Ratzinger clashed over how to deal with Groër, Sodano prevailing as he left without a word of con-demnation from John Paul in a show of Vatican unity.[18] On a 1998 trip to Austria, John Paul avoided mention of Groër. A lay group, We Are Church, with 500,000 signatures, had arisen over the Groër scandal as a larger protest of Vatican control.[19] When German bishops arrived for *ad limina* visits, the every-fifth-year meeting with the pope, Kunze prepared dossiers for Castrillón and assisted as translator in the cardinal's meetings.

In the internal politics over celibacy, Kunze sided with Castrillón, Tony McDaid, and others while a liberal camp supported the option for priests to marry. When Cardinal Castrillón was away, Archbishop Ternyak hosted a visiting nuncio from Hungary. Kunze says, "He told ev-eryone how great they were doing with a married clergy in Hungary"—an offshoot of the Communist resistance. "A group of us were looking at our feet, red in the face, while others smiled. It was a small show of power on Ternyak's part."

No one discussed the economic impact from the long tide of men leaving the priesthood, many of whom had raised funds and managed parish budgets. The exodus was like that of a college losing seasoned professors or a newsroom its veteran editors, forcing an operation to do more with less, sacrificing quality in the process.

Monsignor Mauro Piacenza, a native of Genoa, slender, bespectacled, a devotee of opera, handled much of the Italian writing for Castrillón. Words poured out of Piacenza, written or spoken. The topics that animated him—theology, saints, a desire to shift control of the Curia from the Secretariat of State (under Sodano) to the Congregation for the Doctrine of the Faith (under Ratzinger)—were a tad sublime. But Kunze, who admired Ratzinger, shared Piacenza's view of the CDF, the office where theologians' works were judged for doctrinal purity, as a preferable high point of power in the Curia.

Father Maciel was quite close to Cardinal Sodano, but the Legion's more important champion was Pope John Paul II himself.

In January 1979, on his first trip as pontiff, John Paul visited Mexico. Maciel sat on the plane with him, a reward for extensive advance work. Thanks to a Legionary priest who said private Masses for the First Lady, President José López Portillo decided to greet John Paul at the airport—a potent symbol in a heavily Catholic nation with a history of persecuted priests.[20] Six months later, John Paul showed his appreciation with a visit to the Legionaries in Rome.[21] A video camera captured priceless moments of Maciel with the pope.

Troubled by the liberal drift of religious orders since Vatican II, John Paul was determined to restore the moorings of orthodoxy. As the priest shortage worsened, Maciel was competing with Opus Dei to recruit young men committed to papal teachings. The Legion had a financial engine in Regnum Christi, which had sixty thousand members, mostly laypeople, many of them upper middle class, some quite wealthy. One wing of Regnum Christi consisted of "consecrated women" who lived in communities, rather like nuns, staffing Legion prep schools. "One of the most powerful demonstrations of strength by the Legion," the Spanish journalist Alfonso Torres Robles has written, "was its fiftieth anniversary celebration on January 3, 1991, at St. Peter's Basilica in Rome, when John Paul II ordained 60 Legionaries into the priesthood, in the presence of 7000 Regnum Christi members from different countries, 15 cardinals, 52 bishops, and many millionaire benefactors from Mexico [and] Spain."[22]

The pageantry filmed at ordination ceremonies was vital to the Legion's Web and mail marketing, selling videocassettes or bestowing them on donors. "People who wanted to give money were quick to do so if they found that the group was united to the pope," explains Glenn Favreau, who left the Legion in 1997 after thirteen years and had frequent dealings with Maciel. A 1991 film sequence shows a vibrant John Paul, clad in white, greeting a vast crowd of Legionaries and Regnum Christi members at a Vatican audience, amid waving banners and crescendo cheers as the Holy Father, with a deep voice and satisfied smile, calls out Father Maciel.

The Legion had a $650 million annual operating budget, according to a 2006 *Wall Street Journal* report.[23] An ex-Legionary who had held a high position says, "The budget was well over $1 billion, easily. How all the pieces operate is a mystery." Whatever the budget, it was substantial for a small religious order with only 450 priests and 2,500 seminarians—the Jesuits numbered about 18,000. Wearing traditional cassocks or double-breasted blazers, walking in pairs, the Legionaries cut a distinctive image in Rome with their close-cropped hair.

Christopher Kunze's family had flown down to Mexico City for his ordination in 1994. He walked in file with fifty-three other Legionaries wearing white robes, each in turn pausing before Father Maciel for the ritual embrace in procession to the altar for a bow and a blessing by the papal nuncio, Archbishop Girolamo Prigione. The men lay prostrate, forming a vast white semicircular fan in symbolic obedience as forty thousand people in the domed stadium looked on. The Legion took out a half-page advertisement in *El Universal* and six other Mexico City dailies on December 5, 1994, featuring a photograph of Maciel kissing John Paul's ring and an open letter from the pope calling him "an efficacious guide to youth," in celebration of Maciel's fifty years as a priest.

In 1995 one of Kunze's twin sisters, Elizabeth, joined the Movement, as Regnum Christi members called it. A former retail buyer with Neiman Marcus, she was twenty-nine, recently split from a boyfriend, hungering for a life with more meaning. "My parents divorced after my ordination," Chris reflects. "I think that had something to do with Lizzie's decision to join." She began her immersion in Regnum Christi in Wakefield, Rhode Island.

THE COURTING OF GABRIELLE MEE

The Legion's Rhode Island expansion was built on the legwork of Irish-born Father Anthony Bannon. Bannon oversaw Regnum Christi in North America from the Connecticut headquarters; he sent seminarians with priests on fund-raising calls to potential donors. Genvieve Kineke, who joined Regnum Christi in the midnineties, recalls a Bannon visit: "We'd break into groups, brainstorm, and then give a report on projected growth. We had about twenty women at the time, although some women from Massachusetts joined us for that event. Rhode Island is quirky and parochial. You can get around the state in an hour and a half, but people won't go to Providence without an overnight bag. Rhode Islanders looked upon Regnum Christi with suspicion. Our numbers were low. I gave a summary presentation, outlining these human obstacles, laced with humor. Bannon gave me the look of death. He was furious. I sat down with my tail between my legs."

Bannon and another Irish priest, Owen Kearns, "were like a road team, raising money and seeking recruits," says Kineke. "Things took off in the 1980s. They built a new wing for the novitiate in Cheshire, Connecticut, thanks to a seven-figure donation from [Reagan administration CIA director] William Casey and his wife. The Legion installed a plaque honoring their support."

Bannon arranged with Bishop Louis Gelineau of Providence and Mrs. Gabrielle Mee to host a reception for the Legion in March 1990 at the Narragansett home of former governor John Joseph Garrahy and his wife, Marguerite. Gabrielle Mee and Marguerite Garrahy attended daily Mass together. "This announcement and endorsement by the diocese was critical to the [Legion's] securing of funds to purchase a facility," observed the *Rhode Island Catholic*. In 1991 the Legion acquired a former convent in Wakefield, which became a Regnum Christi girls' school, and two other religious estates. Overbrook Academy in Warwick Neck, a middle school for girls from Latin America and Spain, had a $35,000 tuition in 2009.[24]

With high tuitions and low faculty salaries, Legion schools generated revenue for operating expenses in Rome, according to several ex-Legionaries. The widow Mee was a breakthrough in the Legion's growth. A daily communicant since childhood, Gabrielle Dauray was thirty-seven and childless when she married Timothy Mee, a wealthy widower. The year was 1948. Each had a trail of sorrows. Timothy's wife and children died when a hurricane destroyed their beach house ten years earlier. Gabrielle, the sixth of nine children, was raised in a fatherless home and had never known great comfort. Devoted to the church, Timothy Mee was a bedrock investor in Fleet National Bank. In 1982 he established trusts for himself and his wife. Since they had no direct heirs, the trusts would benefit charitable causes after their deaths. In 1985, when Timothy died, Gabrielle was seventy-four. Two years later, she established her own charitable trust, naming Fleet Bank as joint trustee.

Gabrielle Mee was a classic Legion target—a devout, wealthy widow with scattered younger relatives. At a 1991 ceremony in Rome she joined Regnum Christi. In Rhode Island, as a consecrated woman, she made a promise of obedience to her superiors. She drew up a will to benefit the Legion. In 1994 she amended her trust, and Fleet amended the Timothy J. Mee Foundation (which had $15 million in assets) as a charitable trust: interest revenues from both were designated for Legion of Christ of North America, Inc.[25] Besides $7.5 million gained from the Mee trusts, the Legion borrowed $25 million from Fleet to purchase a corporate complex in Westchester County, New York, for an envisioned university. Mrs. Mee was eighty-nine in December 2000 when she changed her will, leaving the estate to the Legionaries of Christ, and appointed Father Bannon the executor of her will. She named Fleet Bank as coexecutor.

Dave Altimari of the *Hartford Courant* recounts the next step:

> But soon the order and Mee filed a lawsuit against Fleet Bank, disputing how the bank was distributing the funds from her trusts. In 2003 she changed her will again, removing Fleet completely and naming Christopher Brackett, another Legionaries priest, based in Cheshire, as the co-executor.
>
> One of Gabrielle Mee's two trusts was dissolved by a court order in 2003 with the remaining funds—more than $2.1 million—turned over to the Legionaries, records show. In June 2003, the Legionaries became the sole owners of a condominium she owned in Narragansett, R.I., assessed at more than $850,000.[26]

The lawsuit with Fleet was settled out of court. As Mee lost contact with her family, a niece named Jeanne Dauray began to worry. In 2001 Dauray visited the Regnum Christi center. In five days she had not an hour alone with her aunt: another RC woman was always present, diverting the conversations from anything they didn't like or at odds with the movement. When Mee wanted to visit a sister who was ill, Legion priests said no, disappointing the old lady. Dauray left disillusioned. Regnum Christi members called, beseeching *her* to join the Movement—the last thing she wanted. She had a few more phone calls with her aunt. "The feeling I had was that they had found a cash cow and they were never, ever going to let it go," Dauray told Altimari.[27] After Mee died, Dauray's cousin sued to overturn the will.[28]

Genvieve Kineke withdrew from Regnum Christi when she became pregnant with her fifth child. Soon thereafter, negative news coverage of Maciel, and conversations with other women leaving the Movement, bestirred Genvieve Kineke to launch a remarkable blog: life-after-r.c.com.

THE MODEL IMPORTED FROM MEXICO

Maciel's strategy of targeting wealthy women and oligarchs had been field-tested in Monterrey, the industrial capital of Mexico. Courting elite families, Maciel established private secondary schools, one for boys, one for girls. He exported to America a model for private schools to attract well-heeled families who would join Regnum Christi and give money and their children as future Legionaries or RC women. RC groups discussed Nuestro Padre's letters. The highest level, lay celibates, lived in communities. Maciel's order emulated Opus Dei, the order founded in Spain in the 1930s, whose lay celibates, called numeraries, donate portions of their salaries. But where Opus Dei's founder stressed the sanctification of work by laypeople,[29] Maciel's goal was *gaining wealth* for the Legion. RC consecrated women, a cheap workforce, revered Nuestro Padre, and were, with designated priests, relentless fund-raisers.

Maciel's competition in Monterrey was with Jesuits, who had close ties to the upper class. Liberation theology gained popularity in Mexico in the 1960s. "The Jesuits would soon give up educating the wealthy," writes the historian Enrique Krauze, "and turn their attention to 'the Church of the poor.' "[30] In major Mexican cities, Maciel's schools would compete, but with a goal of capturing affluent supporters. In 1968 Eugenio Garza, a benefactor of the university Instituto Tecnológico y de Estudios Superiores de Monterrey, put pressure on the bishop to expel Jesuit chaplains from the campus and the order itself from the Nuevo León diocese. Five years later, in an unrelated event, Garza was killed by guerrillas in a botched kidnapping downtown. His funeral drew 200,000 people. "The murder shocked the business community, and chaos seemed imminent," the *New York Times* reported later.

> The family soon broke up its holding company, the Monter-
> rey Group, into four businesses that could be managed—and
> protected—more easily. Alfa, one of the four, grew so fast in the
> mid-to-late 70's that it soon became Latin America's largest pri-
> vately owned company, with $2.49 billion in sales [in 1994]. Three
> of its divisions are steel, petrochemicals and prepared foods.[31]

Eugenio Garza's brother, Dionisio, grew close to Maciel, as did other members of the Garza family, which the *Times* likened to the Rockefellers. "One of my aunts gave Maciel a house," says Roberta Garza, the youngest of Dionisio's eight children. Born in 1966, Roberta Garza became an editor with *Milenio* newspaper in Mexico City. Her late father, "a conservative Victorian gentleman," gave millions to the Legion. "Our family rarely watched TV. We came together after dinner and we talked."[32]

As a girl Roberta spent hours reading in her grandfather's library. "Neither my grandfather nor his brother were close to the Legionaries—they thought them pompous," she continues. "After my uncle expelled the Jesuits, that left a void. The Legion went house to house, assigning a particular priest to a family. Father Maciel stressed, *You must do much for the church since God has given much to you.* He was flanked by a young priest or two. They would let slip, out of earshot, *Nuestro Padre is so close to God, he can see through your soul* . . . I was convinced he was a holy priest. But some things made me skeptical. I didn't like the way people adored him without any question. Women *loved* him."

When Roberta was eleven she went to France to board at an Academy of the Sacred Heart school. She read voraciously and began to write. During that time she received benevolent letters from Father Maciel. One of her older brothers, Luis Garza Medina (born in 1957), graduated from the Legion's Irish Institute, a prep school in Monterrey. Under Maciel's vision of a chosen elect, teachers encouraged students to see themselves as future priests or Regnum Christi servants. Roberta says that when Luis revealed his intention to become a priest, their father insisted he go to college first. At age sixteen Luis entered Stanford University and studied industrial engineering. "To make sure his vocation wasn't lost amid California campus life," explains Roberta, "the order sent a Legionary to room with him."

"That was Maciel's standard policy," explains a longtime friend of Luis's. "When you are a third-degree Regnum Christi member, you cannot live on your own—you need to go in pairs. At the end of sophomore year, Father Maciel sent someone to live with him." After graduating from Stanford in 1978, Luis Garza joined the Legion. He was ordained in seven years; most Legionaries took ten. Another Garza sibling, Paulina, joined Regnum Christi and moved to Rome.

Roberta returned from Europe in 1980 for high school in Monterrey. She found it "rigid, highly traditional, but not analytical. One of my in-laws had a daughter who was not learning English. She complained to the Legionary priest. He actually told her: 'The final judgment will not be in English.' They were grooming us for the Movement. If your family had money, power, influence, they wanted you . . . It was crushing to come from France, where I could think freely. Their whole discourse was that whatever good you have is given by the grace of God—*you must give back and fight the forces of evil*. They sell you this paradise of moral rectitude. I was crying every night, thinking, *This is my family, my home, but I don't want to be here*. I almost cracked up."

After the patriarch's death, Maciel courted the widow Garza. "My mother gave him jewels and a lot of money," says Roberta. "He targeted women in Mexico of a certain class who were not allowed to work. I had to fight to go to college. For cultured women who were bored, Maciel offered a sense of purpose." With Luis a Legion priest and Paulina a consecrated RC woman in Rome, Maciel secured a flow of money from key members of the family. An electrifying speaker, Maciel could work a room of donors like a senator with silk between the fingers. Luis Garza—reserved, dignified, aloof—donated $3 million of his inheritance to the Legion, according to a colleague at the time. Roberta cannot confirm the figure but says it is within her brother's means.

Luis Garza declined my requests for an interview in e-mail replies.

"One of my brothers hates the Legion more than I do," explained Roberta, who left the Catholic Church after college. When the Garzas gather at holidays, they use good manners to avoid discussing the Legion.

The eldest sibling, Dionisio Garza Medina—paternal namesake and longtime CEO of Alfa, the business founded by the grandfather—became a Legion benefactor. He told Jose de Cordoba of the *Wall Street Journal:* "The Legion is the only Mexican multinational in the world of religion."[33] It made business sense for Maciel to appoint thirty-five-year-old Luis Garza as vicar general in 1992. He functioned as the chief financial officer, "responsible for overseeing key areas of logistical governance," according to a Regnum Christi profile, "often behind a desk, involving constant analysis of numbers and personnel structures and organizations, risks and opportunities."[34]

Christopher Kunze found Luis Garza determined, driven, and cold.

"In one of his talks," says Kunze, "he explained how successful heart surgeons worked. They'd have highly trained people do the prep work on the patients; the surgeon would then come in to do so many procedures a day, close the arteries, and earn all the money. He held that out as an example for the Legion, like a business model. We were supposed to work with leaders in the world, wealthy and powerful people we should convert for Christ."

In early 1997 Father Garza traveled to various Legion centers, "giving a talk, telling us that some information had been made public about Nuestro Padre in a newspaper," explains Kunze, "that it was all lies, *curiosidad malsana*—an unhealthy curiosity. And if anyone should send us a newspaper clipping we should not read it, but put it an envelope and send it immediately to him in Rome." Kunze was in Mexico City, living in the religious community at the Legion's Anáhuac University, working with a Regnum Christi center in the vast smoggy metropolis. For months he had been suffering from insomnia and a sadness he felt uncomfortable discussing. The warrior mystique had given way to a loneliness he had never known. In keeping with the internal vows, to avoid slander as moral cancer, Kunze gave little mind to the prohibited article.

"We had no idea what the false accusations were about," he continues, "except that there had been a conspiracy against Maciel from the early days of the Legion, and we must show our allegiance. We renewed our vows twice a year. They made us sign an agreement that we'd never sue the Legion . . . I was starting to wonder about all this when Father Maciel called me in Mexico and said there was a job for me with Cardinal Castrillón in the Vatican."

THE ASCENDANCY OF NUESTRO PADRE

The youngest of five boys, Marcial Maciel Degollado was born on March 10, 1920, into a family of nine children. His hometown, Cotija de la Paz, lies in the southwestern state of Michoacán, which today is a front line in Mexico's grisly drug wars. His father, Francisco Maciel Farías, a Creole of French-Spanish descent, owned a sugar mill and several ranches. Ridiculed by his father for being a sissy and subjected to whippings by his brothers, he kept close to his mother, Maurita, who was reputedly pious. "There will be no faggots in my house," snapped Francisco, sending his son to work with mule drivers for six months to shape up as a man. The mule drivers sexually assaulted him and another boy, according to an informant of the Mexican scholar Fernando M. González.[35] The story tracks what Maciel confided to Juan Vaca, among the first Legion seminarians he abused.[36] Hungry to vanquish the shame, Maciel entered the seminary at sixteen in the aftershocks of a society that had been crippled by war.

The Mexican Revolution of 1910 began when Francisco Madero, a reform-minded patrician, raised a small army against the dictator Porfirio Díaz. Díaz, a former general who descended on one side from Zapotec Indians, had become a figure of Victorian pomp and ruthless power after ruling for thirty-four years. Speaking of men he had had executed for stealing telegraph wires, he told a reporter, "Sometimes we were relentless to the point of cruelty. The blood that was spilled was bad blood."[37] Porfirio Díaz gave huge land concessions to local gentry and foreign individuals and firms, driving rural masses deeper into poverty, while inciting war with the Yaqui and Mayo Indians. "He had the chieftains of the latter tribe put on a warship, chained together, and dumped into the Pacific Ocean," writes Carlos Fuentes. "Leaders of the Yaqui rebellion were murdered, and half of the tribe's total male population (30,000 people) were deported . . . Where was this barbarism coming from? From the city, from the countryside? One thing was certain, the ideology of progress overrode all objections."[38]

In 1907 the American economy crashed. Drought and poverty worsened in rural Mexico. Seven months after Madero's revolt, as bombs blew rail-cars off the tracks, Díaz fled to Paris. Madero was elected president in 1911 and murdered after a coup in 1913. The revolution erupted in regional uprisings rather than a mass rebellion, though many states saw attacks on mines and big haciendas.[39] The 1917 constitution codified labor rights, state control of natural resources, and, in reaction to a powerful Catho-lic hierarchy, the banning of monasteries, Catholic schools, and denial of voting rights for clergy. Two more presidents were assassinated. By 1919 a wrecked economy had left 1 million of Mexico's 15 million people dead.[40] Plutarco Elías Calles gained power, a pro-labor revolutionary who prized industry over land redistribution. Calles improved public education and used the church as a whipping post.

Maciel as a boy saw men hanged in public. The Michoacán of his child-hood was a hotbed of Catholic resistance. Cotija was called "town of the cassocks" for its many priests. Maciel came from "good blood." Of his four uncle-bishops, Rafael Guízar Valencia ran a 1930s clandestine seminary in Mexico City and is memorialized in a statue in Cotija's plaza. Father Ma-ciel would nominate Guízar, and his mother, Maurita, for sainthood, and later anticipate his own. ("Don't start my canonization process until I've been dead thirty years," he told aides at a 1992 ceremony in Rome.)[41] An-other uncle, Jesús Degollado Guízar, was a pharmacist-turned-general in the Cristero uprising. In 1922 the Mexican bishops launched the Catholic Labor Confederation (CLC) to counter Calles's manipulation of unions. That enraged Luis Napoleón Morones, the labor minister. As the CLC mushroomed to eighty thousand members, Calles and Morones sent armed thugs against priests and churches.[42] The bishops closed the churches on July 31, 1926. Four hundred men bunkered into a Guadalajara church, firing at federal troops. As the revolt spread across southwestern Mexico, many bishops and priests fled. Cristeros rallied behind the slogan *Viva Cristo Rey!*—Long Live Christ the King! Landowners, working families, peasants, and Indians fused interests "like a fire deep down in the earth," writes the historian Jean A. Meyer. "The army was a federation of repub-lics and communities in arms. Sometimes it really was a case of a village republic, or the confederation of an entire region . . . and sometimes the women and children followed the men into the desert and abandoned the village."[43]

Calles had greater firepower, but the vast sweep of lower Mexico posed a huge logistical challenge. The Cristeros reacted "against the social law-lessness that was becoming the rule . . . It was neither conservatism nor revolution, but reform."[44] As the battles intensified, bishops who fled (many to San Antonio, Texas) were aghast at soldiers wearing Christian crosses who cut off the ears of Communists. Fernando M. González writes pejoratively of Cristero priests who died in battle and were turned into martyred saints decades later.[45] Despite the small number of clerics who actually fought, and the scorn of some intellectuals for its "orthodox uto-pia,"[46] the Cristeros drew unlikely allies, campesinos and hacienda own-ers, forging religious liberty as a common cause.

In 1929, six months after the Vatican's Lateran Pact with Mussolini, the U.S. ambassador to Mexico, Dwight Morrow, brokered a truce after discussions with the Holy See. Mexico agreed to respect Catholic rights without purging its anticlerical laws. Excluded from the talks, Cristero leaders disbanded because of a treaty endorsed by the pope. Degollado protested by telegram to Pius XI; he spent several years in hiding as other Cristero leaders were systematically murdered. Graham Greene's novel *The Power and the Glory* is set in the Cristero struggle. "The peasants got into the churches in Veracruz," Greene wrote on a 1937 research trip, "locked the doors and rang the bells; the police could do nothing, and the governor gave way—the churches were opened."[47]

In 1941, with Mexico comparatively calm, twenty-one-year-old Mar-cial Maciel Degollado organized a community of thirteen boys in the base-ment of a house in the capital. Their families had no idea he had been expelled from two seminaries for reasons never disclosed. No Mexican seminary would accept him, despite his quartet of uncles in the hierarchy. The house belonged to Talita Retes, a benefactress who guided Maciel to well-to-do families with memories of clandestine Masses and priests shot by goons. In 1944 Bishop Arias ordained his nephew. "Maciel had this in-credible charisma," one of the original disciples recalled.[48] To the affluent Mexicans, Venezuelans, and Spaniards living in Mexico he approached, the idea of an elite order of priest-educators—soldiers for Christ—had powerful appeal. In 1947 the textile-manufacturing brothers Guillermo and Luis Barroso helped him purchase an estate in Mexico City's Tlalpan area that had previously been owned by Morones, the labor potentate and Cristero enemy. With fields for sports and lagoons for boat rides, Maciel named it Quinta Pacelli, honoring Pius XII (Eugenio Pacelli).

In the 1950s Maciel gained the support of Flora Barragán de Garza—a precursor of the widow Mee and Roberta Garza's mother (no relation). Flora's late husband, Roberto Barragán, a Monterrey industrialist, left her a fortune. She gave Maciel a Mercedes and funds for expansion. From Spain, Legion seminarians wrote her letters on their progress. After she died, her daughter Florita, embittered, told José de Jesús Barba Martin that Flora had given the Legion $50 million over the years. A college professor in Mexico City, José Barba cannot verify the figure, but says, "Flora's support was substantial."[49]

Like many of the apostolic schoolboys, José Barba came from a family of Spanish ancestry. Barba was eleven when he entered the Legion in Mexico City in 1948. He left the order in 1962 and later earned a doctorate at Harvard in Latin American literature. He has done extensive research on the Legion. "Maciel was in the habit of buying things in cash," states Barba. "He was twenty-seven when he purchased the Morones estate. In 1950 he began construction on the Instituto Cumbres (the first prep school in Mexico City, on land Flora provided). That summer he also inaugurated Collegio Massimo in Rome. He was thirty. In 1953 he tried to start construction of a college in Salamanca. I was there. The bishop was sick; he failed to lay the cornerstone. He began the work in 1954 and completed it four years later. It was also in 1954 that he purchased the old spa in Ontenada, Spain, which had its own lake, for another seminary. Again, he paid cash. Father Gregorio López told me he delivered the money, wrapped in thin paper, to Leopoldo Corinez, representing the brothers who sold one of the last family properties. I do not know the exact amount."

The first boy Barba met in 1948 at Tlalpan was eleven-year-old Juan Vaca, the son of a Cristero–turned–village undertaker. When the youths arrived in Spain, brimming with esprit de corps, Maciel had arranged for classes at the Jesuit-run Comillas Pontifical University. Juan Vaca was twelve the night Maciel summoned him to his quarters: Nuestro Padre was in bed, writhing in pain, beckoning Vaca to come and massage his stomach, then guiding the boy's hands down into a coercive psychosexual entanglement that gripped Vaca for the next twelve years and haunted him thereafter. Sometimes Maciel had two boys at once.

In 1950 the Jesuit authorities forced Maciel to take his charges and leave Comillas. Maciel was trying to steal recruits from the Comillas diocese seminarians, and the Jesuits knew of Maciel's sexual abuses.[50] Maciel arranged for the youths to study in nearby Cobreces, and later Ontenada. As they moved on to Rome, Vaca, Barba, and other apostolic schoolboys (not all of them sexual victims) watched Maciel wallow in addiction to a morphine painkiller called Dolantin. Injecting himself and dispatching young couriers with bribes for doctors in Rome, he fell into stupors. In 1956 a strung-out Maciel landed in Salvator Mundi International Hospital in Rome. Cardinal Valerio Valeri, a reed-thin former diplomat and prefect of the Congregation of the Affairs of Religious, was incensed over letters from Tlalpan's rector and an older seminarian in Mexico City who had seen Maciel self-inject and worried about his behavior with boys. Entering the hospital room, eyes narrowed, Valeri told Vaca, "*Get back to your place!*"[51]

Cardinal Valeri suspended Maciel as the Legion director general; he arranged for Carmelite priests to assume control. They began questioning the boys, eight of whom admitted years later to Gerald Renner and me how they lied to protect Maciel and their own vocations lest the Carmelites deem *them* sinners.[52] "We didn't know what to do," said Vaca. "Our lives *would have ended.*" In keeping with clerical custom, Valeri was discreet about Maciel's suspension. Out of the hospital and persona non grata in Rome, Maciel followed the money between Spain and Latin America, raising donations for the big project in Rome that loomed as his salvation: Our Lady of Guadalupe Basilica.

Still in ecclesiastical limbo, Father Maciel in 1958 completed a seminary in Salamanca, Spain, with financial help from Josefita Pérez Jiménez, the daughter of a former Venezuelan dictator.[53] Despite Valeri's suspension order, Maciel suffered no loss of standing in his travels. His drug use would ebb and roll for decades. In 1958 Maciel got his break when Pope Pius XII died. Cardinal Micara, now the vicar of Rome, signed an order reinstating Maciel—something for which, in the interregnum between popes, Micara had no authority. Canon law puts the decision making of most Vatican officials on hold until a new pope is elected. What was Cardinal Valeri to do? Expend his version of political capital with the new pope, John XXIII, by protesting the reinstatement of a druggie priest who had lines to enough cash to erect a basilica? Maciel regained power on an illicit order from a cardinal he had given $10,000 to twelve years before. As Fuentes wrote of the dictator, "The ideology of progress overrode all objections."

Micara had blessed the basilica's cornerstone. Maciel had the money to finish it.

Like the captive American soldiers brainwashed by Communists in *The Manchurian Candidate,* a cold war film, the Legionaries bore the psychological scars of Maciel's tyranny for decades to come. Unlike the movie characters, dozens of ex-Legionaries never forgot what Maciel did to them—nor his confiding that he had permission from Pius XII for his sexual relief. The idea of clergy abuse survivors speaking out lay many years in the future.

In 1972 Maciel sent Father Juan Vaca to Connecticut to guide the Legion's American operations. In 1976 thirty-nine-year-old Vaca left the Legion and joined the clergy of the Rockville Centre, Long Island, diocese. Vaca wrote Maciel a searing twelve-page letter listing twenty other victims. He also gave the letter to his bishop, John R. McGann.[54] Bishop McGann questioned a second ex-Legionary priest in his diocese, Felix Alarcón, who admitted that Maciel abused him, too. McGann sent their statements to the Vatican. Nothing happened. Vaca petitioned the Vatican to take action in 1978, again to no avail. In 1989, having left the priesthood, Vaca sent his original document with an impassioned letter to John Paul II, via Vatican channels. He asked for official dispensation of his vows, arguing that his ordination was invalid; he wanted a church blessing for his civil marriage. In 1993 he got the dispensation but nothing on the allegations.

Vaca's classmates took years to reconnect and admit among themselves what Maciel had done. A languages professor named Arturo Jurado, after reading *Lead Us Not into Temptation,* contacted me in 1993 and put me in touch with José Barba. When the *Hartford Courant* reporter Gerald Renner called to see if I knew much about the secretive religious order in Connecticut, I had sworn statements from eight men. Renner's call led to a joint assignment.

Our lengthy report on Maciel's abuse of Legion youths ran in the *Courant* of February 23, 1997. Refusing to be interviewed, Maciel denied the accusations through a Washington, D.C., law firm, which sent documents by Regnum Christi members accusing Vaca and the others of a conspiracy against Maciel. The conspiracy charge lacked the salient fact of a motive. The *Courant* published Maciel's letter reasserting his innocence, praying for his accusers. A website LegionaryFacts.org, and the Legion's newspaper, the *National Catholic Register*, defended Maciel, counterattacking the accusers (and journalists). The Vatican refused to answer our calls, not even a "no comment." But the silence meant no assertion of Maciel's innocence. Most of the mainstream media ignored the story until the 2002 abuse crisis; however, in Mexico City, the daily *La Jornada* did a follow-up series and a cable station, Channel 40, ran a documentary interviewing Barba, Vaca, and others. An advertisers' boycott nearly killed the station.

Ironically, Father Kunze's computer in the Congregation for the Clergy gave him the first taste of freedom: in 1999 he followed a Google link to the forbidden article and was astounded to read the allegations of men, by name, including "a priest, guidance counselor, professor, engineer and lawyer."

> Some of the men, now in their 50s and 60s, wept during the interviews. All said the events still haunt them.
>
> They said they were coming forward now because Pope John Paul II did not respond to letters from two priests sent through church channels in 1978 and 1989 seeking an investigation, and then praised Maciel in 1994 as "an efficacious guide to youth."
>
> "The pope has reprimanded Germans for lack of courage during the Nazi era. We are in a similar situation. For years we were silent. Then we tried to reach authorities in the church. This is a statement of conscience," said Jose de J. Barba Martin, one of the men . . .
>
> Each one said Maciel was addicted to painkilling drugs despite his being cleared of that accusation in the Vatican investigation.[55]

The flashback hit Kunze like a gust of freezing wind: in a hotel room near the Legion center in Les Avants, Switzerland, in 1992, Kunze stares at Nuestro Padre's open suitcase, lined with tiny, white-capped orange plastic bottles filled with powder, no prescription labels. Kunze thinks, *I know Father Maciel's sick, but why does he need all these drugs?* His superior, Father Fergus O'Carroll, says Maciel has doctors' permission to mix his own drugs.

Kunze read on. "Maciel would summon a boy to his room at night and be in his bed, writhing in apparent pain, and ask the boy to rub his stomach." And the memory Kunze had tried to stuff welled up again: still in 1992, himself at the wheel of Father Maciel's favored Mercedes, the priest in the backseat telling him to "pull over" just before they cross into Belgium. Nuestro Padre leans forward, his fingers reaching onto Chris's right forearm, his hand stroking him. "Oh, how strong you are," purrs Maciel. "The nurses help me, they give me massages when I have pain." The strapping young celibate, ever-sensitive to sexual stoicism, thinks, *He's not only touching me, he's talking about massages—is he really coming on to me?* Kunze's resistant body language sent Maciel sinking softly into his seat. When Kunze returned to Germany, his Legionary brothers were full of wonder about his lucky drive alone with Nuestro Padre. Obedient to the private vows, he told them how good the trip had been, the weight of his mendacity so thick that some nights he cried in his room. *We are all sinners,* he told himself, even Father Maciel. He had stayed in the Legion despite Maciel's advances: *Why did I do that?* His family, two years after the encounter in the car, had gone to Mexico City for his ordination ceremony. His sister, Lizzie, was a Regnum Christi celibate teaching at a girls' finishing school in Switzerland while he, stricken with doubt, reeling from memories of Maciel he had failed to expunge, read how Juan Vaca "hand-delivered" a letter to Maciel "with a list of 20 victims." Father Owen Kearns, to whom Kunze made his cathartic forty-five-minute confession in Cheshire, told the newspaper, "Vaca is seeking revenge because he was incompetent in his job and was being demoted." Vaca disputed that claim but acknowledged that despondency over years of abuse had affected his ministry. (Vaca, in fact, resigned with a hand-delivered letter to Maciel in Mexico City on April 4, 1976.)

These are the conspirators Luis Garza warned us against, Kunze realized, *but this sounds true!* Obedient to the private vows, he said nothing to his fellow Legionaries. A lonely sense of futility haunted his identity as a priest. As the days rolled down to Christmas, he watched seminarians in the basement prepare the gift baskets for Legion friends in the Curia. The spectacle of fine wines, liqueurs, and cured hams deepened Kunze's sadness. *What am I doing here?* He had no idea other Legionaries felt guilt about the Legion's materialism.

The Christmas gifts were divided into categories by declining levels of importance, a Legion priest told me in Rome in 2009. "Legionary brothers are sent in cars to deliver them to cardinals and other allies, always for a purpose—to gain power for the Legion and Maciel," he said. "A small gift, I understand; but a large gift is a bribe . . . Fine Spanish hams cost quite a lot—30 euros per kilo. You can spend a thousand dollars for a large one."[56]

AN ELEGANT WAY OF GIVING A BRIBE

First Things editor Father Richard John Neuhaus had come out swinging in a March 8, 1997, letter to the *Courant*, denouncing "the scurrilous charges that have been lodged against Father Maciel" and praising the Legionaries. The Vatican gave a more Olympian endorsement that fall: John Paul named Maciel one of twenty-one papal delegates to the Synod for America in Rome. The *National Catholic Reporter* called it "a distressing message . . . [that] the church does not really take sex abuse accusations seriously."[57] Maciel mingled with hierarchs and lay notables like Harvard law professor Mary Ann Glendon, who also lectured at Regina Apostolorum. Neuhaus, since his early years as a Lutheran pastor arrested at 1960s antiwar protests, had swung to the right, becoming a Catholic, a priest, and a Republican polemicist, forging ties with evangelical leaders like Chuck Colson and gaining support from conservative foundations.[58] At the synod he sat by Maciel. "Most of the secretarial and logistical assistance here seems to be handled by the Legionaries," wrote Neuhaus.[59] "Events with their seminarians and priests are marked by a festive sense of delight, complete with ample wine and exuberant mariachi bands, reflecting a sheer joy in being invited to throw away their lives for Christ."[60]

Throwing away their lives is how several Legion priests, unaware of Kunze's gloom, had begun to feel about Maciel's use of money. None of them knew that in October 1998 José Barba and Arturo Jurado filed a canonical case in Cardinal Ratzinger's office, seeking Maciel's expulsion for absolving "sins" of his victims in confession, an issue over which the CDF had a tribunal on which to rule. An official asked the men to keep silent. As they left, the Mexicans saw Ratzinger and knelt in respect, kissing his ecclesial ring.[61]

Accusations against the head of an international religious order were a rarity for the Vatican justice system. Each congregation has its *competenza*, or responsibility. Most congregations fielding requests from bishops or superiors to punish sex abusers did not have tribunals, legal arenas to pass judgment. The 1997 accusations should have put Maciel's fate in the CDF, which has its own tribunal, apart from the major canonical courts at the Signatura, the Rota, and the Apostolic Penitentiary. Canon law is administrative and does not provide open trials or jury deliberations. Tribunal cases dragged on for years. The real issue was whether *anyone in the Vatican* wanted to take action against a high priest. The few cases to cross Kunze's desk were passed to Castrillón.

The Maciel accusations also confronted the *competenza* of Cardinal Eduardo Martínez Somalo, the Spanish prefect of the congregation overseeing religious orders. His office, one floor above that of Clergy, should have launched an inquiry: Maciel was superior general of an order. Martínez Somalo had presided at a 1985 ordination of Legionaries at Rome's Our Lady of Guadalupe Basilica.

Because Maciel was highly favored by the Holy Father, the accusations concerned Sodano as papal chief of staff. John Paul's 1994 praise of Maciel as "an efficacious guide to youth" now called his judgment into question.

Maciel had used large sums of money to insulate himself from justice.

In 1995, according to former Legion insiders, Maciel sent $1 million to John Paul, via Monsignor Stanisław Dziwisz, when the pope traveled to Poland. As papal secretary, the Polish-born Dziwisz (pronounced Gee-Vish) was the man closest to John Paul for decades. Handling money was part of his job. In the Vatican's 1980s alliance with Solidarity, Dziwisz persuaded Polish authorities to overlook customs duties on trucks with imported goods, many of which carried up to $2,000 cash, in small bills, to help the resistance.[62] Dziwisz slept down the hall from John Paul in the papal living quarters.

Maciel had previously arranged for Flora Barragán to attend a private Mass said by John Paul II. The chapel in the Apostolic Palace seats forty people in a milieu graced by Michelangelo's frescoes *The Conversion of Saul* and *The Crucifixion of St. Peter*.[63] Mass there was a rare privilege for the visiting dignitary, like British prime minister Tony Blair and his family. "Mass would start at 7 a.m., and there was always someone in attendance: laypeople, or priests, or groups of bishops," Dziwisz wrote.

> They often found the pope kneeling in prayer with his eyes closed, in a state of total abandonment, almost of ecstasy, completely

unaware of who was entering the chapel . . . For the laypeople,
it was a great spiritual experience. The Holy Father attached extreme importance to the presence of the lay faithful.[64]

"I accompanied a wealthy family from Mexico for a private Mass and
at the end, the family gave Dziwisz $50,000," explains Father A, who left
the Legion and spoke on background. The $50,000 payment was in 1997,
the year Maciel was publicly accused. "We arranged things like that," the
priest said of his role as go-between. Given the pope's ascetic lifestyle and
accounts of his charitable giving, such funds could have been routed to
a deserving cause. Did Dziwisz salt away some for himself? His book says
nothing about donations and does not mention the Legion. Father A
brooded about the Legion's pipeline to the pope: "This happened all the
time. Dziwisz provided frequent appearances for Legion supporters, which
was huge" in helping the order.[65] "It was always cash. And in dollars. You'd
need too many notes for lire. Even in Mexico they preferred using dollars
over pesos."

Maciel threw out the stops for a lavish reception in 1998 honoring Dziwisz's elevation as a bishop, down to the festive Mexican music played,
Mariachi-style, by a small Legionaries' orchestra.

Father B, who also steered payments to Dziwisz for Legion patrons, says,
"It's not so much that you're paying him for a person to go to Mass. You're
saying, 'These people are fervent, it's good for them to meet the pope.'
The expression is *opere de carità*: 'We're making an offering for your *works
of charity*.' In fact, you don't know where the money is going. It's an elegant way of giving a bribe."

On assignment for *National Catholic Reporter*, I tried to reach Dziwisz,
now a cardinal in Kracòw, for comment. Iowana Hoffman, a Polish journalist in New York, translated a letter with questions and faxed it to Dziwisz's press secretary; he reported back that the cardinal "does not have
time for an interview"—nor, indeed, for a statement defending John Paul's
use of the funds.[66]

Father B, who called the gifts an elegant bribe, explains why he left
the Legion: "I woke up and asked: Am I giving my life to serve God, or
one man who had his problems? It was not worth consecrating myself to
Maciel." Cardinals and bishops who said Mass for Legionaries received

payment of $2,500 and up, according to the importance of the event, the men said.

Do large sums of cash to a Vatican official constitute bribery? The money from Maciel went to heads and midlevel people at congregations through the 1990s. Such exchanges are not bribes in the view of canonist Nicholas Cafardi, the dean emeritus of Duquesne University Law School in Pittsburgh. Cafardi, who has worked as a legal consultant for many bishops, responded to a general question about large donations to priests or officials in the Vatican. Under canon 1302, a large financial gift to an official "would qualify as a pious cause," says Cafardi. The Vatican has no oversight office; funds should be reported to the cardinal-vicar for Rome. An expensive gift, like a car, need not be reported. "That's how I read the law," Cafardi explains. "I know of no exceptions. Cardinals do have to report gifts for pious causes. If funds are given for the official's personal charity, that is not a pious cause and need not be reported."

"Maciel wanted to buy power," says Father A, in explaining why he left the Legion. Morality was at issue. "It got to a breaking point for me [over] a culture of lying. The superiors know they're lying and they know that you know. They lie about money, where it comes from, where it goes, how it's given."

With prescient calculation, Maciel had sunk money into the Congregation for Religious and Secular Institutes by paying for the renovation of the residence of its prefect from 1976 to 1983, the late Cardinal Eduardo Francisco Pironio, according to Father A. Raised in Argentina, the youngest of twenty-two children born of Italian émigré parents, Cardinal Pironio enjoyed meals and socializing with the Legionaries. Renovating his home was "a pretty big resource, expensive, widely known at upper levels of the Legion," says the priest. Maciel wanted Pironio's approval of the Legion constitution, which included the private vows—never to speak ill of Maciel, or the superiors, and to weed out internal critics. The private vows were Maciel's chief tool to conceal his sexual abuses, to secure lockstep obedience. Pironio had ordained fifty Legionaries to the priesthood. But cardinals on the consultors' board at the Congregation for Religious balked at approving the constitution.

"Maciel went to the pope through Monsignor Dziwisz," says Father A. "Two weeks later Pironio signed it."

Whether John Paul read the document is doubtful. Dziwisz's swift delivery suggests he was financially beholden to the Legion well before the $50,000 gift. For Maciel, the encoded trampling of individual rights *approved by the pope* was a huge victory. Several years after Pironio's death, John Paul appointed Martínez Somalo, a diplomat, to head a renamed Congregation for the Institutes of Consecrated Life and Societies of Apostolic Life. Maciel dispatched Father A to Cardinal Martínez Somalo's home with an envelope. "I didn't bat an eye," he recalls. "I went up to his apartment, handed him the envelope, said good-bye." He says the envelope held $90,000. "It was a way of making friends, ensuring certain help if it were needed, oiling the cogs, so to speak." Martínez Somalo ignored the 1997 allegations against Maciel. John Paul later named him camerlango, or chamberlain, the official in charge of the papal conclave. Martínez Somalo rebuffed my interview requests put through the Vatican spokesman, Father Federico Lombardi, and the receptionist at his home.

"Martínez Somalo was talked about a lot in the Legion . . . *un amigo de Legion,*" recalls Glenn Favreau, a Washington, D.C., attorney who left the order in 1997 after seven years in Rome. Favreau, who was not abused by Maciel, explains: "There were cardinals who weren't *amigos*. They wouldn't call them enemies, but everyone knew who they were. Pio Laghi did not like the Legion." Cardinal Laghi, a former nuncio to the United States, was prefect of the Congregation for Catholic Education.

Of all the cardinals in the Curia, Sodano was the closest to Maciel. Their relationship dated to the Pinochet years in Chile, ideological soul mates from the start. In 1980 the Legion needed Cardinal Raúl Silva Henriquez's permission to establish schools in Santiago. A critic of the Pinochet regime for its human rights atrocities, Silva had misgivings about "*los millionarios de Cristo,*" as some Mexicans derisively called them. Still, he met with the Legion emissaries, including the rector of Mexico's Anáhuac University, which Maciel had founded in 1964. Several advisory bishops begged Silva not to admit them. "In a society as polarized as Chile at the time," the journalist Andrea Insunza and Javier Ortega report, "the Legionaries found a key ally: the apostolic nuncio, Angelo Sodano."[67]

Sodano backed the Legion and Opus Dei in Chile not just to blunt liberation theology advocates on the left. Neo-Pentecostal sects were wooing conservative Catholics who liked the scripture classes and felt a sense of mutual care in the emotional fervor of services. Catholic-style prosperity theology embraced orthodoxy, papal loyalty, and free-market capitalism. Wealth-as-virtue begat gifts to the church. The tradeoff was tolerance of Latin American political repression versus the Soviet Communist brand. Silva, who helped labor unions in the police state, made human rights an issue. Sodano, who supported Pinochet, pressed the Legion's case. Silva capitulated. Later, a Jesuit asked him why. "Don't talk to me about it, please," Silva said ruefully.[68]

Maciel put Father Raymond Cosgrave, an Irish Legionary, at Sodano's disposal as a virtual aide-de-camp at the nunciature in Santiago. In 1989, on track to become secretary of state, Sodano took English classes in Dublin at a Legion school. He went on holiday at a Legion vacation home in Sorrento. Back in Rome, explains Favreau, "Sodano came over with his entire family, two hundred of them, for a big meal when he was named cardinal. And we fed them all. When Sodano became secretary of state there was another celebration. He'd come over for special events, like the groundbreaking for the Center for Higher Studies performed with a golden shovel. And a dinner after that.

"Cardinal Sodano helped change the zoning requirements to build the university in Rome," continues Favreau. Sodano's brother, Alessandro, was a building engineer caught up in Italian corruption charges in the early 1990s.[69] The cardinal's nephew, Andrea, the building engineer and later vice president of the Follieri Group, did work on the Regina Apostolorum. Two Legionaries on the project thought Andrea's work was inadequate. When they suggested to Maciel that the bill not be paid, he yelled, "You pay him and you pay him now!" They did.

Maciel approved separate gifts of $10,000 and $5,000 to Cardinal Sodano, according to former Legionaries. These priests consider these funds the tip of the iceberg for Sodano. Sodano's photograph hung in the Regnum Christi center in Rome, embroidering the cardinal's persona as champion of a growing lay movement. Regnum Christi's success was his success, too.

Sodano declined my interview requests through the papal spokesman, Father Lombardi. Calls to Sodano's residence were referred back to the Vatican.

Maciel wanted Vatican approval for Regina Apostolorum as a Pontifical Academy, the highest level of recognition by the Vatican. This would put the freshly minted university on equal footing with the much older

Lateran and Gregorian universities. So it was, in 1999, that the Legionaries offered a Mercedes-Benz to Cardinal Pio Laghi, then-prefect of the Congregation for Catholic Education (and former papal ambassador to the United States). Laghi, who has since died, was appalled and spurned the offer, according to Father B, who witnessed his outrage. Laghi's successor, Cardinal Zenon Grocholewski, refused to grant the academic status. Regina Apostolorum lacked credentials in research, faculty, and international prestige, according to a knowledgeable official. The Lateran University, which was established in 1773, had received pontifical standing in 1910. In denying Maciel his university's distinction, Grocholewski bucked the powerful Sodano. But Grocholewski, a Pole who had come to Rome as a seminarian in the cold war and never left, was a former prefect of the Signatura, confident of his position and ties to John Paul.

Sodano did Maciel a greater favor by pressuring Ratzinger to halt the canonical case in the CDF, as José Barba learned from his canon lawyer, Martha Wegan. Ratzinger, as archbishop of Munich and then as prefect of the CDF, had moved haltingly on other cases of sexual predators; the Vatican under John Paul had no uniform approach.[70] His ideal of the priesthood as a chivalrous caste, resisting godless Communism, left him myopic, if not blind, to the cold truth of the 1990s as victims, lawyers, and journalists in English-speaking countries dug out evidence of appalling crimes in a clergy sexual underground.

Sodano was Machiavellian, Ratzinger a moral absolutist. Sodano's reputation stood to suffer if Maciel were punished. By Sodano's lights, the Maciel record of supplying vocations outweighed accusations from the 1950s on which Rome had already ruled. Truth didn't matter anyway. This was Sodano's logic in pushing a Vatican silent front as they eased out Groër, the pederast cardinal of Vienna. But Ratzinger could not have tabled a case as grave as Maciel's without the approval of John Paul. The pope *is* the pope; they had a standing Friday lunch. In what now seems face-saving, Ratzinger told a Mexican bishop that an investigation of Maciel might not be "prudent," as he had attracted so many men to the priesthood.[71] How tepid a rationale from the law-and-order prefect who had waged intellectual war against Leonardo Boff, Hans Küng, and Charles Curran: humiliate prolific theologians, but look the other way when it was time to condemn a pedophile?

On a visit to Regina Apostolorum, Ratzinger refused a pay envelope after a lecture on theology. "Tough as nails in a very cordial way," says Father A.

Maciel maintained his power courtesy of a warped tribunal system. He continued traveling from Rome to Madrid, on to Latin America and North America, visiting Legion centers, meeting the donors. Father Stephen Fichter, today the pastor of Sacred Heart parish in Haworth, New Jersey, coordinated the Legion's administrative office in Rome from February 1998 until October 2000. Fichter left the Legion for the diocesan clergy, earned a doctorate in sociology from Rutgers, and today is a New Jersey pastor and an associate at a Georgetown University research center. "When Father Maciel would leave Rome it was my duty to supply him with ten thousand dollars in cash—five thousand in American dollars, and the other half in the currency of the country to which he was traveling," explains Fichter. "It was a routine part of my job. He was so totally above reproach that I felt honored to have that role. He did not submit any receipts and I would not have dared to ask him for a receipt . . . As Legionaries, our norms concerning the use of money were very restricted. If I went on an outing I was given twenty dollars and if I had a pizza I'd return the fifteen dollars to my superior with a receipt."[72]

Besides Regina Apostolorum and the Center for Higher Studies, where Chris Kunze lived, Maciel built Mater Ecclesiae, a seminary in Rome for various dioceses; newly named bishops stayed there for training. Maciel grounded the Legion into the church infrastructure of Rome. Sitting at a 2000 celebrational lunch on the campus, Maciel saw Sodano, seated at another table, and snorted to a Legionary: "*Este hombre no toma paso sin guarache*" (This man does not make a move without having his feet covered; that is, getting something in return).

When Chris Kunze went to the Legion vacation house at Santa Maria de Termini near Sorrento, on the Mediterranean, for the 2000 summer break, his loneliness was acute. While there he met a young woman who was divorced with two children. As she confided about herself, his pastoral front softened; he spoke about his doubts. He kept his vow of celibacy, but in the emotional freedom realized that Legion life was eating at him like acid on the soul.

In the warm glow of an August evening he sat alone with Maciel in the house, both of them wearing Mexican guayaberas. He said he had to leave; he was simply not cut out for life in the priesthood. He wanted to go back to America. "You're wrong," replied Maciel. "You have an important position. You must follow God's will." But, said Kunze, his loneliness was not new, he'd struggled with it years ago in Germany. Maciel frowned. "If I'd known that I wouldn't have recommended you for the Vatican, Father Christopher." *He doesn't remember what I confided in letters from Germany,* realized Kunze, *because Legionary brothers ghostwrite his letters. How could he keep up with the deep personal details of so many men, so many letters? But I know he kept the letters . . .*

Maciel jabbed a finger on the table. "If you don't fulfill God's will, you will go to hell!" Kunze told him chastity was a burden he could no longer bear.

Maciel sat back with arms folded, legs extended, a dripping scowl.

Soon, though, Legion superiors proposed that Father Christopher spend a sabbatical period of discernment in Cheshire, Connecticut. He agreed.

In September he accompanied Maciel on one of his walks around the campus the superior general took most days he was in Rome. Recalling pleasant experiences of his religious life, particularly the Vatican work, Kunze thanked him. Maciel glowered. "When you leave the Legion don't you ever join league with the conspirators against me!" Never before had Kunze seen Maciel vulnerable. He realized the letters that he and others had sent, revealing innermost thoughts and sins, gave Maciel leverage should anyone criticize him.

The Vatican paid Kunze $8,000 in severance, which he kept for himself. He told his Clergy colleagues he was returning to America; his mother was ill.

With avuncular kindness, Cardinal Castrillón wished him well.

Maciel's cynicism extended to using "espionage" against other officials. The respected Spanish journalist José Martínez de Velasco published a book based on internal documents given to him by a disgruntled Legionary who took files as he walked out of the Legion forever. Cardinals and bishops who attended the conferences and receptions at Regina Apostolorum had no idea seminarians were writing reports about them. Martínez de Velasco quotes a seminarian's October 10, 2000, memo on Maciel's friend Cardinal Castrillón. Legionary brothers "went to pick up the Cardinal for his conference. He proved amiable and open enough. Along the way he commented to us about his region of Colombia and the region where he had worked." After greeting other bishops, Castrillón marveled at the beauty of the campus.

> The Cardinal grumbled a little about his predecessor in Colombia who had sold a house near the seminary and it would have been wonderful to have the seminarians nearby . . . The Cardinal told us who had donated the house and how a wealthy gentleman in Colombia had given the old bishop money . . . The Cardinal continued to tell us how when he was young he was "very tough" and sometimes he now felt sorry and ashamed for things he had done as a bishop.[73]

Another seminarian reports on Bishop Onésimo Cepeda of Ecatepec, Mexico, saying that calm had come to Chiapas (where Zapatista guerrillas captured three cities in 1994) and Bishop Samuel Ruiz "had ceased his propaganda." The seminarian sneers at Ruiz as "a supporter of the rights of natives and liberation theology, and fighting against the Legionaries." Ruiz, who preached nonviolence to Zapatista rebels, was beloved among the poor.[74]

The seminarians' sophomoric reports display a sycophancy in seeking favor with superiors. Portraying a bishop allied with the poor as a Legion enemy fits Maciel's formula: the Legion on the right side, conspiracies on the other.

Glenn Favreau felt regret for the role he played in developing files on North American College seminarians in the early 1990s. Maciel told "specially chosen brothers" to befriend men "who were likely going to be officials in their dioceses one day, or even bishops," says Favreau. Legionary brothers filled out reports to "the superiors on progress with each seminarian, about the potential we saw in each one. It was a well-organized system of espionage." One seminarian in the files was a son of Supreme Court justice Antonin Scalia.[75]

As the 2002 abuse crisis intensified, Maciel exposed fault lines in the Vatican. From his *First Things* office, Neuhaus reacted to news coverage of the charges against Maciel in the CDF. (José Barba, incensed at four years' delay, had broken the Vatican-requested silence.)[76] Neuhaus denounced "vicious gossip" and praised Maciel for "virile holiness of tenacious resolve

that has been refined in the fires of frequent opposition and misunderstanding." He continued: "A cardinal in whom I have unbounded confidence and who has been involved in the case tells me that the charges
are 'pure invention, without the slightest foundation.' " Neuhaus, now deceased, never revealed his source, but the cardinal "involved in the case"
was probably Ratzinger, who had confronted nothing like it in his storied
career. Neuhaus insulted Maciel's victims: "After a scrupulous examina-
tion of the claims and counter-claims, I have arrived at *moral certainty* that
the charges are false and malicious."[77]

As Neuhaus's defense spread via Legion websites into translations for
Spanish and Latin American supporters, Maciel became an albatross for
Ratzinger who was, ironically, one of the few cardinals who didn't take
the money. When ABC reporter Brian Ross and a camera crew surprised
Ratzinger outside a Vatican doorway and asked about Maciel, the cardinal
slapped Ross's wrist, fuming, "Come to me when the moment is given. Not
yet!"[78] The footage was indelible.

The Legion disinformation strategy was fraying as more men left the
order, connecting via the Internet with Genvieve Kineke, who saw Regnum Christi as a scam, and Paul Lennon, a family therapist in Alexandria,
Virginia, who had left the Legion in 1984, not as a sexual victim, but in
protest against Maciel's domineering behavior. Lennon formed ReGAIN
Network to post information and probe the cultlike dynamics. Maciel, age
eighty-four, had his last hurrah at a 2004 banquet at the Waldorf Astoria,
cohosted by Citigroup chairman Sanford Weill, raising $725,000 for Le-
gion schools. Chatting with Carlos Slim, Maciel ran his fingers admiringly
down the billionaire's tuxedo lapel, as filmed by Televisa.

In summer 2004 Chris Kunze, three years out of the priesthood, attended a ReGAIN conference in Atlanta. He embraced Juan Vaca in
common cause. Three years later in the Georgia capital, Jeb Bush spoke
at a Legion–Regnum Christi conference. Among those present, Cardinal Franc Rodé, the Vatican prefect in charge of religious orders, was a
champion of Regnum Christi. Rodé flew on to Cancun for a vacation on
the Legion's dime, according to Legion insiders.

Maciel scored another coup in 2003 when Archbishop Tarcisio Bertone of Genoa wrote an illustrious preface to *Christ Is My Life,* Nuestro
Padre's book-length interview with Jésus Colina. The book was Maciel's

self-defense against the pending CDF charges. Colina, a member of Regnum Christi, founded Zenit, the Legion-sponsored news agency. In the soft questions, Colina proved himself a willing dupe. So did Bertone, who had worked for Ratzinger in the CDF as a canon lawyer before his appointment in Genoa. In the Italian preface, Bertone wrote of Maciel:

> The answers that Fr. Maciel gives in the interview are profound and simple and have the frankness of one who lives his mission in the world and in the Church with his sights and his heart fixed on Christ Jesus. The key to this success is, without doubt, the attractive force of the love of Christ. This has always encouraged Fr. Maciel and his institute not to allow themselves to be conquered by controversy, which has not been lacking in their history.[79]

Bertone would succeed Sodano as Pope Benedict's secretary of state.

RATZINGER BREAKS RANKS

John Paul in his twilight showed a surreal dissociation from the abuse crisis. As the Irish scandals worsened, California bishops faced more than nine hundred civil lawsuits filed under a 2002 law that extended the statute of limitations in reaction to Law's cover-up in Boston. The Vatican had no real plan. The CDF by then had seven hundred cases of priests whose bishops wanted them ousted. Ratzinger was slowly laicizing the worst offenders. But John Paul's lavish praise of Maciel marked Sodano's chessboard move against the CDF case. If the Holy Father extols him, how can Father Maciel be bad? On November 30, 2004, the pope gave the Legion administrative control of the Pontifical Institute Notre Dame of Jerusalem Center, an international conference center and hotel school. John Paul praised Regnum Christi for fostering a "civilization of Christian justice and love" and approved their statutes to Sodano's smile. Did the ailing pontiff read what he endorsed?

> 103. Recruitment happens in stages, going successfully from kindness to friendship, from friendship to confidence, from confidence to conviction, from conviction to submission.

494. No one shall visit outsiders in their homes, deal with them frequently or speak with them by telephone without justifiable reasons or for apostolic purposes . . .

504.2. No one shall attend public spectacles or sporting events, even under the pretext of accompanying outside persons or groups, especially if such groups are mixed.

509. The center's Director or Manager shall review all correspondence from members of the center and release that which he or she judges to be opportune.

514.1. Live your consecration with a sense of removal as it relates to dealings with your family and try to fundamentally channel this relationship into conquering them for Christ.

"I think the only honest answer is that the pope and his senior aides obviously do not believe the charges," John Allen, the *National Catholic Reporter*'s Vatican correspondent, wrote on December 3, 2004.[80] In a striking coincidence, Archbishop Harry Flynn of St. Paul, Minnesota, released a letter to his pastors that banned the Legion and Regnum Christi from the archdiocese and criticized Father Anthony Bannon as "vague and ambiguous" on the Legion's agenda; Flynn saw Regnum Christi as "a parallel church." That same week, Ratzinger broke ranks with Sodano and ordered an investigation of Maciel. With John Paul dying, Ratzinger knew that whoever the forthcoming conclave might elect should not enter the papacy saddled by the scandal of a sheltered Maciel. "Under a 2002 policy adopted by the U.S. hierarchy, an American priest facing allegations such as those made against Maciel would be suspended immediately while an investigation was conducted," reported Gerald Renner for the *Hartford Courant.*[81]

And so, during the first week of December 2004, Maciel stepped down as the Legion's superior general. The Legionaries elected Álvaro Corcuera, a forty-seven-year-old priest from Mexico City and a frequent visitor in the Apostolic Palace, courtesy of Bishop Dziwisz. A product of Legion schools, Corcuera was popular within the order, adulated Maciel, and was hardly prepared for what was to come.

The pope was too ill on Good Friday so Ratzinger led the Stations of the Cross in the Colosseum. His words shot across the media grid: "How much filth there is in the Church, and even among those who, in the priesthood, ought to belong entirely to Him." As journalist Robert Blair Kaiser wrote, Ratzinger was "nailing down a campaign theme" in his pursuit of the papacy.[82]

Born in Malta, Monsignor Charles Scicluna cut an unlikely figure as Ratzinger's investigator. In his early forties, short, stout, with thinning black hair, cherubic cheeks, and tiny hands, the canonist cut an ironic counterimage to his title: promoter of justice. But Scicluna was tough. He had briefed American canonists on how to send their nightmare cases to the CDF. His punitive approach clashed with the clubby circles of clergy in Rome who saw priests' rights under assault. Scicluna spoke English with a British accent; his Spanish bore traces of Italian, as Juan Vaca noticed when he gave his testimony at an Upper East Side church on April 2, 2005. Scicluna asked questions, a priest-secretary typed on a laptop, Vaca recounted the horrors of his past. During a break, they learned the news from Rome: John Paul had died.

Chris Kunze watched the solemn majesty of John Paul's death from his home in Waco, Texas, in mourning for the pope he revered. Now married and the father of a toddler, Kunze had written John Paul about his encounters with Maciel. On the flight to Mexico City, where he would join Barba and others as witnesses, Kunze thought, *I don't want Father Maciel to go to hell. This is a chance for him to repent, do penance, to say he is sorry to victims who have waited decades. Imagine their suffering! Mine is nothing compared to what they went through.*

Monsignor Scicluna took the testimony of more than twenty men in Mexico City. He returned to Rome with a satchel of books on Maciel published in Spanish and English, and videotapes of news investigations Barba had culled. The canonical prosecutor arrived in the Vatican where his boss had become the new pope. Barely a month into Benedict's papacy, the Legionaries issued a May 20 news release disclosing that the "Holy See" had informed them that "there is no canonical process under way regarding our founder . . . nor will one be initiated." The Vatican Press Office confirmed the statement. The Legion pronounced Maciel "exonerated," just as other witnesses were arriving in Rome to testify before Scicluna. But the case-closed document, as John Allen reported, came not from Scicluna's office, which had jurisdiction over the case, but from the office of Cardinal Sodano, in a fax bearing the Secretariat of State's seal.[83]

Then irony dealt Maciel a fateful hand. In 1995 he had nominated Bishop Rafael Guízar Valencia, his uncle, for sainthood. In 2006 the Congregation for the Causes of Saints gave its approval. The document for Guízar's sainthood was on Benedict's desk to sign as the pope mulled the contents of Scicluna's report. For a Vatican-protected pederast to attend his uncle's beatification would invite a media bloodbath. On May 18, 2006, the ruse ended with a terse Vatican communiqué. It said that the Congregation for the Doctrine of the Faith

> decided—bearing in mind Fr. Maciel's advanced age and his delicate health—to forgo a canonical hearing and to invite the father to a reserved life of penitence and prayer, relinquishing any form of public ministry. The Holy Father approved these decisions. Independently of the person of the Founder, the worthy apostolate of the Legionaries of Christ and of the Association "Regnum Christi" is gratefully recognized.[84]

As a cardinal, Ratzinger would have laicized an ordinary priest with so many victims. Sodano intervened again, according to a well-placed Vatican official, to soften the punishment and make sure the language praised RC and the Legion, despite the nine-year campaign attacking the victims. The Legion statement had no hint of apology: "Fr. Maciel, with the spirit of obedience to the church that has always characterized him, has accepted this communiqué with faith, complete serenity, and tranquility of conscience . . . Following the example of Christ, [he] decided not to defend himself." Comparing a pedophile to Jesus was hubris more inflated than anything in the media circus of celebrities or politicians snared in sex scandals who apologize, pick themselves up, and keep getting airtime. As Maciel, age eighty-six, slouched out of Rome, the Legion took down its website attacks, though for months it maintained the biographical hosannas to the founder, having little else about the Legion to promote.

Money is a mighty force in any religion. The Legionaries had their script with Sodano's fingerprints: Father Maciel was never tried, the Vatican never stated that he abused anyone. Banking on the illusion of things unsaid, the Legionaries unofficially told people that Maciel had been wrongly accused and would one day be vindicated. As part of its mop-up campaign, the Legion in 2007 sued ReGAIN Network and Paul Lennon for posting the private vows, the constitution, as allegedly stolen intellectual properties, and in a spectacular display of projection, accused the ex-Legionaries of "malicious disinformation."[85] The nuisance suit threw ReGAIN into a fund-raising scramble. Although the constitution still circulated on the Internet, Lennon gave a copy to Legion lawyers and, in order to settle the case, halted the discussion board, the real target of the lawsuit, as it drew ex-supporters, with fresh facts, like steel filings to a magnet. In Rome, Benedict XVI ordered the Legion to abolish the private vows.

Elizabeth Kunze was in her thirteenth year as a Regnum Christi consecrated woman, teaching in Ireland, when Maciel's health gave out in late January 2008, in Florida. Legionaries took him to a hospital in Miami. A report in Madrid's *El Mundo* by Idoia Sota and José M. Vidal reconstructs his final days. Father Corcuera, Maciel's successor as superior general, gathered in the hospital with several other Legionaries. They wanted Nuestro Padre to make a final confession in keeping with the Catholic faith. He refused so emotionally that one priest reportedly summoned an exorcist, but no ritual took place.

Amid the black emotions of his ebbing life, the women appeared: Norma Hilda Baños and the daughter she had had with Maciel, twenty-three-year-old Normita. "I want to stay with them," said Maciel. According to the account in *El Mundo:*

> The Legionary priests, alarmed by Maciel's attitude, called Rome. [Father] Luis Garza knew right away that this was a grave problem. He consulted with the highest authority, Álvaro Corcuera, and then hopped on the first plane to Miami and went directly to the hospital.
>
> [Garza's] indignation could be read on his face. He faced the once-powerful founder and threatened him: "I will give you two hours to come with us or I will call all the press and the whole world will find out who you really are." And Maciel let his arm be twisted.[86]

The priests got Maciel to a Legion house in Jacksonville, Florida; he reportedly grew belligerent when Corcuera tried to anoint him, yelling,

"*I said no!*" According to the reporters, he "did not believe in God's pardon," an opinion to which his biographical facts lend large support, but for which, in truth, we have no proof. What mattered to the Legion as he died was sealing the history known to insiders of his financial arrangements for Norma Hilda, with whom he had begun a common-law relationship in Acapulco in about 1980, and their child, Normita. Later on he moved them to Madrid and provided financial security.

Upon his death, the Legion said that he went to heaven.

In Cuernavaca, Mexico, Maciel's three sons saw the news of his death on TV with their mother, Blanca Lara Gutiérrez, whom he had met and wooed in 1977, when she was nineteen and he, at fifty-seven, told her he was an agent for the CIA. He had been out of touch with that family for several years.

CHAPTER 8

BORRÉ in ROME

Peter Borré's strategy of drawing the Vatican into responsibility for Boston parish closings registered in March 2006. Cardinal Castrillón responded to the parishioners' appeals by writing Bishop William Skylstad, the USCCB president (whose Spokane diocese had taken bankruptcy protection because of abuse litigation). With no reference to Boston, Castrillón's message was clear.

> *Your Excellency:*
>
> *This Congregation deems it opportune to write to you regarding the closure of parishes in the dioceses of the United States, since in recent times certain dioceses have wrongly applied canon 123 CIC and stating that a parish has been "suppressed" when in reality it has been merged or amalgamated.*
>
> *A parish is more than a public juridical person. Canon 369 defines the diocese as a "portion of the people of God which is entrusted to the bishop to be nurtured by him" . . . In this light, then, only with great difficulty, can one say that a parish becomes extinct.*[1]

The proceeds from closed churches should follow parishioners to the "enlarged parish community." But the Boston archdiocese wanted church assets to sell and plug the deficit. For Borré it was all very simple: Castrillón was covering his ass. Officials in the Congregation for the Clergy were advising the Boston archdiocese on how pastors of parishes shutting down could "voluntarily" surrender funds. Castrillón's chief concern was not the injustice of suppression orders, but *how* to help Seán O'Malley meet his financial needs.

Other prelates secured closures predicated on fleeting media coverage. On a February night in 2007 Borré bedded down in a pew of Our Lady Queen of Angels in Harlem in a show of solidarity with forty people at a vigil. The next day, with the vigil established, he caught an evening shuttle to Boston. A few hours later police officers responding to Cardinal Edward Egan's office hauled off the leaders, most of them women, releasing them after the archdiocese locked the doors.[2] Egan, a Chicago canonist trained in Rome, had come to New York from the diocese of Bridgeport, Connecticut. In a 1997 deposition over an abuse case and his recycling of perpetrators, Egan, in trying to contain financial damage, actually testified, "Every priest is self-employed."[3] Three years later he went to New York, with 2.5 million Catholics, after the death of Cardinal John O'Connor. "New York Catholicism was practically an Irish-run Establishment overseeing a mosaic of stable ethnic enclaves," wrote the religion writer David Gibson.

> But now those old-time Catholic communities were spreading out to suburbs while new, poorer immigrants back-filled city parishes that had fewer priests to staff them and little money to support them. Churches and schools would have to close, creating a sense that after 200 years of surging numbers and clout, New York Catholicism had become a mature industry, religiously speaking, and was facing a discouraging phase of downsizing . . .
>
> O'Connor's popularity was owed to the fact that he never denied anyone who came begging for a new program or for him to halt the closing of an old parish and he left the archdiocese with a $20 million-a-year operating deficit and an infrastructure that needed a serious overhaul. During his tenure, O'Connor

blew through tens of millions in reserves. "O'Connor spent like a drunken sailor," as one priest said.[4]

Not so Ed Egan. The cardinal who adored opera courted donors at small fund-raisers by playing piano. Egan wouldn't dream of emulating O'Malley by posting archdiocesan financial statements. "Do we want to leave ourselves open?" Egan mused to the *Times*, rolling his eyes. "Oh, what fun people could have." Church officials said Egan had erased the deficit, paying down $40 million of internal debt at $3 million annually, but there was no way to check.[5] When Egan suppressed Our Lady of Vilnius, a Lithuanian parish in Manhattan, he called in the pastor, told him his church was being padlocked as they spoke, and that ended the 107-year-old parish.[6] Bad news would pass.

Three Boston area parishes that filed canonical appeals to Rome had been occupied twenty-four hours at a time since 2004, despite Clergy's rejection of their requests. Two other parishes had had their appeals rejected by the Boston archdiocese for failure to file in thirty days; their appeals never went to Rome, but people slept in the pews anyway, making five vigil parishes in 2006.

For an appeal to the Apostolic Signatura the groups needed well-positioned counsel. Borré saw that only twelve people were qualified as advocates at the Signatura listed in the Holy See's *Annuario Pontificio*. Only two lay canonists had the standing to bring a recourse, or ultimate appeal, to the Holy Father. One was Martha Wegan, the Austrian who had filed the 1998 case against Maciel in Ratzinger's tribunal; the other, Carlo Gullo, an Italian, taught canon law at Pontifical University of the Holy Cross, which was affiliated with Opus Dei. (Gullo insisted to Borré he was not an Opus member.)

Born in 1942 in Tuscany, Carlo Gullo was married with four grown children. After law school at the University of Messina, in Sicily, he had taken a canon law degree from the Gregorian in 1968. Canon lawyers gained a role in Italy's legal system with the 1929 Lateran Pacts by which Mussolini gave the church authority over marriage in civil affairs. Divorce was illegal until the 1970s; dissolving a marriage required an annulment. In 2002 the Pontifical Lateran University had seven hundred students pursuing degrees in canon law, most of them laywomen and laymen.

Canonists could earn $20,000 or more by resolving property issues in complex annulments.[7] Gullo practiced with his daughter, Alessia, one of the youngest advocates admitted at the bar of the Signatura. She also oversaw the computer system in her father's home office.

"Dottor Borré"—Doctor—was the salutation in Gullo's e-mails, while Borré's opened "Egregio Avvocato," Distinguished Attorney. In their get-acquainted conversations, Borré spoke Italian, since his counterpart did not speak English. Alessia, who was conversant in English, occasionally assisted on arcane points of law. In the exchanges with Gullo, Borré was summoned back to his Latin studies as a schoolboy in Rome, for Gullo wrote his briefs in Latin. On the telephone Gullo spoke so softly that Borré at times strained to hear. Gullo was an elegant voice in explaining how hard it was to reverse an archbishop's decree. But, it had happened some years ago when a Chicago parish persuaded the Signatura to overturn a suppression by the late Cardinal Joseph Bernardin. Borré asked if he could read the decision.

"This is classified," Gullo replied gravely.

Borré was curious about the give-and-take among the cardinals and judges during Signatura proceedings.

"I have no idea," said Gullo.

He explained that it was forbidden for the advocates to be in the room when the judges met. The Signatura had twenty-five canonists, most of them cardinals (including Egan of New York) on its board of consultors. The Rome-based judges, led by the prefect and assisted by the court secretary and a "promoter of justice," constituted a tribunal called the Congressio, which screened appeals to determine which should go to the full bench. The Signatura covered administrative decisions of other tribunals and congregations. Parishioners who might travel to Rome would never be admitted to a session; nor were they allowed to read the briefs in Latin submitted by parties other than their advocates.

Borré pictured Dante's arrival at the river in the *Inferno* and the sign saying "Abandon All Hope, Ye Who Enter Here!"

Gullo explained that if they proceeded in a Vatican process, the decisions would not come fast. The first stage of an appeal, read by the Congressio, involved a counteropinion from the Advocate for Public Administration, whose job was to defend the Congregation for the Clergy's rationale. As it turned out, the canonist who filled that role in these cases was Martha Wegan. Borré assumed that Congressio canonists would not overrule Cardinal Castrillón's dicastery. That meant filing a detailed appeal to the full bench. They were looking at an uphill slog to question the moral logic of parishes-as-assets before cardinal-jurists. Borré had no doubt of the resolve by people in their round-the-clock vigils.

After a discussion of finances, Gullo agreed to a fee of 4,000 euros per parish, or about $6,000 under the exchange rates. Over time, ten parishioner groups from the Boston archdiocese took this route, which translated into roughly $60,000 for work that was likely to extend three years or longer. The fixed fee also covered an appeal against sale of a church, should the suppression per se be granted. Borré calculated the hourly rate at less than $100, which was affordable to the parish groups, and a form of leverage in driving up the cost to the Boston archdiocese each month a given church could not be sold. When the two men finally met in the winter of 2007, the appeals Gullo had filed in the preceding year were still pending at the Signatura; he would eventually have eleven Boston parishes as clients.

Carlo Gullo lived on the third floor of an apartment building in an eastern suburb of Rome, several miles beyond Porta Pia, the sixteenth-century gate crowned with ornamental crenellations that stood as Michelangelo's last monumental work. In 1870 Italian troops blasted through Porta Pia in seizing Rome from Pope Pius IX. As the bus passed the sight, Borré saw a bronze-and-marble monument to a Risorgimento rifle regiment that Mussolini had erected in 1932, a reminder of triumphal Rome.

The night before, at dinner with a Jesuit who had taught him decades earlier in middle school in Rome, Borré vented about parishes being sold to pay for clergy crimes. "You Americans," the old Italian grunted. "Always the sex!" But shutting these churches was driving away the faithful, insisted Borré. "If in ten years the American church is half its present size," the Jesuit retorted, "we will be a better church." Borré sized him up as a Ratzingerian, loyal to Benedict XVI's view of a purified church, small, leaner, more obedient to orthodoxy, a view that conservatives cheered.

Tall and slender, with a full head of gray hair, Gullo greeted him at the door. They sat in the book-lined office. In his soft, courtly voice, Gullo emphasized the importance of language in the petitions to convey a sense of the spiritual integrity in people occupying the churches. Gullo conceded that they were on a hard road, but the financial ethics intrigued him as an issue the Vatican offices had to confront. "You must put aside any notions of jurisprudence from Anglo-Saxon systems," Gullo explained. Despite the strict time limits for appellants, the Vatican congregations and courts could take as long as they wished.

Borré conceived the Council of Parishes as an organization capable of expanding as financial convulsions hit other dioceses; this was neither perverse nor wishful thinking, rather a realization that the Boston crisis turned on Lennon, then O'Malley, shielding information on Law's mismanagement of money and predators—a system corroded by protection rituals. Catholics deserved honesty on church finances. Parishioners in Scranton and Allentown, New Orleans and Cleveland, among two dozen dioceses, contacted Borré in hopes of halting parish closures. Nationally, the large majority of parishes closed without great protest, as many churches had too few members. But where protests arose, they shone a spotlight on how bishops managed money with little or no accountability. Borré prepared folders with plastic labels, comparative information on different dioceses, accounts of media coverage, and a how-to explanation on filing a canonical appeal to the Congregation for the Clergy if the bishop did not respond in thirty days, and how the process worked up to the Signatura.

Borré was careful not to offend Carlo Gullo by going on a tear about the injustices of American prelates. For Gullo, the Vatican legal system was a business, the structure in which he practiced his profession.

At home, Mary Beth was amused when her husband, putting down his Latin dictionary, began speaking in Italian. At least he wasn't yelling at TV news or stewing in boredom like some men who retire with little self-knowledge. Despite her estrangement from the church, Mary Beth had once gone to a Bible study class with Rosie, telling herself, *I am doing this because I love my mother.* Peter's journey into church officialdom engaged her intellectually; she liked his focus on the property dynamics. She felt for the people sleeping in pews.

"Why am I doing all this?" Borré said aloud to his wife one day.

"You've got parts of your skill set you've never used," she replied.

He rolled the idea over, wondering why it was so.

CHAPTER 9

SECRECY AND LAMENTATIONS

The road that led Peter Borré to Cleveland ran from Boston to Rome and back again. The big Ohio diocese was mired in a financial scandal when he met Sister Christine Schenk. Chris Schenk had been working for years to expand ministry as parishes lost priests; she anticipated the day when bishops would sit down for practical discussions on how to rejuvenate the church by allowing married Catholics and women to become priests. In 1991 the Cleveland diocese had accurately forecast a decline of 480 priests to 340 within the decade, as part of a 40 percent drop since 1970.[1] History had taught Sister Chris that Rome would accept change when reality was clear to everyone else.

Schenk and Father Lou Trivison founded FutureChurch in 1990 after an eight-month study on the impact of the priest shortage by Trivison's Church of the Resurrection in Solon, an affluent Cleveland suburb. The motto was: "We love the church . . . We're working to make it better!" Years later, as the Boston vigil movement radiated into the heartland, the agenda was well in place:

> FutureChurch, inspired by Vatican II, recognizes that Eucharistic
> Celebration (the Mass) is the core of Roman Catholic worship

and sacramental life. We advocate that this celebration be available universally and at least weekly to all baptized Catholics.

FutureChurch respects the tradition of the Roman Catholic
Church and its current position on ordination [of celibate males
only] and advocates widespread discussion of the need to open ordination to all baptized Catholics who are called to priestly ministry by God and the people of God.[2]

Beloved by his parishioners, Lou Trivison had good ties to Bishop Anthony Pilla. The bishop allowed FutureChurch to seek out supportive pastors for its workshops and speakers. At any time Pilla could have halted
the group, though at the cost of a broken friendship with a priest he liked.
Independent groups, like religious orders, need a bishop's approval to meet
in parishes.

Born in 1932, Tony Pilla had grown up in an Italian neighborhood on
Cleveland's east side. Pilla graduated from John Carroll, the Jesuit university in Cleveland, then went to St. Charles Borromeo, the diocesan seminary. Short, with dark hair and bedroom eyes, he was a popular bishop,
the hometown boy made good. The affable Pilla was politically astute;
he served in the midnineties as president of the national bishops' conference. While never endorsing such ideas, Pilla seemed unthreatened by
optional celibacy or women priests. He was resolutely pro-life and a critic
of nuclear arms. Pilla's great concern was dying neighborhoods. Cleveland
was a case study of the rust-belt economy in existential panic.

Founded in 1796 on Lake Erie near the mouth of the Cuyahoga River,
the port town grew into a city as railroads expanded the navigational arteries to carry coal, crops, and timber. From a core of 1830s Irish settlers,
the church had a growing German community in 1846 when the pastor
Peter McLaughlin got involved with a choir girl and "proved himself a
cad," notes a diocesan history, "declaring the woman had seduced him!"[3]
The new priest, Maurice Howard, set tongues wagging over the housekeeper, a young female cousin. Protesting his innocence, Father Howard
wrote: "Thank God, I am succeeding with my people here . . . there is neither card-playing, dancing, party or frolic."[4] Cleveland diocese, founded
in 1847, spun off from the Cincinnati archdiocese.

Shipyards and iron plants burgeoned after the Civil War. John D.
Rockefeller's oil refinery controlled 90 percent of U.S. refining capacity

in the 1890s. His mansion was one of many on fabled Euclid Avenue.[5] Working families in the late nineteenth and early twentieth centuries came from south central Europe, and there were pockets of black people. Settlements in the Haymarket district followed "village chains" in southern Italy, clustering families and folkways in urban enclaves. St. Anthony of Padua church, built in 1887, held yearly celebrations of patron saints of villages with bands, fireworks, and cuisine. The parish had ten thousand Italian residents in 1900, the year that the First Catholic Slovak Union was founded.[6] Serbs, Croats, and Poles enriched the urban mosaic; tribal loyalties formed around the parish. "Even a street merchant, whose jaded mare was dragging a wagon through the muddy street, cried his wares in Czech," recalled a blacksmith of his 1889 arrival. "And it truly did look like a Czech village . . . Children, chickens, ducks, dogs and cats ran about, and there was not a blade of grass to be seen."[7]

Jews came from Russia and central Europe. By 1930 African Americans numbered 71,890, or 8 percent of the 900,429 population.

Cleveland's ethnic churches served as cultural sanctuaries for people rooted in Old World ways. "Saint Stanislaus Church cost its Polish congregation $150,000 to build in 1889—when the average wage at the Newburgh Rolling Mill, which employed many of the members, was $7.25 per week," writes historian Michael J. McTighe. Three years later the pastor resigned, leaving a debt exceeding $90,000, which the parish and new pastor paid down.[8]

Conflicts flared in early-nineteenth-century America over parish control by lay trustees and the bishop's power. In a number of larger dioceses the bishop was a "corporation sole," a legal term that means the bishop literally owns all church property. Bishops gathered control of parishes as presumably benevolent rulers. An 1888 Ohio Supreme Court decision, *Mannix v. Purcell*, considered the sale of parish property to satisfy a bishop's debts.

> A panic in the 1880's having made depositors fearful, the Bishop of Cincinnati, John Purcell, created a "bank" for Catholic depositors. Somehow, he and his brother ran the bank into three million dollars of debt, and the creditors took an assignment from Bishop Purcell of "all Diocesan property."
>
> The creditors of the Bishop sought a ruling from the Ohio

Supreme Court that they could sell the property of the parishes within the diocese of Cincinnati to satisfy the debt, as they were "Diocesan property." The Court ruled that such property was only held in trust by the Bishop for the benefit of the congregation of worshippers . . . and consistently named the congregation of persons worshipping and supporting the individual churches as the beneficiaries of the individual trusts in which the churches were held.[9]

As *Mannix* saved the Cincinnati churches from liquidation to cover a bishop's bad debts, Cleveland's ethnic churches fell into the old European pattern of hierarchical property, albeit in an era when a bishop's challenge was to *expand,* while braiding the mores of varied parishes into a common culture of Catholicism. As Cleveland became a muscle of the industrial Midwest, the diocese educated growing numbers of youngsters and helped people adrift in the city. In 1911 Bishop John Farrelly designated an Orphans' Week collection with a quota on each parish to support orphanages across the diocese. Other dioceses emulated it.[10] But as the city grew, so did dozens of inner-ring townships that should have been sending taxes downtown to a central city hall.

"Cleveland did not incorporate inner-ring suburbs, as Columbus did," explains Father Bob Begin, the pastor of inner-city St. Colman parish. "We have all these little suburbs with a fire department, mayor, and school system. Integrating schools didn't mean a lot because by then there weren't many whites. When Interstate 90 was built in the fifties it took out four hundred houses from this parish and St. Ignatius. In those days the parish was the center of life. St. Ignatius is at West 100th Street, we're at West 65th. St. Ignatius seats a thousand people. We're about the same. On a given Sunday we have four hundred people. Sixty percent come back from the suburbs and they assist in programs that help the poor, as part of the mission."

White flight escalated after two riots in the late 1960s tore through black neighborhoods. The city population began a steady decline from 900,000 to 450,000. The economy lost 86,100 industrial jobs between 1970 and 1985. Poverty surged by 45 percent in the 1980s in Cuyahoga County; nearly one-fifth of the county residents were poor. By 2000 Cleveland proper had a poverty rate of 32 percent, or 215,700 people, while inner-ring townships hummed along via tax bases of their own, delivering better services on a tighter grid. Churches that once anchored the families of Italians, Irish, Poles, Slovenians, and Czechs when factories were at full steam sat in neighborhoods that had become poorer, darker, and less Catholic, even as people drove in from the townships for Sunday Mass. As state funds supported lakefront parks, Cleveland's revitalization in the 1990s via tax concessions to developers helped draw an educated workforce to downtown jobs. But a crumbling public school system and scourges of a drug economy revealed the bleak fault lines between city and suburbs.

The Cleveland diocese by 2000 had 802,000 Catholics, some 28 percent of the eight-county population. Philanthropy, government grants, and the rise of ethnic generations made Catholic Charities of Cleveland reputedly the world's largest diocesan system of social services, leveraging donations with government contracts for a 2004 budget of $85 million, facilitating 4 million annual meals to the hungry and a range of social service programs.[11]

In a 1996 speech to Cleveland's influential City Club, Bishop Pilla took aim at regional sprawl as a drain on city revenue and vital services. With "growing concentrations of poverty in our urban cores, fiscal resources are strained, if not scarce," said Pilla. "We basically have flat regional population growth, yet we spread out over more and more land . . . sprawl without growth."

> Does this well established trend represent good stewardship of our valuable agricultural lands? Does it lead to a cleaner environment? Does it strengthen the social fabric of our communities? Does it make cohesive, vibrant family life easier? Does it foster greater civic participation? Does it wisely utilize our fiscal resources? Does it increase our economic competitiveness? . . . Does it help bridge the widening gaps that separate rich, poor and middle class? Does it advance social justice? I don't think so.

Pilla worked tirelessly to fund Cleveland Catholic schools—Ohio's largest school district, with many inner-city students from non-Catholic homes. "How we live proclaims what we believe," he told the assembled movers and shakers. Citing the struggle of blacks in slavery and segregation, and Hispanics in immigration, he got personal: "My own father came to this country with a nickel in his pocket. Literally one nickel. Growing up in the city, I know well the struggles he faced and so many others like him and my mother, good hard-working people of all races, religions and backgrounds. They built our cities brick by brick. Today we their sons and daughters are called to build and rebuild not so much buildings and streets as lives and relationships, one by one."[12]

Pilla's vision of the church as an urban anchor was rooted in Catholic social teaching, a shared responsibility to the Other. Sister Schenk and Bishop Pilla were poised to be natural allies in helping at-risk parishes as the priesthood lost greater numbers of men. Six months after his City Club speech, Pilla voiced worries of "the graying of the priestly fraternity," in a presidential address to the national bishops' conference in Washington, D.C. Priests, he said, "worry about the slow fade-out for the priesthood, at least as we have known it."[13] But Rome's hand in church politics required that Pilla praise the "promise of celibate chastity," even though celibacy was driving away men in record numbers. Sister Chris Schenk had no inkling that the bigger problem for FutureChurch was the mess surrounding Pilla himself.

LOOKING FOR JESUS

Born in 1946, Chris Schenk was the eldest of four daughters raised in a close family in Lima, which is nestled in Ohio farm country. Her father, a decorated war veteran, sold life insurance; her mother, whose nursing studies had been cut short by the war, influenced Schenk, her sister, and two cousins to choose nursing over teaching, she recalls.

People drawn to the religious life often experience the sweep of a spiritual force, a beauty suggesting God's love, seeding the imagination with a passion for the search, finding grace in service to others. As a young girl, sitting alone on the front steps, she was overcome by a feeling of primordial mystery in the radiance of trees, the leaves in early sunlight shimmering in the breeze. At Mass, the Latin antiphons *Introibo ad altare Dei*, the quavering bells, the aromas of incense, and the luminous colors of the stained-glass windows filled her with wonder for a loving God. "I just couldn't figure out how Harry Miller got to swing the incense when he wasn't nearly as smart or as well behaved as I." At Mass, she thought, *If only I were a boy, I would be a priest. But I can't. I'm a girl.*

During senior year in high school, while teaching catechism to the children of Latino farmworkers, she was struck by the families' purity of faith. She headed off to Washington, D.C., on scholarship at Georgetown University's nursing school. In the social tumult of the 1960s, Chris Schenk's notion of a loving God "clashed with America's role in the Vietnam war, rampant racism and urban riots."[14] She found solace in the dirgelike rhythms of T. S. Eliot's *The Waste Land*. A Jesuit chaplain for medical and nursing students, Father William Kaifer, counseled her as she wrestled with betrayal. *If God is loving, why is the world torn by violence and corruption?* They discussed free will; she tried to square her despair with her "industrial-strength Ohio Catholicism." One day Kaifer said, "What would it mean if you found that God *did* exist?" She knew immediately: she would dedicate her life to that Being, try to bring love to a sinful world.

In college she discovered the works of Pierre Teilhard de Chardin, the Jesuit evolutionary philosopher. As a paramedic with French troops in World War I, Teilhard found an essence of Christ crucified in the carnage. He went on to do pioneering paleontological work in China. Church authorities suppressed Teilhard's writings, which treated scientific findings on planetary growth as expressions of God's design.[15] He died on Easter Sunday 1955, in New York, exiled from his community in France. His posthumously published books quickly became classics. Chris Schenk found inspiration in Teilhard's words.

> I know that the powers of evil, considered in their deliberate and malign action, can do nothing to trouble the divine milieu around me. As they try to penetrate into my universe . . . temptations and evil are converted into good and fan the fires of love.[16]

Three days before her 1968 graduation, she was shattered by the assassination of Senator Robert F. Kennedy. But faith is idealism regenerated. Back in Ohio, working as a hospital nurse, she found herself managing a night ward with one aide and thirty-six patients, a milieu so different from Georgetown's hospital with its interns and residents and collegial atmosphere. She had read the studies that showed poor staffing affected survival rates. Searching for a way to apply her ideals, she went to Boston College for a master's in nursing.

Soon thereafter, she met several members of the Medical Mission Sisters, an order founded in 1925 with a history in north India, where thousands of Muslim women and children died for lack of medical care. The sisters as health providers considered themselves "a healing presence at the heart of a wounded world." Chris Schenk's studies of theology reinforced the sisters' embrace of the Other, finding grace in the poor. She met brilliant, idealistic nuns opposed to U.S. policy that perpetuated poverty in countries where America supported dictators, often to plunder the natural resources.

Her religious life began in Philadelphia, a teaching job at Temple University; she returned her $28,000 salary to the community; however, she soon soured on academic politics. With the support of the Mission Sisters, she became an interfaith organizer with the United Farm Workers (UFW). At a UFW event she met the Peruvian priest Gustavo Gutiérrez, author of A Theology of Liberation. "To be converted is to commit oneself to the process of the liberation of the poor and oppressed," he had written. "We can stand straight, according to the Gospel, only when our center of gravity is outside ourselves."[17] She found her center in Kentucky, where she trained to become a midwife. The region's poverty drove her to join a campaign to change state law so that nurse-practitioners could write prescriptions, an acute need in areas without doctors. In a difficult decision, she left the medical sisterhood, realizing that her need to be rooted somewhere geographically did not mesh with life as a foreign missionary.

In Kentucky, she found a mentor in Baptist midwife Elsie Maier Wilson, "the most enlightening revolutionary of my life. She taught me to trust Jesus's power."

> Some members of the nursing board saw our expanded roles as an abandonment of nursing. Many times as I made the long drive to big-city Louisville from the remote simplicity of the mountains I prayed for God's help to present our case well. We changed the law because of the common decency of ordinary Kentuckians. But it was Jesus's power to empower the powerless, and the organizing skills I learned from the Farm Workers, that gave me the courage to try.[18]

In 1978 she moved to Cleveland. She had romance, a boyfriend, but a spiritual quest for justice ran deep. As a nurse-midwife among the poor, she lobbied for legislation to expand prenatal care services. In time, she was drawn to an activist sensibility in the Congregation of the Sisters of St. Joseph, the order of Sister Helen Prejean. For a second time, Chris Schenk became a nun.

SANTIAGO FELICIANO JR. AT WORK

Cleveland in the 1980s was a crossroads for refugees from Central America. Bishop James Hickey, who had ministered with Mexican farmworkers before his studies in Rome, was aghast at the March 1980 murder of El Salvador's archbishop Óscar Romero while he was saying Mass. The funeral was disrupted by gunshots: twenty mourners were wounded as Hickey and others took shelter in a cathedral. Hickey, who was about to become archbishop of Washington, D.C., encouraged Clevelanders Jean Donovan, a lay missionary, and Ursuline sister Dorothy Kazel to continue their work in El Salvador. Just before Christmas, they, too, were murdered.

The FBI and the Immigration and Naturalization Service harassed New Mexican and Arizona churches in the Sanctuary movement that aided people fleeing civil wars and death squads. Reagan administration CIA director (and Legion of Christ benefactor) William Casey steered money to right-wing militias in El Salvador, Guatemala, and Nicaragua.[19] Hickey's successor, Bishop Pilla, supported a diocesan ministry in El Salvador—and Cleveland. Pilla often quoted Pope Paul VI: "If you want peace, work for justice."

"Pilla wasn't ambitious in the clerical sense," explains Father Bob Begin, the activist. "Pilla was happy to be Bishop of Cleveland. Priests liked that and had loyalty to him. He also had a real sense of mission for the poor." Begin went to Bolivia to learn Spanish and returned to start a house for refugees from Central America. "Six hundred people moved through that house," says Begin. "Most found asylum in Canada."

One of Hickey's last hires, a young attorney named Santiago Feliciano Jr., became general counsel to the diocese and Catholic Charities. "Charlie" Feliciano advised Pilla. In 1984 the Community of St. Malachi, a group affiliated with the parish of the slain missionary women, decided to assist refugees seeking asylum. When Charlie Feliciano gave them a briefing on legal issues, Sister Chris Schenk, who had gotten involved with St. Malachi, was impressed.

Feliciano was a year old in 1952 when his family left Puerto Rico. His father worked in a steel mill providing for a wife and four kids. As the first Hispanics in the neighborhood, they endured hostilities. Sitting by the window of his rented home on a summer afternoon in 2009, his feet tapping nervously, Feliciano recalls "a church that was elemental to our lives." From parochial schools he went to John Carroll, then to Cleveland-Marshall College of Law. Charlie Feliciano read prayers from the altar at Pilla's installation as bishop. Pilla said grace before dinner at the home Charlie and his wife, Rosa, made in the good years. "My kids sat on his lap. This was not a casual relationship." He pauses. "Pilla was upwards of seventeen years my senior. I never called him by his first name."

Meeting Feliciano opened a lens on my own bruising encounter with the Cleveland diocese, and the enigma of Anthony Pilla.

In 1987 the diocese clashed with the *Plain Dealer* newspaper over an article I had done on a freelance assignment about Father Gary Berthiaume. The report drew on documents from a lawsuit against the Detroit archdiocese. In 1978 Berthiaume spent six months in jail in Michigan for molesting a boy of thirteen. Eight years later, the victim's lawyers negotiated a $325,000 settlement. Berthiaume had been a paternal figure to the boy and his older brother after their parents divorced. Unbeknownst to police, the priest abused the older boy *and* four brothers in a second family. The mother of the second family moved south with a $60,000 settlement for one child, never pressing charges. After a trail of shattered lives, Berthiaume took the Fifth Amendment some two dozen times in a deposition when asked about sex with minors.[20]

In the ever-forgiving clerical fraternity, Hickey and Pilla gave Berthiaume a new start in Cleveland. Putting a man fresh from prison in a parish unaware of his criminal past fit well with the culture's benefits package. When I knocked on Berthiaume's rectory door in November 1986, he refused to speak on the record. Nor would Bishop Pilla, when I called the diocese. But church attorneys gave *Plain Dealer* editors a message: to expose Berthiaume would destroy his ministry and be grounds for him to sue for invasion of privacy, since he had paid his debt to society years before. As amazing as the argument seems today, no large daily newspaper back then had done an investigation of bishops helping such a priest. The *Plain*

Dealer's lawyer told the editors that no Ohio judge would dismiss such a suit outright, the legal fees would reach $500,000, and they couldn't predict a jury's response.[21] At the editors' behest I sent a letter with questions to Pilla. The answers came back by letter from Auxiliary Bishop A. James Quinn, a canon lawyer who had a law degree from Cleveland State.

"Quinn drove the decision on Berthiaume," a grim-faced Charlie Santiago told me twenty-three years later. "Quinn had a lot of influence over Pilla."

Quinn's letter to me read in part:

> I respect the moral repentance exhibited by Father . . .
>
> I recognize that Father has paid the criminal and civil consequences that the Court and the Church imposed on him. The victim has been compensated to the satisfaction of the Court . . . [The priest] has undergone extensive psychological counseling and has been recommended as an individual who can begin anew to function as a parish priest. Father continues to cooperate with this diocese through periodic reviews. To date, Father has ministered successfully in the parish to which he is assigned.[22]

Unwilling to engage Pilla in an off-the-record exchange, the *Plain Dealer* published a lengthy Sunday commentary on March 15, 1987, crediting my work, but under a joint byline of the publisher, editor, and managing editor.[23] "The Parish Must Be Told the Truth, Bishop Pilla," read the headline. They called on Pilla to identify the priest. Disappointed to lose an article, I nevertheless supported the decision. The paper treated me fairly; I was back in New Orleans as the drama played out. The face of the diocese in that crisis became Auxiliary Bishop Quinn instead of Bishop Pilla.

"Probably no churchman in America," *Plain Dealer* investigative reporter James F. McCarty later wrote, "has come to personify the [hierarchy's] split personality more succinctly than Auxiliary Bishop Alexander James Quinn."[24] Jimmy Quinn, as friends called him, was a Cleveland native son who had come back from studies in Rome with a Romanità cast of mind. He called the cops to the cathedral in 1969 to eject Bob Begin and another priest as they gave Communion to antiwar protesters. In 1985 Quinn previewed a ninety-three-page secret report that forewarned

U.S. bishops of a pedophilia crisis, coauthored by Father Thomas Doyle, the canon lawyer at the Vatican embassy. Quinn disparaged Doyle to the nuncio, Archbishop Pio Laghi, writing that the "pedophilia annoyance [will] abate."[25] Doyle, an American in the Dominican order, lost his job for pressing the issue. By 2002 his warnings had become prophetic.

In shielding Berthiaume, Jimmy Quinn and Tony Pilla did just what Tom Doyle and his 1985 coauthors had said *not* to: stonewall. They warned about huge civil settlements if bishops were found concealing abusers.[26] Pilla and Quinn relied on Jones Day, the biggest corporate law firm in Cleveland, and Father John Wright, the diocese's secretary for financial and legal affairs. Wright had earned a law degree from Georgetown in 1969 before becoming a priest. "Quinn as a bishop had the stature to be the front man," says Joseph Smith, a CPA who was diocesan treasurer at the time, going to law school at night on the diocese's dime. "But you didn't do anything in our diocese without running it through Bishop Pilla." Wright was uncomfortable in tense situations with the bishop, and in 2000 arranged for Smith to take his own place as CFO, making Smith Pilla's closest adviser.

Back in 1987, as people wondered whose parish had the ex-convict, Quinn told the *Plain Dealer*, "The fact that the priest has been clean for ten years is a very good sign of his rehabilitation." But the standoff spurred victims of other priests to call the newsroom. In July 1987 Karen Henderson reported that the diocese had bargained with three families to keep silent about three *other* priests, who had also been reassigned, and were identified by the *Plain Dealer*.[27]

"Quinn had an awful lot of power, and not for the good," recalls Charlie Feliciano, gazing at the mauve twilight, his feet jittery on the rug. "I went out to tour the Paracletes' facility in New Mexico [that treated pedophiles]. I came back and told Pilla, 'Don't send them there, or [to] St. Luke Institute.' I told him to send the priests to Johns Hopkins [Hospital Sexual Disorders Clinic] under Dr. Fred Berlin. I trusted him. We began sending priests there. The reports coming back weren't so good. The internal debate was, *Do we force them out of the priesthood?* I said, Yes! I am a father of four children. Quinn wouldn't say anything directly. He thought one way, I thought another. I called him Bishop Quinn."

After the *Plain Dealer* coverage, several journalists at the diocese's *Catholic Universe-Bulletin* felt they should write about the church abuse cases.

Pilla, as bishop, was the publisher; the editorial staff were members of the AFL-CIO-affiliated Cleveland Newspaper Guild (as were *Plain Dealer* journalists). Lou Pumphrey, a Vietnam veteran who had worked at the *Universe-Bulletin* since 1977, was among the four staffers summoned to a 1988 meeting with Pilla, Quinn, and Father Michael Dimengo, who oversaw the paper. According to Pumphrey, "It was an interrogation. Pilla was very calm, like Al Pacino in *The Godfather*—no threats, just clear the air. I said we as journalists should be autonomous and have the interests of people in the pews uppermost. Pilla said, 'Well, we are going to have to change that.' Quinn was crimson. He said that if he were in Pilla's shoes he wouldn't be so diplomatic." Pilla overruled the project. The journalists withdrew their bylines from one issue as a protest. Despite the union security, the diocese managed to fire them on one hour's notice.[28] The *Universe-Bulletin* handled the printing of the Youngstown and Toledo diocesan papers. The IRS got wind of disputes among the dioceses and did an audit.

Quinn had a circle of friends, couples he had known for years, and a longtime female secretary who were deeply loyal to him. But sociable Jimmy Quinn could be one tough customer. In a 1990 speech to the Midwest Canon Law Society (an audiotape of which landed in my mailbox), Bishop Quinn declared that personnel files under subpoena

> cannot be tampered with, destroyed, removed. That constitutes obstruction of justice and contempt of court. Prior, however, thought and study ought to be given if you think it's going to be necessary. If there's something you really don't want people to see, you might send it to the Apostolic Delegate (Vatican ambassador) because they have immunity.[29]

In the 1985 report Doyle had bluntly warned *against* such a move, fearing the Vatican would lose diplomatic immunity if the nunciature became a safe house for incriminating files. Quinn's cynicism was alpine.

As victims contacted the diocese, Charlie Feliciano went home at night, torn by a horror show of priests he had never imagined. As he told me in 2009, "I wanted to fashion a remedy for victims to get compensation. I'd say, 'You go out and find a lawyer. Here's what I'm offering.' " Feliciano reported to Father Wright, the financial and legal secretary. Coming from a wealthy local family, Wright had spent part of his childhood in Rhode

Island. He was a nephew and namesake of the late Cardinal John Wright, who had been prefect of the Congregation for the Clergy, and who, in the 1950s, as a Boston auxiliary bishop, had dined at the Borré household in Rome. "Wright told me, 'Quinn thinks you're being too generous with the victims,' " says Feliciano. "Quinn began to handle settlements."

Gary Berthiaume, in 1988, quietly moved to the Joliet, Illinois, diocese, where he was welcomed by an avuncular friend, Bishop Joseph Imesch.[30]

In 1990 a subdued Pilla told his staff that the Vatican had contacted the Cleveland diocese to host World Youth Day with Pope John Paul II in the summer of 1993. From Washington, the bishops' conference sent people for a briefing. "We were assured of good cooperation from county leaders, law enforcement, and the governor's office," explains a high-level person involved in the decision. "It would have cost the diocese a few hundred thousand dollars, and involved about 100,000 youth. Many would stay at college dorms, others in private homes. But internally, there was a serious concern about any sexual abuse to a young person . . . Pilla did not seem eager to have it."

Most bishops would seize the chance to host the Holy Father. By giving the decision to his staff, Pilla sent a message; the staff voted the idea down. World Youth Day 1993 went to Denver, with the attendant commerce and media coverage of an American visit by John Paul. Denver archbishop James F. Stafford subsequently landed a Vatican job and a cardinal's red hat.

Feliciano confirms the account, calling himself "among those worried, saying, 'Can we handle this?' But I was not on the staff that cast the vote."

When a priest abused the son of a deacon on a trip out west, Feliciano felt he had to report the cleric to the county Department of Children and Family Services (DCFS). "Father Wright said Quinn and Pilla didn't want me to report it, since it happened in another state," says Feliciano, who made the report to DCFS. "They thought I was difficult, squawking about the treatment centers."

As Wright outsourced the legal defense work, Feliciano turned to Cleveland Catholic schools—with sixty-five thousand students, the state's largest system. He drafted the protocols to ensure child safety and took complaints of misbehavior by lay teachers, priests, nuns, and workers, reporting at least fifty people to DCFS. "Seven or eight were prosecuted," he says. "The church bureaucracy was a state unto itself." Stacie White, a child rape victim of Father Martin Louis (who went to prison in 1993), sued the diocese as an adult. A defense motion by outside counsel devastated White's parents by blaming them for letting the priest get too close to her. Feliciano crafted a settlement of $385,000 to White. Later, she visited Louis in prison and forgave him.[31]

ROME DEMANDS ASSENT

The issue of priestless parishes entered Sister Chris Schenk's life through conversations with Lou Trivison, the priest who got his parish to focus on the shortage issue and pass a resolution that said what the bishops would never dare to: "There is no lack of vocations to the ordained priesthood if we consider priests who have married and are willing to lead the community in worship, married men who desire to be priests, and single and married women who feel called to the ordained priesthood." John Paul and Cardinal Ratzinger were closing the Vatican II window on a collegial relationship between bishops and pope. The papacy wanted "willful assent"—obedience—from the hierarchs on policy defined by the top. As the priest shortage worsened, Mass attendance rates sank in Western Europe. Any priest who favored optional celibacy was immediately disqualified in the vetting of bishops. (Trivison had no such goal.)

As FutureChurch forged ties with sympathetic parishes for discussions on changing the celibacy law and ordaining women, the first wave of clergy sex abuse cases in English-speaking countries magnified a double standard. John Paul stood aloof, offering no leadership, no plan, while bishops faced lawsuits and searing press coverage. A bishop couldn't defrock a pedophile in prison. Thanks to expensive treatment centers, many priests evaded prosecution. The process to laicize such men in Rome often took years. Many bishops tried to keep victims' settlements under wraps. And church finances were secret.

Of the scandals in the 1990s, says Sister Chris Schenk, "I think we were inclined to give the diocese the benefit of the doubt, rightly or wrongly. We thought that they had tightened up, that they revamped their procedures."

FutureChurch worked on fostering pastoral life coordinators, men and women who took on parish duties once reserved for priests. In 1993, 263 deacons, sisters, brothers, and laypersons had such positions. (By 2004 the number would be 566.)[32] FutureChurch leaders met with the bishop.

"Pilla made clear to us that his job was not only to represent us to Rome but to represent Rome to us," Sister Chris explains. "As long as we did not question faith and morals, he took a benign neglect approach toward us."

As she continued her midwife's work in the poverty of East Cleveland, Chris Schenk enrolled at St. Mary, the diocese's graduate school of theology. Delivering the babies of teenage girls at night, she caught naps on a couch at school by day during breaks. She felt a pull of kinship across the vales of time with women who were early Christian leaders. Their history, erased from Catholic memory, was her focus at the theologate. The girl-mothers she helped to give birth were unconsciously socialized into seeing their value as an extension of the boy-fathers. Catholic women had historically seen themselves as a rung below men as sacred figures of worship. Yet now, many women took classes alongside the men who were on track to become priests. Many of the young men were gay, some in harmony with their sexual identities, others not. Ratzinger in 1986 had deemed homosexuality "an intrinsic moral evil," but he could not explain (nor bishops openly discuss) why the priesthood had become a huge closet, or address the complexities of a pronounced gay priest culture.[33]

"I commend unto you Phébe, our sister," Paul writes in Romans (16:1), calling her "a servant of the church . . . at Cenchreae." As Chris Schenk found on deeper reading, Phoebe was a *diakonos,* or minister, who had hosted Paul at Cenchreae, a seaport at Corinth.[34] In *When Women Were Priests,* the scholar Karen Jo Torjesen writes that Phoebe "carried Paul's letter to the Romans. She was a woman of some wealth and social status." Paul acknowledged Phoebe as a patron (*prostatis*) to Rome's Christians. Of the twenty-eight distinguished people Paul singles out in his letter to the Romans, ten were women.

> Among these women leaders of the Roman congregation was a woman apostle, Junia, whom Paul hailed as "foremost among the apostles" (Rom. 16:7). She and her husband, Adronicus, traveled teaching and preaching from city to city. The turmoil and riots occasionally provoked by Christian preaching landed her and her husband in prison, where they encountered Paul. She was a heroine of the fourth-century Christian Church, and John Chrysostom's elegant sermons invoked the image of Junia, for the Christian women of Constantinople to emulate.[35]

As a female priesthood emerged in the Anglican Church, John Paul in 1994 issued *Ordinatio Sacerdotalis*, a letter forbidding women's ordination. Although he acknowledged a "debate among theologians and in certain Catholic circles," the pope ignored the issues in explaining, simply, that because the Blessed Virgin Mary was not a minister, it "cannot mean that women are of lesser dignity, nor can it be construed as discrimination against them."

> In calling only men as his Apostles, Christ acted in a completely free and sovereign manner. In doing so, he exercised the same freedom with which, in all his behavior, he emphasized the dignity and the vocation of women, without conforming to the prevailing customs and to the traditions sanctioned by the legislation of the time . . .
>
> Moreover, it is to the holiness of the faithful that the hierarchical structure of the Church is totally ordered.[36]

Pared to the essentials, John Paul said that it was Jesus's *intent* that only men—through all of time to come—should serve as priests. But as scripture scholars pointed out, the New Testament never says that Jesus "ordained" His own apostles. Nor does scripture say that Jesus banned women, who were vital figures in His public life, from the ordained ministry. By evading the scriptural findings, John Paul's stance is antihistorical. In that sense he echoes Paul VI's 1967 encyclical on celibacy, which calls clerical chastity the "brilliant jewel" of the church, with "a maximum psychological efficiency." Pope Paul cited no psychological studies on maximum efficiency because none existed.[37] Like celibacy, the male-priests position is not doctrine, but "legislation of the time." John Paul wanted legislative permanence: "I declare that the Church has no authority whatsoever to confer priestly ordination on women and that this judgment is to be definitively held by all the Church's faithful."

Sixteen months after John Paul's letter, Cardinal Groër "retired" as archbishop of Vienna, engulfed by accusations that he had made sexual advances on young men in a monastery years before. Admitting nothing, Groër provoked a huge scandal. John Paul was silent. The financial impact took a while to register. Within weeks, 500,000 Austrians and 1.8 million Germans sent petitions to the Vatican asking for married priests and women priests. Catholics in Austria had the option of resigning from the church and renouncing a portion of their taxes designated to the church. Forty thousand resigned that year. By 2009 the Austrian church had declined from 78 percent to 66 percent of the population. Tax revenues to the church had fallen from 394.2 million euros in 1994 to 295 million euros.[38]

A key factor behind those figures was the release of Ratzinger's decree in support of *Ordinatio Sacerdotalis*, on November 18, 1995, which all but said to the incensed Catholics of Austria and his homeland, *Your views don't matter:*

> This teaching requires definitive assent, since, founded on the written Word of God, and from the beginning constantly preserved and applied in the tradition of the Church, it has been set forth infallibly by the ordinary and universal magisterium.[39]

Ratzinger's insertion of "infallibly" as part of the magisterium, or teaching office, caused bonfires of criticism. The Cambridge divinity professor Nicholas Lash decried the infallibility reference as "a quite scandalous abuse of power."[40] Sister Joan Chittister, the prolific Benedictine lecturer from Erie, Pennsylvania, wrote with surgical precision:

> Can an office of the Vatican declare a papal statement infallible?
> And can they do it ex-post facto? Any time they want to? Maybe hundreds of years after it was written?
> Why is it that when bishops all over the world ask for this issue to be discussed, they are simply ignored?
> I am now more convinced than ever that this subject is not closed, in fact it has not even been opened. It has only been suppressed.[41]

Chris Schenk was feeling numb when a call came from Auxiliary Bishop P. Francis Murphy of Baltimore, who had found sympathetic bishops with whom the women's ordination advocates could have dialogue. In 1991, after ten years of internal discussion, the bishops' conference was finishing a pastoral letter on women when Ratzinger demanded strict language against female priests. "For the first time in the entire history of the conference," writes David Gibson, "the bishops spiked the entire project."[42] On October 27, 1995, three weeks before Ratzinger's decree, Bishop Murphy had spoken at a dinner for FutureChurch. "It is critical that we who hold some authority in the church listen to the base, to the people much more than we give directives," he declared. "I have grave concerns that the official teaching church has forgotten about learning."[43]

Now on the phone, Frank Murphy said gently, "How are you doing?"

"Angry and depressed," replied Sister Christine Schenk.

"So am I," said the bishop, with a ragged sigh.

When Murphy died later of cancer, at sixty-six, she wept for many reasons, not least the loss of so committed an ally within the hierarchy.

THE CHURCH'S MONEYMEN

As Charlie Feliciano's influence receded on the handling of abusive priests, so did his distance from Pilla, who had taken to working in an office suite that was adjacent to an old dormitory of St. John College, formerly a nuns' teaching facility, behind Cathedral Square. The college was torn down; the diocese leased the land to investors who built an office tower. The bishop who had once dined at his home was remote. Feliciano, his secretary, and an assistant shared space in the chancery. Pilla had a kitchen cabinet that included Sam Miller, a Jewish real estate developer and Democratic Party potentate, and Patrick McCartan, a managing partner of Jones Day.

Joe Smith, the diocesan treasurer, had a sideline business, Tee Sports, that organized golf tournaments and corporate events. Smith organized the Bishop Pilla Golf Classic that raised money for inner-city school scholarships. One day Father Wright's secretary let slip that Joe Smith was getting paid to put on the golf event. Feliciano's brother was a partner in Baker Hostetler, one of Cleveland's biggest law firms. "Joe wanted me to sell them an ad for ten grand," Feliciano says. "I knew he was getting a cut, so I took a pass on that one."

In midsummer 1999, a lawyer from Jones Day paid a visit to Feliciano's small office. "You're unhappy," she said. "We have a proposal." The "we," he realized, was his employer, which paid the lady from a firm with steep

hourly rates to offer him a church job assisting illegal immigrants in another county. Feliciano said no, immigration law was not his specialty;
the humiliation added to his stress. Besides the internal battles over the
sheltering of pedophiles, the finances smelled bad to Feliciano. "Smith
kept saying we couldn't get pay raises, we had to cut back. It didn't make
sense to me," says Feliciano. Feliciano sat in a chancery meeting where everyone other than himself reported to Joe Smith. (Feliciano's boss was still
Pilla.) Father Wright all but swooned over Smith. Pilla worked in another
building. *What am I doing here?* thought Feliciano. *This place is like Oz.*

"Charlie did very good work in the eighties," recalls Joe Smith. "But in
that system you learn that you're always secondary to the clergy. Charlie
liked attention. In that environment you had to know when to open your
mouth and when to shut it. You swallow your pride; that's how you had to
operate. I felt bad for Charlie. I liked him. Pilla wanted him fired. Wright
was reluctant."

Feliciano was casting lines for a new job on February 17, 2000, when
his body convulsed, the left side suddenly ran stiff: he keeled over with
a stroke. Two women rushed him to the hospital. None of the chancery
priests or Pilla visited him in the weeks it took him to regain his speech
and mobility. He had long-accrued sick days, but when he recovered, the
job was gone. He got in a dispute with Wright over the severance pay
offer, and left without a settlement.

That fall Feliciano joined the law firm of Gallagher Sharp to establish a practice assisting Catholic schools. "The diocese sent out a letter
that implied if any [school] hired outside legal counsel, it could jeopardize
their insurance coverage," reported the *Cleveland Free Times*.[44] The job
dried up. As Feliciano searched for new work, his son had a severe medical
emergency; the family drained their savings. As debts mounted, they lost
their home to foreclosure.

Joe Smith took over as financial and legal secretary in midsummer 2000.
A delighted Father Wright devoted himself full-time to the less-stressful
work of the Catholic Cemeteries Association, far from the chancery.
Smith, a former college football quarterback, was a 5-handicap golfer married to the niece of a priest quite close to Pilla. Charlie Feliciano had seen
swaggering Joe Smith as one of Pilla's elite. "John Wright got tired of Pilla
calling him at two a.m.," explains Smith. "Pilla's management style was
reacting to whatever popped up. He's a charming guy. When he prepares

for a speech, he's magnificent. But he's an introvert; he worried endlessly, and it was all about his image. He got angry when the *Plain Dealer* did a story on Cleveland's ten most powerful people and he wasn't number one. The late-night calls didn't bother me as much. I'm a workaholic, but I had a family, so he wouldn't call as often."

Feliciano's disillusionment shifted to a sense of vindication when the media chain reaction triggered by the *Boston Globe* reports of 2002 hit Cleveland. The *Plain Dealer* exposed the diocese's cynical tactics. James F. McCarty and David Briggs finally identified Gary Berthiaume in a report that March:

> Berthiaume had been "watched like a hawk" during his stay at Ascension Church, with no reports of illegal behavior—a strong indication, Auxiliary Bishop Quinn said at the time, that Berthiaume had been cured of his disease.
>
> But it turned out the hawk watching Berthiaume at Ascension was the Rev. Allen Bruening—who himself would become the target of several allegations that he sexually molested Catholic grade-school children during his 20-year stay in the Cleveland Diocese.
>
> In a lawsuit filed last year, a former Ascension student accused Bruening and Berthiaume of teaming up to molest him in the school's shower over three years in the 1980s.
>
> Berthiaume . . . now works at the Centacle Retreat House in Warrenville, Ill. Berthiaume did not return calls seeking comment.
>
> . Bruening was quietly forced to resign as Ascension pastor in late 1984, after another parish family accused him of a pattern of child abuse covering the previous two decades . . . Shortly thereafter, Bruening was reassigned to another Cleveland-area parish.
>
> In 1990, the Cleveland Diocese sent him to a parish in Amarillo, Texas, but diocese officials say the bishop there was fully informed of the earlier Bruening allegations.[45]

Reporter Bill Sheil of WJW TV, Fox 8, began interviewing victims and diocesan sources. Sheil, who had a law degree, prepared a long report on Quinn, utilizing audio of his 1990 speech telling canon lawyers to send files to the nunciature, or Vatican embassy. Quinn avoided Sheil. Pilla, who happened to be in the studio for an unrelated taping, agreed to an interview. Pressed by Sheil, Pilla awkwardly denied ever sending secret files to the nunciature, or that he recycled predators. After the broadcast, the parents of a youth whose perpetrator had gone to a new parish in the 1980s, called Sheil. In a subsequent report, they accused Pilla of lying.[46]

Calls from abuse survivors to the chancery sent Joe Smith searching into clergy files, contacting therapists, dealing with reporters, signing six-figure monthly checks to Jones Day for legal help in the $300-an-hour range.[47] "Pilla called me at home many times during the abuse crisis, saying he was going to resign," says Smith. "I calmed him down." The diocese eventually negotiated victim settlements with Jeff Anderson, a St. Paul lawyer and pioneer in clergy abuse torts. As the scandal drove a shift in public opinion, Cuyahoga County Prosecuting Attorney William D. Mason convened a grand jury to investigate the diocese. As Joe Smith gathered boxes to comply with Mason's subpoenas he was taking calls from a frantic Pilla well past midnight. The bishop appointed a lay task force to evaluate the response to victims. On Holy Thursday he washed the feet of Stacie White, who had been raped as a girl by the now-imprisoned Martin Louis. Charlie Feliciano had wept on meeting with other victims of Louis. Now, as Pilla suspended other priests, Feliciano, who had slowly rebuilt his legal career, wondered if Pilla had taken his advice as a $90,000-a-year staff attorney, back in the day, he might have avoided all hell breaking loose.

By the spring, Pilla had suspended twelve priests on past accusations and identified thirteen former or retired priests so accused. Of those twenty-five clerics, the county Department of Children and Family Services had received "just eight reports," wrote McCarty in the Plain Dealer, "over the last fourteen years. But five of those reports have arrived since mid-March."[48] Feliciano broke his silence on the clergy cases, speaking to the Plain Dealer and to Ed Bradley of 60 Minutes.[49] The CBS interview aired during the June 2002 bishops' convention in Dallas, where they adopted the youth protection charter and voted to raise the petition threshold at the Vatican for selling property.

Money secrets started spilling out in August. A Plain Dealer report on Catholic Charities, the largest social service agency in Ohio's largest county, found high-end donors incensed about whether funds meant to help the poor had been routed for abuse settlements. Several major contributors revealed that Pilla in 1999 had requested $4 million from

Catholic Charities, which emptied "a discretionary fund that had been used to pay for various social service projects."

> Sources said at least some of that money was used to pay off a multimillion-dollar deficit that built up in the late 1990s during the diocese's abortive attempt to centralize and modernize its computer system.
>
> Diocesan spokesman Bob Tayek said the $4 million transaction was meant to combine two of the bishop's charitable discretionary funds.
>
> None of the money was spent on the late 1990s computer deficit or sex-abuse settlements, Tayek said.[50]

James Mason, the board chairman of Cleveland Catholic Charities, wrote Pilla, asking him to confirm that charitable funds would go to charitable uses. "These are difficult times for all," replied Pilla in a hazy understatement. "Leadership and trust have been damaged. Only concerted action over time can restore that trust." He pledged to do "everything in my power"—but gave no full promise on the use of money.[51] A culture of passivity was too entrenched for well-heeled Clevelanders to rise in unison, asking Pilla to resign, though several high-end donors did so in protest.

"None of that money was used for settlements," says Joe Smith, who was secretary for financial and legal affairs at the time. "We had built up a significant reserve in our Property and Casualty Fund. In the 1990s we had great markets, those reserves tripled in value. That was the risk pool. Timing can be everything. We were fortunate we had that money available. I never touched Catholic Charities' funds for settlement monies."

"So where did the $4 million go?" I asked.

"Mostly subsidies to parishes and schools that ran short. It happened a lot."

Roughly 60 percent of the parishes paid their assessments, or taxes, to the bishop. For the other 40 percent, expenses often exceeded the revenues from Sunday collections.[52] This situation had been building for years. Church in the City grants, handled by a separate foundation, did not go for deficit shortfalls. But diocesan finances had a chaotic side.

Michael Ryan, who has researched church embezzlements (see page 10), criticizes an embedded practice of pastors who take "walking around money" before collection funds make it into the bank. Joe Smith points to a corollary in Cleveland: "In old-school parishes, priests created slush funds. I'd say that 90 percent of the time they really had a good intention. Priests were afraid bishops would take their money. Guys would put new windows in the school or a new roof and start these funds. You have a culture of priests doing this. You have guys from parishes who end up downtown in management spots and they carry the same ideas. A lot of stuff was off the books [concealed from auditors and accepted accounting procedure]. That was the culture we dealt with—a personal culture, a business culture, a diocesan culture . . . It's the way things were always done, a way for folks not to tell anyone. Priests didn't want to deal with inconsistencies. *Priests hate confrontation*. They do what they want to.

"Pilla used to give out crisp $100 bills at Christmas to staff," Smith continues. "Maybe twenty or thirty of them; all the secretaries got one. The idea was, take your spouse to dinner on me. As bishop he'd go places, confirmations, weddings. He'd get an envelope with four hundred bucks. As his tax preparer I never saw that. What am I gonna do, beat him on the head and say, *Now, Bishop, you know you're getting money from those Masses* . . . You knew not to press it. This was a norm not only in his office. Pastors gave money to secretaries and people for Christmas. That's the way it's done in parishes."

LAMENTATIONS

To Cleveland's many priests and nuns, the news reports about clergy sex abuse were like a daily beating. The church in which they believed, the bishops they obeyed—how much worse could it get? Sister Christine Schenk was astounded at Pilla's behavior when an inkling of hope came in the person of "Stephen" (his real name withheld), a former seminarian who had been abused by a priest. Stephen had done therapy, had a good job, and had sustained a spiritual life, an excruciating challenge to most victims. (Mark Serrano, a Notre Dame graduate who grew up in a close home in the pastoral town of Mendham, New Jersey, told how seeing a priest on the altar made him think of Father Jim Hanley's genitals.)[53]

Stephen handed Sister Chris a service of healing prayers he had written. He wanted FutureChurch to sponsor a prayer service for victims. She thought his intermingling of scripture, songs, and hymns was a godsend. Joe Fortuna, the priest who had taught her master's level class in liturgy, had recently become pastor at Church of the Ascension—the parish where, years earlier, the predators Bruening and Berthiaume shared the rectory. Fortuna and the pastoral associate, Laurel Jurecki, helped Stephen and Sister Chris shape the prayer service called Liturgy of Lament for the Broken Body of Christ. Two hundred people, including many survivors and therapists, attended on October 14, 2002.[54]

Father Fortuna began:

> We have come here tonight from many places . . .
> We come together for one thing only: To raise our hearts and voices and
>   very bodies to God,
> In the hope that in the very act of raising them in lament yet in faith,
> They may be touched in their brokenness
> And know the transforming and surpassing power of God's love.

Then the choir rolled out "Were You There," a Negro spiritual.

> Were you there when they crucified my Lord?
> Oh, sometimes it causes me to tremble, tremble, tremble.
> Were you there when they crucified my Lord?

Fortuna, Schenk, and other men and women in robes lay down on the altar, an act of obeisance to God, and a ritual expression of repentance to the abuse survivors. Sister Christine took the podium. "Why would a supposedly good God allow such a terrible thing to happen to one so innocent—you as a child?" she began. "Why did God allow you to lose your childhood so early? How could this grievous betrayal happen at the hand of one from whom you had every right to expect nurture, respect, and wisdom about the ways of God? Instead, you learned fear, self-hatred, and numbing confusion about yourself and about God."

Everyone present was stunned at the galloping pace of the scandal. "Many of us here tonight," she said, "never experienced childhood sexual abuse or clergy sexual abuse, but we feel wounded and betrayed by church leaders who made decisions more protective of institutions than of persons. We want to say in some way that we are sorry. Perhaps we are like the women of Jerusalem in the gospel who witness Jesus's crucifixion and death. Watching from a distance, we come to offer what comfort we can in our presence, our sorrow, our lament, our mourning over what our institution has done to individuals."

She paid tribute to Stephen and other survivors present for affirming

> that yes, there is a God who is good and able to heal even the horrible wound of childhood sex abuse. You, more than any here, know what it is to be an earthen vessel carrying within your body the death of Jesus. And you know as well the wondrous gift of carrying within your body the life of Jesus . . . You witness that yes, there is a balm in Gilead as the old hymn says.
>
> Believers know that Jesus' suffering did not end in death but in resurrection—in new life. A dear friend once told me to never look at the cross without seeing the resurrection. When we venerate the cross we are acknowledging the reality of evil and death but even more so venerating God's power to save. This is the life journey of every believer, not only those who have been touched by the evil of clerical sexual abuse, or by the grievous structural evil which allowed such abuse to continue. All of us are journeying to a deeper, richer life as we slowly, slowly loose the power that evil holds through our belief in Christ.
>
> Matthew tells us that after crying out on the cross, Jesus "yielded up his Spirit . . . and the veil of the temple was torn in two." I wonder if we are not in that place now as a church. The veil of our sacred structure has been torn and we see it for what it is—a flawed human institution. But since we want our church structures to reflect the goodness of the God we serve, we must cry out for repentance, renewal and rebirth. We trust this Spirit to make all things new. And we claim our Church and our wounded persons once again for Christ.

The priests and female pastoral ministers in robes lay hands on the congregants in a prayer for healing.

A DIOCESE RUN AMOK

Three weeks before Christmas 2003, the county grand jury indicted one priest for child sexual abuse and, in a separate set of events, six men who had worked at Parmadale, a youth home under the auspices of Catholic Charities. Cuyahoga County Prosecuting Attorney William D. Mason seemed frustrated to some journalists as he explained that his staff had found 145 priests with accusations in their files. "But for the statute of limitations, many more would have been indicted," he said. An assistant prosecutor had presented charges of obstruction of justice and racketeering against Pilla and Quinn, but the nine-member grand jury lacked the seven votes to indict them.[55]

Although Mason's office had gotten the 145 names from the diocese, the grand jury proceedings were secret. Bill Mason, a husky fellow with reddish-blond hair and a potent political machine behind him, could stand tall for the cameras, while the faceless grand jurors bore responsibility for giving the bishops a pass. State laws long predating child abuse as a social issue shielded most of the alleged sex offenders from punishment. Cleveland was a near washout compared with Boston, where a judge had released files, abusers were identified, several prosecutions were under way, half a thousand victims were in court, and Cardinal Law had resigned in proverbial disgrace.

Ironically, Ohio had one of the better public records laws. Bill Sheil wanted the list of priests; so did Jim McCarty at the *Plain Dealer* and other journalists. Sheil lodged a request with Mason's office for documents on the priests. The diocese then threatened to sue Mason if he released grand jury information. "We are looking to protect the identity of persons who are investigated but not charged," a church spokesman offered.[56] With overhanging questions of about 145 priests, Mason, who had failed to indict the bishops, did a pirouette to become a target of the church's legal hammer. Having gained in the public media sweepstakes, Mason had his staff petition the court: would Judge Brian Corrigan, who had overseen the grand jury, release the names and files? The motion referred to "more than one thousand (1000) possible victims and four hundred ninety-six (496) possible offenders," most of them lay workers.[57]

In March 2003, the diocese's financial picture worsened. The *Plain Dealer* reported that Catholic Charities had taken a $1.4 million loss in recent donations. Catholic Charities' donor base had dropped from 104,000 individuals in 1996 to 79,000 in 2002. Pilla met with one hundred diocesan staffers to outline pay cuts, freezes in office expenditures, and selling "unused church property." Blaming the nation's economic decline since 9/11, he assured the staffers that insurance had covered the Jones Day legal bills for its help in the abuse crisis.[58] How much had the scandal cost in lost donations?

Bill Sheil persuaded his TV station to fund a law firm to research and file a motion with Judge Corrigan, seeking release of the church records reviewed by the grand jury. Prosecutor Mason's brief "lacks the courage of its own convictions," opined the WJW–Fox 8 attorneys, Michael McMenamin and Kenneth Zirm. "The requested issuance of a mere advisory opinion by this Court" would give Mason's office the leeway to decide which documents to give to law enforcement. Federal law allowed disclosure of grand jury files for compelling reasons. The TV station attorneys asked Corrigan to do the same.

> The breadth, depth and duration of sexual abuse of children within the Catholic Church, both here and across the nation, make this a matter of public and historical significance, present special circumstances and weigh heavily in favor of disclosure . . . Exceptions to grand jury secrecy are well-recognized and the First Amendment protects the right to gather as well as disseminate news.[59]

The prosecutor and diocese "may know which of these priests and other employees remain in unsupervised contact with children [but] the public does not, especially the parents of children" in Catholic schools or programs, they argued. Sheil flew east and interviewed District Attorney Paul F. Walsh Jr. of Bristol, Massachusetts, who had released the names of twenty priests with allegations too old to prosecute, citing the common good. The TV station attorneys referenced prosecutor Walsh's position, among other new precedents:

> In September, 2002, Cardinal William H. Keeler publicized the names of 83 priests accused of sexually molesting in the Baltimore Archdiocese over a period of 70 years, saying in a letter to

180,000 Catholic households, "At times we have let our fears of scandal override the need for the kind of openness that helps prevent abuse." The conduct of the Cleveland Diocese in resolutely resisting this Court even contemplating the Prosecutor's modest request for an advisory opinion stands in marked contrast to the courage and responsibility displayed by Cardinal Keeler.

The attorneys proposed the naming of a special master to review all files to ensure that no victim or pivotal witness's identity would be involuntarily disclosed. The issue was under review by the court as the year drew to a close.

THE CHRISTMAS BOMBSHELL

A central figure in the handling of Cleveland diocese finances was Anton Zgoznik, a totemic young man of six foot three who weighed nearly 300 pounds. A defensive tackle in high school football, he was a first-generation American of Slovenian descent. (His last name is pronounced Zuh-*goz*-nick.) Numbers sang for Anton Zgoznik. After studying business and accounting at John Carroll, he worked as a diocesan auditor in the early 1990s, then formed his own accounting and tax practice. Joe Smith outsourced lots of work: "We had a small staff for hundreds of entities doing audits and reviews. Anton's firm grew from a three-person office to thirty people and more than $2 million annual billing of the diocese. Anton's results were impeccable. It was all documented through our comptroller with engagement letters. Our books were regularly audited with no adjustment or review comment."

But auditors did not see off-the-books accounts, transactions apart from normal payroll or invoiced payment by standard procedure. In a sense, the off-the-books accounts were like the little parish "slush funds," only larger—sometimes, much larger.

The work between Smith and Zgoznik led to lunches, golf outings, the occasional dinner with their wives. Joe Smith, a dozen years older, had learned to submerge his ego around Pilla; he took some afternoons off to coach his two kids in sports, making up the hours at night. Pilla relied on Smith as a troubleshooter. When two of Pilla's nephews tried to get lucrative business as diocesan insurance brokers, says Smith, "I told the bishop,

'You're gonna get killed on this.' The commissions for a diocese of that size run half a million dollars and it's publicly documented. Legit or not, no good would come of it for him. He thought about it, then said: 'I don't want anything to do with it—but you take care of it.' I had to tell the nephews no. They weren't happy."

Anton Zgoznik, with an infant at home, put in marathon hours building his company. He drove his employees mercilessly, leaving a trail of people who quit or were fired. The list included the best man at his wedding, Zrino Jukic (pronounced Joo-kich). Zrino was not as tall as Anton but was nearly as large. Zrino idolized Anton. He, too, had an accounting degree, though Zrino Jukic's work ethic was more casual. He never bothered to take the ethics portion of the CPA certification test, and he neglected to file his own tax returns for several years.[60] Catholic high schools had been outsourcing their financial record keeping to Anton Zgoznik's company. Zrino Jukic assisted the education secretariat of the diocese, as a kind of outsourced CFO. The job overwhelmed him. When Zgoznik slashed his handshake share of the company, Jukic was livid, yet he held Anton Zgoznik in a mixture of awe and fear. Zrino Jukic's bad feelings spilled out in late December 2003 at a bar with several church employees who were also hostile to Anton. As drinks flowed, they recalled Anton's blowout Christmas parties: work them like a tyrant all year, then turn up the friendship, booze, good tidings to all come Christmas—a sentimental boss. The guys decided to send Anton a Christmas present he would not forget.

The anonymous letter dated December 24, 2003, was addressed to Jay Milano, an attorney who had seven abuse lawsuits against the diocese. The letter criticized a pattern of "consulting payments" by an "extremely large vendor of the Diocese of Cleveland . . . Mr. Anton Zgoznik." The letter listed seven corporate names Zgoznik used and also took aim at Joe Smith.

> The person in charge who chooses to give the work to Mr. Zgoznik is Mr. Joseph Smith, who receives such payments under JHS Enterprises ($451,596) and under Tee Sports ($226,635) as indicated in the attached material . . .
>
> [Zgoznik's] firms have been paid a few million dollars each year for the last few years to perform services for the Diocese that

some feel are either not needed in the fashion as prepared by the consulting firm[s], totally unnecessary at all, or somewhere in the middle . . . [T]he Diocese has been paying the millions per year in bookkeeping/accounting/computer/consulting fees when the Diocese could easily hire employees for a small fraction of that cost. In addition, this would probably explain why there were no raises for the dedicated employees of the Diocese this year, thus further explaining why this particular consultant is so disliked by those here at the Diocese office. I understand the Diocese has been advised to make payments to Mr. Zgoznik's companies in small enough amounts as not to raise any red flags with the auditors.[61]

Jay Milano knew the legal equivalent of lava when he saw it. So did Jim McCarty of the *Plain Dealer* and Bill Sheil at Fox 8: both found the same hot package on their desks after Christmas. Obligated to disclose a potential crime, Milano sent copies of everything to the U.S. Attorney and the diocese, whose documents had landed unsolicited on his desk. On January 6, 2004, the Feast of the Epiphany, Joe Smith was summoned to Pilla's office. Sitting with the bishop were two attorneys. Steve Sozio, of Jones Day, was a former federal prosecutor who had worked closely with Smith in steering the diocese through the abuse crisis. Peter Carfagna, a Harvard Law graduate, chaired the diocesan financial council. Carfagna, formerly with Jones Day, was a corporate counsel in professional sports. His face telegraphed huge dismay. "Joe," said Bishop Pilla, "I have something terrible to tell you." Pilla got flustered and left the room. Steve Sozio showed Smith the documents sent by Milano and said, "I think you better get a lawyer, Joe." Sozio hoped an internal investigation would find a reasonable resolution. Smith was suspended with pay for a month; he never returned.

The *Plain Dealer* soon reported that Joe Smith had raked in $750,000 from Zgoznik's firms in outsourced church accounts. Smith's Tee Sports Inc. received more than $225,000 as "a marketing firm that runs golf tournaments," wrote McCarty and Joel Rutchick. On TV Sheil magnified the image of a diocese reeling from a sex scandal that toppled into a financial debacle.

"Smith made false representations to a member of the Diocesan Financial Advisors and a Diocese attorney," a Jones Day attorney wrote to

a claims analyst with AIG Technical Services in New York, as the diocese sought a settlement from its crime insurance policy for "Employee
Dishonesty—Joseph H. Smith." The letter, which surfaced much later as a
public document, telegraphs the strategy that emerged in the early months
of 2004:

> In records created for [the Cleveland diocese], Mr. Zgoznik eu-
> phemistically characterized his hundreds of thousands of dollars
> of payments to Mr. Smith as part of some so-called "executive
> compensation package" . . . Smith apparently will claim that at
> least some of the so-called "executive compensation package" was
> authorized by Father John Wright, who until late 1999 preceded
> Smith in the position of Financial and Legal Secretary of the Dio-
> cese. Father Wright categorically denies ever doing so, however.[62]

By then, the diocese had commissioned an Ernst & Young audit that
accompanied the letter.[63] Insurers do not usually pay a settlement to a
financially victimized client without a verdict. Insurers will, however, in
some cases pay legal fees as part of a settlement, since it takes legal work
to prove theft. The church later issued statements saying it had been paid
a claim, but did not say how much.[64] By the agreement, AIG relinquished
its right to sue guilty parties to recover the insurance loss, according to
Smith. If AIG launched discovery depositions against Smith and Zgoznik,
the two defendants would seek church documents by subpoena in return.
Steve Sozio, wisely, did not want that.

FBI investigations of complex financial transactions often move slowly.
Gathering documents is laborious; investigations on different cases can
overlap. Federal attorneys want a full grasp of evidence before bargaining
plea agreements (if such are to be) or distilling documents into a story line
for a jury. A jury can better grasp Olympian greed if the documents fit neat
patterns.

On February 27, 2004, Judge Corrigan denied WJW TV's motion for
the grand jury documents on the 145 priests, ruling that without a legal
proceeding to compel the evidence, he lacked the authority on a media
request.[65]

The next day Bishop Pilla, looking sad, held a news conference to
provide data on the diocese's handling of abusive priests. Pilla produced

numbers in accordance with the national bishops' conference youth pro-
tection charter as adopted in 2002. That very morning in Washington,
D.C., the National Review Board for the Protection of Children and
Young People, made up of twelve prominent lay Catholics (including
Leon Panetta and Washington attorney Robert Bennett) who had been
commissioned by USCCB to research the crisis, released their report. The
USCCB president, Bishop Wilton Gregory, made headlines in saying,
"The scandal is history."[66] The bishops released data on perpetrators, vic-
tims, and financial losses as tabulated by the John Jay College of Criminal
Justice. Pilla was giving a local report with numbers already reported to
the John Jay researchers. Pilla announced that 117 priests and one deacon
had been accused of sexually abusing youngsters since 1951.

Bill Sheil of Fox 8 asked Pilla how many priests with accusations
he had sent to new assignments. Since 1989, said Pilla, "about three."
(Berthiaume left in 1988.) Haltingly, the bishop added, "I don't want to
misspeak."

"He's lying," Charlie Feliciano told *Cleveland Free Times*. "He transferred them out of state and within the diocese." At least fifteen priests,
he said.[67]

Quite a story lay in the numbers. The Boston archdiocese had agreed to
an $85 million settlement for 542 victims. The Cleveland diocese, for 285
people making abuse charges, said it had paid $14.4 million for "compen-
sation, treatment and legal costs." Three million dollars had gone to legal
fees; the church did not say how much of the $11.4 million was absorbed
by clergy treatment costs. Compared with the Boston abuse survivors, the
Cleveland survivors received a pittance.[68]

Plain Dealer columnist Regina Brett drew a bead on the 117 unnamed
priests and one deacon trailed by allegations.

> Where are those men now? Diocesan spokesman Bob Tayek gave
> me a breakdown:
>
> - 20 are on administrative leave waiting for a ruling on
>   whether they can return to ministry.
> - 20 are in active ministry.
> - 28 are deceased.
> - 18 have resigned.

- 19 are priests from religious orders not under the diocese.
- One was a diocesan deacon who has resigned.
- Eight are priests not identified by their accusers.

The remaining four priests are from outside the diocese or returned to ministry when allegations could not be substantiated. That accounts for all 118 accused. Except the Cuyahoga County Prosecutor Bill Mason came up with a different number: 145. Tayek doesn't know who those 27 are. Mason knows but by law can't tell him.[69]

The cover-up under Quinn, Wright, and Pilla had recycled predators, kept most of them unprosecuted, saved the diocese major costs in providing settlements to victims, and with Judge Corrigan's timely boost, kept most of the abusers unnamed and gave the diocese control over those still in ministry.

PAYBACK

As his public image took a drubbing, Pilla caved in to traditionalists in the chancery and punished FutureChurch. Here was a way for Pilla to prove his defense of the church; he felt no allegiance to the group. Future-Church had grown to five thousand dues-paying members with a $260,000 budget and a small paid staff that organized Catholic groups to sponsor educational programs, prayer services about Mary Magdalene, and discussions regarding the future of priestly ministry and women's roles in the church. After fourteen years of live and let live, Pilla announced on April 1, 2004, that FutureChurch's activities were "not appropriate" for church facilities.[70] "We are both sad and puzzled," the group said in a response Schenk and Trivison posted. "During Pope John Paul II's papacy, the number of priests in the world declined by 4% while the number of Catholics increased by 40%." Restricting the priesthood to celibate males "makes celibacy more important than the Eucharist." They called for "respectful discussion" on "systematic inequality of women in the Catholic Church."

Through Cleveland's aching scandal, Schenk had held back from criticizing Pilla. The promoter of Church in the City had betrayed people who had shared his vision. As the media drubbing intensified, the nun had

even written Pilla a personal letter of support. Now Pilla was making FutureChurch a scapegoat. The *Plain Dealer* in covering the story published a
leaked e-mail Schenk had sent her board. She was blunt. If pastors refused
to ban FutureChurch, she said, and if John Carroll University and her
religious order gave them a welcome mat, "what can the diocese do? Kick
out a priest for allowing discussions when they haven't kicked them out
for sexually abusing kids?"[71]

"I console myself that Jesus was rejected by his own tradition," she
told Tom Roberts of the *National Catholic Reporter.* "So was Paul. He was
thrown out of all the best synagogues in the Mediterranean world, so when
I get upset that one diocese or the other won't let me speak on church
property, I just remind myself that it's all part of it."[72]

That August, Joe Smith had his five-bedroom house on the market
for $579,000, when Charlie Feliciano opened his newspaper to read that
Smith had a new job: CFO of the Columbus diocese! Feliciano detected
an old pattern: as the bishops had shuffled the pederasts, so now with the
money-grubbers. Feliciano thought again, *Joe Smith must have a lot on Pilla.*
Columbus bishop James Griffin "said that he had spoken to Pilla about
Smith and that a Cleveland auxiliary bishop had strongly recommended
Smith," the *Columbus Dispatch* reported.[73] Feliciano knew that Jimmy
Quinn and Jim Griffin had been classmates in seminary and law school.

The Ernst & Young audit had satisfied the Cleveland diocese's insurance company to pay "an unspecified damage claim," the *Plain Dealer*
reported. The insurer "then filed a claim against Smith to recoup the
money."[74] If Smith had lied on January 6, 2004—as the Jones Day letter
to AIG stated in laying out the theft-insurance claim—why did Pilla recommend the man his diocese accused of lying and theft to oversee church
finances in Columbus?

Smith says he was never sued by AIG.

How did he get the Columbus job after being sacked in Cleveland?

Smith told me that Matt Brown, the Columbus diocese's outgoing fi-
nance director and a longtime friend, arranged for him to meet with
Bishop Griffin. Griffin in 2002 was the first prelate to ban the Legion of
Christ and Regnum Christi from his diocese. "So I go down and talk to
Griffin," states Smith. "He says, 'Joe, you're probably overqualified. Tell
me what happened.' For an hour and a half I told him everything, how
I wanted to leave for a better-paying job. I'd had an offer [in 1996] to

sit on the board of Blue Cross for $30,000 a year. Pilla wouldn't allow it. John Wright wanted to keep me. He told Anton to find out how much CEOs in similar positions were making. He said to cover [the difference] in off-the-books accounts. Wright wanted it that way. When I finished, Griffin said, 'I know Tony Pilla. You got caught up in a Tony Pilla mess.' "

Griffin, who is retired, refused to make any comment when I called him. But Griffin's hiring of Smith, after the explosive media coverage, is all the more striking because *Griffin was a lawyer*. Signaling his trust in Smith *despite* the messy compensation package, Griffin obviously did not think he would get indicted.

Charlie Feliciano had another take. The diocese's internal dynamics reminded him of the mafia. On June 5, 2005, he filed suit on behalf of thirty-seven Cleveland parishioners as plaintiffs in state court against Pilla, Smith, and Zgoznik, accusing them of defrauding the diocese, seeking $1 million in restitution, and demanding that Ohio's attorney general conduct a full investigation of the diocese "as a charitable trust."[75]

The court dismissed the suit on the grounds that Feliciano's clients "must claim that they personally have a particular interest in the substance of the trust." But, tellingly, Judge Stuart A. Friedman opined: "The Court finds that it does have jurisdiction over allegations of fiscal mismanagement, even when the alleged misconduct relates to the operation of a hierarchical church, so long as matters of faith, dogma and religious practice are not impinged."[76] Disappointed, Feliciano had nonetheless magnified the ties between Pilla, Zgoznik, and Smith, who was then at work in Columbus.

In January 2006 Bishop Pilla, age seventy-three, two years shy of mandatory retirement, decided to retire. "It's time for a change," his statement said.[77]

Sister Chris Schenk flew to Rome in late March, leading a pilgrimage of thirty-one women on a tour of ancient Christian sites. A second-century fresco in the catacomb of Saint Priscilla depicts a woman breaking bread, the Eucharist, with six other women. "We would like to talk to our leaders," she said in an NPR interview, "and tell them of our experience—how we can begin to re-institute that wonderful balanced leadership we had in the first three centuries of both women and men leading the communities."[78]

Still in Rome, on April 4, 2006, she heard the news: Pope Benedict had appointed Bishop Richard Lennon of Boston to take Pilla's place. Schenk had gotten an earful on Lennon in late February at a conference in Boston, where she met Peter Borré and others in the vigil movement. When a reporter called Borré for comment on Lennon's new position, he blurted out, "God help the people of Cleveland." To the best of his knowledge the quote never ran.

CHAPTER 10

PROSECUTION AND SUPPRESSION

For a second time, Richard Lennon assumed control of a diocese damaged by dishonest bishops, concealed sex offenders, and mismanaged money. Lennon's mentor Cardinal Law had left financial craters, and although Archbishop Seán O'Malley was now himself a cardinal, Boston's debt hole had grown steadily deeper. In Cleveland, Lennon found a different milieu. Despite the abuse scandal and overhanging financial questions, many people thought fondly of Pilla for his pastoral warmth and Church in the City agenda. Retired in his hometown, Bishop Pilla was still saying Masses as the FBI investigated Joe Smith, Anton Zgoznik, and the web of diocesan finances.

Despite the agonizing inner-city poverty and issues of deferred maintenance in Lennon's new diocese, Cleveland Catholic Charities had a budget of $92 million, nearly three times Boston's. The programs afforded a bishop access to media photo ops and events to meet donors and politicians to establish his presence. Dick Lennon was an introvert. Although he made public appearances, he typically got to his desk before dawn, toiling some nights till eleven. His formal manner was often brusque; the thick Boston accent held few hints of joy. At a meeting for clergy dialogue he spoke for nearly three hours, leaving a brief window for priests' comments. Most priests had found Pilla warm and approachable. Lennon was cold, though he gave Cleveland his workaholic best.

Lennon arrived as a virtuous counterweight to the sleazy, unfolding narrative about church finances. On August 16, 2006, a federal grand jury indicted Anton Zgoznik and Joseph Smith (who then resigned as CFO of the Columbus diocese) on an array of counts for money laundering, mail fraud, and filing false income tax returns. A pivotal charge centered on a 1996 agreement in which Father John Wright, identified in the indictment only as "the then Financial and Legal Secretary," agreed to pay Smith $270,000 above his salary, as a bonus for staying on the job. The bill of particulars stated:

> The understanding was that the payment would be in lieu of any additional raises for the next five years, other than cost-of-living increases. ZGOZNIK participated in the arrangement by helping to urge the Financial and Legal Secretary to agree to the payment and by helping transfer the Diocese funds under the arrangement.[1]

An attorney for Wright said he had been "duped" and "unfortunately placed his trust in individuals that [sic] abused that trust," reported the *Plain Dealer*. "He didn't give Smith a raise and then say, 'Go put it in a secret fund and don't tell anybody about it.'"

> Zgoznik's companies got $17.5 million from the diocese between 1996 and 2003, prosecutors said. In return, Zgoznik paid $784,000 to companies owned by Smith. Those payments were kickbacks, prosecutors said.[2]

Reading the account, Charlie Feliciano shook his head. Father Wright, who idolized Joe Smith and played golf with him and Anton, needed *urging* by Anton to embrace Joe's sweetheart deal? Wright officiated at Anton's wedding; he baptized his baby boy. Although Feliciano was glad to see the wheels of justice finally turn, the indictment was odd in its reliance on the passive voice. A special investments account "was set up" using the diocese's not-for-profit tax ID. The only check signers were Joe Smith—and Father Wright.

Every indictment has a narrative strategy. Prosecutors develop a story line for judge and jury as the investigation settles on its targets. The prosecutors choose the key witnesses, and documents, to build a case. If necessary, some witnesses get immunity. Successful testimony typically comes from people who were victims, witnessed crimes or the steps that led to crimes, or had a role in such acts and are eager to avoid prison. If Father John Wright was "duped," why was Pilla passive about Joe Smith's heading down the road to manage diocesan finances in Columbus after being sacked in Cleveland?

Catholic Charities and the Catholic Diocese of Cleveland Foundation issued a joint statement that funds were "being properly managed to benefit children, the elderly, people who are poor and so many other important ministries." Financial reports were posted. The diocese announced full cooperation with the U.S. Attorney and said it was "taking steps to recover lost funds . . . Any suggestion that the Diocese of Cleveland or its leadership approved or knew of the conduct alleged in the indictment at issue is flatly wrong and inaccurate."[3]

LENNON'S AGENDA TAKES SHAPE

On January 30, 2007, Bishop Lennon, his spokesman, and a nun on his staff met with the FutureChurch founders Father Lou Trivison and Sister Chris Schenk, along with two of their colleagues. They wanted to strike a dialogue for preserving parishes and foster cordial ties without conflict or censure from the bishop. In Pilla's final year, the diocese had forced FutureChurch to vacate rented space at St. Mark parish; the group moved to a storefront office in the inner-ring town of Lakewood.

Bishop Lennon listened, nodding occasionally as Sister Chris cited a national study which found that 40 percent of merged parishes lost members, while churches that stayed open with "parish directors" did better.[4] When she was done, Lennon noted that he'd been in Cleveland for eight months; why hadn't he seen them before? Unsure whether it was a threat or a compliment, she took the question as rhetorical. The priest shortage, he said, was *not* the problem. "It's all about demographics and finances." (In Boston, with its soaring debt, he had told Father Josoma's group it was not about money. In Cleveland, it *was*.)

Schenk and her colleague Emily Hoag pointed out that the diocese's Vibrant Parish Life Committee had cited the priest shortage in its statement.

Lennon reiterated: the problem was *not* the priest shortage—42 percent of Cleveland's parishes were in the red; *that* was a problem. When two priests were serving ten thousand people in the suburbs, and fourteen worked in a small radius in the city with far fewer parishioners, he had to assess the assignments. Schenk replied that urban parishes anchor neighborhoods; they could keep on with pastoral life coordinators, trained laypeople and religious sisters. Lennon gave an example of three urban parishes that agreed to merge. For that, said the bishop, "People thanked me." In contrast, he continued, another parish had spent down its savings to $218,000. How wise was that?

Three years prior to Lennon's arrival, the diocese had embarked on a process called Vibrant Parish Life, in which groups in small geographic areas met to assess their strengths and needs. In Boston, clustering had been the first step to closures, merged parishes, then Suppression. Like a dutiful debater, Lennon cited data, rebutting his visitors in a respectful manner that was nothing if not resolute. Schenk took comfort that he had refrained from criticizing FutureChurch for being at variance with church teaching, as Pilla had done in the swamps of scandal. Still, she couldn't shake the impression that Lennon was rehearsing his talking points for later consumption. Sometimes, said Lennon, it took someone coming in from another place to have a fresh vision. In Boston he had closed or merged sixty-two parishes, with only a 2 percent drop in Mass attendance! Some Catholics in Boston had *thanked* him.

Not the ones I've spoken with, thought Sister Chris.

Lennon ended the meeting, saying the hour they had requested was up.

Several days later the Cleveland Catholic Diocese released a financial statement. In 2006 the diocese reported revenues of $269.2 million, up $6.4 million from the preceding year. The diocese was in the black. Collection baskets had yielded $106.1 million, a 2 percent increase and "the highest since 2002 when the church first began to feel the impact of the clergy sex abuse scandal," reported David Briggs in the *Plain Dealer*. The parochial schools, however, had a $26 million deficit. Spread across the parishes, from affluent to poor, church expenses had risen by 3.8 percent, while revenues lagged at 2.4 percent. Nevertheless, compared with Boston's financial disaster, and the New Orleans archdiocese's free fall after Hurricane Katrina, when 80 percent of the city flooded, Cleveland was in decent shape. Briggs scrutinized problem areas:

The more than 20 percent jump in parishes operating in the red shows the wealth was not evenly shared. Many parishes in cities or inner-ring suburbs trying to hold on to their elementary schools face a particularly difficult road. The mixed financial results come as the diocese is going through an extensive process . . . in which all parishes will be placed in a cluster with up to five other churches.

The clusters will work on plans for shared ministry. The changes could range from staggered Mass times to the closing or mergers of some parishes and schools.[5]

On January 16, 2007, the PBS series *Frontline* aired a documentary by Joe Cultrera, *Hand of God*, that followed the Boston crisis through the long impact on Cultrera's family, from his brother's childhood abuse by a priest through his parents' despair as the archdiocese closed their parish in Salem. As Bill Sheil watched the film, the reporter-anchorman was mesmerized by a sequence that opens with Lennon, in a Roman collar, smothering the lens with his hands. After watching the film, Sheil secured permission to air the scene on Fox 8, which ended Lennon's honeymoon with the Cleveland media.

As Lennon backs away from the camera, a short, bearded guy in a baseball cap enters the viewfinder: Joe Cultrera, with the Boston chancery building in the background. Cultrera tells Lennon, "I'm doing a film here. Doing a film about my family and the church . . . and need some shots here. This building—it was ten years ago my brother came here to report his abuse. Do you have a problem with me shooting here?"

"Well, sir, it is private property," says Lennon, who stands a full head taller than the filmmaker. At this point Lennon is not identified.

"I did twelve years of Catholic school," says Cultrera.

"That does not—"

"My family put so much money into this church."

"No, no, that has nothing to do with it," replies Lennon, turning away, waving his hands in a dismissive motion.

Provoked, Cultrera starts mimicking Lennon. "No, that has nothing to do with nothing. It's always *take, take, take*."

Lennon turns. "Sir," he says icily, "if you think you're going to make me feel bad about this, you're not."

"No, I know you guys don't feel bad. You don't feel anything."

"No, that's not true. You can say whatever you want. The thing is that this man"—the cameraman—"had been asked to leave."

"Then he asked me, and I said, 'Don't worry, go ahead and shoot.' "

"As if *you* have authority," retorts Lennon.

"I do have authority."

"No, you—"

"Same as *you* do. How much money have you put into the church?"

"That— Sir, that—"

"My family has paid for the church. All you've done is taken."

Again, Lennon turns to leave.

"You've got to walk away," Cultrera calls. "You have no argument!"

Taking the bait, Lennon turns again. "Sir, you have nothing to say. You've paid for nothing. Your family paid for nothing."

"We've paid with our souls, paid with our cash!" he cries in a near-operatic retort.

"*Nahhh,*" sneers Lennon.

"—paid with our church—"

"Nice try," replies the bishop dismissively.

"You took our church."

"Nice try. Nice try. It's all in your head, sir. You're just a sad little man. Sad little man."

Lennon walks toward the office. Cultrera snaps: "You're a sad big man. You're a sadder big man."[6]

The film excerpt then cuts to the home of Cultrera's parents in Salem, and the family's realization that the priest who argued with Joe was Bishop Lennon, the architect of Reconfiguration, the man who shut their own parish.

For the broadcast of the segment in Cleveland, Lennon refused Bill Sheil's request for an interview. The diocese sent a statement by the bishop:

> I went outside to ask the people to leave this property. The parties involved were never identified and the sole issue in our exchange involved their presence on private property. I was taunted and treated in an extremely unprofessional manner, resulting in the exchange as portrayed in the documentary.

The camera can be cruel to one caught off guard. Perhaps Lennon had no idea why the cameraman was there. Cultrera, quickening to the chance for spontaneous drama, says, "It was ten years ago my brother came here to report his abuse. Do you have a problem with me shooting here?" Lennon at that point in time had met with some of Boston's abuse survivors, but as the archdiocesan building looms behind him, the bishop offers not a word of sympathy for Cultrera's brother. Nor does he try to finesse a new start for the hungry camera. Why *not* let some guy in a baseball cap film exteriors of a building that TV news has shot countless times? Instead, making it a turf war, Lennon projects his response to protesters bunkered down in Boston churches he wants to sell—*it's private property!*—and comes off an insulting bully.

Several days after that embarrassing clip on Fox 8, it could not have been easy on Lennon as he entered the City Club of Cleveland for a scheduled talk. Eleven years had passed since Pilla condemned regional sprawl, promoting Church in the City. Could Lennon charm Cleveland's civic elite? "There are many things that a bishop is engaged in internally," he began. "Preaching and teaching, celebrating the sacraments and pastoral care . . . I entitled our little talk today, 'The Church Going Forward.' " The transcript suggests Lennon spoke extemporaneously or possibly from notes. The syntax is excruciating:

> Certainly, one of the things that strikes me but also strikes many people as looking for the church's attention at the present moment is the need for education and formation within the Catholic community . . .
>
> We are in need of solid religious education in the parish programs for youth in our Catholic schools and, in particular, as the Catholic bishops in the United States increasingly have focused on is adult education and formation. There's a crying need for all of us within the Catholic community to know our faith so that we in turn may live it as fully as possible.[7]

Declaring "no shortcuts" for adult religious education, Lennon mentions his work for vocations. Then he cites two phases in Vibrant Parish Life.

The first one was to invite parishioners of their diocese as parishioners of parishes to reflect on the vibrancy, the vitality, the energy of their particular parish to really come to understand who they were and what they were doing with the idea that the second phase would be when parishes would then begin to work together to enhance and to better what their internal life had been.

There are all kinds of concern about what may happen with the clustering. I must say in the past week and a half since the letters went out, we have received only four replies, two of which was congratulatory, one was questioning and one asked for reconsideration.

I think the low response is reflective of how the process was done and the respect with which the various parish requests as to who they would be clustered with were respected.

To a very large percent, the parishes were clustered with those who they had mentioned in their own report. My hope is that this will be an opportunity for all of our parishes and all the people in the parishes to enhance their own Catholic life . . . The clustering process with the good will of the people and their energy will in fact do what Bishop Pilla had envisioned to be an opportunity for the church to revigorize itself going forward.

Returning to "the church's interaction in the larger community," Lennon assessed Catholic education:

The schools, especially as we see them, but not exclusively in the inner cities, the church is committed to not only educating, but helping people to give them an opportunity . . . I have visited now twelve of our Catholic high schools, many of which have large numbers of nonCatholic students, and I feel confident that the contribution we're making is indeed a helpful contribution and a significant one. It does challenge us, however, as a church to be able to continue to offer this because of resources and personnel, and yet I personally would want us to be able to always offer what we're offering today.

Turning to Catholic Charities, with its large budget, he was on surer footing, reviewing various programs, and thanking members of the development office in the audience "for all that they have done . . . so that we, as a diocese, can make a contribution to the larger community."

Bishop Lennon cited scripture to convey his idea of faith.

> As we go forward as a diocese, we do so in a dual relationship, as I see it. One relationship as a bishop, I call the Catholic community to a deeper relationship with God. First and foremost, we are a religion. We are a faith community. So, as a bishop, my concern is a relationship with God that, in turn, enlivens the lives of individuals so that they in turn may have a committed relationship with all of their brothers and sisters in these eight counties. When Our Lord was asked what is the greatest commandment, he answers very succinctly, to love God and love your neighbor. And that is still our charge today. That is my charge as a leader of the Catholic community—to work with those in the church to deepen those relationships so that we're ever more faithful with the mission that the church has been given, that God's kingdom will be on earth as it is in heaven.

In the question period, someone asked if the clustering would see a shift from the city "out in the suburbs and rural parishes." He said, "I don't see where that needs at all to be, you know, exclusionary of the—you know, the Church and the City. One of the first things I did when I came here, I read all those documents . . . I did not see where clustering a group of parishes in a section of the city precludes relationships with the parishes in the suburbs . . . I think the two can go along, you know, side by side." To a similar question, he responded, "In this year's financial statements to the diocese, again sent to everyone, shows that forty-two percent [of parishes] are operating in the red. So I think that clustering at least since mid-summer if not before, I have consistently spoken that the main reasons are threefold. Demographic shift, number one. Number two, is the whole question of financial viability, and number three is the decreasing number of priests."

Out of the mangled sentence structure, Lennon at least acknowledged what he did not say to FutureChurch leaders: the priest shortage *was* a factor.

VICTIMS FOR THE PROSECUTION

Judge Ann Aldrich, who would preside over the Smith-Zgoznik trial, had been appointed to the federal bench in 1980 by President Carter. With a law degree from New York University, staff experience at the Federal Communications Commission, and twenty-seven years on the federal bench, Judge Aldrich was nearly eighty. Despite her reputation as a liberal with a sympathy for civil liberties, she denied the request by Zgoznik's counsel to learn whether the prosecution had given immunity to any witnesses.

In another motion seeking evidence, Smith's attorney, Philip Kushner, took a knife to the diocese's Achilles' heel: "The indictment takes no position regarding whether Father Wright was authorized to pay Mr. Smith additional compensation, or to not disclose it on the [diocese's] financial records, or to conceal it from others within the Diocese." Kushner made no issue of Smith's $270,000 off-the-books compensation. Smith, however, was accused of taking $784,624 in other fees. "Father Wright was not duped," declaimed Kushner.

> [Wright] is a financially sophisticated attorney. He arranged for other Diocesan employees to receive compensation through the Zgoznik Entities, so that it would not be disclosed on the [diocese's] books and records.[8]

In 1996, while financial and legal secretary, Wright also became CEO of the Catholic Cemeteries Association, which had 170 employees and seventeen sites. Wright left the chancery in 2000 to handle Cemeteries full-time. "Cemeteries was a cash cow," Charlie Feliciano told me with a shrug. People buy in, die, loved ones follow. Kushner's motions suggested he owned a map of where evidentiary bodies lay buried. Moreover, the digest of an FBI interview with Zrino Jukic stated that

> the reason this money was given to Smith was because he was invited to be on the Board of Directors for Blue Cross Blue Shield and other companies; however, Bishop Pilla would not permit him to sit on these boards. Because of this, Smith was going to leave the Diocese while he still had the opportunity to pursue other more lucrative business ventures. Jukic went on to say that

Marilyn Ruane, secretary of the Diocese Cemeteries Association, was on the payroll of Resultant Corporation but didn't work
there. Ruane was Father Wright's girlfriend.[9]

"John was in love with Marilyn," says Smith matter-of-factly. "I did
Marilyn's tax returns. John met Marilyn at St. Bernadette's. I always
thought he'd leave the priesthood and marry after his dad died, but he
stayed a priest."

"The defense of this case centers on whether Mr. Zgoznik believed he
was authorized to make the payments to Mr. Smith and what the Diocese
knew about those payments," asserted Zgoznik's attorney, Robert Rotatori, in another evidentiary request. Certain payments "were, in large part,
for Father Wright" because Wright's "friend . . . needed work."[10] Marilyn
Ruane began work at Cemeteries in 1997 on a salary of $31,500, which
ramped up to $81,000 by 2004, prompting the scornful tone of the jour-
nalist Bill Frogameni, writing for the *Cleveland Scene*: "If the raises seem
a bit outsized for a religious entity funded by the dollar donations of little old ladies, Ruane isn't talking. 'I really don't want to comment about
that,' she said sweetly when contacted by *Scene*, 'but thanks so much for
calling.' "[11]

Whatever the precise nature of Wright's relationship with Ruane, he
helped her find work, routing funds through a subcontractor for compensation, according to Kushner. Kushner charged that the diocese "routinely
gave additional compensation to employees" outside the conventional
payroll methods, "including many of the witnesses in this case, such as
Father Wright . . . . [and] Bishop Pilla." John Wright and Joe Smith had
played golf together, sometimes with Anton Zgoznik. Now, it was every
man for himself. Smith was pulling out what he knew about the clergy
old-boy network and its ethical liabilities to mount a defense. Kushner
wanted the diocese's copy of IRS findings from a late-1990s audit because,
he alleged, "the IRS determined that the Catholic Universe Bulletin had
consistently failed to report additional income paid to individuals"—
more off the books! As the evidence scrimmage pitched back and forth,
Kushner accused the diocese of destroying records, a charge unproven.
His discovery requests did not yield all of the materials he suggested would
exculpate his client;[12] but he planted the unmistakable impression that

Pilla had a rewarding relationship with his ex-quarterback on money, Joe Smith:

> The Anthony M. Pilla Charitable Account [has] assets in excess of $500,000 . . . It has never appeared on the [diocese's] books and records. Bishop Pilla withdrew money from the account for his own use in a manner designed to conceal the transactions and his use of the funds.[13]

Jones Day attorney Stephen Sozio accused Kushner of a fishing expedition. Kushner had indeed tossed juicy bait to the press: "After the indictment in this case, Bishop Pilla resigned and filed amended tax returns which account for some of the activity in this account." Pilla had written a check payable to cash for $180,000 from the account and deposited it with the diocese, asserted Kushner. The diocese attacked Kushner's "scurrilous accusations." But for all of the church's pushback, the persona of Pilla–as–gentle pastor faced a competing image: the bishop who lived like a lord. For as the *Plain Dealer* tracked the money, some $78,000 that attorney Kushner said "was secretly funneled" to the bishop, reported Mike Tobin, went to

> furnishing and remodeling a spacious Geauga County home that was to be used as a getaway spot. Pilla kept many of the household items—including a large-scale television—after the diocese sold the Munson Township house and 30-acre lot in 2003. Movers took the furnishings to a home Pilla owns in Cleveland Heights . . .
>
> Diocesan spokesman Bob Tayek said private donations paid for improvements at the Munson property. After the sale, items in the home were split among diocesan headquarters, St. John Cathedral and the Cleveland Heights residence that Pilla inherited after his mother died.
>
> "The diocese is responsible for a retirement residence for him," Tayek said.
>
> The Munson home was donated to the diocese in 1995 by Larry Dolan, now the owner of the Cleveland Indians, who suggested it

be used as a retreat house for the Cleveland bishop. The house was intended for whoever was serving as bishop of the Cleveland diocese, not just Pilla, Tayek said.[14]

The diocese had sold the house in 2003 for $696,000 to a company managed by Peter Carfagna, a board member of the Catholic Diocese of Cleveland Foundation and a high-level professional sports attorney. Of the $383,000 in renovation to the large home, Tayek said that it had all come from private donations. Jim McCarty of the *Plain Dealer* had done research on the house for an earlier report.[15] The reporter had spoken with one of the six Dolan siblings who had grown up there. "I kind of ambushed Matt Dolan, a lawyer and former assistant county prosecutor," McCarty told me, "and asked him about the decision to give the estate to the diocese. Dolan said the intention was to convert the home into a diocesan retreat house or an old priests' retirement home, although those provisions weren't written into any sort of agreement."

Joe Smith told me, "Pilla felt he had earned the house through his time as bishop. His mom would stay out there with him. The Dolans were pissed at us and they should have been: the purpose was for priests to get away from the parish, and relax—a house in the woods with six bedrooms upstairs, a pond and a creek and tennis courts. Pilla wanted the property in his name. I went to see Pat McCartan, Jack Newman [another Jones Day top partner], and Peter Carfagna to figure a way to do this without all of us winding up in the can. It was the damnedest thing. Pilla had complete access to the place; he was afraid that when the next bishop came he would throw him out. He wanted the house in his name. Then it came out in the press, so we're selling it. I think Peter Carfagna decided to help Pilla out of the jam. Pilla tells me, 'You go out and clean it up.' So I'm spending days in this fricking house, making sure it's cleaned, bills paid, overseeing Jimmy jobs on repair . . . He wanted someone he could trust. He was so concerned about his image."

The evidentiary motions fed deeper coverage in the *Plain Dealer*. "The Anthony M. Pilla Charitable Account wasn't a secret fund but rather the former bishop's personal savings account," reported Mike Tobin, referring to a fund at $500,000 plus. Stephen Sozio of Jones Day, for the diocese, accused Joe Smith of trying "to impugn Bishop Pilla by arguing that the transactions . . . on which he actually advised the bishop were somehow untoward. They were not."

But why was Pilla's account secret? Why so many secret accounts? And how docs a bishop amass half a million dollars plus in private savings?

"Smith was comfortable receiving additional compensation in this fashion because Bishop Pilla had a similar investment account," wrote Kushner, implying a bishop in harmony with secret payments to upper-echelon personnel.

On June 14, 2007, Judge Aldrich ordered the diocese to provide many of the financial records the defense requested, though not the IRS findings. The files included payments of $27,200 to the family of a deacon who had lost his job at a high school for making sexual advances to girls. The disclosure of payments included a loan approved by Father Wright for $60,000 in church funds to another female secretary. Kushner was taking off the gloves as Jones Day lawyers positioned Pilla and Wright *as victims*.

Judge Aldrich framed the core issue of the approaching trial:

> The defendants' position is that while the evidence sought would cast doubt on the credibility of Bishop Pilla, Father Wright and the Diocese, it *also* and *primarily* serves to rebut the factual assertions Bishop Pilla and Father Wright make—that the Kickback Scheme could not have been authorized, was not authorized, and was not similar to common, questionable practices used by the Diocese.[16]

"Bishop Pilla, Father Wright, Joe Smith, they were all stealing," Charlie Feliciano told the *New York Times*. "It was a corporate culture that was corrupt at almost all the top levels."[17] Disappointed that Pilla and Wright escaped indictment, Feliciano took comfort that his thwarted civil case of defrauding a religious charity would be distilled into a federal criminal proceeding.

A thorny legal issue arose: a tape recording as prosecution evidence.

In January 2004, with the diocese in damage control over the secret files, Anton Zgoznik was at a conference in Las Vegas. Stunned to hear Joe Smith had been sacked, Zgoznik made his first call to the priest who had blessed his marriage and later his infant son: John Wright, who confided that he had gotten an attorney. *Hang in there*, he recalled the priest saying. *Remember that Joe worked for you.* Anton Zgoznik felt alone on an island.[18] When he reached out to Zrino Jukic, both men smelled trouble. On January 12, two days after the story broke, Zrino lodged a digital tape recorder into his right sock. Anton, as he said later, "was the type of person that could have tried to blame me."[19]

They met in a parking lot, which is rarely a good sign.

"The fucking assholes," Anton snarls to Zrino. "See, this is what happens when nobody communicates. Okay, Joe's trying to claim it's a consulting fee from us." Anton confides that lawyer Steve Sozio, for the diocese, has asked him why he paid Joe Smith all that money. "Obviously, you and I would never give a kickback," Anton says. To which Zrino says, "No."

"It was executive compensation," continues Anton Zgoznik. "Cause that's exactly what we have to say."

"Right."

"Father Wright is behind this. You know that as well as I do."

"*He is?*" blurts Zrino Jukic.

"They hooked us into their system," says Zgoznik, of the diocese.

"Right."

Zgoznik gets down to the point. "But you gotta help me out with Joe and Father and say that they authorized this."

"They did," replies Zrino Jukic.

Anton tells Zrino to confect a document to show that.[20]

Zrino Jukic drove home in the toxic residue of a Christmas dirty trick and put the tape in his dresser drawer where it slept for several months until he met with the federal prosecutor, John Siegel. As Anton Zgoznik's business crashed, Jukic hoped his tape would keep him from being indicted.

Judge Aldrich ruled that the recording was hearsay damaging to Smith, who was not present. Thus, separate trials for Zgoznik and Smith.

Anton Zgoznik's trial began the last week of August 2007.

Joe Smith sat in the audience, taking copious notes each day.

Zrino Jukic, as the prosecution lead witness, testified that while in Zgoznik's employ, Anton "told me that Joe was asking for a percentage of the business that the company was getting from the Diocese . . . ten percent." Jukic claimed to have no "control over the situation. So I can't say I challenged him." Pressed by prosecutor Siegel as to whether it "would be legal for you" to help facilitate such payments, he said, "No."

Siegel rejoined: "Did you agree to go ahead and do it anyway?"

"I did."

As he gave more answers, Zrino Jukic showed himself still hurting from the jilt.

> I started to realize that I was not an owner in the company . . . I was being reviewed and treated like an employee just like everyone else. My salary was determined by Anton. I didn't come in and say, "These are my clients and [I] brought in so much as revenues; as a partner, that's mine." No, that was not the story.

Jukic several times mentioned "kickbacks" to Joe Smith, finally eliciting an objection from defense attorney Robert Rotatori over a term yet unproven. Rotatori jabbed at Jukic for his failure to file personal income taxes "in 1997, 1998, 1999 and 2000"—he had finally filed them, several years later. A detached observer might see why Zgoznik subjected him to a job review, and wonder how a guy who failed to file his tax returns qualified as a financial adviser. Rotatori in trying to attack his credibility sought to portray Zrino Jukic as a snitch.

> ROTATORI: *What's your expectation as you sit here today about your being prosecuted with regard to your personal tax returns that you described in your testimony?*
> JUKIC: I have no expectations.
> *You don't believe you will be prosecuted?*
> I don't control that. I have been asked to cooperate as a witness, and that's what I've done . . . Nothing was promised to me.

In contrast to the corpulent Jukic who double-crossed his friend, the slender Father Wright in his Roman collar was a bland personality. He wore glasses; his silver-gray hair was carefully parted. He had entered seminary after law school and a broken romance. By virtue of his background and education, Pilla had made him secretary for legal *and* financial affairs. The job ran nineteen years. Cemeteries was less demanding than the chancery post: more time to be a pastor, more time to be with friends. From lawyers' huddles came the agreement not to grill Wright about "the girlfriend," since he was not on trial.

"We were friends," Wright said of Joe Smith. "I relied on him totally for his financial experience. I felt Joe was a hard worker and he did a good job."

When Rotatori questioned him about payments to a computer consultant with money routed through Zgoznik's company, Wright said, "I was not aware of that." Did he know how the subcontractor was paid? "I never really inquired . . . I assumed the diocese was paying him directly."[21]

Wright admitted to arranging a $60,000 loan for one of his secretaries, Maria "Mitzy" Milos in the late 1990s. He cleared it with Pilla: "We didn't work out the specifics, but he told us to work it out." Mitzy Milos's loan was not on church ledgers; when she fell behind on payments, Wright paid the $50,000 balance from Cemeteries. Mitzy Milos repaid it through paycheck deductions.

Against the image of a benevolent boss, Wright was a cipher on questions of deep money. He had no recollection of Zgoznik's contractual ties to the diocese; he did not remember signing the first $185,000 bonus check for Smith in 1996, when his salary was $70,000. When Smith assumed his job as Wright moved on to Cemeteries, in 2000, he knew Smith was earning $135,000. "He said that he was going to negotiate his salary with the canonical advisors," said Wright. That much, he remembered.

On the fulcrum issue of why and how in 1996 Wright approved a total bonus of $270,000 for Smith not to seek private sector work, he was hazy.

> ROTATORI: *Did you not ask Anton Zgoznik to check with universities and hospitals and see what they were paying their chief executive officers?*
>
> WRIGHT: No. I don't recall doing that. I just recall Anton saying Joe would be making twice as much out in the public.

Wright did allude to a twist of regret. He had met with another priest, his spiritual director, to discuss whether to tell Pilla about a $270,000 off-the-books bonus. That dialogue of entombed secrecy (his spiritual adviser had passed on) confirmed for the Georgetown law graduate that he could, in conscience, keep mum on how Joe Smith got his money. Despite that nebulous notion of guilt, Wright's memory hole deposited the ethical burden onto Anton Zgoznik.

Bishop Pilla took the stand. The smooth, dulcet tones of a homilist yielded to terse answers as a witness. "I considered it a very close relationship," he said of Smith. "He was of great assistance to me because I'm not a business person. I have no training in that."

Bishop Pilla's use of money, secret accounts, the foiled grab for the Dolan house, were off-limits for questioning. His motives and behavior were not on trial. In the prosecution script, Tony Pilla was a victim. What, asked Assistant U.S. Attorney Siegel, did the bishop think of that anonymous letter that spilled out the news of payments between Smith and Zgoznik?

"Shocked," testified Pilla. "I had complete trust in Mr. Smith. He was a valued co-worker in whom I had great confidence and trust."

Shocked, registered Charlie Feliciano of testimony that recalled for him the scene in *Casablanca* when the police chief in Humphrey Bogart's nightclub orders a probe of backroom gambling, saying *Round up the usual suspects!* just as someone hands the chief his winnings. But Charlie Feliciano was not on the jury.

Pilla said he knew nothing of the Wright-Smith agreement for the off-the-books bonus of $270,000. Nor, testified the bishop, had he known that Wright allowed a longtime executive at Cemeteries, Tom Kelly now, to retire, draw a pension, and continue to work, billing the diocese as a subcontractor off payroll. Father Wright felt for Tom Kelly: his wife had Alzheimer's; her care costs were skyrocketing. Still, when Rotatori asked Pilla if he had discussed Tom Kelly's deal with Wright, the bishop had no memory.

The silence between Father Wright and Bishop Pilla on diocesan finances hovered like a monolith, damp in folds of fog.

Only after the scandal broke had Pilla discussed Smith's bonus with Wright, "expressing my serious concern, that I was not informed or consulted, in a reprimanding way, and my disappointment," asserted the bishop.

"It would have been nice to hear more from the bishop," one juror remarked after the trial. "He played deaf, dumb and blind up there."[22]

One hurdle to Pilla's victim-credibility was the job Smith got in Columbus. Pilla testified that Bishop Griffin had called him several weeks after Smith resigned—a surprising phone call, said Pilla, who then read from a letter he had sent Griffin: "At no time did you ask for, nor did I give a recommendation." Griffin did not testify: Smith's job was irrelevant to Zgoznik's charges. And so Pilla read the letter—his self-defense—on how another bishop had hired Joe Smith.

As prosecution and church lawyers sparred over what various witnesses should or could not say, more hushed huddles ensued at the bench.

"I'm beginning to feel like the judge in the O.J. Simpson case with all of these sidebars," Her Honor said at one point. "I don't normally work like this."[23]

When Zrino Jukic's secretly taped conversation was presented, Anton Zgoznik's scramble to keep himself from being the fall guy was on full display. "We'll say they wanted us to keep a confidential payroll going on," Anton tells Zrino, "because they wanted to compensate the key executives of the diocese. It's gonna be our word against theirs."

Later, he says, "Zrino, we did not kick back any money."

"I know, I know," replies Zrino. "We got sucked in. We didn't do anything"—though Zrino was sucking in Anton via the digital device in his sock.[24]

When Anton Zgoznik took the stand his biggest challenge was to rebut the black image of himself from the tape and Zrino Jukic's knifing testimony.

"I was the only one of my family born here," he began. "My father died when I was in college. And, you know, we had no aunts or uncles, so in essence, I had to finance a lot of my education . . . with the support of my mother." Recounting his employment history, the founding of his firm as chief diocesan vendor of financial services, he began rushing, giving longer, nervous answers, apologizing to judge and jury. But Anton Zgoznik was emphatic on having met with Wright to review Smith's job and the contested payments of $185,000 and $85,000. In those discussions, he learned the diocese had assets of $3 billion. Details like that do not come from thin air. How had he gotten the money to pay Smith?

> Basically, what I did is find unrestricted money that was sitting in the Finance Office, and basically, you know, I found that pocket of money and moved that money into their checking account.
>
> Now, that money was held as like a liability on their books, but it was really unrestricted. Once the money was moved from that investment account, for that liability into their checking account, the Diocese would have enough to make a payment to cover funds for Mr. Smith.

Under Siegel's questioning, Zgoznik grew flustered, volunteering, "I was not happy about taking money off the books, and I told Smith and Father Wright, you guys have to go another way. Taking money off the books is not right for me or the Catholic Church, Mr. Siegel. I was concerned about the appearance of doing something like that behind closed doors."

Emotions welling, Zgoznik went far beyond the question about how the second check was written: "I am on trial because they don't want to take responsibility for their decision making. And you know what? They are human beings, but they are *blaming the wrong person!*"

Huge and shaking, he spun into a choking carousel of self-defense: "Yes, I had good understanding of the Diocese, but I earned my work unequivocally, categorically. Anton Zgoznik would never buy the work! I would never buy the work. *I would rather take a gun to my head than steal from my own religion!* This is my church we are talking about, my church to House of God that I love. *I would rather take a gun to my head, and if I get convicted, Mr. Siegel, kill me, please.* Because anybody that takes money from his own religion should die! *I deserve to die.* Anton Zgoznik doesn't deserve to live—"

"Sir!" interjected Judge Aldrich.

"—if he pays the kickbacks," groaned Zgoznik, in near hysteria.

"Would you please calm down?" said the judge.

Anton Zgoznik composed himself.

In closing arguments his attorney Rotatori had to maneuver around the devastating taped conversation in which Zgoznik tried to confect a defense for himself and Zrino Jukic. Rotatori outlined Zrino Jukic's many problems saying, "That's why he made up these lies." But after his client's overflow of self-pity on the stand, Rotatori stopped short of a full attack on the diocese's cozy world of financial insiders. "Never, ever, ever question the clergy" is how he explained his client's flaw. So had Anton been taught as a boy, so had Zgoznik worked as a man. "Never doubt the priest. Whatever the priest tells you to do, you accept."

In contrast, federal attorney John Siegel told the jurors in his summation: "There was no way Bishop Pilla would know, the diocese would know."

When the jury returned, Anton Zgoznik was convicted on fifteen counts of fraud, kickbacks, and tax charges. His wife was weeping.

Judge Aldrich let him stay free on bond till sentencing. Rotatori promised to appeal in remarks to the press more barbed than his closing argument: "The diocese permitted this type of program to go on. They permitted the improper transfer of charitable funds for noncharitable purposes."

He hit that one dead on the money.

EVIDENCE OF THINGS UNSPOKEN

When Joseph Smith stood trial ten months later, Zgoznik was still free on bond. Judge Aldrich wanted the second case done before meting out prison time for the two defendants.

Too smart to testify in his own defense, Joe Smith had a paramount advantage over Zgoznik: the Smith jury would not be exposed to Zrino Jukic's taped conversation with Anton. Judge Aldrich ruled it inadmissible as hearsay evidence: Smith was not present as the two men schemed on how to defend themselves in entanglements with him. Nor would Smith's trial be subjected to messy fireworks by Anton Zgoznik giving testimony: the prosecution could not gamble with so volatile a witness.

Without a secret tape to convey his would-be probity against Anton's desperation, Zrino Jukic made a weak witness. Kushner chopped like a butcher on Jukic's failure to file income taxes, the bypassed CPA-ethics test, his role as a cooperative witness hoping to not get nailed. When Kushner maneuvered Jukic into a statement on Wright's girlfriend, Aldrich told the jury to disregard gossip. Kushner then asked Jukic, "And did you have personal knowledge that that was true?"

"No."

"What was the source of that information?"

"I had a conversation with Anton—"

Besmirching a priest on hearsay!

In cross-examining Wright, Kushner had a witness whose vanilla personality nevertheless gave answers as a sinner might reveal in confession.

> KUSHNER: *You didn't need to report to anyone the decisions you'd made regarding Mr. Smith's salary, correct?*
> WRIGHT: Correct.

And you were concerned that if you didn't give him a raise he would leave, correct?

Correct.

And you did not want him to leave?

I did not want him to leave . . .

And, in fact, it is fair to say that you regarded him as your right-hand man?

I would say that's true.

. . . but you didn't want anyone to know, because you were concerned that they would want a raise, too, if they knew. Is that right?

That's correct.

And so you concealed the fact that you had agreed to give Mr. Smith a raise from others, true?

Correct.

And you concealed it from the Payroll Office?

Correct.

And the Benefits Office?

Correct.

And from your secretary?

I did not tell my secretary.

And you concealed it from the Finance Council?

I did not tell the Finance Council.

You concealed it from the diocese attorneys and outside lawyers?

Correct . . .

Nevertheless, Wright insisted that Smith and Zgoznik had presented *him* with the payment plan: "They said no one will ever find out."

Cemeteries was making good money but falling short of funding the perpetual care of certain plots when Wright assumed the reins in 1996. "And you offered [Smith] a thousand dollars a month if he would help you with turning things around . . . true?" asked Kushner. "That is correct," said Father Wright.

By 1997 Joe Smith as CFO had a base pay of $70,000, plus $12,000 from Cemeteries, plus the $250,000 bonus to cover five years of raises. Moreover, testimony from a witness given immunity confirmed that Smith pulled in $1,200 a month in a sweetheart deal from a church insurance vendor on his Florida condo. If we factor the bonus at a per annum $50,000, Smith was earning $146,400 before the profits from Tee Sports, which ran the Bishop Pilla Golf Classic and such functions. In 2000 his base pay rose to $135,000. In sum, the church was paying Smith as well as the private sector that Father Wright wanted to prevent him from joining.

The trial elicited similar testimony from Pilla as before. The jury had to decide between the prosecution's version of a financial cover-up and kickbacks by Smith and Zgoznik—or the defense's version of a secret deal between Father Wright and Joe Smith, with Zgoznik as the outsourced vendor routing the money, all done according to the diocese's secret methods. The jury acquitted Smith on the fraud and kickback charges; he went down on six charges of filing false income tax returns, including failure to report $150,000 in earnings.

"At the end of the trial I thanked the judge," says Joe Smith. "She told me, 'I know you're not guilty of the diocesan stuff—in fact you're the victim.'"

The self-serving words of a convicted felon? That is one interpretation. Judge Aldrich, who ordered Smith (and Zgoznik) to make financial restitutions, died before I was able to contact her about Smith's comment. Well before that, the prosecution presented Aldrich with federal sentencing guidelines for the scope of charges on which Anton Zgoznik was convicted: ten years in prison. Aldrich gave Zgoznik the identical one-year-and-one-day sentence as Smith. A year and a day means eight months if an inmate shows good behavior. Smith and Zgoznik each served the short sentence, returned to their families, and began picking up their lives.

What does the legal resolution tell us? Pilla and Wright were never punished for running a religious charity like a set of fiefdoms, making their own rules for spending Catholic donations. Under oath, Wright admitted keeping Smith's bonus a secret from Pilla and the supplemental pay of $784,624 over seven years. Why was Wright afraid to tell Pilla what he confided to another priest, his spiritual director? The most plausible answer is that he feared Pilla would not approve—Wright didn't want a bishop's scrutiny on how his barony facilitated funds to his girlfriend or Cemeteries' Tom Kelly, just as Pilla did not want others snooping into his $500,000 savings account or the deed he coveted for the house donated by the Dolans. Secrecy ruled the financial baronies.

In the end, Judge Aldrich saw Zgoznik as a fall guy for church officials' dishonesty. The winner was the Jones Day law firm. All those billable hours! Steve Sozio did what high-dollar defense attorneys do for dirty clients: he turned them into witnesses against smaller fish. The U.S. Attorney did what prosecutors do: move the case with the strongest evidence. The big piece was Zrino Jukic's secret tape recording; the weak link, Wright and Pilla as victims. Had Rotatori done a better job cross-examining Jukic and Wright, and had Zgoznik never testified, his trial may well have ended differently. The Smith jury rejected the charge that his nearly $785,000 off-the-books were kickbacks. Smith told me his attorney's fees exceeded $1 million. The Cleveland diocese surely spent several times that to protect Pilla, Wright, and what credibility they had.

ASSETS TO THE SUBURBS

As the financial scandal receded, Bishop Lennon got down to business. In March 2009 the diocese announced it would close twenty-nine Cleveland parishes outright and an additional forty-one would merge with others. Across the eight counties, fifty-two churches in all would close. The inner-city and inner-ring suburbs accounted for thirty-eight closures, the poorest neighborhoods bearing the brunt. Akron, Elyria, and Lorain—which was poorer than Cleveland, since a Ford plant downsizing—lost twelve parishes among them.

"Some were big surprises—St. Ignatius of Antioch, St. James in Lakewood and St. Colman in Cleveland," wrote Michael O'Malley in the *Plain Dealer*:

> Shutting down Colman and Ignatius means the darkening of two brilliantly lighted West Side steeples, both of which are prominent landmarks reaching into the city's skyline . . .
>
> "The suburbs are isolated from the poor," said Colman parishioner Carol Romansky of Berea, noting how inner-city neighborhoods took the biggest hits in the downsizing. "Would Jesus have stayed in the suburbs?"[25]

"We're just too big for the number of people that we have," Lennon told Mike O'Malley, as emotions roiled in many of the targeted parishes.

Cleveland did not have the black hole of deficit financing Law had left Boston. Indeed, for all of his petty greed and secrecy, Tony Pilla, like a wily ward boss, had paid attention to the real estate; he kept old churches open, even as maintenance costs and unpaid assessments rose. Catholic Charities would counter the worst ravages of urban decay. Although his diocese did face tough realities that a prudent plan of limited closures could have mitigated, Lennon's rationale stemmed from Boston, liquidating assets to cover the operational shortfalls. For Cleveland, Lennon took preventative steps. But Cleveland in 2006—four years after Pilla's frantic midnight calls to Joe Smith—had *gained* $1 million in parish Offertory donations, taking in $106.1 million, while Boston since 2002 had steadily registered losses and deficits. Cleveland had seen a drop of $2 million from 2002 in reaction to the pedophilia cover-up. But in 2004, the Sunday plates began a steady climb and in 2005 registered $104.5 million. In 2006—the year the secret files on Zgoznik and Smith made headlines—the collections rose again, by $1.6 million.[26] Quite the opposite happened in Boston, which one could take as a popular repudiation of Lennon's Reconfiguration plan. Cleveland's numbers track the national data cited in the prologue of Catholics who kept giving *to their parishes* despite the spectacle of their bishops slogging in scandal muck.

Lennon approached Cleveland like a banker redlining loans in poor neighborhoods. As chief executive officer he would follow the trail of prosperity, shift priests to suburban parishes, recapitalize the diocese. Shuttering inner-city churches and historic gems in old enclaves was pragmatism. In Boston he had suppressed wealthy parishes in order to sell churches in plugging a deficit that trailed back to the 1990s, exacerbated by the abuse cases. In Cleveland he would prevent deficits with early, tough chopping-block decisions.

"He was clueless about Cleveland philanthropy," explains Sister Christine Schenk. "In Los Angeles, the archdiocese does an annual collection for the urban parishes. We mentioned that at our meeting with Lennon. But he came with his own mind-set to do it his way without recognition of the safety net woven by Church in the City. This diocese was used to interactive decision making. Some parishes needed to close, perhaps fifteen rather than fifty-two."

Lennon sketched his logic in a sequence of short pages resembling a PowerPoint presentation via the diocesan website. The Catholic population had declined by 19 percent since 1975. Mass attendance was down 56 percent, to 29 percent.[27] Despite the cost of maintaining inner-city churches, Cleveland had a tradition of people from the suburbs driving in for Sunday Mass in the old neighborhoods, which undergirded Pilla's Church in the City program. Pilla's plan became Banquo's ghost for Lennon: he could not escape the urban church in the memory of Catholic Cleveland. Instead of summoning the hope inherent in faith as an appeal for hard-times generosity, Lennon tried to sell people on fear.

An Overview of Key Diocesan Realities
Financial Erosion

- Some parishes are using savings to fund deficit spending
- Deferred maintenance of many parish facilities is a big and increasing concern
- Catholic assets are being used in our Diocese just for the purpose of maintaining more buildings than we can realistically support due to the changed demographics
- 60 parishes have negative net savings (liabilities exceed savings)—27 do not involve mortgage debt
- 17 other parishes have positive net savings of less than $60,000 (low reserves for emergencies)
- Parishes own these assets; yet, it is the Diocese that is compelled to respond to the emergencies[28]

A parish owned its assets but, like a slave in the antebellum South, it did not own itself. This reality radiated from Boston to New Orleans, from Scranton to New York City, back again to Cleveland and elsewhere as shuttered parishes joined Peter Borré's Council of Parishes. Canon law calls the parish a "juridic person." Conflicting opinions of canon law in diocesan bankruptcy cases demonstrate that the bishop has the power to suppress a juridic person, take its assets, and issue a death warrant for sale or demolition of the physical plant.

FutureChurch flew into action with e-mails to area parishes and information kits, matching sympathetic canon lawyers with protesting parishes.

In Cleveland, twenty-eight Catholic churches had already been designated as historical landmarks. Under Lennon's order, eight would be closed. "St. Casimir, one of the biggest and most beautiful churches in the diocese, also learned its Polish Masses will be coming to an end," reported the *Plain Dealer*.

> "St. Ignatius is everything a Cleveland diocese should be," said Cleveland City councilman Jay Westbrook. "It's like the United Nations here. They have an integrated school and church. This is where the diocese should be taking its stand."
>
> "Understandably, there will be sadness and upset," Lennon said in a statement posted on the diocese's Web site. "There may well be questioning why us and not them. And even for some there will be anger."[29]

The "upset" extended to Father Joseph Mecir, pastor of Sacred Heart of Jesus in Slavic Village, who said in a sermon, "This is a real blow to us. We were not expecting this at all. We are the only parish in Slavic Village whose bills are paid. We are not in the red at all. We have no idea why this came about."[30]

Lennon's plan, for all of its foreboding tone, had no data from urban planners, public officials, priests, or nuns. It was Lennon all the way.

An Overview of Key Diocesan Realities
Sense of Urgency Needed

- In total, the finances of the Diocese and most parishes are not in a crisis state . . . *today*
- However, there are indicators of immediate or pending crisis for many of our entities
- All parishes must proceed with a sense of urgency before there are more crises than we can handle
- Often the process of closing parishes appears to be about finances
- Granted, finances often create the final sense of urgency
- However, finances are a trailing indicator of stress in a parish
- The leading indicators and real causes are the demographic shifts that began long ago in our area, continued for many years, are still occurring at present[31]

Removing icons, statues, and paintings was like "ripping out copper plumbing in foreclosed houses," bristled Councilman Westbrook. "If the diocese is going to make closing announcements and just let the community suffer the consequences, it will require us to enact stricter legislation."[32]

Michael Polensek, a city councilman for more than thirty years, represented Collinwood, a lakefront ward and ethnic quilt that included old Slovenian streets where he had been raised. "I went to see the bishop," Councilman Polensek told me. "Even though I'm a lifelong Catholic I made it clear this would be a massive fight and it would not be pretty. Lennon said, 'The numbers aren't there, the flock has moved.' Many of the figures I wouldn't dispute."

But Polensek knew the four parishes in his ward were in the black. "They were maintaining the racial stability," he said. "Here's my Catholic Church telling me we're going to vamoose from the old, the poor, the indigent, and above all a racially diverse neighborhood. Is that the message you really want to send? Lennon is not very warm. I don't know if the diocese is better off financially because you've got so many angry people. He's caused so much animosity."

Lennon was flanked by police officers when he went to officiate at the final Mass of the Hungarian church, St. Emeric. A group called Endangered Catholics protested outside, singing "God Bless America."

"The St. Emeric community wanted to buy the church for a cultural center," continued Polensek. "He wouldn't sell it to them. It's that kind of in-your-face stuff that's so insulting and unsettling. These are people who fled from Europe, came here for religious freedom; I heard the stories as a kid of men and women who carried the bricks and raised the money. He comes here without respect to knock down churches. Some of these architectural gems were abandoned. My great-grandmother's church, St. Andrew's at Fifty-fifth and Superior, I drove down there when it was demolished. They didn't even take the bells out of the tower. It was one of only two examples of Spanish Mission architecture in the city. They never took the wrought-iron cross out of the tower. My mother sent me over to get some bricks. I wanted to drive down Superior Avenue with one of those bricks and say, 'You know what, you SOB? You couldn't take the bell and cross out of the tower! That's a sacrilegious act!' "

Polensek did not finish the metaphor of brick usage when we spoke in the fall of 2010. "Collinwood used to be a stand-alone village," he continued. "It's predominantly African American but we have a lot of Italians, Irish, and Lithuanians. Senator George Voinovich still lives in the neighborhood. We have a high concentration of city employees, working class, a great sense of pride. We presented documentation to the bishop on each parish. We started a campaign—letters, e-mails, eliciting support from Baptist and Jewish leaders to say these are not just houses of worship, these are neighborhood institutions. If you close these it has an impact on stability. Because of pressure we were the only neighborhood not to have a closure."[33]

Father Bob Begin, who had helped Central American refugees in the 1980s, was pastor of St. Colman. Begin had been studying Arabic in his off hours for several years, anticipating work with Iraqi refugees in America. He hoped for a sabbatical to further his study, but when the closure list came out, his parish was on it. Begin went to see the retired bishop Pilla.

Did Pilla have friends in Rome?

Rome will never reverse a bishop, Pilla told him. Solve the problem locally.

Begin asked if Pilla knew Archbishop Pietro Sambi, the papal nuncio in Washington. "I do know Sambi and you should write him." But, added Pilla, "you need to think of the church as your mother. You may not agree, but she's your mother—you love her."

Archbishop Pietro Sambi made a good impression on embassy row in Washington. The nuncio had silver hair and deep forehead creases that lent dignity to his image after four decades as a diplomat. An Italian trained in canon law, he spoke English, French, and Spanish and had previously served as a nuncio in Indonesia, Cyprus, and Israel. He had worked with Cardinal O'Malley in arranging for Benedict to meet several Boston abuse survivors on his 2008 trip to America. Before that, Sambi had negotiated with Palestinian militants to free people in the siege of a Bethlehem basilica. Lennon's Darwinist plan for Cleveland may have seemed small by comparison, but Sambi took Begin's letter seriously. A priest who writes the papal delegate about his bishop knows the letter will go right back to the bishop, who can make his life hell.

"I am deeply troubled," began Begin. After the cluster groups' many meetings, "the Bishop made decisions that completely disregarded our recommendations," he wrote.

The inner cities are places where you are most likely to find the very poor, the homeless and the near homeless . . . The neighborhoods are very fragile. The inner city parish then provides a lot more to the social fabric of the neighborhood than a place to worship. To be sure the great artistic miniature cathedrals that the various immigrant peoples have built at great sacrifice are a real oasis of beauty that the people truly appreciate.

Each parish to some extent has developed and organized leadership in the community to provide safety, sustenance, emergency assistance, and programs for children, etc. When a Church closes, that component of society is removed with the landmark buildings and the already fragile social fabric rapidly disintegrates.

The bishop was ignoring these factors, wrote Father Begin. (Meanwhile, several parishes had appeals in motion to the Congregation for the Clergy.) "For the inner city residents of Cleveland this is a grave scandal," continued Father Begin to Archbishop Sambi, "a real abandonment not only of Church property of inestimable worth, but also as a real abandonment of truly needy people."

On the West Side of Cleveland, the recently arrived refugees from Somalia, Liberia, Congo, Sudan and other parts of Africa who have found a welcome in our Churches and a place at the table are devastated and confused by the news of closures. Many of them became Catholics in refugee camps because of Catholic Relief Services. Others are becoming Catholic because of the welcome they are given in our inner city parishes (the only place they can afford housing) . . .

I have a forty-year history of working with the poor in the inner City of Cleveland and I myself am dismayed. It seems that in one or two years, the work of 40 years can be destroyed by the arbitrary action of Bishop Lennon.[34]

Four thousand people filled out forms on the importance of the parish, which Begin sent to the bishop. "Lennon had no idea that 30 percent of people in this neighborhood do not have cars," Begin told me later. "Every day at least fifty people come to our door in need of something. The phone rings all day. We need a full-time outreach worker. I explained this to him. If you're from Boston and look at Cleveland, it's kind of the way Cleveland looks at Alabama: you're surprised if someone from Alabama has a good idea. At another meeting, he said if I was still interested in studying Arabic, 'talk to your friend Sambi.' Council members Jay Westbrook, Dona Brady, and Matt Zone showed him a map of the Lorain Avenue Corridor—four square miles without a church. State Senator Tom Patton talked with Lennon. He helped defeat a motion in our legislature to remove the statute of limitations on pedophilia—which Ohio bishops lobbied hard against, having seen California dioceses lose hundreds of millions in lawsuits after a 2002 state law opened the statutory filing window."

Lennon reversed his decision on St. Colman and St. Ignatius of Antioch, another inner-city parish. "I now have a more complete understanding of the extent of social and community services at the parish and the outreach of the diverse neighborhoods," Lennon said in a May 1, 2009, letter, rescinding the two closure orders.[35] "The reprieve comes with conditions," wrote Tom Roberts of the *National Catholic Reporter:*

> Fr. Robert Begin has been placed on a four-year clock to end a trend of deficit spending and complete needed capital repairs; to continue growing "in households and in Mass attendance"; to strengthen parish finances and to establish "emergency reserves and build preservation reserves"; and to "remain dedicated to its outreach ministries while becoming a more financially viable parish."[36]

"Lennon is a hard man to figure out," Begin told me, months later, as more priests contacted Sambi to complain about Lennon. "Lennon has a fixation about what he wants to do. He evidently read a book about franchise management. He makes his decisions as if parishes are franchises. If there's enough room in one church to worship, why have more than one? A particular mission, ethnicity, none of those things mean anything if the customer base can be satisfied by one church."

BEATING THE DRUMS IN ROME

Leaders from a large swath of parishes were enraged at the bishop when Peter Borré pulled into Cleveland for a June 27, 2009, meeting at the public library of Westlake, an inner-ring town. Had Cleveland controlled the water distribution to its near suburbs, as Columbus did, the city could have annexed dozens of townships like Westlake, amplifying the tax base to benefit the core. Instead, the diocese helped the mayor's office with lifelines to the inner city. Forty people from Voice of the Faithful, Future-Church, and the upstart Endangered Catholics came to the event. Eleven parishes had taken the path of canonical appeals, most of which would end up with Carlo Gullo as he framed the arguments, often in dialogue with Peter Borré, in pleadings to the Signatura. Lennon had shuttered parishes with pivotal neighborhood ministries in Akron and Lorain, too.

Borré, comfortably tanned, wearing jeans and a red button-down shirt, began self-effacingly, "I know a talking head from out of town is not what you need." He turned to the closures. "Lennon was the architect of what happened in Boston. Now you have him—"

"How did you get rid of him?" asked a lady.

"It took us two years," he said, shaking his head. "A Boston auxiliary bishop told a group of priests, 'This is a disaster we will never repeat.' That is Lennon's legacy. One cannot be cynical about losing one's spiritual home."

Other bishops had been ruthless, too. Anthony and Noreen Foti of Scranton presented a numbing portrait of the suppressions under Bishop Joseph Martino. Two months later, the sixty-three-year-old Martino abruptly resigned after a six-year tenure "distinctive for an almost non-stop round of battles with Catholic academics, Catholic teachers' union, Catholic politicians and a range of other groups, including his own peers among the Catholic hierarchy," noted the *National Catholic Reporter*.[37]

New Orleans archbishop Alfred Hughes had gotten Mayor Ray Nagin to order reluctant policemen into two vigil churches, one of them on the National Register of Historic Places, hauling several parishioners into patrol cars.

In Boston, explained Borré, with eighty-three closures announced, the archdiocese stopped at sixty. "We mobilized nine vigils. The press thinks of vigils as people with candles. This is civil disobedience. After all of this in Cleveland, Lennon spared two parishes 'on reflection.'

"As I've gone around, I've been very clear that the chances of success are low. Then why do it?" He paused. "Even the Communists did not destroy churches in the Eastern bloc. They turned them into houses of the people which have slowly been returned to the church."

He mentioned Archbishop Raymond Burke, prefect of the Apostolic Signatura, who in 2004, while yet in St. Louis, suppressed a Polish parish. St. Stanislaus Kostka had an 1891 charter under which the then-archbishop allowed a parish board to control their finances. The board in 2004 claimed its properties and assets totaled $8 million. Although the amount was never independently verified, Burke wanted to fold the parish into a common structure of nonprofit parish corporations in order to limit the assets available to sex abuse lawsuits. The parish council spurned Burke's suppression order; unable to negotiate an agreement with him, they hired a Polish priest as pastor. Burke excommunicated the lay leaders and the pastor, Marek Bozek. The Vatican dismissed Bozek from the priesthood; he continued on as pastor. By 2010 Bozek's support had splintered, with some parishioners joining the archdiocese in a civil lawsuit against the parish.[38] Burke, ensconced in Rome, oversaw the Signatura cases as American parishes tried to reverse their bishops.[39]

"We are concerned with keeping churches viable," said Borré. He stressed the importance of filing appeals to keep the issue before the Vatican.

People from the various groups voiced their frustrations, citing well-functioning parishes that stood to lose their funds (Cleveland suppressions netted about $9 million to the diocese the first year). A woman complained, "He is destroying the ethnic parishes." Heads nodded across the room. Borré reviewed the history of O'Malley's struggle and his 2004 letter "in which he said there are nights when I go to sleep and pray for the Lord to take me home. O'Malley stopped meeting with Lennon. You're dealing with one of the most extreme personalities of the American bishops—Lennon stays in his own cocoon. He hates people standing outside, protesting. He *hates* that."

Nancy McGrath, a founder of Endangered Catholics, was nodding. Their group mounted continuing protests.

"If you get your foot in the door with a supplemental brief at Congregation for the Clergy," said Borré, "make sure you do it as registered parishioners, not as a committee." He traced the steps a case would travel in the Vatican labyrinth. "We are pushing up the caseload. Burke has issued a regulation that cases will not be screened by a panel of the Signatura, but by the secretary of the tribunal. Carlo Gullo, our superbly trained canon-ist, is up in arms; he considers this a gross violation. He will challenge this at the Council for Legislative Texts, which is like a Supreme Court for procedure in the Vatican."

FutureChurch's package on canonical appeals was on its website. As time passed, Sister Chris Schenk followed the increase in download patterns.

"Preserve every scrap of paper with postmarks," Borré told them. He cited Bishop Skylstad's position in the Spokane diocese bankruptcy pro-ceeding; and the affidavit by canon lawyer Nicholas Cafardi. "Even if the title is held by the bishop, under canon law, Skylstad said in effect, 'I am a trustee and it would be terrible if I took this property for my own.' He said he did not own the parishes under canon law. But more than a few bishops are despotic."

"We think church closures is a policy issue the Vatican needs to ad-dress. No human institution except the Boston Red Sox is entitled to eter-nal life."

Only a few people chuckled. "But the notion of a vibrant, financially stable parish just thrown under the bus is wrong, and it's where I'm making my stand. The leadership that emerged from the pews has largely been by women."

Amid the experiences recounted of people with the poker-faced bishop, a lady said, "You shouldn't have to work this hard to be a practicing Catholic!"

Of the many parishes in the struggle, St. Peter on Superior Avenue downtown, catty-corner to the *Plain Dealer* newsroom, was a sturdy Gothic Revival church. It was also a model parish for a city confronting a cycle of decline. Founded by German immigrants in 1853, St. Peter had for gen-erations been a church school. As people moved away from the old urban core, the parish lost membership, and as the population flow to suburbs accelerated, the school closed. As the downtown area grew more commer-cial by day, the walking poverty increased by night. In 1991, a young pas-tor, Father Robert Marrone, oversaw a $300,000 renovation of the church thanks to resilient parishioners—some of whom pushed wheelbarrows of concrete to repave the floor.

Marrone's eloquent sermons drew new followers. A liturgist who saw rare ceremonial potential in the large, shabby space, Marrone had the vaulted interior painted white, "revealing the simple elegance of the structure," writes theologian Joan M. Nuth, "reminiscent of a Cistercian monastery chapel."[40] Pale Corinthian pillars stood in symmetry with the slender stained-glass windows. Marrone dispensed with padded kneelers and extraneous furniture to accentuate the altar as spiritual anchor of the large floor, particularly as the congregants walked in processions. The beauty of the space exuded a deep serenity. By the midnineties, St. Peter had seven hundred parishioners; most members drove in from the suburbs to the deserted downtown for the Sunday liturgies—attorneys, arborists, teachers, physicians, academics, and professionals whose generosity anchored outreach ministries, including one with a public school for tutoring, clothes, books, library assistance, and mentoring help for parents.

Lennon's chessboard changes to the churches and the city put St. Peter in a clustering group. Marrone's parish was an easy walk from the Cathedral of St. John the Evangelist, where Lennon said Mass. As the jolting news of the closures spread, a benefactor contacted Marrone to offer the parish $2 million to ensure its survival. Bob Marrone was thrilled. With permission from the diocese, he had financed new refurbishing for St. Peter's 150th anniversary as the city's oldest Catholic church and oldest pre–Civil War religious house, holding back the assessments rather than taking out a bank loan. Now he could pay $750,000 to the diocese, pay for demolition of the old school as part of a master plan for the physical plant, and put $1 million into the outreach ministries.

Lennon told him no, turn down the money. His parish would close.

Attorneys in the parish were familiar with the 1888 *Mannix v. Purcell* decision, in which Cincinnati parishes successfully appealed to the Ohio Supreme Court, against a bishop's plan to sell the churches to cover the debts of a church bank run by the bishop and his brother. But in the Toledo diocese, St. James parish in the rural farming community of Kansas, Ohio, had used *Mannix* in a civil case seeking to overturn their 2005 suppression by Bishop Leonard Blair. The state court sided with the Toledo bishop.[41]

The parishioners did not appeal the state decision. "The overriding issue was that the bishop padlocked the church and took the money," explains Columbus attorney Nicholas A. Pittner, whose firm represented the parish. "The parishioners who contributed money were beneficiaries of a trust. We argued that the bishop, as a trustee, couldn't appropriate the funds. The bishop argued that yes, he was a trustee, but under canon law the beneficiary was a juridic person"—the parish and bishop as one. Pittner continues: "What is a juridic person? The state court of appeals was loath to say that a juridic person is a fiction. Whose law do you apply? Is it Ohio property law? Or is there a federal right to have your claim decided on a body of law other than canon law?"

"We spent more than $100,000 in legal fees, trying to get the property back," Virginia Hull, a St. James parish leader, told me. "The $77,957 we had in the parish account all went to Bishop Blair. The diocese provided our attorney with statements that showed that most of our parish funds went to pay the attorney representing them against us. They offered us use of the church for meetings or social activities but not worship. The Methodist church has provided us space and a time to have our Sunday liturgy. A married Franciscan priest drives in to say Mass and provide us the sacraments. We used to have about 160 people each Sunday. Now we have about 45. Some people have gone to parishes in nearby towns, others left the faith. We did not want to join a church seven miles away; we do a lot of outreach to the needy right here. The diocese tore down our church. They allowed us to keep the steeple and bell. The land is for sale. We feel closer to God than we ever have. I don't think the bishops know what a community is."

Virginia Hull's words describe Bishop Lennon, the self-taught canonist who used the Suppression strategy that backfired in Boston on his new territory. "The Diocese of Cleveland fails to provide parishioners with the audited financial information needed to assess the economic state of the diocese," comments Western Michigan University professor of accountancy Jack Ruhl, an authority on diocesan financial statements. Weighing the disclosures by the diocesan Finance Office, Foundation, and Catholic Charities, he says: "What is the dollar amount of diocesan assets and liabilities? What is the diocesan liability for post-retirement obligations? Is there any liability for clergy abuse settlements? While Bishop Lennon did publish a 'Report to the Community' in 2009 that listed total parish revenues and expenses for two years, the information was unaudited. The Finance Office has been so narrowly defined that financial reports for it exclude 'troublesome' accounts like the Property and Casualty Reserve

Fund, which pays sex abuse claims. They don't list it. This is not transparent financial reporting. Too much remains hidden."

A St. Peter's civil case would cost hundreds of thousands of dollars in a city and state court system that had long shown its subservience to the Catholic Church; even if a court sided with the parish on the ownership issue, Lennon could refuse to provide a pastor. No court could make him do that.

St. Peter's leaders filed an appeal at the Vatican over the Suppression order, though they knew the Signatura could take years to make a decision, and, as one member told me, "the Vatican sides with bishops, not people in the pews." A core group of parishioners formed the Community of St. Peter and incorporated as a 501(c)(3) nonprofit charitable organization under IRS regulations. They settled on a renovated car dealership in downtown Cleveland, the area where their hearts were, raising $200,000 to cover the rent, administrative expenses, outreach ministry, and supplant the salary and health insurance for Father Marrone, who took a leave of absence from the diocese to be their pastor. Four hundred people joined, nearly two-thirds the number of parishioners, as Sunday services resumed.

Cleveland's clergy retirement fund was well capitalized, at about $90 million as of 2006, according to Joe Smith. Whatever his rationale, Lennon failed to provide a persuasive argument for the destructive policy toward the city's struggling neighborhoods.

St. Peter closed on Easter 2010. At the final Mass, Marrone recounted its remarkable history. He scored the "tragic and even sinful decisions" made by certain church leaders. As people wept, he spoke of the parish as "an empty tomb," while admonishing any who would "confuse blind faith with faithfulness . . . [and] allow more churches to become tombs of the living dead.

"The power of fear which has caused this injustice is not the last word, must not be the last word and will not be the last word. I know it seems unbearable to us but we can bear it. Go forth into the world and be living stones. God will tent with us where ever we go."[42]

CHAPTER 11

THE DEBTS of APOSTOLIC SUCCESSION

Marcial Maciel Degollado's burial in early 2008 in the family crypt at Cotija de la Paz, in the hinterlands of Mexico, was a world away from the tomb he had had built in Rome's Our Lady of Guadalupe Basilica—the vault for his sainthood candidacy. The saints who founded religious orders, like Francis of Assisi and Ignatius Loyola, stand as spiritual models for their followers across time. Maciel's canonization quest sank in 2006 when the Vatican ordered him to renounce public ministry for "a reserved life of penitence and prayer." That communiqué, which in effect banished him from Rome, signaled Pope Benedict's break from the denial of John Paul, a mind-set that inured the Polish pope to prosecuting Maciel and taking forceful action against the larger abuse crisis.

Cardinal Sodano, the secretary of state, made sure the 2006 communiqué from the Press Office praised the Legionaries of Christ and Regnum Christi. Ignoring the thirty men who testified about the sexual abuses they suffered before Monsignor Scicluna, the promoter of justice dispatched belatedly by Ratzinger, the Vatican whitewashed the Legion's eight-year disinformation campaign against Maciel's victims, even as outraged ex-Legionaries and disaffected RC members sent new information to Scicluna. Ratzinger, who had become Benedict, approved the communiqué.

Maciel flew off to Mexico for a reunion with Norma Hilda Baños and their daughter, Normita, who was in her early twenties. A March 2005 photograph of Maciel and the Normas in Cotija surfaced well after his death.[1] Maciel's legacy—and John Paul's failure to stop him—would detonate like land mines as Benedict confronted the Legion of Christ.[2]

Sodano had appeared with Maciel several months before the 2006 decision at a religious conference in the beautiful Tuscan town of Lucca. Sodano was pulling out the stops to include Maciel in the de facto immunity given to bishops and cardinals by the logic of apostolic succession. The Vatican considers members of the hierarchy as spiritual descendants of Jesus's apostles. A cardinal or a bishop can be removed from his position under canon law, but in reality, only the pope as the supreme authority can render such justice. The singular lesson undergirding the quarter century of abuse scandals and financial debacles is that cardinals and bishops stand above their severe mistakes or moral crimes. Cardinal Hans Hermann Groër of Austria made "strong homoerotic gestures to most of his students" for years before he became archbishop of Vienna, reports Leon C. Podles, the author of *Sacrilege*.[3] Groër suffered no demotion in ecclesial rank when accusations forced his retirement in 1995. John Paul uttered no public criticism, yet announced prayers for Groër several years later upon his death. He had no words for Groër's victims. For all of Maciel's financial power as the leader of an international religious order, he was neither bishop nor cardinal.

Bernard Law, Darío Castrillón Hoyos, and other cardinals who concealed pedophiles had caused financial disasters. Prelates of lesser rank, like Bishop Lennon, the self-taught canonist, destroyed parishes and took their money through incompetence. "It is to the holiness of the faithful that the hierarchical structure of the Church is totally ordered," John Paul stated in forbidding women's ordination.[4] Ecclesiastical tradition sees the men of the hierarchy in a descending line from Jesus's apostles, fostering holiness as an expression of God's kingdom. Many bishops work dutifully to do so. Bishops of recent memory who stand out as moral exemplars—the martyred Óscar Romero of El Salvador, Samuel Ruíz of Chiapas—embodied solidarity with the poor. But the hierarchy spares no expense to defend a compromised prelate in secular courts. As this self-protective logic evolved, apostolic succession created a caste system. Cardinals stand as nobility, each prince a potential pontiff; archbishops and bishops hold elite standing above the lower clergy and, at bottom, ordinary Catholics whose donations finance the church.

Inspired by the Second Vatican Council, the 1964 Dogmatic Constitution of the Church, *Lumen Gentium,* gave ordinary Catholics an elevated status as People of God. A body of theological writing on People of God has arisen since then, auguring hope for pluralism in church governance, tapping a wisdom born of married life.[5] But the last two papacies have devalued the People of God idea like a poor foreign currency. Pray, pay, obey is Rome's expectation. John Paul and Benedict blunted the ethos of a collaborative role for People of God through the selection process for bishops. As Cardinal Law wielded great influence on American candidates for the episcopacy, John Paul imposed a litmus test to eliminate any priest who supported optional celibacy or women priests. When the abuse scandals erupted, the subsurface story was a legacy of episcopal yes-men and theological reactionaries who recycled child molesters, kept silent on the burgeoning gay culture in seminaries, and rarely lost rank for mismanaging church money. Suborning moral conscience to papal supremacy was the currency for episcopal advancement. As the CDF in the Palace of the Holy Office became the citadel of moral truth, John Paul's indifference to traumatized abuse victims, and the impact of the crisis on people in the pews, was symptomatic of the hubris embedded in the apostolic succession.

Cardinal Ratzinger punished theologians who embraced the complexities of conscience in the real lives of People of God: Charles Curran on birth control, Hans Küng on papal infallibility, Leonardo Boff on poverty as the prism of liberation theology, among other persecuted intellectuals. In defining moral truth as the province of the Vatican, Ratzinger wanted *obedience*—"definitive assent"—to the magisterium, or teaching office of his congregation. *Curia* comes from the Latin *covir*—men among men. "The freedom that celibacy was supposed to give for selfless action is snuffed out at the most basic level when freedom of discussion is outlawed," Garry Wills has written.[6] A larger anxiety turned on whether the church had "gone too far" in its post–Vatican II encounter with a world that saw spaceships sail to the moon. Doctrinaire conservatives thrilled to the spectacle of John Paul and Ratzinger squelching "dissent," but fell silent on Vatican hypocrisy that protected the guiltiest bishops in the abuse crisis, and Father Maciel.

"The outer purpose always sounds noble, to defend the Church's teaching office," Eugene Kennedy comments in *The Unhealed Wound.* "Holy Mother Church, as it is called, cannot be 'defiled' by false teaching or errant behavior, papal teaching authority cannot be 'violated.' " Nevertheless,

> the underlying psychological and spiritual reality is not difficult to recognize. Men use power against other men to destroy their masculine potency . . . Feeling righteous is a totalitarian emotion and justifies wounding men in their manhood, emasculating them in the name of an institution that does not notice the shadow it casts as it focuses on and overwhelms them. Women must also be controlled and called into their place, but men—the potent male—must be incapacitated, ruined as a man, and shamed and humiliated as well.[7]

Ratzinger voiced his outrage when he substituted for the dying pope at the 2005 Good Friday Stations of the Cross in the Colosseum. The cardinal said scornfully, "How much filth there is in the Church, and even among those . . . in the priesthood"—words that shot across the international media grid. As John Paul's body lay in state at St. Peter's Basilica, the media covered a drama of religious grandeur. Father Tom Williams, a Legionary and a stalwart defender of Maciel, provided commentary on NBC's *Today*, suffering not a question from perky Katie Couric on his accused superior. Irony hung like a thundercloud as Cardinal Ratzinger in his sermon at the Mass opening the conclave gave a cri de coeur on Christian values: "We are building a dictatorship of relativism that does not recognize anything as definitive."

The papacy of Benedict XVI opened into a tense drama between moral absolutes and the concessions that come with governing. The moral absolutist, in a speech at his old college in Regensburg, Germany, quoted an ancient Byzantine emperor's hostile words on Islam. Journalists who saw the advance text warned the Vatican press spokesman "that the talk would cause problems with Muslims," wrote Marco Politi, a biographer of John Paul and a distinguished correspondent for *La Repubblica*. "Cardinal Angelo Sodano warned the Pope of the risks he was taking with the lecture."[8] Undeterred, Benedict gave the speech, which inflamed Muslim leaders and provoked attacks on several churches in the West Bank and Gaza; in Somalia, an Italian nun who worked in a children's hospital was shot and killed. Politi adds:

> When I interviewed him in November 2004, just a few months before the conclave in which he was elected Pope, the then Cardinal Ratzinger said: "It is increasingly apparent that a worldwide Church, particularly in this present situation, cannot be governed by an absolute monarch . . . in time a means will be found to create realistically a profound collaboration between the bishops and the Pope, because only in this way will we be able to respond to the challenges of this world."
>
> Benedict XVI has done nothing to realize this principle.[9]

Perhaps the idea of deeper collaboration convinced Benedict to invite the ultraorthodox Society of St. Pius X—a sect excommunicated by John Paul—back into the fold. The groundwork by Cardinal Castrillón collapsed when one of the society's bishops gave a television interview in Sweden denying the existence of the Holocaust. More embarrassment, another papal apology.

CHARISM IN THE COUNTING HOUSE

Sodano had practical reasons for putting the Holy See's credibility behind the Legionaries. His own reputation was on the line. The cardinal's photograph hung in the halls of the Regina Apostolorum campus and Rome's Regnum Christi center. The Legion had cultivated support from major figures in the Curia through the dispersal of Mass stipends that ranged from $2,500 up to several times that amount depending on the ceremonial importance. With Maciel exiled in Cotija, Legion seminarians drove around Rome delivering the 2006 Christmas baskets laden with fine wine and thousand-dollar Spanish hams for Curial supporters. Maciel was gone but his operation was part of the Vatican infrastructure—a large, troubled asset in the very literal sense.

To sustain its $650 million budget, the Legion had a sophisticated fundraising operation in Hamden, Connecticut, which at its peak in 2005 employed a hundred professionals. "If an employee became ill they'd go out of their way to help," Fredrik Akerblom, a former fund-raiser, told me. "If someone had cancer, they'd keep him on payroll and do everything to help. That was one aspect I respected and liked. But they didn't provide health care for the [Legion] brothers. There was a lot of internal discussion about their culture of young men bearing it out for Christ, and using that to make the families pay for the insurance."

Mary Kunze—Chris Kunze's mother and a hospital bioethicist in Elm Grove, Wisconsin—reflected on her daughter, who in 2010 was living in a Regnum Christi community in Dublin, after fifteen years as a consecrated woman. "I speak to Elizabeth at least once a month," Mrs. Kunze told me. "The last time, I asked if she'd had a pap smear or mammogram. She never has. In her last physical, she didn't have blood work or urine analysis. They neglect the quiet little people like my daughter. She's not getting any money, can't come home unless we send money, and is not even getting basic medical care. She's forty-five, at an age where women need these baseline tests. They have no health insurance. And it's such a wealthy order! She says she's happy and feels she's doing God's work, but I really doubt it; the brainwashing is so deep. These women don't ask for things they need. They feel by asking they are selfish. They don't have the basic human rights. I wish Benedict would really go in and clean it up."

"For the most part, Legionaries and consecrated are self-insured by the Legion," the order's lay spokesman Jim Fair told me. "Most do not have actual insurance, but we simply pay for care."

Roberta Garza, the youngest sibling of Father Luis Garza, the Legion vicar general, said that when her sister in Regnum Christi returned to Mexico from Rome "every couple of years, they would count on us to pay for her medical treatments, and they were not small. I remember she had her spleen removed and another time all her teeth repaired, and I'm not talking just a small filling. She seemed to not have any regular checkups or any preventive treatment whatsoever while under the Legion's care, and she would come home in order to have her long overdue medical needs paid for by her family."

Akerblom had been a Regnum Christi member in Connecticut before returning to his native Sweden. "Over time," he explained, "I realized that our donors interpreted anything critical of the Legion as an attack on their faith. The Legion had a brilliant way of dealing with those criticisms: we never speak ill of anyone who criticizes us. Donors felt the liberal establishment was hounding them. The Legionaries created the idea that they were under siege, that anything negative about them was an expression of that fallen world.

"We sent out millions of fund-raising letters, literally millions," Akerblom told me. "The appeal was young men in cassocks. That conveyed something deep to people, a hope that what they perhaps had grown up with and what had almost disappeared from the church was coming back: young men well groomed, orthodox in their beliefs, conservative in their views. We raised a lot of money. My personal concern when I worked there was that we frankly did not know what happened with money after it left the fund-raising office."

The fund-raising staff in Hamden worked the phones, direct-mail appeals, and personal contacts with donors, refining a database with help from Regnum Christi members to cultivate wealthy supporters.

Another source shared a 2005 Legion study of its database.

This study defined "a critical gift [as] a single, lump-sum cash gift of $10,000 or more." Between 2002 and 2004 (while Maciel's case lay dormant at Ratzinger's tribunal), the study scrutinized 295 Major Donors—as they are called—in that $10,000-and-up category. Direct mail accounted for 48 percent of the contributions.

> To understand the critical path these Direct Mail donors followed, 137 dossiers outlining their cultivation history were compiled and reviewed . . .
>
> Nearly 70% (95 out of 137) of the donors surveyed met with a Legionary priest or brother and in 80 out of 137 (58%) a positive critical incident—that is, an event which made a difference in the way the donor thought about the Legion—could be identified from the notes and actions in the donor's record . . .
>
> However, only in the Major Donors program do donors with identifiable critical incidents outperform donors without them, suggesting that critical incidents—and the intimate interpersonal relationships which often produce them—are more important at the major giving level.

In analyzing "critical incidents," the study explains:

> When donors connect with the Legion at its core—either through
> spiritual direction from a Legionary priest, or by incorporation
> into Regnum Christi—they respond generously. In the words of
> [Episcopal] Bishop Alfred Stanway: "Money follows ministry."
>   In our case, money follows charism.[10]

Charism, according to Cardinal Avery Dulles, the late Jesuit theologian, is "a gift of grace, conferred not for one's personal sanctification but for the benefit of others."[11] Charism in a religious order means the defining trait or vision, its unique character. Dominicans are educators known for preaching; Franciscans for commitment to the poor; Jesuits stress analytical thinking, scholarship, and service as "men for others."

Legion donors, according to the fund-raising study, "respond to that which makes the Legion different from Opus Dei, the Red Cross, or Notre Dame: the apostolic mission and spiritual formation of priests and lay men and women established by Father Maciel."

The Legion distributed a spiritual guide by Maciel, *Psalter of My Days*. After his death the order revealed he had plagiarized from *The Psalter of My Hours* by Luis Lucia, a Christian Democrat in Spain who wrote the work while imprisoned in the 1930s. Lucia died in Valencia in 1943. A Spanish Legionary told Catholic News Agency that Maciel's text reproduced "eighty percent of the original book in content and style"[12]—meaning, he stole it.

Maciel's charism was fund-raising.

The Legion fund-raising report lists seven individuals in descending order of their donations. Listed next to each name is a "Lifetime cash value" and a "critical incident." The highest donor had a $10,686,341 lifetime cash value. The critical incident came at the Legion retreat center in Thornwood, New York—"very strong experience . . . spiritual direction with" two Legionaries identified by initials. "Wants to get active with the LC," the note concludes.

The second-highest donor gave $1,043,629 and "had a critical incident in getting involved" as "director couple for Familia."

Familia was a ministry to families that the Legion wrested away from the founders, Paul and Libbie Sellors. The couple hired counsel and received an out-of-court settlement.[13] Information on this went to Monsignor Scicluna at the Vatican.

The third-highest donor, at $308,435, had a "meeting with LC priest and brother; daughters incorporated into [a youth program] by Fr. Maciel."

Of the fourth-highest donor, at $204,772, the report states: "Incorporated into RC indicates integration, death of husband freed up money."

And so on, down to the tenth major donor, at $145,052, next to whom the Critical Incident reads: "Incorporation into RC"—meaning Regnum Christi, signaling that the deal is closed.

The Vatican communiqué that ousted Maciel gave Legion leaders time to regroup and work with Vatican officials. The Legion, through its news service Zenit, released occasional notices of Father Álvaro Corcuera, the superior general, meeting with Benedict. Picture the pope's predicament. As with the Society of St. Pius X, he confronted a group that was beyond orthodoxy, and in this case trained in obedience to a sociopath. The Legion was moral relativism at the outer edge: the spiritual formation of the priests and seminarians, who took private vows never to speak ill of Maciel, was subjugated to his mental tyranny. Praising and defending Maciel shaped the Legion ethos. As Ratzinger's closest canon law adviser, Scicluna had ample evidence for a shutdown, which would have sent a major signal to the media of a pope committed to reform. Why did he hold back? The new pope had two options; neither one was simple.

Ending the Legion required a plan for retraining the priests, seminarians, and RC members with therapy and pastoral counseling—no easy job. That was the route for a moral absolutist. As Camus wrote, "Super human is the term for tasks men take a long time to accomplish, that's all."[14]

Or, was it preferable to show flexibility, take the route of moral relativism, be patient with the behavior of Legionaries who carried a personal history of warped training, bring the order under Vatican control, get a grasp of its finances, and postpone a decision on the "name brand," its public identity?

For Benedict, the 2006 decision marked a confrontation between the moral absolutist and flexible governance over a corrupt religious group. The pope under Sodano's influence chose to salvage the group, now that its founder was in exile. The Legion immediately showed its schizophrenia by pledging fealty to Benedict while announcing that Maciel felt "tranquility of conscience," and, like Jesus, had chosen not to defend himself.

The Legion launched into a campaign of internal marketing to assure its followers that Maciel *had never been tried*. Ergo, he was not guilty.

"One thing that always struck me about the Legion is how they constantly had to justify themselves," says the attorney Glenn Favreau, recalling his thirteen years in the order. "They defined themselves in opposition to others—critics of Maciel, enemies of the Legion. Take away Maciel, what were they?"

The Vatican's containment strategy of 2006 collapsed in 2009 when the Legion revealed to its followers that Maciel had a grown daughter out of wedlock. Corcuera, the superior general, long afflicted with migraine headaches and insomnia, had gone to the various religious houses, breaking the painful news. How long had he, and the austere Luis Garza as chief financial officer, known how money donated to the Legion was channeled to the support of Maciel's shadow family in Madrid? When did Corcuera tell Benedict? Certain Legion advocates issued apologies for having defended him in the past. "Surprising, difficult to understand, and inappropriate for a Catholic priest," offered a Legion spokesman in mild understatement.[15] Several prominent Legion priests left the order.

And so, in 2009, the Vatican authorized an investigation of the entire religious order, a move unprecedented in modern church history.

The Legion's identity dilemma became a tar baby for the Vatican, a sticky creature spawned in the thickets of mendacity that would vex church officials and Pope Benedict amid the abuse scandals of 2010.

As those events registered in Italy as never before, the Holy See faced a U.S. lawsuit brought in Oregon by the victim of a priest who had been moved from Ireland to America.[16] When an Oregon appeals court refused to dismiss the case, which accused the Vatican of complicity, the lead attorney, Jeff Anderson, gained a foothold he had sought for years. Before the year was out, Jeff Anderson and Pope Benedict would stand at distant poles of the scandal, in an exquisite irony, each seeking justice for Maciel's victims.

CHAPTER 12

ANOTHER CALIFORNIA

The energy that burned through him began before dawn on a blend of liquefied fruit with eighteen powdered vitamins—"the mush," his three young sons called it. The life force that sent him hurtling into each day sometimes ran fourteen hours at a stretch. The years of meeting clients, their lives still raw long after the early trauma, taught him how predators buried the evidence in their victims' psyches.[1] The adult survivor yearned to reach back in time and protect the child victim. Jeff Anderson spent heavily on investigations to find perpetrators; most were never prosecuted, too much time had passed. He alerted cops anyway. Hammering out settlements on the civil cases that took, on average, three years to resolve, he routinely blasted bishops in announcing new cases via Web-streamed video from his office (originally a bank built by a timber baron) in downtown St. Paul. Talking strategy with his co-counsels in other states, he carried a mental map of the many cases, working the cell phone on the forty-minute drive back to Stillwater, where he lived in a Victorian mansion above the St. Croix River. Street jogs after dinner softened the manic edge as he crawled into bed for five hours' sleep.

A wiry five foot four inches, Jeff Anderson had receding silver-blond hair and a perpetual tan to soften his rutted brow. The Cheshire cat grin hinted at a natural ebullience that made an easy slide to flamboyance. "All roads lead to Rome," he told the *Washington Post* on April 19, 2010. "We're chasing them. We're taking bites out of their ass."[2] Three days later he filed a motion in federal court to put Benedict XVI under oath.[3] A Wisconsin priest named in several cases had molested two hundred deaf students over many years; Cardinal Ratzinger had refused to defrock him after extensive correspondence with Archbishop Rembert Weakland of Milwaukee. Anderson and his associate Mike Finnegan obtained the correspondence in discovery and gave copies to reporter Laurie Goodstein of the *New York Times*. The *Times* report raised hard questions about the pope's judgment while a cardinal, and embarrassed the Vatican.[4]

"It all leads to the pope," Anderson insisted to the *Minneapolis Star-Tribune*. "Deposing [the pope] sounds bombastic, but it isn't. He needs to be held responsible for the torture and mutilation of children's souls worldwide."[5]

Torture, mutilation—inflammatory rhetoric, words that made him good copy for journalists. But he had absorbed too much factual tonnage on sex criminals whose white collars had given them a free ride to maintain a calm demeanor. Anderson had been suing the church since 1984, losing almost as many cases as he had won, picking himself up each time, coiled to fight again. In Wisconsin he had been forced to hire his own attorney when church lawyers filed punitive motions in Madison. The perpetrator was defrocked, but the abuse, legally, lay too far in the past. Defending himself had cost $40,000. A 1995 Wisconsin state high court decision had barred abuse lawsuits against the church. In time, Anderson found a way around the statute: he began suing Wisconsin bishops for fraud, on the grounds that passing off pedophiles as good priests was itself a tort—an approach that got him a foot in the door.

By spring 2003 he had about 150 clients. Over the previous twenty years he had settled claims for some five hundred victim-survivors for $60 million. He had won several high-profile trials that resulted in multimillion-dollar verdicts. Anderson was ecumenical in his way; he took cases against Protestant ministers, Hare Krishnas, Jehovah's Witnesses, and Mormons, but, by far, most of his clients were Catholic victims. His take of each successful case was 40 percent, plus expenses, proportionally shared with his law partners, until 2002, when he split off from his longtime firm. By 2003 the larger cases were settling for high six figures and up.

"It was never really about the money for Jeff," his wife, Julie, a willowy blonde who had done heavy lifting in the department of patience, said in 2003. "He liked to play the scrappy little lawyer, a down-and-dirty sort . . . He was an actor on a stage. And he was very good at commanding an audience."[6]

Anderson was a major benefactor of Survivors Network of those Abused by Priests (SNAP), an activist group that pushed the bishops, week after week, to disclose the names of perpetrators. SNAP disseminated leaflets outside churches, naming names, attacking negligent bishops. Media coverage expanded the self-help network. SNAP included parents who had lost children to suicide, ex-cops, a cabdriver, a university professor of English, an office secretary, twin brothers each with a master's degree from Harvard, a portrait painter, computer programmers, real estate agents, a nurse, a subway train driver, an accountant, a physician, teachers, stay-at-home moms, firefighters, several priests, nuns, and recovering addicts or alcoholics of many stripes. SNAP had nine thousand members in 2010. Other plaintiff attorneys donated to SNAP, which relied on donations from victims who received settlements, too. SNAP had a budget exceeding $900,000 in 2006. By 2009 it had fallen to $420,000 against expenses of $490,000. Critics said SNAP should disclose its contributors' list; many survivors wanted privacy, countered the founder, Barbara Blaine.[7]

Anderson's friendship with SNAP leaders Blaine in Chicago, David Clohessy and Barbara Dorris in St. Louis, and Peter Isely in Milwaukee, among others, formed an emotional rudder in his life. Their cause was his cause, their outrage his outrage. He had represented Clohessy, one of three brothers abused by the family priest, in a Missouri case that was thrown out for statute of limitations. One of Clohessy's brothers became a priest who later abused youngsters; he left the ministry. Across the gulf of suffering, the two brothers had not spoken in years. The family was deeply splintered.

"I wouldn't know how much I've given SNAP," Anderson told me, "or how much I have made or lost. I don't focus on my own money . . . I'm committed to the same goals and purposes as SNAP. I help them do their advocacy because they help support our survivors in recovery and deliver a message in the court of public opinion. In these parallel universes our goals intersect. If they were another nonprofit, I'd do the same thing. It's evolved into a loose collaboration."

Anderson had several times pushed his bank credit limit to the brink for the heavy costs in investigations and travel, and to lobby legislatures to open state laws on the time frame allowing victims to sue. Bishops attacked such legislation, arguing it would bankrupt their dioceses; defense lawyers accused Anderson of self-enrichment strategies. He had a gladiatorial approach. "From the New Deal to civil rights, the bishops were allied with social justice," he continued. "Now they're allied with the Republican Party, the insurance industry and U.S. Chamber of Commerce in trying to shut down legislative reform"—meaning laws to extend the statutes of limitations. Insurance companies paid heavily in many church settlements, though dioceses since the 1990s had resorted to self-insurance risk pools. Closing parishes to fund settlements, in his view, was a dodge: the church could raise funds to resolve these cases.

"When a bishop testifies at a committee hearing, the politicians imagine 235,000 Catholic voters. Then the insurance representatives come in and they worry about rates going up. The Chamber of Commerce says these cases will kill business. Martin Luther King said the moral arc of time bends toward truth and justice. I see us trending toward greater awareness with attention on the Vatican."

His wife had a point: it was never really about the money. Battling the church was more about Jeff. He enjoyed what wealth brought—the vacation home in Steamboat Springs, Colorado; the elegantly appointed Rivertown Inn with the wraparound porch and Victorian porticoes he and Julie had renovated just up the street in Stillwater; the collection of religious art he had acquired in a spiritual awakening. But money was more of a means, a weapon to batter corrupted power. "You have to be kind of nuts, or willing to take an enormous amount of risk," he opined on the phone between meetings in Chicago. "From a business standpoint, no one would have thought you could do it this way. I've taken a tremendous number of cases knowing the odds were against us. Of the cases I've filed, 40 percent have been knocked out for statute of limitations."

Born in 1947, he was raised outside St. Paul in a comfortably middle-class home with older and younger sisters. The family attended a Lutheran and later a Congregationalist church. "It made me feel constricted," he recalled. His father, a furniture buyer, was deeply humanitarian, but quietly so; he recalls his mother as emotionally distant. "I don't remember my childhood. I remember being cared for, but there was a lack of bonding I somehow internalized. Maybe some missing element in childhood explains my compulsive behavior."

After high school he entered Simpson College in Iowa. He was nineteen and deeply in love when his girlfriend, Patty, who came from a sprawling Catholic family, got pregnant. They married and had a son. Anderson left school, worked, then transferred to the University of Minnesota just in time for the revolution. His hair grew long, he smoked weed, he marched against the Vietnam War, hungering for a larger part in the 1960s social rebellion. After graduation and several low-wage jobs, he began night classes at William Mitchell College of Law in St. Paul. By then they had an infant daughter, too. He flunked a course, scrambled for readmission, and found his stride in a criminal law class taught by Rosalie Wahl, a future justice of the Minnesota Supreme Court. He thrilled to the idea of fighting the establishment by defending people on the margins. In a faculty-supervised poverty law clinic, he took the case of a black man accused of exposing himself in a church basement. Anderson argued that his homeless client was only looking for a place to pee. The judge agreed. "And I got something that day I'd never felt before," he told me in his elegant office, flanked by pictures of Clarence Darrow and Dr. King. "A *feeling of power*, that I could make a difference in how society treats people."

Starting out as a criminal defense attorney, he established a practice with a former law professor that included personal injury work. In 1983 a blue-collar Catholic couple asked his help. Their twenty-five-year-old son, in prison for molesting a youngster, had revealed to them that he was abused as a boy by Father Tom Adamson. They had met with Auxiliary Bishop Robert Carlson, the chancellor of the Twin Cities archdiocese. Carlson offered mild compassion, and then sent a check for $1,500. "Cash it," said Anderson. "And let me visit your son."

Gazing at the young inmate through the glass partition, he was touched by his sad naïveté, a quality he detected in many criminal clients. Anderson called the cops; they were powerless, the statute of limitations on Adamson's crimes had lapsed. He knew of no lawyer who had sued the Catholic Church.

Minnesota law allows a plaintiff to serve a complaint on a defendant before filing court papers. Discovery proceeds as an inducement to settle a

case without notoriety or court costs. He sent his complaint to the archdiocese. Church counsel called immediately: what did he want? He wanted
the priest removed from his parish. He soon got assurance that Adamson
was yanked. The church wanted to settle. Anderson wanted to take the
deposition testimony of Archbishop John Roach. His opposing counsel
said no. Anderson threatened to file suit and call the media. He got the
deposition, along with church files containing letters that documented
how Adamson had crisscrossed dioceses and parishes trailed by sex abuse
complaints. He took the deposition of a second bishop, Loras Watters of
Winona. Convinced that both bishops had lied to him under oath about
their knowledge of Adamson's history, he probed deeper.[8] The archdiocesan lawyer offered a settlement "in the usual way," a signal to him that
Adamson was not unique. The offer was $1 million to be paid in a struc-
tured annuity, a steady paycheck over many years.

"Sick, scared, upset, and unable to sleep," he says now of the offer as if
it had been made yesterday, "I saw it as a huge amount of money." His client had gotten out of prison when Anderson went to see him. He recalls
crying as he explained the settlement offer, which carried a nondisclosure
clause: hush money. Anderson asked him not to agree to that condition.
"Jeff," said the man, "turn it down—but turn it down quickly, before I
change my mind."

He returned to his office, drafted a complaint, went to the courthouse.

Filing the case made major news in St. Paul. The fall 1984 criminal
indictment of Father Gilbert Gauthe in Lafayette, Louisiana, made bigger news. Gauthe accepted a twenty-year plea bargain in 1985; the diocese settled a dozen cases with the families of boys he had abused. Gauthe
and Adamson were opposite faces of the same coin. Adamson was never
prosecuted. The early Gauthe cases (many more would follow) settled,
on average, for about $400,000 per victim. Anderson settled his case for
$1.2 million as a structured annuity. Other Adamson victims called him.
He settled those cases in the late 1980s for an average of $550,000, some
$10 million in all, of which insurance companies paid about a third of the
costs. Eventually he persuaded the Minnesota legislature to extend the
statute of limitations for child abuse. Along the way, his marriage died
because of his drinking and infidelity. Later, he met and married Julie Ar-
onson, who was fourteen years younger than he. In 1992 Jeff Anderson
had a year-old son, a lovely wife, a beautiful house, and a surging practice

when his eighteen-year-old daughter from his first marriage revealed that she had been abused at age eight by her therapist, an ex-priest. The man had since gone to prison. Throttled with guilt, Jeff Anderson resolved to be a better father. But he was rolling down a jagged hill, drinking so voraciously that on his fiftieth birthday he crashed: blacked out after a dinner with friends. When he awoke his second marriage was on the rocks.

Anderson entered outpatient treatment and began attending AA meetings. As the rescuer peered into the wreckage of his drinking, he felt fear at the specter of something he could not control. The spirituality that kept all those Catholics glued to their church had a million forms, he realized; *he* wanted a spiritual base to overcome the lovelessness that drove his compulsive drinking. How does an agnostic find a higher power? His wife and AA allies helped, but it was a Catholic priest who really got him grounded.

BROTHERS IN BATTLE

Father Tom Doyle, the canon lawyer at the Vatican embassy, had lost his job, and a sure bet to become a bishop, because of the 1985 report he coauthored that warned the hierarchy of the abuse crisis. Doyle was a Dominican, and Dominicans are known for preaching; when reporters called, Doyle spoke his mind about the bishops' inaction, his candor quotient rising like a critical mass. The cleric who had worn French cuffs at embassy functions and gone to White House lunches joined the air force as a Catholic chaplain. In 1988 he had unpacked his books in a cottage on an Indiana air base when a lawyer named Jeff Anderson telephoned. Doyle let him talk. A few days later he sent Anderson the ninety-three-page report he had written with lawyer F. Ray Mouton and psychiatrist Father Michael Peterson, which had gone to every bishop in America. The document was a smoking gun at that juncture for Anderson's lawsuits.

A disillusioned soldier of orthodoxy, Tom Doyle was on his own crash landing from alcohol. After hitting bottom, Doyle never blamed the Vatican or bishops; he accepted his powerlessness over drinking and refocused his spiritual life on the daily path of recovery. He accepted himself as a wounded healer. With a pilot's license and membership in the National Rifle Association, Doyle was as conservative as Anderson was liberal. Tom Doyle became the brother Jeff Anderson never had, bonded in the struggle to live clean and take the battle forward. Doyle had become a priest to achieve closeness with God. Appalled by the hierarchy he had once served, Father Doyle counseled abuse survivors via phone calls and e-mail. Doyle's reflections on spiritual integrity had a huge impact on the attorney, who had never had a confessor. Anderson, in turn, gave the rebel priest a new kind of power: as an expert witness in lawsuits he could use his knowledge to throttle the hierarchy for its transgressions of canon law—and moral values. Doyle considered the power structure toxic: prelates addicted to power, sheltering the guilty. Doyle was radical, from the Greek *redux*, meaning roots, first things. Sober as a judge, protected by his air force status from sanctions that diocesan bishops might take, he gave testimony in cases for Anderson and other lawyers as time allowed. In 2002 he received the Priest of Integrity Award from Voice of the Faithful, an upstart reform group. In 2003 the chief military archbishop, Edwin O'Brien, engineered his dismissal as a chaplain for an obscure technicality in canon law over which the air force had no control.[9] In reality, it was payback. Doyle was forced out of the military chaplaincy, after nineteen years—one year short of qualifying for a pension.

What the retribution against Tom Doyle signified in pettiness it made up for in shortsightedness: Doyle was a sure bet to fight back. He settled in a suburb of Washington, D.C., and began full-time work as an expert witness in clergy abuse cases. For that he was much in demand. Doyle was on a leave of absence from priestly ministry in 2010.

Anderson's turning point came when two brothers, James and Joh Howard, asked him to take their case against the diocese of Stockton, California. In the early 1980s, an Irish-born priest named Oliver O'Grady had ingratiated himself with the Howard family and molested four of the seven siblings. O'Grady also befriended a woman whose nine-month-old daughter suffered vaginal scarring from his abuse. In 1984 another family reported O'Grady to police. A church attorney told police O'Grady would have no more contact with children. Stockton bishop Roger Mahony sent him to a psychiatrist. O'Grady discussed his sexual attraction to boys. O'Grady had a "severe defect in maturation," the psychiatrist wrote. "Perhaps Oliver is not truly called to the priesthood."

At Christmas 1985 Bishop Mahony sent O'Grady to a rural church, with parishioners unaware that the priest was a child molester. In 1993 O'Grady was convicted of lewd conduct with the younger Howard, Joh, who was then fifteen. O'Grady was in prison when the brothers contacted Anderson. The Minnesota lawyer needed a California cocounsel in order to function in the state court. He found his ally in Larry Drivon of Stockton, a highly regarded trial attorney from a prominent legal family. Drivon accepted the expensive, time-intensive preparation for a trial of this sort. Knowing that Jeff Anderson was in recovery, Drivon's wife and sympatico friends helped him find noontime AA meetings during the trial.

Roger Mahony was by then the cardinal archbishop of Los Angeles. He traveled the 9,058-square-mile expanse of his archdiocese in a $400,000 helicopter donated by Richard Riordan, a wealthy businessman and future mayor. Los Angeles was the most populous U.S. archdiocese and the wealthiest.[10] John Paul II teased Mahony gently by calling him "Hollywood," but the needling carried a message: the pope made him give up the helicopter.

In the 1960s, as a priest in Stockton, Mahony befriended César Chávez of the United Farm Workers. He had served as the first chairman of the California Agricultural Labor Relations Board, a pro-labor state agency launched under Governor Jerry Brown in 1975. But Mahony's political liberalism regarding Latinos and immigration issues never translated into theological liberalism, and his social awareness was tempered by a fealty to the church's bottom line. As archbishop in the 1990s he scuttled an effort by the predominantly Latino gravediggers in Catholic cemeteries to organize themselves as a union. "Western Sequoia Corp., the commercial firm responsible for cemetery-plot sales that were once handled in-house by employees of the archdiocese, employs people on an 'at will' basis, meaning they may be terminated for any reason," Ron Russell reported.[11]

Speaking out against the death penalty and abortion, Mahony championed the rights of immigrants, while raising funds from some of California's richest Republicans. In 1996 Mahony purchased a five-acre parking lot off the Hollywood Freeway for $10.85 million, the site for a new cathedral.[12]

His ability to bounce back from criticism or bad press bestirred Los Angeles Times columnist Steve Lopez to call him "the Teflon Cardinal."[13] Mahony, at six and a half feet, towered over Anderson at the 1998 trial in Stockton. Six months into recovery, the attorney felt raw, working late in preparing for each day in court. On the phone at night he drew comfort from Doyle's words: You can do it. You're not alone. A day at a time. Keep it simple.

A 1976 letter in which O'Grady admitted to molesting a girl was in his personnel file. "I was not aware of that letter," Cardinal Mahony told the jury.

"Cardinal, if you had known that he admitted [to an earlier therapist] to touching a 9-year-old boy, would you have committed to him the full care of souls at the church at St. Andrew's parish?" asked Anderson.

"It's a bit speculative," answered Mahony. "In any and all cases we—if there's a suspicion or problem—we refer to competent professionals to assist in making the recommendations. And if the competent professionals do not raise any flag or cautions or concerns, then we act according to their judgment."[14]

When the judge called a recess, the cardinal spoke with reporters in the hall. The proceedings resumed. "Cardinal," began Anderson, "you were just out there speaking to the media. And you told the media, did you not, the following: 'I thought when we placed O'Grady in the parish we did everything we humanly could have done to make sure there was no problem there.' "

"Well I'm not sure that's the exact words, but something similar . . . yes."

"At the time, Cardinal, did you talk to the police?"

"No."

"You could have."

"Well, I'm not sure I could have. But—"

"What was restraining you from calling the police and asking them about your priest?"

"When I was told that an allegation had been made, thoroughly investigated, found to be wanting and dismissed, I had no reason to call the police."

"You could have sent Father O'Grady to a specialist, that is a doctor who specializes in the treatment and assessment of suspected offenders, correct?"

"At that time I was really unaware that there were such specialists."

"You have an education in social work, correct?"

"Yes," said Mahony, who had a master's from Catholic University in Washington, D.C.

"When you sent him to that parish you could have gone to the priest file and looked at what was in there about Father O'Grady, could you not?"

"Yes."[15]

The jury returned a verdict of $30 million, $24 million of which was punitive damages against the church. A judge later reduced the award to $7.65 million, the largest on record for clergy abuse in a California trial.

HOW THE LOS ANGELES ARCHDIOCESE GREW

Born in 1936, Roger M. Mahony grew up in North Hollywood when it still had open fields. His father was an electrician with a poultry farm; the boy mingled with Mexican workers, picking up bits of Spanish, becoming bilingual as a young man. He entered the seminary at fourteen, advancing to the college level at St. John's Seminary in Camarillo, set on a gorgeous estate sixty miles northwest of the city in Ventura County. "In seminary Roger was focused on Mexicans and wanted to work with them," recalls a former classmate, Jerry Fallon, an ex-priest. "But he also had pretty thin skin when it came to criticism."

The Camarillo seminary's huge Spanish colonial library sat on a hilltop with a roof-level loggia. This was a gift of Estelle Doheny, the widow of Edward L. Doheny who had made a fortune in Mexico's oil fields in the early 1900s.[16] In 1921 Doheny gave $100,000 to Interior Secretary Albert Fall, who was imprisoned for bribery in the Teapot Dome scandal. Doheny avoided prison after a ten-year court battle. Irish-born archbishop John Cantwell cultivated Doheny. Doheny, who was second-generation Irish, became Cantwell's largest donor. The American church was like a trunk of Ireland with branches spreading west.

But racial and cultural blending—and geopolitical maneuvering— shaped the great western city from its beginnings. The first official settle- ment, El Pueblo de Nuestra Señora de los Angeles—City of Our Lady of Angels—was founded in 1781 by the Spanish crown to counteract the presumed territorial claims of Russia, which had trading posts and forts down the California coast with names such as Sebastapol. The Spanish governor recruited colonists to a pueblo along the Los Angeles River north of Mission San Gabriel—eleven families, who were headed by two Spaniards, four Indians, two blacks, and three men of mixed race. None of the wives was white; most of the twenty-two children were a mixture of Spanish, Indian, and African blood. In 1821, when Mexico won its independence from Spain, California and much of today's Southwest fell under Mexico City's nominal control. After the U.S. defeated Mexico in 1848, America claimed all the land north of the Rio Grande, extending out to the Pacific Ocean.[17]

Flush with the discovery of gold in the Sierra Nevada foothills, California became the thirty-first state in the Union, admitted as a nonslave state in 1850. California's motto was Eureka—"I have found it." People with gilded dreams came from every corner of America and Europe; after the Civil War, jobs building the railroads drew laborers from Canton Province in China to County Cork in Ireland. A century after the founding of the pueblo at Los Angeles, in the city to the north, San Francisco, some 27 percent of the voting-age populace was Irish-born. Long after the gold fields played out, the ethnic pilgrims kept arriving in Los Angeles. As the population grew, farms became subdivisions. L.A.'s population between 1910 and 1930 grew from 319,000 to 1.24 million, of whom 100,000 were Mexicans who had fled the Revolution of 1910, followed by refugees from the late 1920s Cristero Rebellion.[18] Cantwell took in three dozen exiled bishops from Mexico and established fifty Hispanic parishes. The Cristero war so central to Maciel's identity colored Los Angeles, too. In 1934, writes historian Mike Davis, "Cantwell organized the largest demonstration in Los Angeles history: a giant procession of 40,000 people, many of them Cristero refugees, chanting 'Viva Cristo Rey' and marching behind banners that denounced the 'atheistic regimes in Mexico City and Moscow.' "[19]

In 1947, when Cantwell died, Cardinal Spellman of New York recommended his chancellor, James F. McIntyre, to the Vatican. "Lean and taciturn, with the neat gray hair and rimless glasses of a corporate chieftain, McIntyre was a gifted administrator and rock-hard conservative, who fit perfectly with the Los Angeles Protestant establishment," writes Charles R. Morris. A brokerage executive before his call to ministry, Archbishop McIntyre faced frenetic postwar growth as white Catholics moved into greater Los Angeles at a rate of one thousand per week. Stopping plans for a new cathedral, McIntyre went on to open more than one hundred new parishes and nearly twice as many schools, a seminary, and half a dozen hospitals. This construction agenda stemmed from adroit decisions in real estate, scouting land before housing subdivisions were built, buying tracts and selling the excess to fund new parishes or schools.[20]

In a 1954 report to the Holy See, the cardinal explained that his parishes' indebtedness was $15 million, but only $5.5 million of that was owed to banks. As a corporation sole, the cardinal outlined his strategy for Pius XII:

> 1. In the name of the parish, the money is borrowed from a local bank, the parish giving a promissory note as security. The Corporation Sole then signs this note as a guarantor. This is the only security the bank has.
>
> There is no mortgage placed upon the parish property. The parish then pays the loan by payments at specified times and obtains this money from the general income of the parish.
>
> 2. It is the custom of the archdiocese for parishes to deposit in the Chancery Office surplus moneys which they may possess. This would happen, for example, if a parish were accumulating moneys which they may possess with the intention of erecting a new building a few years hence . . . The Chancery Office, in turn, lends this money to other parishes.
>
> This constitutes a substitute for borrowing from the bank. It also places the Chancery Office in somewhat the position of a bank, at least to some of the parishes.[21]

Unlike Eastern and Midwestern dioceses where ethnic churches anchored urban villages a few blocks apart, the Los Angeles archdiocese was a huge landmass spread over four southern California counties. McIntyre foresaw the patterns of freeways tied to real estate development; he spaced out churches at some distance from one another to create large flocks. The city's 1948 population of 3,961,800 nearly doubled to 7,110,796 in just twelve years; besides the Anglos, Mexicans and Central Americans came to work the fruit and vegetable fields that provided 40 percent of the domestic market.[22] McIntyre's careful grid approach stood the test of time well. In 2004 the preeminent California historian Kevin Starr wrote:

> In Pacoima, Father Tom Rush of Mary Immaculate parish, whose congregation had grown to the point where 8,500 parishioners were attending one of ten masses every Sunday (seven in Spanish, three in English), was completing a $3.2 million renovation and expansion of the parish church and school.[23]

McIntyre in the 1960s had bitter clashes with Latino activists, black protesters, and nuns inspired by Vatican II. His successor, Timothy Manning, was a more flexible prelate. Manning gave the vicar general, Monsignor Robert Hawkes, a major hand in financial control. "Hawkes was feared by many priests," a church insider told me, "for his power and absolute control of money."

"As Manning's vicar general, Hawkes handled dozens of accusations against clergy predators, mostly by covering them up," explains John Manly, a prominent Orange County attorney in clergy abuse litigation.

Hawkes was also a pederast. "He paid boys he abused to work at rectories and secured scholarships at a Catholic high school to keep them silent," says Beverly Hills attorney Anthony Demarco, who represents one of the victims.

In 1985, when Mahony became archbishop, he fired Hawkes, although no reason was publicly given. Hawkes died soon thereafter. His probate shows that he left $30,000 cash and about $100,000 in property, most of which went to relatives.[24] He also left behind at least three youths he sexually abused.[25]

The first native Angeleno archbishop, Mahony came from Irish stock. "I didn't see Fresno as his career move," says Jerry Fallon. "Most priests were against César Chávez. Farmers donated heavily to churches in the San Joaquin Valley." Mahony publicly supported the highly religious Chávez, while privately recycling the pedophile O'Grady, which was an internal matter.

In 1991 John Paul made Mahony a cardinal. With his imposing height, dark eyes, and handsome face, Mahony had the social ease to charm the wealthy who gave and gave again. Among them were the hotelier Baron Hilton; Bob Hope's wife, Dolores; Richard Riordan, the future mayor; and Daniel Donohue, president of the Dan Murphy Foundation (based on his father-in-law's fortune). Donohue held a knighthood bestowed by Pius XII for donations to the Holy See; he liked being called Sir Daniel. In the 1940s his wife, Bernardine, gave $250,000 to St. Vibiana Cathedral.[26] When a 1994 earthquake jolted St. Vibiana, Mahony wanted to demolish and rebuild; preservationists blocked him. He pitched a world-class cathedral to civic leaders on the site off Hollywood Freeway. The Rupert Murdoch Family Foundations gave $10 million. The Wall Street Journal called it "one of the five most significant building projects in the country."[27]

Mahony was an avatar of the building bishops of yesteryear, raising the $190 million for the Cathedral of Our Lady of the Angels, immersing himself in the aesthetic and construction details. Los Angeles was growing into its past as a vast Mexican city outside Mexico, now encompassing a mosaic of Asians, Filipinos, and Latinos from Central America. The city was also a case study of national problems that seemed insoluble: a choked infrastructure, dysfunctional public schools, the yawning maw between wealth and poverty, gang killings in drug-infested barrios, and the recurrent plague of national disasters—fires, droughts, mud slides, earthquakes—so severe they at times seemed biblical.

But like the city it served, the church under Cardinal Mahony was a study in resilience. When he gave his shocking 1998 testimony in Stockton, the archdiocese had 287 parish programs for 4 million Catholics. The previous eight years had seen parishes generate a $299 million surplus to fund renovation or new buildings.[28] Each parish paid for its schools. The cardinal was immersed in the final stages of the new cathedral when the Boston scandal broke in January 2002.

MAHONY IN CRISIS

As the media coverage intensified, Jeff Anderson got a call from a southern California police officer named Manny Vega. A decorated marine veteran, Vega said that he and guys he had grown up with in his hometown, Oxnard, were abused as kids by Father Fidencio Silva. Oxnard lies about halfway between Los Angeles and Santa Barbara. On Easter Sunday in 2002, Anderson and Drivon made the 345-mile trek from Stockton to meet with the survivors' group—eight Latinos, including a probation officer, a social worker, cops, and a lawyer. Anderson explained the statute of limitations hurdle; he wanted to help them seek redress. On the long drive home, Anderson fumed, "We need a window in the law."

"Hell yes!" said Larry Drivon, who had political contacts. "Let's go do it."

Manny Vega's family had come from Yucatán; his father was a *bracero*, a field-worker who had come legally to postwar California and eventually gained citizenship. Father Silva began abusing the boy sexually in sixth grade, and took nude photos of him. As Manny heard kids play outside, he felt dirty inside Our Lady of Guadalupe rectory. To keep the boy from telling anyone of his ordeal, Silva drummed into him the story of Judas, betrayer of Jesus. For years Manny Vega kept silent, shame growing like a tumor.[29] Sorrow lanced his memories of praying with his parents as a boy. As a man he couldn't take his own two kids to church, he couldn't step inside a church. At the state capitol in Sacramento, Manny Vega, an Oxnard police officer of the year, sat down with State Senator Martha Escutia, the head of the powerful Latino caucus. She was appalled to learn what the priest had done, that Vega had no legal recourse. Escutia arranged for a group of survivors to give committee testimony. Drivon knew they needed more help to move a bill of this scope through the legislature; he introduced Anderson to Ray Boucher, one of the state's leading trial attorneys. Boucher had good political contacts and superb experience as a class action litigator. Boucher's law firm in Beverly Hills was in a two-story building with about forty employees. All three men knew that if the bill passed, their small firms faced a daunting commitment of time and money. The legislation sailed through, giving victims—regardless of when they had been abused—one year starting on January 1, 2003, to sue the responsible party.

In response to the bishops' youth protection charter of June 2002, Mahony cast himself as a reformer. "If priests are indicted and some end up in prison or whatever, that's going to be very sad for them, for the church," Mahony asserted. "But if that is required to move beyond, that's what we're going to have go through."[30] The cardinal hired J. Michael Hennigan, one of L.A.'s priciest white-collar criminal defense attorneys, to blunt the criminal subpoenas seeking personnel files of priests. Reading the *Boston Globe,* and Ron Russell's investigative reports in *New Times* (L.A.), Head Deputy District Attorney William Hodgman viewed Mahony as a possible case of obstruction of justice. "There is an inevitability to this investigation," Hodgman told *L.A. Weekly.* "It's like Watergate unfolding. We'll work from the ground up. We will get documents and we will put priests in jail."[31]

In response to the budding criminal probe, Mahony formed a Clergy Misconduct Oversight Board with thirteen members, mostly laypeople, and three former FBI agents on call to investigate any charges that might arise. He instituted a Safeguard the Children Program for eighteen thousand church and school employees. But if his reforms and rhetoric suggested an outstretched healing hand to people hungry for justice, his other fist gripped a shield. Mahony and his lawyers knew that the decision of one judge in Boston had released clergy files to the *Globe*, and that as a result Cardinal Law's reputation lay in wreckage.

Sizing up the media dynamics, Roger Mahony launched the most expensive legal battle in American church history to thwart subpoenas for files of accused priests. He would not sit still as prosecutor Bill Hodgman's staff investigated his own complicity in shielding crimes. The assertion that clergy files were privileged under freedom of religion, which the Boston court rejected, became the ramrod issue in Los Angeles, stalling the criminal and civil cases in a legal saga that would run for many years.

A *Los Angeles Times* investigation in late summer 2002 mapped out a chronology of priests who had been reassigned after going to treatment facilities, while the church evaded or ignored police—a pattern of hierarchical behavior well documented in Louisiana, Minnesota, Illinois, New England, New York, Texas, and elsewhere. The priests' photographs resembled mug shots. "I'm just horrified by this whole thing," Mahony said. "You get the cross that comes your way, and this obviously for me is a very heavy cross."

> The *Times* identified 32 parish priests and one deacon who, since Mahony's arrival in 1985, have been accused of molesting minors. Seven of the clerics were dismissed by the cardinal in February, six fled, three have been convicted of sex crimes and 17 are under criminal investigation by law enforcement. The *Times* examination also included more than 100 interviews with church officials, law enforcement authorities, alleged victims and their attorneys.[32]

The Cathedral of Our Lady of the Angels opened on September 2, 2002, to a choir singing "Ode to Joy" as Nigerian and Scottish drummers, a family carrying the relics of saints, a train of bishops wearing robes of watered silk, then priests, deacons, nuns—some seven hundred religious figures—moved in stately procession past the three-story bronze doors into a space of soaring beauty. "The fulcrum where the secular and sacred are joined for the glory of God and the good of the city," wrote Larry B. Stammer in the *Los Angeles Times Magazine*. Mahony called it "a symbol evocative of the deepest aspiration and hopes of the whole polis, the whole people of Los Angeles, the earthly city yearning for consummation, the completion yet to come in the new Jerusalem."[33]

The legal front focused on a subterranean city, as suggested in the 1998 Stockton trial. Jeff Anderson and the gathering army of lawyers knew that clergy records would excavate another California, a Catholic terrain of memory, laden with a hidden history of sexual crimes perpetrated on hundreds of youngsters like Manny Vega. Ray Boucher, who had been an altar boy in New England, became the lead plaintiff attorney to negotiate with the archdiocesan counsel, Mike Hennigan, in Los Angeles. The culmination of the 2003 Boston cases—$85 million for 542 clients—averaged out at $156,000 per plaintiff. California dioceses were well financed, with solid real estate holdings and insurers' deep pockets. As the lawyers signed up clients, the cathedral stood for the presence of Christ in time, a structure of breathtaking beauty—Mahony's symbolic legacy.

The archdiocesan annual budget of $116 million was nearly half that of the Vatican. Less than a month after the glowing coverage of the cathedral opening, Mahony cut the budgets of seven church programs "to close a $4.3 million deficit . . . [with] layoffs of roughly 60 employees," the *Los Angeles Times* reported. Five of Mahony's top assistants resigned in frustration.

> Mahony and other archdiocesan officials have said that the cuts in the budget were needed to close a deficit caused by losses in the stock market. Others have pointed to the church's need to set aside money against the future costs of sexual-abuse settlements.[34]

While Jeff Anderson was on a journey toward spirituality, John Manly's faith was crumbling. His law firm was in a high-rise office near John Wayne Airport in Orange County. A Republican who had built a practice on real estate law, Manly had gone through Catholic schools and attended retreats as a University of Southern California undergraduate. After serving as a naval intelligence officer, he went to law school. He and his wife had four children. "There is an evil in all this," Manly brooded in a December twilight of 2004, with a panoramic view of gleaming malls and manicured streets. "We have clients in Alaska who went through stuff that is mind-boggling to someone like me."

In 1996 Manly and Irvine attorney Katherine Freberg had taken the case of Ryan DiMaria, age twenty-one, who was battling alcoholism in the aftershocks of being molested by Father Michael Harris, a popular high school principal from whom he had sought counseling as a teenager, after a friend's suicide. DiMaria told a priest how Harris had abused him: Father G. Patrick Ziemann, the scion of a prominent area family, and a seminary friend of Mahony's. Mahony, in the meantime, arranged for Ziemann to become bishop of Santa Rosa, north of San Francisco. Ziemann squandered the diocesan treasury, left a $16 million debt, and resigned in 1998 when a priest sued him, alleging he coerced him to provide sex. To prevent Mahony from testifying in the DiMaria case, the Orange diocese settled for a whopping $5.2 million, and agreed to eleven demands made by DiMaria and his attorney, notably, a zero-tolerance policy on abusers. In time, Ryan DiMaria became an attorney representing victims. Harris, the perpetrator, left the priesthood but was never prosecuted.

John Manly's firm had one hundred abuse clients. His chief researcher, Patrick Wall, was a brilliant canonist who had quit the Benedictine priesthood in Collegeville, Minnesota, after five parish assignments, each one replacing a pastor who had stolen money or abused children. Wall had recently moved to California when he saw Manly quoted in the press. He called in hopes of sharing a few things he knew. Manly hired him on the spot. Now married, with a child, Wall was a sleuth when it came to church documents—and had become an Episcopalian by 2003. Another expert witness, Richard Sipe of La Jolla, was a psychotherapist and former Benedictine priest who had written books on celibacy. In their overlapping research, Sipe, Wall, and Tom Doyle, with ten advanced degrees among them, formed a brain trust for Jeff Anderson and John Manly. The trio collaborated on *Sex, Priests, and Secret Codes*, a history of how church laws responded to systemic clergy sexual abuse and the hierarchy's latter-day reliance on psychiatric treatment facilities.[35]

"In some dioceses," said Manly, "if you're not part of the sexual culture, you don't get promoted, you don't get choice assignments. No one can talk about it because the consequences for that person are catastrophic."

The darkness John Manly felt cut a sharp contrast with Pat Wall's wit. Both men had the heft of football players from their younger years. Wall was rewriting his idea of faith with intrigue over each new document. "Roger Mahony is crucial to the Vatican," he told me in 2010, by which time he had become a Buddhist. "He was one of the cardinals called to the Consistory for the Study of the Special Economic Problems of the Holy See"—a 1980 convocation under John Paul II to deal with Vatican deficits. "James Stafford, the archbishop of Denver, was on it; he's in the Curia now. Cormac Murphy O'Connor of London was drawn in, and later Ed Egan from New York. These cardinals are some of the best money producers for Rome. Los Angeles pays the largest annual fee to Rome of any U.S. diocese. Factor in Peter's Pence, and the special checks a cardinal takes on trips to Rome, there's Roger.

"Mahony has a big contract with Stewart Enterprises for management of the Catholic cemeteries," said Wall. "They give a cut to the archdiocese on every funeral they do. Stewart was a big supporter of the new cathedral.[36] Burials are a business for the church. If you're a pastor, as I was, you're inundated in winter—that's the burial season. Spring is big for baptisms, summer for weddings. It's the flow of life, the rise and fall of the rivers and rains. You can bet Mahony is laying his groundwork in Rome to make these abuse cases go away."

Mahony was indeed doing business in Rome, as several lawyers deduced from informal conversations with certain judges overseeing the negotiations. Of the three geographic groupings for the settlements—Clergy 1, in northern California; Clergy 2, in Los Angeles; and Clergy 3, in Orange, San Diego, and dioceses to the south—Clergy 2, with 554 cases, dwarfed the others. Mahony made presentations to the Third Office of the Congregation for the Clergy for the alienation of church property. Unlike Seán O'Malley, who had come empty-handed from Boston to Rome, Mahony dealt from a position of strength. The Vatican gave him great latitude on his handling of assets, for besides building the great cathedral, he had otherwise proved his mettle.

GIRDING FOR BATTLE

By spring 2003, eleven clerics had been indicted on criminal charges in Los Angeles. More than nine hundred civil claims were filed that year against California dioceses. The judges were pushing the settlement groups for mediation to avoid a system clogged with endless trials. These were not class action suits; still, coordinated proceedings with many clients move slowly. Besides the forty or so plaintiff lawyers, Hennigan had a large firm billing long hours on the many issues; the insurance companies that held liability policies of the dioceses had their lawyers. Los Angeles criminal defense attorney Don Steier represented accused priests. Procedural delays were strategic. Mahony also retained a public relations firm (with Enron among its clients) to help with damage control.[37]

"The usual process in cases like this is to saddle up, start discovery, and get a trial date," explained Steve Rubino, a New Jersey lawyer who had two decades' experience in suing dioceses and religious orders. "Instead, we fought about what the discovery would be. The church claimed the priests' files were off-limits because of freedom of religion. Then they challenged the state law under which we had filed the cases. It became a tsunami of paper."

Raised in a blue-collar Catholic home and a law school graduate of Catholic University, Rubino had started out as a prosecutor. He began a civil practice; on taking his first case against the church, he was appalled at the unprosecuted criminal behavior. Through a friendship with Tom Doyle he "joined this strange force, out of the church, *into* the church," he told me one afternoon on the Atlantic shore, a short walk from his home. Unlike Jeff Anderson, the conservative Rubino turned down many cases with time-statute problems. *The only thing I can get for you is money,* he told the clients he did take on. *What you've got to do is recover and learn to live well.*

"Mahony and Hennigan led certain of my esteemed colleagues to believe this would be paid by [insurance] carriers; we'll settle all claims in six months," bristled Rubino. "That played well with the judiciary. The judges didn't want discovery in all of these cases: they wanted order and structure to the proceedings. When Mahony claimed First Amendment privilege, that foxed everything. We spent three years circling over whether we *had* a mediated package."

Rubino was allied with Kathy Freberg, Manly's former law partner, on 156 cases and 37 perpetrators. "We said this is it, we know our future's on the line, *let's do it,*" Rubino remembered. "The only way to get a job done is to deal from a position of strength. The defense had an advantage in sheer manpower. We had to borrow $2 million each, and when I say *we were in,* I mean, we were *deep* in, like with houses, pets, trailers. A lot of lawyers are not willing to take those risks. I don't begrudge them. The only thing the bishops respect is when you keep hitting them, all the time. You have to just stay in their faces."

Manny Vega spent Holy Week of 2003 on a hunger strike outside the Cathedral of Our Lady of the Angels with a sleeping bag and picket sign that said "You Can't Hide the Truth from God." A lady entering church hissed, "You're a shame and an embarrassment." Father Silva had fled to Mexico. (When a TV reporter found him, Silva denied abusing any of the eight men.) Refusing to shave, shower, or eat, Vega occupied his slice of sidewalk. On Good Friday, he was asleep on the concrete when Mahony appeared. Light-headed from lack of food, Vega stood up and stumbled. The cardinal gave him a steadying hand. "You need to take some nutrients," said Mahony helpfully.

"Would you have said that to César Chávez?" Vega shot back.

Mahony winced at the reference to the farm workers' legendary hunger strikes, and withdrew.

Later, the cardinal came back, several times, to talk with Vega and a clutch of survivor-protesters. He apologized (though Silva's abuses predated his time as archbishop); he gave them access to the cathedral restrooms. He offered rosary beads blessed by the pope, which Vega accepted, and later regretted, saying it made him feel bought off. Vega asked to meet one-on-one. Mahony said he could not, regretfully, for legal reasons.

In June 2003 the roof caved in on District Attorney Steve Cooley and the lead prosecutor, Bill Hodgman. The U.S. Supreme Court in *Stogner v. California*, on a 5–4 vote, reversed a California law that enabled prosecutors, in certain circumstances, to pursue people for sex crimes committed far back in time. "*Stogner* killed us," said Hodgman. Among those set free, Michael Wempe had gone through the seminary with Mahony. Wempe's indictment on forty-three counts of child molestation was thrown out. His backstory is instructive.

In May 1987 Wempe was accused of having sex with a youth. Mahony sent him to a clergy treatment center in Jemez Springs, New Mexico, for six months. In 1988 he appointed Wempe a chaplain at Cedars-Sinai Medical Center, confiding not a word on his background to hospital officials. Later that year, two young men complained to the archdiocese that Wempe had abused them as boys. He stayed on his job, undergoing therapy. From 1990 to 1995, he molested a boy in his hospital office. In 2002 Wempe was finally fired after his older transgressions made the news. Less than a year after *Stogner*, Wempe was charged in a new case. Without releasing Wempe's treatment files, Mahony blamed the Paracletes' facility in New Mexico, which was driven out of business by litigation in the midnineties.

Mahony gave me a telephone interview on February 12, 2005, for a *National Catholic Reporter* profile. Hundreds of civil cases were grinding slowly forward. The cardinal insisted that the Paracletes' "prognosis" was that if Wempe "continued his spiritual direction and counseling he was getting, that he would not reoffend. And they recommended that he serve in a limited capacity such as a chaplain to a hospital or a prison facility. At the time, I believed their prognosis to be accurate . . . It wasn't until after he was taken out of ministry that someone made a report that has been subject to criminal prosecution."[38]

Here was John Paul's rationalization from the 2002 cardinals' meeting, cemented into an alibi: the therapists are at fault, they gave us bad advice. What happened to moral standards for a religious life? Why were pedophiles recycled into ministries and church jobs with access to new victims? Mahony had unseemly proximity to several men like Wempe. Father Carl Sutphin lived in the same rectory with Mahony in two cathedrals over a span of seven years until a 2002 LAPD investigation of charges that Sutphin molested two sets of brothers, which caused the cardinal to force his retirement. Sutphin had been a classmate of Mahony's at St. John's Seminary on the hilly estate in Camarillo. In 1991 Mahony removed him from ministry when a Phoenix man said that Sutphin had abused him and his twin brother in the 1970s. Mahony sent Sutphin to St. Luke Institute in Suitland, Maryland, but did not report him to authorities; California at that time did not include clergy as "mandated reporters" of abuse. Sutphin came back to be chaplain in a retirement home. In 1995 Sutphin moved into the St. Vibiana rectory with Mahony, and on to Our Lady of Angels, until his 2002 removal.

"Father Sutphin was another example of someone whose prognosis was favorable," Mahony told me calmly. "One of his ministries had been dealing with men in jail, so the old cathedral rectory, which is right downtown near the jail, seemed to be a good place for him to be in residence, and certainly under supervision . . . We have absolutely no report of any reoffense on his part the whole time." He seemed detached from the reality of what Sutphin had done.

Monsignor Richard A. Loomis had been vicar of clergy with the responsibility to investigate sex abuse allegations in the 1990s. He was himself accused in a civil case, as Mary Grant, a California SNAP leader, wrote in a February 23, 2004, letter to the U.S. Catholic Bishops' Office of Child and Youth Protection in Washington, D.C.

> Although Msgr. Loomis was being sued for sexual molestation, the church deemed him innocent, largely because but a single accuser had come forward. On February 8 of this year, SNAP leafleted [Loomis's] church, only to be mocked and scorned by parishioners. But the publicity from the event caused another victim of Msgr. Loomis to come forward, apparently with a story sufficiently credible to cause the removal of Msgr. Loomis from ministry on February 15, one week later.[39]

"The case proves that our procedures are working," Mahony said in his mild, unruffled way. "If there's sufficient credible evidence and the board decides to recommend that he be taken out of active ministry, and they did in this case, I obviously concurred in their recommendation." As to why SNAP had to leaflet in the first place, Mahony said, "You know, I can't remember the exact sequences. A lot of these problems with civil suits filed in 2002–2003 are because we did not have names of victims or any way to talk to them."

"John Doe" names were routinely given to the church, attorneys told me.

The archdiocese cited expenses of $4,871,000 "related to legal fees, and other costs related to sexual abuse claims in fiscal year 2004. As of September 30, 2004, the Archdiocese has received $4,070,000 in reimbursements of legal fees and settlements" from insurance companies—leaving $801,000 presumably covered by church funds. The insurance companies were reimbursing the expenses for Michael Hennigan's white-shoe firm as part of the policy coverage. In January 2005 three insurers asked the court to relieve them of responsibility, on grounds that the archdiocese had withheld documents. In November California superior court judge

Haley J. Fromholz, a yeoman figure in keeping the complex proceedings in motion, ruled for the archdiocese.

In a 2004 *Report to the People of God*, Mahony stated: "I acknowledge my own mistakes"—but he did not explain them. The report summarized charges against several of the 113 priests and 130 religious brothers, deacons, and seminarians accused over seventy years. It said that 16 priests, unnamed, had been falsely accused. "My goal as your Archbishop is to do all in my power to prevent sexual abuse by anyone serving our Archdiocese now and in the future. Moving the healing and reconciliation process forward requires the fullest possible disclosure."[40]

The first survivors' group, involving the Orange diocese, settled on December 3, 2004, with $100 million to eighty-seven victims. "We were up till two a.m. on December second, hashing it out on *not* settling for $99 million," explained Steve Rubino. "Kathy Freberg, Ray Boucher, and I knew the $100 million mark was historical and it would drive up the value of the other cases. It took us four days to push the church and insurance lawyers to $1.2 million per case. It almost came to fisticuffs. We turned down $99,960,000 because it was $40,000 short. We wanted $100 million as a benchmark. We were in year three by then."

"Mahony put huge pressure on [Orange bishop] Tod Brown not to settle," Boucher told me at the time. "Mahony was trying to shut us down."

But the Orange diocese, which had once been a part of the larger archdiocese of Los Angeles, had a $171 million investment portfolio and $23.4 million in cash to tap for the agreement. During the litigation Bishop Brown had suspended the fund-raising to build a new cathedral. A diocesan attorney announced that the sale of property, funds from cash reserves, and loans secured by church assets would raise the diocese's portion of the settlement, shared with eight insurance companies. The Los Angeles archdiocese was still in negotiations with attorneys for 554 plaintiffs. Loyola of Los Angeles Law School professor Georgene Vairo remarked, "It's like a market is being established for settlements and the price can go up or down." Mahony's lawyer, Hennigan, told the *Los Angeles Times* that some of the cases "will just break your heart," and speculated that the fifty worst cases could reach jury verdicts of $5 million.[41]

Those words were like a signal flare to the insurance lawyers. The only way to get insurance companies to settle was by proving it would cost more *not* to settle—gambling on a trial. Insurance covered wrongful acts from early years of a given policy. Few carriers insured churches for clergy wrongdoing anymore. Catholic dioceses sank funds into self-insured risk pools, and prayed for no new perpetrators. Still, the Orange settlements left a key issue unresolved: disclosure of church files on the perpetrators. SNAP leaders were relentless in the media about demanding that the church post all of the relevant clergy documents.

In a complex agreement with the court, Mahony's lawyers agreed to provide the plaintiffs with information summaries, called "proffers," from the requested files. Soon afterward, the archdiocese filed a voluminous motion challenging the law under which the victims had sued. "We had a deal that they wouldn't do that," groused Boucher, sitting in his Beverly Hills office. "Hennigan is a consummate soldier. The guy will burn paper in his hands to show his loyalty. This is part of the appeasement of the insurance carriers."

A GIFT FROM ROME

As Boucher locked horns with Hennigan in Los Angeles, Jeff Anderson was immersed in Bay Area preparations; the San Francisco archdiocese faced sixty cases. The strategy was to take the first few cases to trial, in hopes of inducing settlement negotiations. During the Easter week that Manny Vega protested at L.A.'s cathedral, SNAP members in San Francisco rallied outside Sts. Peter and Paul, the iconic church on Washington Square where Joe DiMaggio and Marilyn Monroe posed for photographs after their 1954 wedding at City Hall.

The North Beach parish was run by the Salesians of Don Bosco, an order founded in Italy in the nineteenth century with a special focus on the care of young people. The young DiMaggio played sports at the Salesian Boys' Club. Now, as reporters gathered, the abuse survivors railed about the Salesians and their associate pastor, Father Stephen Whelan, who were defendants in a civil case Anderson and Rick Simmons had brought for Joey Piscitelli. As a fourteen-year-old at Salesian High in nearby Richmond, Piscitelli had drawn pictures of Jesus regurgitating on the cross and a priest leering at boys in the shower stall. Joey Piscitelli was fifty now: short, bearded, with sledgehammer intensity. "Whelan, the priest who molested me, is in that rectory," he kept saying.[42]

"It's a spurious accusation," Whelan told TV reporter Dan Noyes, who got a moment inside the rectory. The Salesians announced that Whelan had no contact with children, though he was still saying Mass. In the long buildup to the trial—which yielded a $600,000 verdict to him—Joey Piscitelli kept saying, "The priest who molested me is a block away from Bishop Levada, and he has left that priest in ministry with kids."[43]

Born in 1936 in Long Beach, William Levada had gone through the Camarillo seminary with Roger Mahony. As a young theologian he worked for Cardinal Ratzinger at the CDF in the early eighties. Back home in 1985, boosted by Mahony, he became an auxiliary bishop. A man of compact build with receding gray hair, Archbishop Levada lived in the rectory of St. Mary's Cathedral around the corner from the Salesian provincial headquarters, which housed a religious brother who had served time for child abuse and three priests, dripping guilt from civil cases, who were beyond the statutory reach for criminal charges. Religious orders serve at the discretion of a bishop.

Anderson had first encountered the Salesians in St. Petersburg, Florida, in 2002, when he sued one of the religious brothers, who was promptly transferred to a Salesian house in New Jersey. Later that year, he sued the order in Chicago for a Mexican priest who faced accusations from four Latino youths; the priest was packed off to New Jersey, then Mexico. When Joey Piscitelli contacted him, Jeff Anderson engaged a Bay Area attorney, Rick Simmons, as cocounsel. After taking the depositions of Whelan and his superiors, Anderson saw the California Salesians, with sixteen perpetrators, as a hive of corruption. Levada's passivity from that reality, while he lived around the corner from Salesian headquarters in the City by the Bay, weirdly made sense. Anderson had taken Levada's deposition over his decisions as archbishop in Portland several years before. Levada had sent predators in therapy back to ministry. The archdiocesan attorney, Robert McMenamin, had advised Levada to tell church officials about their obligation to report predators to the police. Levada declined. McMenamin resigned; he later began representing abuse victims. The Oregon Supreme Court dismissed Levada's petition to disqualify McMenamin from such cases as a conflict of interest. McMenamin wrote to his successor: "I have loyalty both to my religion and the confidences of former clients, but not to church officials who deny justice to victims."

Stirring his powdered vitamins and liquid fruit, Jeff Anderson pondered the mind-set that linked Levada, Mahony, and innumerable bishops he had deposed across two decades. Levada struck him as remote, affable, and clueless about what had been going on in his own diocese. But he fell right in line with the hierarchs, hiding the secrets of a celibate system that tolerated all kinds of behavior, the worst of which defiled innocent youth. Unlike AA members, they had no higher power to help them change their hypocritical ways. Popes received them with fraternal esteem. Their first responsibility was to a perverse chivalry that cloaked the sickest secrets. The splendor of Mass, the legacy of saints, the Eucharist as table of life had scant meaning for Anderson; he knew the rituals were vital to Catholics, but he had never known the spiritual dimension of the faith in such a way as to mourn its loss. But he saw how that loss tore at his clients. He was sensitive to the struggle of Tom Doyle and Pat Wall, who were regrounding themselves spiritually. He drew strength from their search, their learnedness, their tenacity in resisting the evil, in taking his battle however far he might.

Levada had gone to San Francisco in 1995. Since the 2002 scandal had broken, he had shoveled some of the muck. Among the clerics he had pulled from ministry for sexually abusing youth were a chaplain of the San Francisco 49ers football team, a former head of Catholic Charities, a rector of the cathedral, a head of the office of liturgy, a police department chaplain, and a former dean at the seminary who used the Internet to search for teenage sex partners.

Levada was unique among U.S. bishops for having been sued by a priest who blew the whistle on a cleric for making advances on a teenage boy.

Born in 1944, Jon Conley was an assistant U.S. attorney in Michigan who decided to become a priest in the late 1980s. Done with the bitter midwestern winters, Conley moved to San Francisco, went through the seminary, and was ordained. One night in 1997, as an assistant pastor, he entered his rectory to find the pastor, Father Gregory Aylward, crawling toward the back door. A flustered fourteen-year-old boy scrambled back to his post as phone receptionist. Suspecting the boy was too embarrassed to admit what had happened, Conley met with an auxiliary bishop who told him, "We usually keep these things in-house." With Levada out of town, Conley decided to notify the San Mateo District Attorney's Office. Frightened, the boy told investigators that he and Father Aylward had only been wrestling. No charges were filed.

Conley told the chancery he couldn't live with a pedophile; he moved

into a hotel. A chancery priest told Conley not to say "pedophile" or mention the accusations to anyone. The boy quit his rectory job. Conley met
the family. The mother wept, saying she couldn't force her son to testify
about Aylward's history of sexual advances. When Conley met with Archbishop Levada and a chancery monsignor, he knew the archdiocese was
circling the wagons around Aylward.

When I interviewed Conley in 2005 on a magazine assignment, he said
that Levada had used the word "calumny" when discussing the accusations
against Aylward. In that meeting a monsignor was taking notes; Conley
pulled out a tape recorder to avoid being set up as a scapegoat. "You don't
trust me?" said Levada. He ordered Conley to turn off the tape recorder.
Conley refused. Levada ordered him onto administrative leave, saying,
"Think about obedience."

They met again privately, no tape recorder; Levada wanted Conley to
undergo psychological evaluation. Conley refused. When the *San Francisco Examiner* got wind of Conley's predicament, an archdiocesan statement said that the church had "instructed him to report the incident to
civil authorities, and strongly supports the reporting of all incidents of
suspected child abuse or neglect. It was [Conley's] behavior subsequent
to the reporting which was unacceptable." Conley fired off a letter to the
Examiner: "Why does the archdiocese of San Francisco not have written policies and procedures in place for priests to deal with situations of
abuse?" He sued Levada and the archdiocese for defamation and infliction
of emotional distress. Conley wanted a public apology *and* procedures for
handling abuse allegations to protect whistle-blowing priests like himself.
Levada ordered him to withdraw the suit and seek "a program of reme-
dial assistance . . . [or] I will have no alternative but to impose on you the
censure of suspension forbidding your exercise of all rights, privileges and
faculties associated with the priestly ministry."

Conley's lawsuit was dismissed as an intrachurch matter. The boy's
family sued the archdiocese. Aylward admitted in a deposition that he
had gotten sexual gratification for years from wrestling with minors. The
archdiocese agreed to a $750,000 settlement with the family. Aylward
left the ministry. Conley's attorney appealed his case. A California appellate court ruled that the law mandating that clergy report suspected
abusers superseded the freedom of religion privilege. Conley had a bona
fide defamation claim against Levada. Depositions began; Levada threw

in the towel. The church issued a statement praising Conley for reporting the incident. The archdiocese "prefunded" Conley's retirement.
How much, Conley would not say, but he had a nice apartment in the
chic Noe Valley neighborhood with good views of the city. As we sat
in his living room, watching TV coverage of Pope John Paul's death,
Conley, a stout, bearded chap with a keen sense of irony, murmured, "I
do substitute work for priests on vacation. This church is a little crazy,
you know?"

And then, as if by magic, several days after the white smoke heralded a
new pope, Benedict XVI lowered a rope ladder that would lift Archbishop
Levada out of the provincial muck, up and away to the Eternal City. Bill
Levada would take Ratzinger's place as the prefect of the Congregation for
the Doctrine of the Faith. The new job assured him of a cardinal's red hat.
Why Levada? many people wondered. His credentials as a theologian were
marginal. But Ratzinger realized that his office, backlogged with seven
hundred cases of sex offenders, needed an American who understood the
issue. Levada's messy record in the swamps of scandal mattered little; he
had proved his fidelity to the men of the apostolic succession.

By late summer 2005, four jury trials in northern California civil cases
involving one priest had produced $5.8 million in judgments. Settlement
negotiations yielded another $37.2 million to a plaintiffs' group. Two of
the survivors were women abused as girls by Father Greg Ingels, a canon
lawyer who had advised Levada on abuse issues. On learning of the accusations against him, Levada let Ingels live quietly at a seminary with a retired archbishop, John Quinn. That move so outraged psychotherapist Jim
Jenkins, chair of Levada's clergy review board, that he resigned. A beaming Levada stood in the cathedral sanctuary for his farewell Mass when a
process server handed him a subpoena to testify in a San Francisco case.

Mahony's lawyers used the term "formation privilege" as shorthand for
the religious freedom argument by which that archdiocese shielded sex offenders' files. *Los Angeles Times* reporters Jean Guccione and William Lobdell, who covered the legal saga with tenacious intelligence, wrote in 2004:

> The archdiocese asserts that the privilege stems from a bishop's
> ecclesiastical duty to provide a lifetime of formative spiritual guid-
> ance to his priests. As claimed by the archdiocese, the privilege
> would require that sensitive communication between a bishop

and his priests involving counseling—including documents relating to sexual abuse of minors—be kept confidential.

Any action by the state to breach that privilege would violate
both state law and the state and federal constitutions' guarantee
of religious freedom, the archdiocese's attorneys argue.[44]

Anderson scoffed, "This kind of assertion of a First Amendment privilege has never succeeded elsewhere. Mahony is putting his fingers and toes
in a big dyke, but he can't keep plugging the holes."[45]

Mahony had borrowed a page from the Vatican playbook. Archbishop
Tarcisio Bertone, a top canon lawyer at the Congregation for the Doctrine
of the Faith, asserted in 2002, "If a priest cannot confide in his bishop
because he is afraid of being denounced it would mean there is no more
freedom of conscience. Civil society must also respect the 'professional
secrecy' of priests."[46]

Bertone was a Salesian. His comments were utterly consistent with the
order's concealment of sex offenders in Jeff Anderson's experience. Bertone had left the CDF in 2003 to become archbishop of Genoa, gaining
administrative experience to help him rise in the apostolic succession. On
June 23, 2006, Pope Benedict named Cardinal Bertone to succeed Sodano
as secretary of state.

Only later did the news emerge that while in Genoa, Bertone had written a celebratory preface to the 2003 Italian edition of Father Maciel's
book-length interview, *Christ Is My Life*—a last-ditch effort at defending
himself in the congregation where Bertone had previously worked. *Christ
Is My Life* appeared some months before Ratzinger ordered the investigation. "The answers that Father Maciel gives . . . are profound and simple
and have the frankness of one who lives his mission in the world and in
the Church with his sights and his heart fixed on Christ Jesus," wrote Bertone. "The key to this success is, without doubt, the attractive force of the
love of Christ."[47]

When Bertone's endorsement surfaced in 2010, Maciel's two grown
sons had given an hour-long radio interview to Carmen Aristegui, a leading journalist in Mexico City, claiming he had abused them as boys and
that meetings with Legion of Christ officials had disclosed, alas, that Maciel's estate was empty. By then, Secretary of State Bertone and Cardinal
Levada were waiting for five bishops from as many countries to deliver

reports of their investigation of the entire religious order, a move without precedent in modern church history.[48]

CLOSING THE DEAL IN CALIFORNIA

As Ray Boucher pushed his counterpart Mike Hennigan to embrace an aggregate settlement exceeding $600 million, all of the attorneys with cases in the Clergy 2 grouping saw Cardinal Mahony's role as strategic if they were to prevail. Mahony was being battered in the media (the *New York Times* and *Los Angeles Times*, in disgust at his recycling of pedophiles, called on the cardinal to resign), but the lawyers knew that to close the deal, they needed Mahony on the job, threading the tightrope between insurance companies and the religious orders, particularly the Salesians, who would have to contribute funds for the settlement packages to come together. For all of their clients' fury at the long delays, the lawyers realized that attacking Mahony as author of a cover-up undercut their interests. As Steve Rubino put it: "If a lawsuit says that negligence causes an injury, that's a covered claim. But if proof comes out that these were intentional acts, a cover-up, the carriers don't have to pay. We knew as we prepared these cases, that if we *went to trial* and aggressively argued cover-up, we'd walk right out of coverage: no deep pocket. And we knew Mahony did not have the assets to pay the full value"—which Boucher was pushing for an average of $1.4 million per case.

Jeff Anderson suggested they find a way for Mahony to meet some survivors. As part of this strategy, Boucher hired a producer to film interviews with the clients, edit their testimonies with the reflections of parents or spouses, intercut the memoir sequences with news footage where possible, and provide DVDs of the ten-minute profiles to Mahony and the judges overseeing the mediation process, as a way of turning "clients" and "survivors" into actual people whose stories would inject pathos and real-life issues into the legal mix.

"I've met a very large number of victims," the cardinal told me in our 2005 interview. "I've also looked at the taped interviews the plaintiff attorneys here have developed. Dozens of interviews on DVD. I've listened to those, every single one of them. They just cause you to cry. You simply are in disbelief at what has happened to the lives of these people. It has been a very humbling experience. Spiritually, I was absolutely at the bottom, which means total vulnerability to God's grace. And I began to realize that this is the ministry Jesus Christ is asking of me and others at this time, to repair the damage, to make sure it won't happen again."

Boucher, at a dinner with Mahony and counsel Mike Hennigan in the cathedral rectory, insisted that the settlement numbers for the 554 claims go well north of $600 million, using $1.4 million per victim as the gauge. He knew his counterparts were in a mosh pit with the insurance lawyers. Subsequently, Hennigan suggested they divide the L.A. group into two sequences—one small, one large. For Mahony's planning, they had to cut the first deal before the end of 2006, and give the cardinal some time to corral the rest of the money. On December 1, 2006, the archdiocese agreed to $60 million for forty-five plaintiffs. These cases involved the most recent perpetrators, post-1985, when the archdiocese was self-insured, and the earliest cases, when it had little or no insurance. Mahony announced that $40 million had come from "funds we set aside last year," money from religious orders and limited insurance payments.[49]

Most of the trial lawyers, like Jeff Anderson and Steve Rubino, had been working on these Orange diocese and northern California cases for four and a half years, bearing the cost of hotels, meals, and paralegal help; the long flights between LAX and Minnesota or New Jersey also were a drain on time with their families. As cases settled and clients were paid, the attorneys who carried large loans for the relentless work began repaying their banks, which gave them some breathing room. In the final payout, they stood to pull in fees in the range of $25 million each, if the archdiocese met the target Boucher had set for some 500 remaining cases.

Although the Supreme Court had refused to hear Mahony's appeal on the so-called formation privilege, Hennigan had delayed the documents' release by arranging for a retired judge to read the voluminous files and decide what should be disclosed. Survivors like Manny Vega wanted Mahony to stop hiding the files. The lawyers saw the cardinal scrambling for money.

"Mahony wanted to settle from day one, but the documents got in his way," said Rubino. "He had a delicate balance between cooperating with carriers and not turning over files that would kill your defense. Insurance carriers kept threatening to pull."

Near the end of 2006, Boucher got Hennigan and Mahony to agree on $660 million. "The church had a budget for the number of diocesan cases, and the ones with religious orders," Boucher told me. "I think Hennigan was right that the carriers should have put up more. The handful of major religious orders had adequate resources to cover their obligations, but the archdiocese did not have a buy-in with them as yet . . . Mahony went to Rome to get approval."

At the Congregation for the Clergy, he needed the approval under canon law to alienate church property at a level far greater than did Boston's O'Malley, who faced an $85 million hole in 2003. Benedict had appointed a new prefect, Cardinal Cláudio Hummes, a Franciscan prelate from Brazil. In an interview with John Allen of *National Catholic Reporter* several months after the settlement was announced, Mahony said, "Of our total settlement, we've only needed to get permission to alienate $200 million . . . Cardinal Hummes particularly has been extremely helpful." Mahony told Allen that he had met with Cardinal Franc Rodé, prefect of the congregation that governs religious life, in May 2007. Rodé, a Slovenian who had spent time in a World War II work camp, was one of the more reactionary figures in the Curia, hostile to Vatican II. Rodé ordered a 2010 Vatican investigation of American nuns, the questionnaire for which sought information on their financial holdings, which most of the sisters' superiors ignored. Rodé was a great friend of Maciel's and utterly loyal to Legionaries. Two weeks after the July 15, 2007, settlement was announced in Los Angeles, Cardinal Rodé took a vacation in sunny Cancun, Mexico, courtesy of the Legion, according to a Legionary priest. In the ornamental language on which cardinals thrive, Mahony told Allen that Rodé "gave us the key principle . . . He said the religious institutes must bear full responsibility for their members, and the dioceses for their members. He said that's the only formula that's going to work, and that's the formula we've been following."[50]

Of course, it was Mahony's formula all along. Boucher continued: "He came back from Rome with the authority to settle the cases at the amounts we set, and to apply pressure on the religious orders. The orders had to come up with about $200 million. The Salesians were the worst offenders—the most callous, the least apologetic, the most repellent." In early July, Boucher watched from across Hennigan's office as Mahony worked the phones. "He was dialing for dollars with the religious orders."

But for religious orders to pledge $200 million did not mean they could deliver cash on the barrel: property sales and aggregation of assets take time. In the meantime, the archdiocese had to write the check.

HOW MAHONY RAISED THE MONEY

The cardinal who five years earlier had opened a $190 million cathedral was scrambling for hundreds of millions to satisfy the abuse survivors' claims. Having spent a fortune in legal fees to prevent the release of clergy files, and the real possibility of his own indictment, Mahony did not have access to the $200 million for which, he told John Allen, the Vatican gave him "permission" to raise via alienation of property. That would include cash reserves and liquid assets. He had already committed $60 million seven months earlier, resolving the first sequence of cases. "By our estimate, he didn't have access to more than $40 million in liquid assets," said Steve Rubino. "We got trial dates in 2006 to push the negotiating toward conclusion. A certain judge I bumped into at Starbucks told me Mahony was in Rome—raising money. He had to have gotten at least $100 million in Rome to pull it off."

According to a *Los Angeles Times* analysis:

> More than $114 million has been promised in previous settlements, bringing the total liability for clergy misconduct in the Los Angeles Archdiocese to more than $774 million. The figure dwarfs the next largest settlements in the U.S., including those reached in Boston, at $157 million, and in Portland, Ore., at $129 million.
>
> Hennigan said the archdiocese expected to pay $250 million in cash, with the balance coming from insurers and religious orders.[51]

The archdiocese borrowed $175 million from the Allied Irish Bank in securing the settlement funds.[52] Boucher said he got wind of AIB involvement in spring 2007; although he had no proof, he suspected that the Vatican provided a loan or pass-through support via AIB to the archdiocese. Allied Irish Bank, a registered company in the Republic of Ireland, was formed in 1966 through the merger of three different Irish banks. The firm branched into the United States in the 1980s. AIB helped the archdiocese build the Cathedral of Our Lady of the Angels. "The funds for the [mausoleum] construction were borrowed from the archdiocesan cemeteries with the assistance of the Allied Irish Bank," according to a history of the cathedral.[53] AIB's "core business in America" has been "funding not-for-profit institutions. AIB 'banks' 45 of 194 Catholic dioceses and archdioceses," according to the *Irish Times*.[54]

Eight months after the settlement the archdiocesan newspaper, *The Tidings*, cited "a bank loan of $175 million and liquidated investments worth $117 million. The administrative office was facing a $12 million deficit.

> The $175 million bank loan is expected to be partially repaid with proceeds from the sale of up to 51 archdiocesan properties (estimated at $107 million). The balance remaining at the end of the loan term in 2011 is estimated at $50 million; this amount may have to be refinanced . . .
>
> The loss of this income, as well as the interest on the bank loan and the interest on the settlement guarantee, means that the Administrative Office will incur a budget deficit of approximately $12 million a year.[55]

Cardinal Mahony denied an interview request for this book. The archdiocesan spokesman, Tod Tamberg, declined to discuss Allied Irish Bank. Mahony's approach to the funding crisis for abuse cases stands out in high relief from his counterpart down Interstate 5 in the San Diego diocese. As the settlements there reached an impasse, the judge set a trial date. Bishop Robert Brom had his attorneys file for Chapter 11 protection from bankruptcy in order to halt the trial and presumably bargain down the opposition. Judge Louise DeCarl Adler ordered an independent audit of its assets by a forensic accountant, former FBI agent R. Todd Neilson. San Diego, the fifth-largest diocese in the United States, had vast property holdings. Neilson discovered that the diocese had claimed its ninety-eight parishes as assets in applications to banks and bond markets, but excluded them for Chapter 11 protection. He noted that after the bankruptcy filing, an auxiliary bishop authorized $69,963 in checks from a special foundation to a parish deacon who "supposedly transferred the funds to an individual . . . who had expertise in importing and exporting goods from Colombia"—to help a poor parish in Colombia. "An additional $23,000 was also disbursed," Neilson continued in dry prose, "but the Expert has not received any supporting documentation."[56]

The diocese had nonchurch properties—multiple-unit buildings, condos, property zoned for commercial or industrial use, stores, and parking lots—valued at $115 million by the county assessor. A real estate economist told the *San Diego Union-Tribune* that the diocese had properties "with a market value well in excess of $1 billion."[57]

The judge dismissed the diocese's bankruptcy filing with prejudice, meaning it could not soon refile. She gave a strong rebuke: "Chapter Eleven is not supposed to be a vehicle, a method, to hammer down the claims of those abused."[58] In the end, plaintiff attorneys closed their briefcases with a settlement of $198 million for 144 clients. The Vatican made no punitive move against Bishop Robert Brom.

"Part of our settlement," explains San Diego plaintiff attorney Irwin Zalkin, "was funded by Allied Irish Bank. They also funded the building of a high school here. I don't know if AIB is directly involved with the Vatican Bank, but the grapevine talk among the lawyers is that AIB was a financial arm of the Vatican, that this is how the Holy See is able to fund some of the things they are involved with, including helping to pay for the settlements."

Unlike Lennon and O'Malley in Boston, Mahony acted like a politician in the end. He went to his people, making an impassioned pitch to all the parishes, in personal meetings and letters, asking for money. He had already apologized. His decisions in recycling perpetrators, and living among them, were more egregious than Bernard Law's scandal. But the media-savvy Mahony spent heavily on publicity and used his financial muscle to wage the legal fight to shelter incriminating files, a strategy that caused delays, which drove up the costs all around. The protracted struggle consumed more time and more money, ratcheting up an overall final payout of $750 million. But Mahony was not indicted. Battered again and again in the media, he was still standing. Cardinal Mahony could have given Nixon lessons on survival.

A parish in Woodland Hills donated its cash reserves of $1.5 million to the archdiocese. Another parish offered a $100,000 interest-free loan to be repaid over ten years. A smaller, poorer parish pledged $25,000 over five years.[59] As Mahony worked to whittle down the huge debt, the clergy files were still bottled up in the labyrinthine Los Angeles court system as the 2010 abuse crisis put Benedict in the media crosshairs. Jeff Anderson had a constitutional attorney working on a motion to the Supreme Court *not* to hear the appeal by the Holy See, which was seeking to dismiss the Oregon lawsuit and his motion to take Pope Benedict's deposition. And he had a new client, the thirty-year-old son of Marcial Maciel Degollado, who was livid at how he had been treated by the Legion of Christ.

CHAPTER 13

AMERICA AND THE VATICAN

To advance the canon law cases for the vigil parishes, Peter Borré flew to
Rome, on average, every other month in 2009 and 2010, staying at least
five days each time. He had passed his seventieth birthday; although his
retirement years were darkened by the frustration of dealing with church
officialdom, he loved Rome and found enjoyment in his friendship with
the canon lawyer Carlo Gullo. In developing the appeals together, Borré
had polished his Latin and gained an appreciation of the baroque intri-
cacies of the Vatican legal system. But Borré wanted a way to take the
story—parishioners seeking to preserve their churches from becoming liquid assets—beyond Gullo's elegant Latin briefs and fuse it into the mental
circuitry of other Vatican officials. The Signatura was a vertical process of
appeals; Borré needed a horizontal strategy, a way of depositing the information in other stations of the Roman Curia.

As he spoke with midlevel officials at the Congregation for the Clergy,
the Signatura, and other dicasteries, Borré sensed that many of the priests
were severely overworked and lacked the support staff requisite for the
central office of a church with 1.2 billion souls. The last thing he wanted
was for the church to model itself on some multinational corporation.
God forbid. But the fawning way young monsignors greeted bishops and

cardinals suggested an imperial culture that stultified healthy candor. Raised in Rome and schooled in Italy's social customs, Borré knew the language of indirect references, the importance of gesture—a shoulder raised, the palm uptilted—a vocabulary of inferences to engage a genuine exchange of information. Italians ran the Curia and to put his story on reality's table, he had to be a persuasive Italian.

Borré had lost patience with reformers back home who put dialogue with bishops high on their agenda. By his lights the lessons of the abuse crisis, which begat a financial crisis, were stunningly clear. Bishops were cynical to sweet notions of pluralism, of engaging laypeople, even rich ones, in meetings that posed even the remotest challenge to their control of money. Bishops had Finance Councils or advisory boards who operated in the pray, pay, obey mode, which meant avoiding questions like why don't we have an audited financial statement, Bishop?

In several cities or dioceses with enclaves of affluent Catholics—Naples, Florida, and Rockville Centre, Long Island, for example—the bishops had banned Voice of the Faithful from meeting in any parish. Here was the face of power showing its fear of the truth. Although many pastors supported VOTF's agenda, which called for financial transparency as a means of reform, a priest who disobeyed a bishop's rule faced the loss of his parish, demotion to a marginal job, or losing his faculties, the approval one needed to say Mass, hear confession, minister the sacraments.

"The bishops have been raised in a Roman culture that is military in nature," Patrick Wall, the Orange County canonist–turned–expert witness remarked. "They take a long view of history. Loyalty and faithfulness are rewarded. These men have been raised in the Latin tradition . . . This is all they have. The bishops don't do battle like the Navy SEALs. They aren't looking to bring everyone home."[1]

From his years in the navy, Borré knew that a military culture needed a system of justice in order to maintain discipline and the allegiance of the governed. In the spring of 2009, Borré was closing in on five years' voluntary work in trying to reverse the suppression orders of the nine vigil parishes in the Boston archdiocese. His strategy of flooding the Vatican with appeals had spread to distant cities as Borré traveled, meeting people with the same values who were trying to keep their churches open. Future-Church's website posted information that went buzzing through a new spiritual network.

Looking beyond the dictatorial politics of the Vatican, Borré and Sister Chris Schenk hoped that civil judges in the various states would begin to weigh the Suppression orders that deprived people of their spiritual homes as a religious tradition that deserved its freedom, too.

A priest in Rome who was sympathetic to Borré's efforts suggested he approach the Secretariat of State, and Monsignor Pietro Parolin, the undersecretary for relations with states. This should be done in writing. For several weeks Borré and Gullo collaborated on the letter, which melded the high formalism of the canon lawyer with the American agitator's drumbeat of candor. The final product, dated April 7, 2009, covered eighteen single-spaced pages: a Request for Mediation, asking Monsignor Parolin for "the appropriate dicastery of the Holy See [to] instruct the *Apostolic Signatura* and the Congregation for the Clergy to suspend the reviews of American parishioners' appeals against parish closings." It included the names and dioceses of all the parish groups and their leaders.

The document quoted a 2004 address by the late pope, referred to as "John Paul the Great," during a visit of American bishops:

> The parish, in fact, is "pre-eminent among all the other communities in his Diocese for which the Bishop has primary responsibility; it is with the parishes above all that he must be concerned" (*Pastores Gregis*, 45) . . . The Diocese should always be understood as existing *in and for its parishes* (emphasis in the papal original).[2]

Borré wrote on behalf of thirty-one groups from eight dioceses—Boston; Cleveland; New Orleans; New York; Buffalo; Scranton; Allentown, Pennsylvania; and Springfield, Massachusetts. Remarking on the four Boston groups "inside their churches round-the-clock, peacefully and prayerfully," since October 2004, the letter evinces Gullo's influence in explaining that there "have been no violations of the *Magisterium* or of canon law"—a sober bow of deference to the Congregation for the Doctrine of the Faith. Moreover: "The most striking development within these communities has been an intensified devotion to Our Blessed Mother, with frequent praying of the Rosary during the vigils, something well beyond what was customary before the suppression of these parishes."

The letter rolls between a Romanesque style of religious salute and deference, registering a within-the-cloth sensibility of believers in a dialogue over prudent religious governance, and an American intercutting of facts to support the core argument. "More than one thousand American parishes have either been closed, or are scheduled to close in the near future. And this number will multiply several times over in the years ahead"—a period of great social stress, "of material hardship not experienced since the Great Depression."

Much of the document reviews canonical procedures, decisions already handed down, demographic data on the American church, and a review of the financial impact of the clergy abuse litigation.

In the letter's request for structured meetings, facilitators, "norms of respect and courtesy for all persons involved," and a deadline to convene the mediation with a suggested time frame to address the crisis, the tone echoes the elemental courteousness and mannered ways of the Curia. Nothing about the long document was disrespectful of the Holy See, though the synopsis of decisions by certain prelates, notably Seán O'Malley and Richard Lennon, made clear the feelings of shock caused by their decisions.

Borré was invited to meet with a midlevel official in the Secretariat of State, whose name he shared with me on background. As Borré tells it, he provided a more textured overview of the various parishes, the issues, media coverage, and financial implications, particularly the deepening deficit in Boston. The Vatican official nodded. *He seems to get it*, thought Borré. He left with cautious optimism, hoping that the notes the priest had taken would be distilled into a formal report for his superiors, and possibly reach the desk of Cardinal Bertone, the secretary of state.

Borré's letter to the Secretariat of State made fleeting reference to, as he put it, sending police "to arrest Catholics in their churches" by Cardinal Egan in New York and Archbishop Alfred Hughes in New Orleans. Referencing Boston, he noted, "to call in the police to arrest the vigilers . . . would cause great harm to the archdiocese." The police action in New Orleans nearly provoked a riot.

NEW ORLEANS: WHO ARE THESE PEOPLE?

When Hurricane Katrina hit on August 29, 2005, more than a million people from the greater urban area evacuated; as they returned, people worked frenetically on cell phones to position themselves on work lists of contractors who converged for rebuilding homes and businesses. The flood saturated 80 percent of the city: an area seven times the size of Manhattan sat in saltwater for nearly a month. "God has brought us to our knees in the face of disaster," said Archbishop Hughes. "We are so overwhelmed, we don't really know how to respond. Powerlessness leads us to prayer."[3]

No one doubted the piety of Al Hughes, a short, balding, modest man. His personality exuded humility, but his credibility had been badly damaged three years earlier in the city's clergy abuse scandals, for which he made humble apologies as guilty priests were sent away. Hughes had gotten his start in Boston as an auxiliary bishop in the 1980s under Cardinal Law.

Boston bore scant resemblance to the archdiocese he took over in 2002. Founded in 1718 as a French colonial port, New Orleans was Catholic from the start, unlike the heavily Baptist and evangelical upper South. The city was the nation's largest slave port in the 1840s and a rare social mosaic. "A man might here study the world," a late-nineteenth-century bookseller wrote. "Every race the world boasts is here, and a good many races that are nowhere else . . . The air is broken by every language— English, French, Italian and German, varied by gombo languages of every shade."[4]

Slaves worshipped in the rear pews of antebellum churches, behind planters, merchants, working-class whites, and free persons of color, many of whom owned slaves. Despite a deep presence of black Catholics, the twentieth-century growth of African American vernacular churches, like Church of God in Christ, and the larger Baptist denominations had broadened the demography of faith. Still, when Katrina hit, the Catholic Church was the largest denomination in the eight-parish area, with 480,000 members in a population of 1.4 million. Parochial schools educated 50,000 students (many of them non-Catholic), nearly as many as were enrolled in the city's decaying public school system. Despite huge damages from Katrina, the church's relief efforts were heroic.[5]

Hurricane Katrina gave Archbishop Hughes a shot at redemption

"I am also a refugee," a weary Hughes said on a visit to a homeless shelter in Baton Rouge the second day after the storm. He heard confessions of state troopers and aid workers. "It's not easy to be so drastically dislocated without any early hope of being able to return."

The church initially announced a $40 million deficit. Over the next three years, $107 million poured in from dioceses, bishops, Rome, individual Catholics, philanthropists, and foundations for rebuilding and relief costs. Volunteers from parishes in many states traveled to New Orleans, gutting houses that had taken four, six, eight, ten feet of water. Catholic Charities provided $7 million in direct relief for survival assistance.

But in the winter of 2006, New Orleans had only 40 percent of its population back. Federal funds to assist home owners whose insurance did not fully cover their rebuilding needs were slow to get congressional approval. The church had reopened 107 of 142 parishes, and 81 of 107 schools. Although the archdiocese would, like many agencies, recoup substantial losses from FEMA, the immediate task was deciding how to allocate its resources across the area. Several parishes had been destroyed; others would have to merge as part of a smaller urban footprint. Hughes entrusted a key part of the planning for this job of enormous complexity to Father Michael Jacques, the white pastor of St. Peter Claver, an African American parish in a downtown neighborhood that was heavily damaged. Jacques was not a seasoned urban planner. He was popular in the community, though overshadowed by Jerome LeDoux, the seventy-six-year-old African American pastor at St. Augustine, ten blocks away in Tremé, a neighborhood steeped in cultural traditions, just outside the French Quarter. Early in his career, LeDoux had spent four years in Rome, earning a master's in theology and a Ph.D. in church law.

Now in the autumn of his life, wearing dashiki vestments at Mass, LeDoux, with his mop of gray hair, was a charismatic preacher who welcomed jazz musicians to perform at liturgies. For some reason German tourists regularly showed up at his Sunday Mass, taking photographs in the side garden of the Tomb of the Unknown Slave, an exhibit with a large anchor and chains. In a neighborhood reeling from drug violence, LeDoux said the funerals for any family, regardless of faith. Many were too poor to pay for a wake. His sermons flowed with hope and wit. "Why do we welcome Mardi Gras Indians?" he said one Sunday. "Feathers, tambourines, *war whoops*. Mmm: we hear whoops *of peace* this fine morn. Scripture tells us, 'Make a joyful noise unto the Lord.' " He smiled. "And that, my dear people, is what we now must do!"

He lived in a shambling rectory filled with books and newspapers, a vegan dishing out dollars to homeless people and addicts who came knocking in the night. Many of them he knew by name. LeDoux wrote a column for the African American *Louisiana Weekly*. He was back at St. Augustine three weeks after Katrina, saying Mass. St. Augustine owed $227,000 in assessments—back taxes—to the archdiocese. Gentrification was edging into Tremé. After the flood, with whole swaths of the city devoid of people, real estate prices were soaring. Church, rectory, parish center, and a huge side yard were a developer's dream.

In early 2006 Hughes told LeDoux the parish had to close. The public announcement ignited a furor in Tremé. Activists occupied the rectory and church. The media coverage portrayed an aloof archbishop against a black neighborhood as the broken city tried to get back on its feet. In 2009 Hughes would be pilloried in satirical Mardi Gras floats, his visage mocked on the plastic cups that masked revelers dispense as carnival "throws"—a fate traditionally accorded to politicians on their way to jail.

LeDoux was gone when Jacques entered the church in his robes to say Mass on Sunday, March 26, an act by which the parish would be formally closed, its members welcomed by a group from St. Peter Claver. In the fraught atmosphere, some parishioners wept, others seethed. Ten plainclothes officers accompanied Father William Maestri, the archdiocesan spokesman, who would brook no dissent. When a nervous Jacques took the pulpit to give his homily, people stood and turned their backs; others waved signs in protest. As people began yelling, Jacques could not speak. Maestri made a slicing gesture under his neck, signaling to the cops that Mass was over. "I'm NOPD!" shouted an officer, hustling Maestri and Jacques into a car.[6]

Hughes denounced "the sacrilege" and canceled Masses indefinitely.

LeDoux, who was in the process of moving out, fired back, saying that police in church "reeked of racial profiling. You have racial profiling when you do not understand an ethnic group or a racial group, and you think that because they are upset, because they're even a little angry, they are dangerous."

A French Quarter hotelier from one of the city's prominent families, Michael Valentino, offered to spearhead a $1 million capital campaign, provided the parish stay open. Another parishioner, Jacques Morial, was a political activist whose father and older brother had both been mayor. He joined Valentino to meet with Father Jacques.

"When you negotiate in a tense situation," Morial told me later, "you assume the people sitting across from you have good information and a

reasonable sense of how to proceed. Hughes would not get directly involved. Father Jacques was in way over his head; he had his plan to close
parishes, no appreciation about the impact or really how to achieve it. I
don't think Hughes had any idea of the reaction or that making LeDoux
leave would set off so many folk. Tremé has a history of being stomped,
politically, by the city, and to make a move like that with so many people
just getting back from Katrina, the timing could not have been worse.
Look, I'm a parishioner and I've got an interest, okay? But if I were a neutral consultant, first thing, you look at the facts. A church built in 1842.
Pride of the black community. A pastor everyone loves. Yeah, the guy
drinks carrot juice. LeDoux's eccentric. *New Orleans* is eccentric. But the
city's in the national media every day because of Katrina. The parish owes
two hundred grand plus change to the archdiocese. So what do you do?
Launch a national fund-raising campaign! Call Oprah, Bill Cosby, rally
people who love New Orleans to help. We knew LeDoux would be essential for fund-raising—he's a folk hero. Jacques wanted to pastor the
two congregations. Hughes, from all I could tell, never thought about an
alternative plan."

Father LeDoux moved to Texas. The parish gained a reprieve, condi-
tioned on its meeting future benchmarks. Jacques remained at St. Peter
Claver. Hughes installed a new pastor, Father Quentin Moody who refused to let Mike Valentino, who had already made donations, serve on
the Finance Council. Looking back on the fiasco of being stiff-armed for
trying to raise money, Valentino told me, "For months after that I went
to Mass and sat in the front row, just to let Moody know I was there. I
kept asking myself, *Who are these guys?* We could have raised $2 million
in twelve months. But the campaign never started. How could I assure
donors where the money would go?" Valentino's plan for a full architectural restoration was aborted; by 2010 the rectory had been renovated, but
Valentino no longer went to church. "I didn't want to fight battles in my
own parish or be a source of acrimony in trying to help. The whole thing
was such a failure of leadership, failing to do what could have been done.
My core faith is intact but I'm disillusioned and have no regular parish."

The archdiocese in a 2010 report on Katrina's financial impact cited
$287.9 million in total property loss of which $235.9 million had been
recovered. More than half of that, $125 million, came from insurance; $64
million came from FEMA reimbursements; and $47 million came from

gifts and donations from other dioceses and Catholic Charities USA.[7] The unrecovered loss was $52 million. Although the pie charts and columns put numbers in broad categories, the essay and data fell far short of a fully audited financial statement. Bruce Nolan of the *Times-Picayune* noted that the church was "severely underinsured against flood [damage] . . . with only $29 million" in coverage.[8]

In an urban area that had sustained heavy flooding in 1994 and 1995, and had mass evacuations from hurricanes in the years leading up to Katrina, *why cancel flood insurance?* The policies were backed by federal funds and reasonably priced. "They were having cash flow problems—not enough parishes sending money to Walmsley Avenue [the chancery head-quarters]," explains a prominent pastor. "They realize now that canceling those policies was a huge mistake."

The minutes from a February 26, 2007, closed meeting of Hughes and his priests' council offer an instructive look at the subsequent closure of two financially stable parishes, where vigil protests arose. Our Lady of Good Counsel, in the historic Garden District, was on the National Register of Historic Places. The parish council leader had a pledge of $300,000 for an endowment if Hughes would reverse the closure; he refused. In the wake of the battering media coverage from the St. Augustine events, the priests' council minutes are devoid of financial or infrastructure planning: "The whole plan is a pastoral plan that deals with the parishes, social service and the schools that will be looked at again at the end of April. Part of the layered look involves [the chief financial officer] looking at the financial pieces to see what it's going to cost us to put this plan into effect and what's going to happen with all the buildings and real estate involved."[9]

"The whole plan" was never disclosed to the public. The minutes continue, oblivious to people in pews, but fearful that a process without any cost-benefit analysis or impact assessment might be discovered by the press: "The Archbishop asked for the strictest of confidentiality to avoid sabotaging the process with media coverage before the plan is finalized. If forced to deal with damage control the fear would be that final decisions could not be made in the atmosphere that they would want to be made."

Professor of Accountancy Jack Ruhl of Western Michigan University analyzed the archdiocese's public disclosures: "The 2009 Financial Report included a compilation report by a local CPA firm that states: 'We have not audited or reviewed the accompanying Summaries . . . and . . . do not express an opinion or any other form of assurance on them.' The CPA firm goes on to say that the archdiocese 'elected to omit substantially all of the disclosures required by generally accepted accounting principles.' In other words, the CPA firm performed only compilation services for the archdiocese, checking the numbers for mathematical accuracy."

A full set of audited financial statements means the assertions of management have been tested by experienced auditors. They contact the banks to make sure a given entity actually has funds on deposit. "Since the New Orleans Financial Report was not audited," continues Ruhl, "there is no assurance at all that the numbers bear any resemblance to reality. The Financial Report does not include any notes, which would tell about activities such as bond issues and impending litigation." Perhaps the archdiocese found its way out of the Katrina debt by a 2007 bond issue. Ruhl, who came across the bond issue information through his own research, explains that although the 2009 Financial Report has no mention of it, the archdiocese, working through the Louisiana Public Facilities Authority, issued $69,150,000 of municipal bonds in 2007. As of June 30, 2009, the Archdiocese had an outstanding liability for $68,130,330 of these bonds.

In 2009 Hughes insisted on church property rights, prevailing on Mayor Ray Nagin to order police officers into the two vigil parishes, Good Counsel and St. Henry (which had cash reserves of $150,000). The spectacle of NOPD beating down a door at Good Counsel and arresting people from both parishes was like a whiplash to many people. At his retirement press conference in 2009, Hughes apologized to the community for any harm he had caused. His successor, Archbishop Gregory Aymond, began a dialogue with the two parishioner groups, allowing limited use of both churches, searching for a solution to reconcile the protesters to the archdiocese, with some role for the two dormant parishes.

THE VATICAN TAKES OVER THE LEGION

In June 2009 Borré met again with his contact in the Secretariat of State. He laid out the main points of the eighteen-page Request for Mediation, the terrible damage done to neighborhoods and people of faith when a viable parish was closed because of its immediate material value to a bishop. Negotiating a solution for the Boston archdiocese would likely have a national impact and, if handled fairly for the vigil groups, would position

Cardinal O'Malley as a peacemaker, a prelate with the vision and leadership to uplift a demoralized community. This would mean the "peaceful demobilization of the vigils and the quiet withdrawal of the Boston appeals at the Signatura."

The Vatican official absorbed what Borré had to say and presented the position of the Secretariat of State. The letter's fundamental issue was outside the *competenza* (area of responsibility) of his office; however, he arranged for Borré to meet another Vatican official. As these conversations unfolded, Borré was following the news from Cleveland, aghast as Lennon repeated the destruction he had wrought on Boston.

Carlo Gullo determined that the only remaining avenue for the vigil parishes' canonical prospects was a direct appeal to Pope Benedict.

As one of the handful of canonists licensed to take appeals to the highest level of the Apostolic Signatura, Gullo had the right to send a document to the Holy Father. He had never done so before, but the professor and practitioner of canon law in Rome, who had little experience of America, had absorbed through Borré a metaphysical sense of the people utterly devoted to their sacred spaces at a time when many European churches, for all of their grandeur and iconic presence in the historical memory, drew sparse crowds at times of Mass. The secularization of Europe, a "post-Christian" society, had become a strand of the media narrative. Benedict's cry against moral relativism was a call for Christian Europe to assert its integrity. Certainly, reasoned Gullo, a movement of Catholics to protect their churches would have meaning for His Holiness.

But by Holy Week of 2010, Benedict XVI had suffered a spectacular loss of respect in public opinion as the abuse crisis came home to Europe, "with scandals convulsing Ireland, Belgium, Germany, the Netherlands, Switzerland, Italy and Austria," writes Andrew Walsh, a scholar and former journalist, in a detailed account of the media coverage.[10] The media was relentless on Benedict, particularly the *New York Times*, which quoted the Vatican correspondence provided by Jeff Anderson on Ratzinger's soft-glove treatment of the Wisconsin priest who had abused dozens of deaf students. The credit Ratzinger had gained as a cardinal for taking responsibility of the abuse cases in the CDF teetered against the weight of past decisions, marked by inertia. The pontiff who as cardinal had stood in judgment over theological adversaries, forcing them to answer questions, had no answers to give, and so fell silent.

The Curia took the foredoomed stance of attacking the messenger. *L'Osservatore Romano* scored the media for "an ignoble attempt to strike at Pope Benedict and his closest aides at any cost." But the Vatican had no youth protection charter, as the American bishops had adopted in 2002, nor did the Holy See have procedures that might penalize the world's bishops. Cardinal Walter Kasper of Germany bravely distanced himself from the Curia in telling *La Repubblica,* "We have to seriously clean up the church." But for Benedict to "clean up," he had to change the assumptions of apostolic succession; and if he opened the bishops to a judicial overview on their tolerance of predatory clerics, what would happen to bishops accused of misusing money?[11]

If a single episode framed the moral relativism of Benedict's papacy it came at Easter Mass, on April 4, 2010, in St. Peter's Square when Angelo Sodano, now dean of the College of Cardinals, preached a defense of the pope. The faithful would "rally close around you, successor to Peter, bishop of Rome, the unfailing rock of the holy church," he declared. The cardinal who had pressured Ratzinger not to prosecute Maciel in John Paul's time now said soothingly, "We are deeply grateful to you for the strength of spirit and apostolic courage with which you announce the Gospel." With a backhanded barb at the press, Sodano continued, "Holy Father, on your side are the people of God, who do not allow themselves to be influenced by the petty gossip of the moment, by the trials which sometimes buffet the community of believers."[12]

Sodano on Easter executed a 180-degree shift from being a paid champion of Maciel to a shield of the beleaguered pope. "What we are dealing with now is a cultural battle: the pope embodies moral truths which people don't accept and for that reason the shortcomings and errors of priests are used as arms against the church," Sodano told *L'Osservatore Romano.* "It was not the fault of Jesus if he was betrayed by Judas. Nor is it the fault of a bishop if one of his priests sullies himself with grave crimes. And certainly, it is not the responsibility of the pontiff."[13]

Here was the logic of apostolic succession draped in pearls of self-righteousness: Maciel as Judas to the Christ-like Sodano!

"There is absolutely no strategy, and I say that as a friend of the pope's," an American bishop, unnamed, told the author and PoliticsDaily correspondent David Gibson.[14]

But there was a strategy, of some inchoate sort, for handling the Legion of Christ. On May 1, 2010, the Vatican issued a statement that excoriated Maciel for a double life "devoid of any scruples and authentic sense of religion." Thus had he managed to sexually assault young boys for so many years. "By pushing away and casting doubt upon all those who questioned his behavior, and the false belief that he wasn't doing harm to the good of the Legion, he created around him a defense mechanism that made him unassailable for a long period, making it difficult to know his true life."[15]

Not a word on John Paul's blind praises of Maciel after the accusations.

The Vatican would be naming a special envoy to help the Legionaries "purify" the good that remained in the order, for a "profound revision" necessary to carry on.

The language denouncing Maciel was strong, but how would the Vatican exert the high moral purpose that Benedict called the church to follow on a cultlike operation such as the Legionaries?

Eleven days after the announcement Father Álvaro Corcuera, the superior general, traveled from Rome to New York City for a four-hour meeting with Juan Vaca. Vaca was the first to denounce Maciel, naming victims' names, in correspondence to the Vatican in 1976, 1978, and 1989. He had settled in Long Island. The twelve-year psychosexual entanglement with Maciel, which began when he was twelve, had caused him to study psychology after leaving the priesthood, trying to determine "where sickness ends and evil starts." Trim and hale, with thinning hair and a resonant voice, Juan Vaca had a gentlemanly Latin demeanor. He had made a career as a college teacher and guidance counselor, married late, and had a teenage daughter he adored.

Corcuera denied my interview request. A Legion spokesman, Jim Fair, said, "He did meet with Vaca, and others in Mexico, as part of his outreach."[16]

That outreach was another twist in Pope Benedict's lurching road toward justice, now that the Vatican had taken control of the strange organization. Corcuera, age fifty-three, came from an upper-middle-class Mexico City family; he had been a frequent guest at the Apostolic Palace when the Legion was sending money to the papal secretary Stanisław Dziwisz.

The meeting with Vaca took place at Mercy College in midtown Manhattan, where Vaca was an adjunct professor. The two men sat in a conference room. "He embraced me in a manly, Mexican way and was about to kneel down in asking my forgiveness," Vaca recounted. "I said no, and had him sit at the head of the table, and I to his immediate right."

Corcuera struck him as relaxed, seemingly kind. Vaca called him "Álvarito," a Latin term of endearment. He assumed an avuncular role, asking the younger priest about his background. Corcuera recalled his youth in a Legion school, inspired by Maciel to join the order. He had gone to seminary in Orange, Connecticut, when Vaca was a superior. (The campus was recently on the real estate market, as the Legion began downsizing.) Vaca did not remember Corcuera from those years; he had worked with many seminarians before leaving in 1976 to join the Rockville Centre diocese. "You were nice to me," said Corcuera. He explained that when he became superior general to succeed Maciel, in 2004, the election came as a surprise for him.

"Well, Maciel trained you for the job," Vaca clarified.

Corcuera insisted he was elected at an open chapter, not handpicked by Maciel. "I asked point-blank if Corcuera knew about Maciel's abuses," Vaca told me. "He said no. I said, 'You knew he sent money to the ladies,' meaning the mother in Madrid, Norma and her daughter. He said, 'I learned after 2004.' He didn't give a specific date on when he learned it, and I didn't press him."

After letting Corcuera talk for an hour or so, Vaca recounted how Maciel had abused him and other seminarians decades ago; how he had pulled Maciel, passed out on morphine, from drowning in a hotel bathtub in Tetuán, Morocco, in 1957, the year Corcuera was born. "He felt ashamed. He hung his head, whispering, *I do believe you.* He put his face in his hands," said Vaca.

Corcuera told Vaca that Legionaries were circulating his 1976 letter denouncing Maciel, naming the twenty other seminary victims. If that was true, it marked a striking shift from the summer of 2009, when two Legion priests in Rome told me that the seminarians were still being taught about Maciel's heroic life.

Vaca accepted his apologies, adding, "But this is not a solution." He insisted that the Legion provide fair compensation for the harm and damages to him and other victims. Corcuera replied that the Legion in Rome had formed a committee to explore the issue. He asked Vaca what he thought would be fair compensation. Refusing to name a figure, Vaca told him to

look at what American dioceses had paid in victim settlements. Vaca had a
deeper issue: how the order had engaged in "slandering me" while defending Maciel. "Think about that. Come up with an amount. I'm not going to
tell you how much."

The website LegionaryFacts.org began posting defenses of Maciel—and
criticism of the accusers—after the 1997 *Hartford Courant* report exposing
Maciel's abuse of Legion youths. Father Owen Kearns, publisher of the
Legion-owned *National Catholic Register*, derided the victims for "a coordinated conspiracy to smear Father Maciel." Kearns on LegionaryFacts.org
had called Vaca "a proud, status-conscious man angered and disappointed
at his professional failures," who had wanted "greater power in the Legion." But Vaca had resigned in his 1976 letter to Maciel.

Vaca had been a counselor for disabled students at York College in the
City University of New York, on the fourth year of a five-year tenure track
position, when he was terminated in 1999. He believed the Legion's "attack on my credibility and character" caused the college not to renew the
contract.

LegionaryFacts.org came down from the Internet in 2006 after the Vatican punished Maciel. Four years later, Kearns issued a general apology to
Gerald Renner and me for criticizing our *Hartford Courant* report, but he
did not name any victims.

Corcuera and Vaca said cordial good-byes. The Legion superior promised to work on the compensation issue. At his request, Vaca provided
names and contact information for Maciel's victims in Mexico.

Corcuera's very presence signaled the influence of Benedict and Monsignor Charles Scicluna, the canon lawyer at the CDF who had worked
for two years taking the testimony of the aging men Maciel had coerced
as boys, hearing their accounts of oral sex, sodomy, and masturbation rituals. As part of its "takeover," the Vatican was prodding the Legion into
a position similar to that of many bishops who clenched their teeth and
wrote large checks to lawyers representing abuse survivors. As the Vatican, in its soft-glove way, pushed the Legion toward financial reparations,
in Rome, Jeff Anderson filed suit against the order on June 16, 2010, in
Connecticut, on behalf of Raúl González Lara, Maciel's older natural son
from Mexico, who alleged a long history of incest and emotional distress
by his father, with certain episodes taking place in America.[17]

SUING THE HOLY SEE

Ironically, as the Vatican was prodding the Legion on the issue of compensation to Maciel's older victims, the Holy See was arguing that it deserved immunity from a case Jeff Anderson had filed in Oregon. He had named the Holy See as one of the defendants.[18] The Foreign Sovereign Immunities Act set limits on whether a foreign government can be sued in U.S. courts; it restricts intervention by the White House and State Department. The priest in question had a record of abusing youths in his native Ireland before his transfer to America. Anderson and his Oregon cocounsel William Barton argued that civil responsibility extended beyond the religious order leader and local bishop to the Vatican. The Holy See hired a California attorney, Jeffrey Lena, to defend the case. Lena's motion to dismiss failed; the Oregon court ordered discovery. Lena appealed to the federal court, which sided with the state court. Lena petitioned the U.S. Supreme Court for a hearing.

The lawsuit asserted that the Holy See—the government of the sovereign monarchy, as opposed to the Vatican as administrator of the city-state—engaged in widespread commercial activity and control over its religious servants. The discovery request drew upon the research of the departed priests Patrick Wall, Tom Doyle, and Richard Sipe.

> Each Bishop keeps track of how much money it obtains for the Holy See through the Peter's Pence solicitation . . . Plaintiff made requests of information about Quinquennial Reports. These reports are required by the Holy See to be sent every five years from each Bishop and each religious order superior. The Holy See requires that the document list the financial well-being of the diocese . . . [Religious orders] must detail for the Holy See the financial condition of the Order, including all property acquired, whether any gains or losses have been sustained, whether there is debt, and whether all temporal goods of the Order and each of its provinces is administered according to the Canons.
>
> In 1947 the Vatican updated the requirements for the Religious Orders' Quinquennial Reports. In addition to the financial disclosures, it also required the Religious Orders to answer whether any of the religious members had sexually abused any of the younger students in their care. It also required the Religious

Orders to answer if they had taken precautions against the dangers of priests sexually abusing children.[19]

Marci Hamilton handled Jeff Anderson's appellate briefs on constitutional issues. Hamilton holds an endowed chair at Benjamin N. Cardozo School of Law in New York City. An author and a prolific writer on legal issues, she specializes in religious issues that bear upon the First Amendment. Her husband is Catholic; several years after their son's baptism, she learned that the priest who performed the ritual had been removed for child abuse. When Hamilton read the petition to the Supreme Court in the Oregon case, she told Anderson, "The arguments are weak, I wouldn't dignify it with a response. Jeff Lena's trying to buy time."

Briefs to the Supreme Court can take a year or longer before a decision is issued on whether the court will hear the case. "Then we get a letter from the court, which they rarely write, requesting our response," Hamilton told me. "It was one of the easiest I've written. There is no need for the Supreme Court to hear this; the issue is state law, not a federal issue. The Court normally would have denied the request for review at that point, but the justices wanted more. After they got our response, they asked for the Solicitor General's views. Then I got a call from the Solicitor General's civil division: they want to meet face-to-face. Now it's political."

The Solicitor General, Elena Kagan, a former Harvard Law dean, was on President Obama's short list for the next available Supreme Court seat, and subsequently won appointment.

Hamilton had written the plaintiff motions challenging Cardinal Mahony's claim of "formation privilege"; she prevailed at every level, save for engineering the enforcement of the decision in California courts. As a young attorney, Hamilton had clerked for Justice Sandra Day O'Connor; she was seasoned in Washington's mores and knew people in Elena Kagan's office. Who exactly would be at this meeting? she inquired. "Just a few," her contact said.

On a snow-shrouded day in March 2010, Hamilton caught the train near her home in Bucks County, Pennsylvania, and on arrival at Union Station met Jeff Anderson, his associate Mike Finnegan, and Bill Barton from Oregon. They went to the Justice Department and in the room found thirteen people, she recalls. "They had obviously been meeting before we arrived. Kagan was there, with her chief deputy Edwin Kneedler. So was Harold Koh, the legal adviser to Hillary Clinton. He's a former Yale dean. The agreement going in was that only I would discuss the case. For two hours they grilled me as if I was going through oral arguments on the merits, even though the ostensible reason for the meeting was to discuss whether the Court should take the case. The genius of Jeff Anderson is that he chose Oregon to sue the Vatican. Oregon has the best state tort law in the country. The only issue to this case was state law. If you get hit by a car driven by a foreign official in your state, you can seek redress. It's the foreign government—and not the officials—that is liable. The officials can create the liability but don't pay out of their pocket.

"Kagan was not as intensely engaged as Koh," says Hamilton. "Koh was trying to push the envelope to find a way to make the case about something other than state law. He seemed to be searching for a federal rule that would be the subject of this case and even control all cases against the Holy See. It just was not there. My assumption is that this was another example of how the Clintons do politics. Bill Clinton was the most pro-religious administration since Grant tried to Christianize the Indians . . . I kept saying, *This is an issue of Oregon state law.*"

After Kagan's nomination, the acting Solicitor General, the Justice Department, and the State Department sent an amicus curiae brief to the Supreme Court, arguing that the case should go back to the federal appeals bench for having misunderstood Oregon tort law.[20] The Supreme Court did not accept the argument; the case was slowly moving forward as this book went to press.

BORRÉ AND THE NUNCIO

As Carlo Gullo sent ideas and draft passages for the appeal to Pope Benedict via e-mail, Peter Borré's contact through the Secretariat of State, after several meetings, suggested that Borré might wish to meet with an archbishop who did have interest in these issues, as they fell in a general sense within his *competenza*. This was Pietro Sambi, the papal nuncio to the United States.

In April 2010, as he caught a flight from Logan Airport to Reagan National, Borré realized that he was on the last leg of his journey: *I keep trying to find something redemptive in the plight of the Roman Catholic Church, whether in Rome's congregations, which I have frequented, the many American dioceses which I visit, or the dozens of Boston parishes where I have assisted. But today I see wreckage all around, a deepening despair among good people, prelates and laity, a widening divide between the flock in the pews and the hierarchical superiors.*

The Congregation for the Clergy had denied every single parishioner appeal against parish closings of which he was aware during the last decade, including the seventy-five of which he had direct knowledge. The Signatura had denied every one of the eleven parishioner appeals from Boston with the same Olympian language in as many decrees. Lawyers for abuse victims were clobbering the church in America because of arrogant decisions by bishops, most of them dating back many years, while in Rome a legal arrogance blunted the very people the church so desperately needed, people who loved the faith and gave in its support—people now spending funds to *save* their churches. These weren't abortion activists with hidden cameras.

For all of his fuming about church reformers seeking dialogue with bishops, Borré had started thinking about Seán O'Malley, his own archbishop. "Why don't you try to talk to him?" his wife, Mary Beth, the political consultant, said one day. The thought of bipartisanship, a consensus of some kind, appealed to him. Do what Congress can't: sit down, talk it out, find a real solution.

Borré was convinced that O'Malley had no idea how to rebuild the finances. The money was going down because people didn't trust the leadership. Law had begun that poisoning; Lennon worsened it. If O'Malley would show some flexibility on the closed parishes, Borré was willing to help swing the public relations his way. But he knew the cardinal considered him an adversary, if not an outright enemy. As the cab dropped him at the stately embassy on Massachusetts Avenue, opposite the vice president's residence at the Naval Observatory, Borré realized that any endgame to benefit the cause he had advanced would probably rely on the man he was about to meet.

Pietro Sambi had wavy silver hair and a firm handshake. As they stood in the foyer, lined with oil paintings of popes and a photograph of the nuncio presenting his credentials to President Obama, Borré knew that he had previously been the Holy See's envoy in Jerusalem, a diplomatic minefield.

As they exchanged amenities in Italian, he could see that Sambi was delighted to converse in his native tongue. The nuncio's eyes lit up at the sight of Borré's new iPad. He handed it to the archbishop, who pulled up *The Divine Comedy.* Knowing that Sambi came from the district of Romagna, next to Emilia, where Borré's maternal grandparents had grown up, Borré casually mentioned that Cardinal O'Malley needed to cross the Rubicon.[21]

"The river Rubicon runs through my village!" Sambi said, smiling.

"Yes, Excellency, I know."

Sambi handed him the iPad. As they walked into his office, the nuncio said, "The cardinal thinks you're a wolf in sheep's clothing."

Borré countered that hundreds of Catholics supported the vigil parishes, and many more people were in full sympathy.

Sambi remarked that in Jerusalem, where he had previously been posted, most people knew what a given solution should be, but none were willing to set it in motion. *Everyone there is guilty of the sin of pride.*

Sambi was voicing O'Malley's view of Borré as an outsized ego who considered the vigil movement an extension of himself.

Borré would rejoice if the cardinal would open five parishes temporarily as chapels. That would give the people a means to repair ties with an archbishop they never wanted to dislike. Borré at that point could willingly phase out. But he picked his words carefully. *If the cardinal will follow through, I'm ready to resign and dissolve the organization. My first and strongest allegiance is to these five groups who are still in vigil.*

Borré explained that he wanted a peaceful but just solution. He was willing to cease his public activism. But for this to work, the cardinal needed to take the first step, a unilateral reopening of one of the vigil parishes.

He assured Sambi that the Council of Parishes members would not react by gloating in the media, declaring a victory.

The meeting ended on a warm note, Sambi agreeing to communicate with O'Malley. After an exchange of letters, Sambi agreed to see Borré again.

Back to Rome, in early June, he worked with Carlo Gullo in refining the language of the appeal that would go to Pope Benedict, one copy in Italian, the other in English. This was for the benefit of Monsignor Peter Wells, who handled the English-language desk in the Secretariat of State and was a native of Tulsa, Oklahoma. Borré had never met Wells, but hoped he would give favorable commentary and recommend that the pope actually read it. In Rome it was no secret that the Holy Father was deep at work on the second volume of his study of Jesus.

The Boston archdiocese had just posted its financial statement. The *Globe* noted that the parish collections had declined 2 percent, while parish operating expenses rose 3 percent. The worst recession in decades was certainly a factor in the downturn; so was the continuing impact of the clergy sexual underground. "In all, the archdiocese has spent $145 million to settle 1,097 civil abuse claims, including 800 since O'Malley's arrival in 2003," reported Lisa Wangsness.[22]

Accountancy professor Jack Ruhl, as part of his research on American diocesan finances, found, "The Boston archdiocese financials show a total operating loss for 2009 of $24,299,645. The change in net assets is analogous to bottom line net income in a corporation. This includes operating income or loss, plus other 'unusual' items, such as a gain on sale of land. The 2009 financials show a change in net assets, a loss, of $4,650,797. The total aggregate operating losses for the fiscal years 2004 to 2009 are $7,484,274."

Coming off such losses, the biggest problem facing O'Malley in his challenge to rebuild finances was the 30 percent decline in church attendance since 2002. The base of support was shrinking as expenses rose. O'Malley had made a forthright effort at transparency, posting detailed financial statements on the archdiocese's website. "I continue to be optimistic," noted Chancellor James P. McDonough in introducing the 85-page report. "We are making significant progress in improving our operations and will build on that success as we adjust our operating model and ministries to the realities of the present time."[23]

Peter Borré did not share the optimism. Besides the archdiocese's operating losses, he saw the priest pension fund underfunded by $104 million. McDonough, a former banker, had taken a 10 percent salary cut because of the precarious finances; still, he earned $225,000. Borré's long-ago Harvard Business School classmate David Castaldi saw nothing wrong with paying competitive salaries for the right people. Borré had no personal grudge against McDonough, who had been on the job for four years, but he thought it absurd to pay anyone that much money when the operation had such bleeding losses.

The Boston archdiocese was generous to people at the top. The secretary of education earned $292,500, according to the *Globe*. Parochial school enrollment had dropped from 50,000 students in 2007 to 46,000 in 2010.[24] As parishes strained to support schools, the top educator earned $42,500 *more* than the superintendent of New York City's public schools, which had 1.1 million students. The associate superintendent of Boston parochial schools earned $176,000. Why such salaries with money leaking like a sieve?

When Borré returned to Washington for his next meeting with Sambi, he was angry about the archdiocesan finances. He gave a memorandum on the matter to the nuncio, whose interest piqued at the numbers and analysis. Sambi the diplomat kept his thoughts close to the vest as he absorbed the information. Borré's idea on reform began with restoring priests' morale; but mobilizing them to help shore up finances turned on changes at the top and slashing big salaries.

Father Bob Bowers, once the pastor at Borré's now-dormant parish, had taken a leave of absence from the priesthood in 2005. Bowers had gone through a long disillusionment before joining the Paulist Center, just off Boston Commons, as an outreach minister to disaffected Catholics who were inching back toward the faith. Disillusioned with Vatican officials as "very, very old men who can't grasp what's happening," Bowers nevertheless wanted Pope Benedict on the job, to work for healing. His own job was to "help people deal with conflict better, help them realize that forgiveness sets them free and that letting go can make them whole again."[25] Since the bruising loss of his parish, Bowers's goal was "*never* to get people to return to participation in the church. My goal is very simple: to listen. That is where God is."[26]

Borré, who had been out of touch with his former pastor, was ambivalent about reconciliation after six years of pushing at the rock of church officialdom. Sitting with Sambi in the nuncio's office in Washington, Borré wanted the Boston archdiocese to slash the six-figure salaries at the top and shed jobs that were not necessary. Here was a religious charity swimming in red ink.

Sambi listened. He read the document carefully as Borré reviewed the high points. Borré's blood was racing as he compared St. Frances Cabrini parish in Scituate, with all that rich waterfront acreage, the good people in their sixth year of vigil now, and the St. Peter parish in Cleveland, where the people had let Lennon take over the building, splitting off to form a new parish, taking their priest with them. Were these examples of schism, offered Borré—of people splitting from the church in breakaway sects, like the Society of St. Pius X? He left it there for Sambi to chew on.

This is the legacy of Bishop Lennon, he told Sambi. The disasters of Reconfiguration were a huge factor in the sapping of money from the Boston archdiocese. He was doing the same thing in Cleveland.

"Lennon is protected," said Sambi.

"By Cardinal Law?" replied Borré.

The slight shrug said it all.

Law protected Lennon so that Law's disastrous handling of the money would be sealed away.

After a third meeting with Sambi, Borré saw little chance that O'Malley would make a first move, or any reciprocal gesture. Lennon, however, had become an issue for Sambi, as the nuncio told him of angry letters from priests in Cleveland. Sambi said he would authorize an apostolic visitation, an investigation of Lennon by another prelate. The lesson of Boston was that if priests revolt against a bishop, his chances of survival go down.

The larger lesson that Peter Borré carried out of his final meeting with the nuncio was that the power structure did not know how to change. So many well-educated Catholics who had the skills to rebuild a listing church were shunned by bishops fearful of facing the failures of the hierarchy. The scandalous handling of money was symptomatic of a larger institutional breakdown. The layers of denial in the Romanità mind were as thick as stone. This came home to Borré in the elegant language of understatement to which he had become so accustomed in Rome, via an e-mail to him from Archbishop Pietro Sambi:

> It is necessary to make known to the Cardinal [O'Malley] that your activity, perhaps undertaken in an erroneous manner, was not a struggle against him, but a manifestation of attachment to the Church, and to which She represents your faith in God . . . As proof positive of this, dissolve the organization and make yourself available to the Cardinal, who has a mandate from God to guide our Church, to collaborate with him for the purpose of holding open the greatest possible number of churches, as the presence of God in the community and the city. We are certain that this is also the innermost desire of His Eminence.

Perhaps some breakthrough with O'Malley might in time be possible, but dissolving the Council of Parishes without a quid pro quo was not in Borré's deck of cards.

In the fall, on another trip to Rome, Borré drew encouragement from a priest in the Congregation for the Clergy who told him to continue with the parishioner challenges of their churches' relegation "to profane use." Puzzled, he replied that if parishes were closed, wasn't the raising of a canonical issue like "profane use" little more than arguing over a cadaver? No, said the cleric. He explained that a bishop had the power to shut down a parish for any just reason, but the bishop's authority to reduce the church to profane use (nonreligious status) and to order that it be sold *could* be challenged. The bishop needs a *grave* reason, the priest emphasized. In Italy the attitude was not to sell a church unless it was falling down. Italy had closed parishes in villages, but the churches remained churches. A priest might visit once a month, say Mass, baptize infants. The church had limited use, but the larger church wanted to maintain its presence by keeping these small churches.

In the first week of 2011, a different legal shift was registered in a U.S. federal district court. After the diocese of Springfield, Massachusetts, closed Our Lady of Hope Church, the city council through its Historical Commission gave the church protected status to halt its demolition. The diocese sued the city, arguing that its rights under canon law had been abrogated. Judge Michael A. Ponsor ruled in the city's favor. "This lawsuit places the court at the intersection of two important, protected rights: the right of a religious entity to manage its places of worship in accordance with church law without oversight by secular authorities, and the right of the larger community to have a role in the preservation of a beloved landmark that was once a church," the judge ruled. The city council had taken action after the diocese had demolished another church, St. Joseph, "without really an opportunity to protect that church, which was of great historical significance to the city's French immigrants and culture," the city attorney, Edward M. Pikula, told the *Springfield Republican*.[27]

The diocese had accused the city of "religious gerrymandering," but a spokesman said the bishop would not take further action on the site until the Vatican ruled on the parishioners' appeal of the closure. Judge Ponsor, it seemed, had echoed the logic of the Congregation for the Clergy priest who endorsed the maintaining of old churches in Italian villages.

Fourteen parishes in the Pennsylvania diocese of Allentown had pressed appeals at the Congregation for the Clergy, expecting first to be denied and then to appeal to the Signatura. Meanwhile, Sister Christine Schenk had learned that fourteen parish appeals in Cleveland filed at the Congregation for the Clergy were on some sort of standby.

But in early 2011, Borré's strategy, carried out on the many trips to Rome—meeting with officials in Clergy and the Secretariat of State, working with Gullo in generating appeals to the Signatura—was bearing fruit. In January, Cardinal Raymond Burke, the prefect of the Signatura, in a speech to a gathering of clergy from England and Wales, said that closing a church should only come "as a last resort."[28] In early March, Congregation for the Clergy overruled the diocese of Allentown, Pennsylvania, on the shuttering of eight parishes out of the fourteen that had appealed. "It does not bring the parish back to life, but it puts on the table what could be a workable compromise: to physically reopen the locked-up church as a Catholic place of worship," Borré told the AP.[29] He was feeling good about three other Clergy decrees that allowed as many churches to stay open in the diocese of Springfield, Massachusetts. At the same time, eleven of nineteen parish appeals to Clergy had decisions to reopen their doors as churches, if not as operating parishes. The distinction between sacred and profane use had become leverage against a real estate sale, although the bishop was under no order to send a priest to say Mass. Seven closed parishes in Boston had appeals at Clergy protesting the relegation of their churches to profane use. Cleveland parishes had fifteen appeals pending. In the six months since Borré had last seen Sambi, Lennon had become more beleaguered.

Pope Benedict refused to intervene in the cases after the appeal by Carlo Gullo. Yet to Chris Schenk it was clear that Rome was searching for a response to the rising tide of people protesting the church closures. She had had many cordial dealings with bishops over the years, even prelates who did not share FutureChurch's agenda. She knew those men had to show their obedience to the Vatican even when they did not agree, as in endorsing a celibate priesthood while the worsening shortage of priests forced them to close churches. But with so many outcries from the grass roots as people demanded that their sacred spaces not be shuttered and sold, the signal sent to Rome was that bishops had not shown pastoral leadership. In Cleveland the various groups had sent thousands of letters to the nuncio in Washington. Sambi told a Cleveland priest that he had gotten more letters from Cleveland than any other diocese. Schenk knew that St. Patrick parishioners had sent three thousand letters in one day.

These stirrings of pluralism were part of a larger shift. An investigation, or "apostolic visitation," of the women's religious orders had been ordered by Cardinal Franc Rodé in Rome. Even if the women who led their congregations had not known Rodé was a loyalist to Father Maciel and the Legion of Christ, they would have resisted questions about their finances. The investigation did little to hurt the nuns, with no great Roman show of power. Someone at the Vatican realized that if you lose the nuns, you lose a big piece of the American church. Bob Bowers telling the *New York Times* that "very, very old men" in the Vatican were deeply out of touch was more than a display of courage by a gutsy priest who had lost his parish. Bowers was saying what Catholics could see: the Vatican had no mystique of religious elitism or even the shield of secrecy to combat the media coverage of clergy child molestation cases and the complicity of cardinals like Sodano and Castrillón. American bishops could not shelter Vatican letters from the subpoena power of lawyers like Jeff Anderson.

Chris Schenk had changed her view of letter-writing campaigns. Several years before, FutureChurch members had written letters to Rome about the need for opening ordination beyond the male-only celibacy law to preserve access to the Eucharist; the advancing shortage of priests meant that Mass attendance would drop—the data pointed toward exactly what came to pass. In the 1990s pastors who circulated appeals in their churches, seeking a change in the celibacy law, had generated two thousand letters to the Vatican. The letters went to Bishop Pilla, who held a stance of silent passivity as the priest shortage deepened.

The parish-closing protests galvanized deeper issues of spiritual integrity and money, striking the central nervous system of the church. Archbishop Sambi responded to many of the people who wrote to him. "He sent a letter to one parishioner with information about how to appeal," explains Sister Schenk. "The nuncio is the pope's eyes and ears in America. It is a serious issue when fifty parishes are closing in Cleveland while many of them are solvent. Cleveland is a heartbeat of the church in America. How can leadership maintain credibility while it threatens the very lifeblood of the church?"

The Reconfiguration plan that Lennon had grafted onto the Boston archdiocese backfired on O'Malley. In Cleveland it backfired on Lennon. Neither bishop knew how to change course: the issue for them was submission by the people to the selling of churches, upholding their authority and preventing further disclosure on Cardinal Law. In Boston, people voted with their feet; financial losses deepened. In Cleveland, Lennon defiantly said final Masses at parishes he suppressed with police escorts. Was this a sign of Christ on earth?

"I grieve for the capacity of the clerical system to denigrate basic human rights," said Sister Chris Schenk. "As Catholics we are supporting a wall of corruption with our money, whether we want to or not. Our job is to do something about it or risk being complicit. It's not enough to say, 'The bishop—or pastor—will handle things.' Lay leaders, particularly good Catholic businessmen, have to recognize what this corrosive secrecy is doing to us and be part of the solution. I think Mike Ryan's plan to safeguard the collections must be implemented from the parish to the diocese, up to the USCCB and Peter's Pence. We need transparency."

Well, sure, I countered. But how does "transparency" happen in a power structure afflicted with such rot and inertia? In 2010 Italian authorities had impounded funds from the Vatican Bank for alleged money laundering. An investigation of the bank by Italian authorities was under way as Pope Benedict made apologies to clergy abuse victims; but he retreated into a cocoon of silence as cardinals in his Curia were exposed for shielding pedophiles or facilitating schemes to profiteer off church sales. With his hands dirty from the Follieri scandal, Sodano had scoffed at the abuse crisis in an Easter sermon. Popes, cardinals, and bishops betraying human rights are more than mere cracks in a power grid, I told the good nun. How much worse could it get?

"With Cleveland I cry and lament," she replied. "And yes, I get depressed; however, this will lead to something better for the universal church. I always go back to Saint Paul: 'But where sin abounded, grace abounded even more'—Romans 5:20. God finds a way to bring good out of evil. That is the meaning of Jesus's crucifixion and resurrection. This is the core of my Christianity. Jesus stood against unjust authority. We push against the rock of injustice in our own church. Evil does not have the final word."

BENEDICT XVI: POPE
of IRONIES

─────────────

In 2008 the global economy plunged, thanks to titanic greed on Wall Street. Investment bankers created an arcane vocabulary of credit swaps, derivatives, and mortgage-backed securities to mask a riverboat gambler's monopoly on the table money. For years, bankers donated heavily to well-chosen political troughs and reaped rewards with the dismantling of federal regulatory practices, a legacy of Franklin Roosevelt's response to the Great Depression. In gutting oversight standards, particularly at the Securities and Exchange Commission, the Clinton and George W. Bush administrations abetted a bankers' gambling culture in which only the risk was missing. Wall Street built a wall of fictional value on assets gleaned from the buying and reselling of mortgages in a bonanza of easy lending. The wizards pulled bonus money off the top. When the housing bubble popped, the wall of assets crumbled. Lawyers—expensive ones—materialized from the dust to keep executives out of prison. The U.S. Treasury under President Bush and President Obama used taxpayer billions to save banks and revitalize lending. By 2011 credit was still tight, unemployment was high, the national debt had soared, but the recession appeared to have passed. The bonuses still flowed like wedding wine.

The Catholic Church's financial convulsions are another take on the spoils of deregulation, but the church fisc was never regulated much to begin with. The Vatican Bank is not included in the Holy See's financial statements. How much of Peter's Pence actually goes to the needy is a mystery. So is Allied Irish Bank's role in American dioceses that struggled to pay abuse settlements. Was AIB a pass-through for Vatican funds to help certain dioceses while others had no such advantage?

Politics is the movement of money. Every system has its players. The Vatican deemed Cardinal Sodano a descendant of Jesus's apostles. Certain congregations were his to manipulate for Maciel and Follieri. The scheme in which Follieri routed at least $387,300 to the Vatican Bank would have destroyed Sodano's career in a democracy, if not sent him to prison. Follieri pleaded guilty to money laundering in New York. How did the money circulate after it entered the Vatican Bank? Was it, in a legal sense, laundered? Stepping down as secretary of state, Sodano became dean of the College of Cardinals.

The church financial system resembles a constellation of medieval fiefdoms in which each bishop manages his fisc ideally to serve his people but with an eye riveted on Rome. Few dioceses subject their finances to robust auditing. Every five years the bishop sends a secret statement to the Vatican, which has scant interest in "transparency." The culture of passivity by which most Catholics receive the sacraments and give their dollars is a bedrock. As long as the people ask no questions about their money, the bishop can ban reformers from church grounds. The issue is not faith but fear that people might see where the money goes.

The beatification ceremony of John Paul II slated for May 2011 was an ironic way of avoiding that pope's call for "the purification of memory." Why beatify a pope whose faith in Maciel and myopia on the abuse crisis left a trail of human wreckage? The rush to spectacle cannot airbrush facts from history.

The Catholic Church's great problem is structural mendacity, institutionalized lying. The church that fosters Christian witness through the values of peace and reaching out to the world's poor is also saddled with bishops who, like Father Maciel's Legionaries, cannot criticize their cardinals, and with cardinals who fail to uphold the human rights of children. Under heavy media pressure, the U.S. bishops in 2002 adopted a youth protection charter. "In 1985 I didn't know anyone else who had been molested by a priest," says Barbara Blaine, the founder of SNAP. "Today, bishops have removed hundreds of predators from ministry. Survivors who speak up are more likely to be believed and to receive sympathy from parishioners and compassion from church officials. Secrecy is still a top priority for bishops; but the church has safe-touch programs for children. Teachers and lay workers are taught to report inappropriate behavior. The climate is safer for children and better for survivors who report abuse." Yet, as Blaine points out, the hierarchy's concealment of perpetrators is still a reality. Cardinal Francis George of Chicago, three years after the youth charter was adopted, put an accused pedophile back in ministry over warnings from his advisory board. The priest reoffended, went to jail, the archdiocese paid heavily to the victims—and Cardinal George was elected president of the USCCB.[1]

Rewarding failure is so embedded in the good old boy culture of the ecclesial princes as to suggest that bishops think the church will always be rich. Demographics do not bode well for maintaining double standards. A Pew Forum on Religion and Public Life survey found that Catholicism is still America's largest single religion—about 25 percent of the population identify themselves as Catholic—but the numbers are in decline. The second-largest cohort polled, at 10 percent, consisted of ex-Catholics, people who left the church.[2] The monetary losses in the Boston archdiocese with so many believers gone may be seen as a worst case or the shape of things to come. The pivotal group is women of child-bearing age; if they continue to leave, the church loses their children. The rise of an Irish American and Italian American middle class took several generations to achieve, but the early-twentieth-century migrations fostered a booming church. Although the influx of Latinos has thwarted a steeper Catholic population loss, today's church is scaling back, struggling to provide care for aged clergy and nuns. As bishops shut churches against the people's will, questions of financial ethics hover like black clouds.

By the lights of apostolic succession, the American bishops' youth protection charter of 2002 prevented lay review boards from investigating bishops. Cardinals, too, must be protected from the intrusions of justice. But the assumptions of immunity for prelates collided with Pope Benedict's concern for the secularization of Catholic Europe. His agenda for evangelizing Europe and renewing the church ran headlong into the 2010 news coverage of clergy abuse cases and European bishops who concealed perpetrators, just as in America.

The European bishops might heed a prescient American legal scholar. Patrick J. Schiltz published an article in *America,* the Jesuit magazine, in 2003. At the time he held a chair at the University of St. Thomas School of Law in Minneapolis. Citing his background in doing defense work for dioceses in abuse cases, Schiltz wrote: "I must confess that the church will not restore my trust until it holds negligent bishops accountable for the incalculable damage that they have inflicted on the church." Schiltz was writing as litigation began to surge, just as the second wave of Boston plaintiffs received an $85 million settlement. A billion dollars more in church payouts from other states was yet to come. Schiltz recommended a reverse-class-action strategy.

> The church should set up a national tribunal—a group of extremely well-respected people who are completely independent of the church—to arbitrate sexual claims against the church. A diocese that wanted to "opt in" to the system would invite victims who appear to be telling the truth about being sexually abused—which is about 98 percent of them—to use the tribunal. The diocese would essentially tell the victims that, if they forgo litigation and instead present their claims to the tribunal, the diocese will pay the victim whatever the tribunal decides is fair. Such a system would have major advantages for both victims and the church.
>
> Victims would be certain of getting compensation. The diocese would agree not to raise the statute of limitations or any other defense. In other words, the question before the tribunal would not be "whether" but "how much?" Dioceses would recognize that regardless of what the law says, they have a moral obligation to compensate victims fairly. Moreover, victims could get quick compensation. In the court system, cases often drag on four or five years . . .
>
> The most important benefit of this system is that it would let the church and the victim work together in a common cause— achieving a just and healing result—rather than pit them against each other through several years of litigation. Needless to say,

there would be a lot of details to work out, but unless the church takes bold and creative steps such as these, it is in for a grim few years in the legal arena.[3]

Schiltz was right about the grim legal arena ahead. Eight years later, lawsuits continue. Bishops in Europe could embrace his plan, reduce losses, and gain respect in the eyes of their followers and the news media. It might yet work in parts of America. Schiltz, who is now a federal judge, declined to be interviewed.

Benedict XVI's ascetic personality and history, as a cardinal, of punishing church intellectuals hardly suggest a reformer who would embrace Schiltz's proposal; but as the annus horribilis of 2010 drew to a close, Benedict took a calculated risk with the Legion of Christ. He installed Cardinal Velasio De Paolis as papal delegate to the order—read: overseer. De Paolis is a canon lawyer, former secretary of the Signatura, and president of the Prefecture for the Economic Affairs of the Holy See, the office that audits the balance sheets and budgets of other curial departments. As he began the process of drafting a new constitution for the Legion, De Paolis had to locate its assets. Benedict was gambling that it was better to salvage the organization than to dismantle it, despite its many disillusioned ex-members and the opinions of six U.S. bishops who banned the Legion and Regnum Christi from their dioceses. The pope ordered an investigation of Regnum Christi. Benedict began prodding the Legion to compensate Maciel's victims, especially older ones who no longer had legal recourse. Jeff Anderson sued the Legion in Connecticut on behalf of Maciel's son for allegations of incest committed on U.S. soil. The Vatican has no mechanism for compensating victims per se, but the pope wanted the Legion's coffers to do that; he was, in a way, acting like a judge pushing two parties to settle a dispute—a wise use of power. Bishop Ricardo Watty Urquidi of Tepic, Mexico, one of five apostolic visitators who had investigated the Legion for the Holy See, told reporters in Mexico on May 18, 2010: "We need, then, to take care of [Maciel's] victims, as much inside as outside the Legion, and to compensate them for damages. This is something we all agreed on, and the pope accepted—just as he has been doing, and bravely so."[4]

The Vatican monarchical system has no separation of powers, nor a bona fide court system for criminal prosecution or property rights. Benedict in theory had the power to punish or call down cardinals, though to do so would violate the unwritten laws of apostolic succession. Benedict seemed ill-suited for the hard choices of reform during the debacles of 2010, as exemplified by his refusal to accept the resignations offered by two Irish bishops for their complicity in harboring predators. But his design that Legion assets be used to compensate victims, if achieved, would set a precedent. The Legionaries as a religious order are subject to papal obedience. To punish Sodano would be a greater act of justice.

The Vatican cannot be reformed without an independent court system to supplant the tribunals that cater to bishops. An international commission of Catholic constitutional scholars could craft a system to codify children's rights, the preservation of parishes, and oversight of bishops. The alternative is a recurrent spectacle of parish-closing protests, while victims' lawyers target diocesan assets, notably in Europe, with more shame heaped on the Vatican.

The financial accountability of bishops is an issue that seems destined for more activity in the civil courts. Corporation sole—the bishop owns all—is an anachronism prone to abuse. When American parishioners have sought rights as beneficiaries to their churches, judges have largely bowed to canon law, as in the Ohio decision that gave ownership of St. James Parish in the town of Kansas to Bishop Leonard P. Blair of Toledo. The Ohio court allowed Bishop Blair to pay his lawyers from the parish bank accounts, close the church, demolish it, and put the land up for sale. And the parishioners' recourse? A sovereign monarchy that bars them from sitting in the court, since there are no open arguments anyway. The Apostolic Signatura and the Congregation for the Clergy make a mockery of justice. As American judges learn how the Vatican system works, a few of them, perhaps even in Ohio, may emulate Mr. Ponsor of the federal bench in Springfield, Massachusetts, in recognizing religious property as a more complex issue of democratic jurisprudence.

VATICAN BANK IN TROUBLE AGAIN

The Institute of Religious Works, or Vatican Bank, has 40,000 account holders from among the members of religious congregations, and cardinals sit on its board of directors. Church officials over the years have said it should not be considered a bank, but rather a massive trust to manage the capital of religious orders, relief organizations, and church charities, getting the best returns on funds invested, thereby promoting charitable and other works. But from its small suite in a medieval tower near the courtyard leading to the Apostolic Palace, IOR has also functioned as an offshore bank by virtue of its status in Vatican City, a sovereign state. Italy exerted little control after the Vatican paid a $242 million fine a quarter century ago to resolve IOR's role in the money-laundering scheme involving Archbishop Marcinkus, Roberto Calvi, and Michele Sindona that caused Banco Ambrosiano's collapse.[5]

Monetary wire transfers is a serious issue for central banks of various countries in trying to thwart terrorist groups and organized crime. In September 2010, Italian authorities impounded $30 million in IOR assets on suspicion of money laundering and ordered an investigation of the IOR chairman Ettore Gotti Tedeschi and his chief deputy. It was a bitter pill for Tedeschi, an economics scholar, daily communicant, and Opus Dei member with an image of rectitude. Italy's central bank flagged transfers from an IOR account in Credito Artigiano to JP Morgan Frankfurt for $26 million, and to Banca del Funcino for $4 million, for insufficient documentation under European Union laws. The Holy See stated it was "perplexed and astonished" that that information was available to Italy's central bank. Tedeschi voluntarily spoke with prosecutors and pledged to work with the international Organization for Economic Cooperation and Development to put the IOR in full compliance.[6]

For all of its religious clients, and the funds it provides the Holy Father for his charitable uses, IOR had "an unknown number of private Italian account holders who use the Vatican as a tax haven," according to the *Financial Times*. A month after the $30 million impoundment, Guy Dinmore reported that police in Sicily made six arrests linked to

> Father Orazio Bonaccorsi allegedly using an account in the name of the Vatican bank to help his father launder €250,000 ($350,000) he had obtained from European Union funding for an allegedly non-existent fish farm project.
>
> After passing through the account as a "charity" donation in 2006, the money allegedly returned to Sicily to be withdrawn by an uncle previously convicted for mafia association . . .
>
> "IOR cannot work like this any more," an Italian official said.

"People have used IOR as a screen," he added. "What is behind the screen? That is the mechanism we are trying to dismantle," he told the *Financial Times*.[7]

The $30 million was in a state of banking limbo when the Holy See issued a statement by Pope Benedict on December 30, 2010, promulgating a law for the Vatican city-state "concerning the prevention and countering of the laundering of proceeds from criminal activities and the financing of terrorism." The pope created a Financial Information Authority to ensure that IOR and all Vatican departments adhered to European regulations on money laundering. He named Cardinal Attilo Nicora, who administers the Vatican real estate and financial holdings, as its chairman. The Vatican appointed a four-member board of prominent academics in relevant fields to sit in Rome.

A POPE OF IRONIES

As the years of prosecuting theologians sink into his past, Benedict XVI stands as the pope of ironies. The cardinal whose tactics drove Hans Küng to compare him to Dostoyevsky's Grand Inquisitor ("he fears nothing more than freedom") must, as pope, balance the agenda of moral absolutes with the politics of restraint.[8] In *The Brothers Karamazov*, Dostoyevsky uses the inquisitor's cameo to condemn the church for abandoning Christ: Jesus appears in Seville during the Spanish Inquisition. The sinister monk who has been burning heretics puts Jesus in a cell and lays on a cynical lecture about power and why the fearful masses must be subdued. Jesus stands silent. Then, in a sublime gesture of forgiveness, Jesus kisses the inquisitor and leaves. For Dostoyevsky, the Church of Rome will betray the conscience of Christ anew.

Ratzinger-as-prosecutor peers over Benedict's shoulder, repulsed by the structural sins and crimes. The pope, as chief pastor, must weigh flexibility for the greater good. Does he fear a faith unmoored by prosecutions let loose?

Creating a commission to clean up the Vatican Bank, like the punishment of Maciel and takeover of the Legion, suggests a pope gaining confidence with his powers. The powers are supreme. How far should he go? To let the likes of Cardinal Sodano simply age and slip away is a passive sign that justice is a ritual of half measures. The pope cannot be an authentic voice for peace, affirm the dignity of human life, and preach the values of a greener planet if people see that Vatican justice is a farce. Will justice sink beneath the weight of popes forever bound to the hubris of apostolic succession? Questions hang; a hungry people wait.

The miracle is that the Eucharist endures.

NOTES

AUTHOR'S NOTE
The many interviews for this book involved countless follow-up calls and e-mails; to have listed each interview as a citation was impractical. Most direct quotations are not cited as footnotes. I have kept background sources, who spoke with assurance of anonymity, to a minimum; but investigative reporting, particularly at the Vatican and in high levels of the Catholic Church, relies on some sources with careers to protect, hence their insistence on not being identified. The notes list a small number of interviews that were germane to specific points like a published citation. Many of the news articles and documents cited in this book can be found in the online library archive www.bishopaccountability.org.

PROLOGUE: PRINCES OF THE REALM
1. Hans Küng, *The Catholic Church: A Short History* (New York, 2001), p. 181.
2. Message of Pope Paul VI, Celebration of the Day of Peace, January 1, 1972, www.vatican.va.
3. Luigi Accattoli, *When a Pope Asks for Forgiveness: The Mea Culpa's of John Paul II* (Boston, 1998), p. 96.
4. Ibid., p. 118.
5. James Gollin, *Worldly Goods* (New York, 1971), p. 492.

6. Sam Dillon and Leslie Wayne, "Scandals in the Church: The Money," *New York Times*, June 13, 2002.

7. Ibid.

8. Brian Ross, "Archbishop Settles Sex Assault Claim," *Good Morning America*, May 23, 2002.

9. Tom Heinan, "Rome Endowments to Honor Weakland," *Milwaukee Journal Sentinel*, November 22, 1997.

10. Rembert G. Weakland, *A Pilgrim in a Pilgrim Church: Memoirs of a Catholic Archbishop* (Grand Rapids, MI, 2009), p. 341. Weakland's account of the legal settlement with Paul Marcoux—whom I interviewed as part of the ABC News investigation—is a study in self-pity, riddled with inaccuracies.

11. James A. Brundage, *Law, Sex, and Christian Society in Medieval Europe* (Chicago, 1987), p. 214.

12. Douglas MacMillan, "A Business Plan for the Catholic Church," *Business-Week*, September 30, 2008.

13. *The Catholic Church in America—Meeting Real Needs in Your Neighborhood* (Washington, DC: United States Conference of Catholic Bishops, 2002), pp. 13–14.

14. Harris provided his opinion in a telephone interview after extensive dialogue on his interpretation of data.

15. Harris utilized the data from Georgetown University's Center for Applied Research in the Apostolate (CARA). He explains: "Estimates for the total parish Offertory collection for the years 2002 through 2006 were calculated as follows. CARA annually collected Offertory collection data from members of the International Catholic Stewardship Council (ICSC). In addition to estimates for the Offertory collection, ICSC members also provided estimates of the number of households by diocese. The response rate for these data requests was approximately 65 percent. The data were organized according to a structure of seven geographic regions: Northeast, South Atlantic, South, Great Lakes, Midwest, Mountain, and Pacific. We first developed an average household donation by diocese for every responding diocese. The regional average statistic was then multiplied by the number of households in a diocese that did not report Offertory collection data. The reported data and the calculated data were added together to form an estimated total Offertory collection for every diocese in the region. The process was repeated for all regions to form an estimated Offertory collection for the fifty states and the District of Columbia."

16. John Jay College of Criminal Justice, *The Nature and Scope of the Problems of Sexual Abuse of Minors by Catholic Priests and Deacons in the United States* (Washington, DC: United States Conference of Catholic Bishops, 2004), p. 105, table 6.

17. Joseph Claude Harris, "The Sexual Abuse Scandal in the United States: What It Cost" (unpublished, 2010). Harris draws his data from annual studies on data related to the abuse crisis by CARA.

18. In a personal communication with the author, Mary Gautier, Ph.D., of CARA explains a discrepancy: "Dioceses are not consistent in what they report to *The Official Catholic Directory,* which is the only source of those data. If a diocese merges three parishes into one, it should report that it has closed three parishes and created one new parish. Too often, they do not report this accurately." A "new" parish formed by a consolidation of existing ones, however, is not the same as a church developed and built to be a Catholic parish.

19. James Freeman, "Pennies Backed by Heaven," *Wall Street Journal,* May 16, 2008.

20. Ralph Cipriano, "Lavish Spending in Archdiocese Skips Inner City," *National Catholic Reporter,* June 19, 1998.

21. "A Continuous, Concerted Campaign of Cover-up," excerpts from the Grand Jury's Report, *Philadelphia Inquirer,* September 22, 2005.

22. Robert West and Charles Zech, "Internal Financial Controls in the U.S. Church" (Villanova, PA: Villanova University, Center for the Study of Church Management, January 2007).

23. Susan Spencer-Wendel, "Bookkeepers Believed Priest Was Skimming from Church," *Palm Beach Post,* February 18, 2009; and "Jury Finds Priest Stole Collections," *Palm Beach Post,* February 23, 2009.

24. Anemona Hartocollis, "Monsignor Gets 4-Year Sentence for Large Thefts from His East Side Parish," *New York Times,* September 23, 2006; Associated Press, "N.Y. Church Sues Insurer Over $1.2 Million Thefts Blamed on Priest," *Insurance Journal,* January 26, 2005; Veronika Belenkaya, "Priest Who Swindled East Side Parish Released from Prison," *New York Daily News,* September 22, 2007.

25. Michael Ryan draws on parish population data from the Center for Applied Research in the Apostolate (CARA), a Georgetown University–affiliated research center, and financial figures drawn from media reports he has culled in more than twenty years of research on Catholic church embezzlements. Ryan estimates that nearly $90 million was embezzled from Sunday collections in the calendar year 2010.

"News articles concerning specific embezzlements occasionally include a reference to the stolen funds being replaced by the diocese acting as its own insurer," writes Ryan. "I am amazed that any commercial insurers are or would be willing to indemnify the church or a particular diocese without requiring them to implement readily available procedures that would prevent virtually all Sunday collection embezzlements. Insurers often pay out large sums of money when an embezzlement is discovered, and many diocesan officials are quick to announce that the loss suffered by the victim parish is being recovered through insurance. Whether such losses are paid for by a commercial insurer or a fund created and maintained by the diocese, it is still a loss that need not have been sustained."

Ryan continues: "The $90 million estimated to have been lost from collection plates in 2010 was arrived at by estimating that the average

Sunday collection embezzlement totaled $25,000, or about $500 per week, and that such embezzlements are ongoing in 20 percent of parishes at any given time. For 2010, 20 percent of CARA's reported 17,958 American parishes comes to 3,592 parishes. Multiplying that number by the estimated average loss per affected parish results in a total estimated loss of $89.8 million in 2010 alone.

"The key years ('65, '74, '75, '84, etc.) were computed using the 2010 estimate of $89.8 million as the base year and applying the Consumer Price Index (CPI) calculator to determine the equivalent 'real dollar' value for each of the key years. The average yearly loss for each of the five multiyear periods was then determined by adding the beginning and ending years' estimated losses and dividing the total by two."

ESTIMATE OF LOSSES DUE TO SUNDAY COLLECTION EMBEZZLEMENTS IN THE U.S. CATHOLIC CHURCH

YEAR	ANNUAL LOSSES* (ADJ. FOR INFLATION)	AVG. ANN. LOSSES FOR PERIODS SHOWN	TOTAL LOSSES FOR PERIODS SHOWN	EXISTING PARISHES†	AVG. ANNUAL LOSS PER PARISH*
1965	$12,740,000	1965–74	1965–74	17,637	$3,612
1974	$19,707,000	$16,223,000	$162,230,000	18,427‡	$5,348
1975	$22,248,000	1975–84	1975–84	18,515	$6,008
1984	$44,961,000	$33,604,000	$336,040,000	19,171‡	$11,727
1985	$46,919,000	1985–94	1985–94	19,244	$12,190
1994	$65,220,000	$56,069,000	$560,690,000	19,322‡	$16,879
1995	$66,998,000	1995–2004	1995–2004	19,331	$17,330
2004	$80,799,000	$73,898,000	$738,980,000	18,935‡	$21,336
2005	$83,233,000	2005–10	2005–10	18,891	$22,031
2010	$89,800,000	$86,516,000	$519,096,000	17,958	$25,000

ESTIMATED CUMULATIVE LOSSES 1965–2010: $2,317,036,000

* Annual loss figures are based upon an estimation that collections in 20% of existing parishes lost an average of $25,000 in CY 2010. Losses for other years shown in left column were computed by applying the Consumer Price Index to the CY 2010 estimation.
† Center for Applied Research in the Apostolate, http://cara.georgetown.edu/CARA Services/requestedchurchstats.html.
‡ Estimated from trend reflected by CARA figures.

26. Alan Gomez, "Bishops Look at Fleecings of Flocks," USA Today, February 18, 2007.

27. Julie Shaw, "Priest Admits Stealing from School: Sex Abuse, Drug Use Alleged," *Philadelphia Daily News*, March 10, 2009; Joseph A. Slobodzian, "Judge Calls Priest Liar; Sends Him to Prison for $900,000 Theft," *Philadelphia Inquirer*, May 22, 2009.

28. Andrew Greeley and William McManus, *Catholic Contributions: Sociology and Policy* (Chicago, 1985), pp. 2–3.

29. The study by Joseph Claude Harris, *The Cost of Catholic Parishes and Schools* (Kansas City, MO, 1996), is cited in Charles E. Zech, *Why Catholics Don't Give . . . and What Can Be Done About It* (Huntington, IN, 2000), p. 13.

30. Zech, *Why Catholics Don't Give*, p. 71.

31. Jack Ruhl, personal communication with the author.

32. See "Mercer Actuarial Study," National Religious Retirement Office, www.ncchuscc.org/nrro.

33. Fred Kammer, SJ, "The *Jaynotes* Interview," *Jaynotes: The Magazine of Jesuit High School in New Orleans, Graduation 2008* 34, no. 2 (2008): 28.

34. Fred Kammer, SJ, *Faith. Works. Wonders. An Insider's Guide to Catholic Charities* (Eugene, OR, 2009), pp. 63–64.

35. Cindy Wooden, "2006 Vatican Budget Closes with Surplus; Peter's Pence up $42 Million," Catholic News Service, July 6, 2007.

36. Robert Mickens, "Church with a Midas Touch," *The Tablet*, September 27, 2008.

37. *The Nature and Scope of the Problems of Sexual Abuse of Minors by Catholic Priests and Deacons in the United States*. The report underreported the number of victims; John Jay researchers did not interview attorneys with long experience in litigation for victims, nor groups like Survivors Network of those Abused by Priests to cross-reference what the bishops reported. For a solid analysis of the report, see Mary Gail Frawley O'Dea, *Perversion of Power: Sexual Abuse in the Catholic Church* (Nashville, 2007).

CHAPTER 1: BOSTON IN THE FAULT LINES

1. Walter V. Robinson and Michael Rezendes, "Geoghan Victims Agree to $10m Settlement," *Boston Globe*, September 19, 2002; Kevin Cullen and Stephen Kurkjian, "Church in an $85 Million Accord," *Boston Globe*, September 10, 2003. The settlement negotiated by attorneys was $85 million, covering 542 victims. The archdiocese later came to terms with a small number of victims who filed their own claims without counsel, boosting the final settlement to an estimated $90 million for 552 victims.

2. For a concise account, see *Boston Globe* Investigative Staff, *Betrayal: The Crisis of the Catholic Church* (New York, 2002). The authors—Matt Carroll, Kevin Cullen, Thomas Farragher, Stephen Kurkjian, Michael Paulson, Sacha Pfeiffer, Michael Rezendes, Spotlight Team Editor Walter V. Robinson—and Deputy Managing Editor for Projects Ben Bradlee Jr. shared a 2003 Pulitzer Prize and other awards.

3. Michael Paulson, "Diocese to Mortgage Seminary, Cathedral," *Boston Globe*, December 9, 2003.

4. Phyllis Berman and Lea Goldman, "Catholics in Crisis," *Forbes*, September 19, 2005.

5. Michael Paulson, "Diocesan Headquarters Sold to BC," *Boston Globe*, April 21, 2004.

6. Marie Roth, genealogical tree and personal communication with the author, May 16, 2009.

7. Paul L. Williams, *The Vatican Exposed: Money, Murder, and the Mafia* (Amherst, NY, 2003), p. 81.

8. John Pollard, *Catholicism in Modern Italy: Religion, Society and Politics Since 1861* (New York, 2008), p. 122.

9. Thomas Powers, *The Man Who Kept the Secrets: Richard Helms and the CIA* (New York, 1979), p. 31.

10. Tim Weiner, *Legacy of Ashes* (New York, 2007), p. 27.

11. Ibid.

12. John Cornwell, *Hitler's Pope: The Secret History of Pius XII* (New York, 1999), p. 329.

13. John Cooney, *The American Pope: The Life and Times of Francis Cardinal Spellman* (New York, 1984), pp. 159–60.

14. Nino Lo Bello, *The Vatican Empire* (New York, 1968), p. 143.

15. Weiner, *Legacy of Ashes*, p. 27.

16. Christopher Duggan, *The Force of Destiny: A History of Italy Since 1796* (London, 2007), p. 478.

17. Thomas H. O'Connor, *The Hub: Boston Past and Present* (Boston, 2001), p. 8.

18. Thomas H. O'Connor, *Boston Catholics: A History of the Church and Its People* (Boston, 1998), pp. 4–5.

19. O'Connor, *The Hub*, pp. 33–35.

20. J. Anthony Lukas, *Common Ground* (New York, 1985), p. 75.

21. On the French missionaries and the first Catholic Church, see O'Connor, *Boston Catholics*, pp. 19–22, 24; on the riots, see O'Connor, *The Hub*, p. 150.

22. On Protestant Charlestown, see Lukas, *Common Ground*, p. 76; on Beecher's sermon, see James Hennessey, SJ, *American Catholics: A History of the Roman Catholic Community in the United States* (New York, 1981), p. 122; on drunks feeding bonfires, see Charles R. Morris, *American Catholic: The Saints and Sinners Who Built America's Most Powerful Church* (New York, 1997), pp. 56–57.

23. For Great Famine emigration data, see R. F. Foster, *Modern Ireland: 1600–1972* (London, 1989), p. 345. The *Bunker Hill Aurora* quote is in Lukas, *Common Ground*, p. 77.

24. Thomas H. O'Connor, *The Boston Irish: A Political History* (Boston, 1995), p. 150.

25. St. Catherine of Siena Parish, *Ninetieth Anniversary Celebration, 1887–1977* (Boston, 1977), no page numbers.

26. John Henry Cutler, *Cardinal Cushing of Boston* (New York, 1970), p. 214.

27. Lukas, *Common Ground*, p. 25.

28. Cutler, *Cardinal Cushing*, p. 82.

29. See Jason Berry and Gerald Renner, *Vows of Silence: The Abuse of Power in the Papacy of John Paul II* (New York, 2004), p. 65.

30. Dante Alighieri, *The Divine Comedy: The Purgatorio*, trans. John Ciardi (New York, 2003), p. 431, canto XVII.

CHAPTER 2: ORIGINS OF THE VATICAN FINANCIAL SYSTEM

1. "Papal Donations Bring Hope to Needy Worldwide," Catholic News Agency, July 22, 2010.

2. According to USCCB.org, the website of the U.S. Conference of Catholic Bishops, "the Peter's Pence Collection supports the Pope's philanthropy by giving the Holy Father the means to provide emergency assistance to those in need because of natural disaster, war, oppression, and disease."

3. Information at www.thepapalfoundation.com.

4. Alessandro Speciale also reports for a religious news service in Rome, among other outlets, and worked as a research associate for this book.

5. On the Vatican II debt burden, see *Communiqué on the Fifth Meeting of the Council of Cardinals for Studying the Organizational and Economic Questions of the Holy See*, Press Office, March 9, 1985; translation of Italian from *L'Osservatore Romano* to English, dated March 10, 1985. On the deficit figure, see *Holy See General Final Balance Sheet and Profit and Loss Account, 1985*, p. 7. Copies of both were provided by a background source.

6. Philip Willan, *The Last Supper: The Mafia, the Masons, and the Killing of Roberto Calvi* (London, 2007).

7. "Outline of Remarks by Cardinal Krol on Vatican Deficit," November 18, 1987, unpublished.

8. Praefectura Rerum Oeconomicarum Sanctae Sedis, *Statement of Income and Expenditure of the Holy See, Year 1987*. The financial figures cited are taken from a three-page letter addressed "Dear Brother Bishops," dated October 14, 1988, and signed by seven cardinals, including Krol of Philadelphia; John O'Connor of New York; Edward Clancy of Sydney; Albert Decourtray of Lyon; Joseph Cordeiro of Karachi; Eugenio de Araújo Sales of Rio de Janeiro; and Paul Zoungrana of Ouagadougou. Copies were provided by a background source.

9. Thomas J. Reese, SJ, *A Flock of Shepherds: The National Conference of Catholic Bishops* (Kansas City, MO, 1992), p. 282.

10. Jerry Filteau, "Vatican's Financial Head Says Catholics Not Giving What They Can," Catholic News Service, November 12, 1991.

11. Sandro Magister, "For Peter's Cash, a Calm Amid the Storm," trans. Matthew Sherry, January 30, 2009, www.chiesa.espressonline.it.

12. On Peter's Pence figures, see Peter R. D'Agostino, *Rome in America* (Chapel Hill, NC, 2004), p. 31. On Rome real estate, see John F. Pollard, *Money and the Rise of the Modern Papacy* (Cambridge, UK, 2005), p. 62.

13. Nicholas P. Cafardi, "The Availability of Parish Assets for Diocesan Debts: A Canonical Analysis," *Seton Hall Legislative Journal* 29, no. 2 (2004–2005), p. 362.

14. David I. Kertzer, *The Kidnapping of Edgardo Mortara* (New York, 1998), p. 15.

15. Eamon Duffy, *Saints and Sinners: A History of the Popes* (New Haven, CT, 2006), p. 286.

16. David Kertzer, telephone interview with the author, May 8, 2009. See also David I. Kertzer, *The Popes Against the Jews: The Vatican's Role in the Rise of Modern Anti-Semitism* (New York, 2001), chap. 3.

17. Pollard, *Money and the Rise of the Modern Papacy*, p. 24.

18. Charles Dickens, *Pictures from Italy* (New York, 1974), p. 165.

19. Tommaso Astarita, *Between Salt Water and Holy Water: A History of Southern Italy* (New York, 2005), p. 75.

20. Massimo Franco, *Parallel Empires: The Vatican and the United States—Two Centuries of Alliance and Conflict* (New York, 2008), p. 32.

21. Kertzer, *The Popes Against the Jews*, p. 79.

22. James Carroll, *Constantine's Sword: The Church and the Jews* (New York, 2001), p. 379.

23. Kertzer, *The Popes Against the Jews*, p. 115.

24. Pollard, *Money and the Rise of the Modern Papacy*, pp. 32–33.

25. "Peter's Pence," www.britannica.com.

26. D'Agostino, *Rome in America*, p. 31.

27. James M. O'Toole, *The Faithful: A History of Catholics in America* (Cambridge, MA, 2008), p. 132.

28. David I. Kertzer, *Prisoner of the Vatican: The Popes' Secret Plot to Capture Rome from the New Italian State* (Boston, 2004), p. 5.

29. Kertzer, *The Kidnapping of Edgardo Mortara*, p. 79, quoting Jan Derek Holmes's *The Triumph of the Holy See* (Shepherdstown, WV, 1978).

30. Anthony Rhodes, *The Power of Rome in the Twentieth Century: The Vatican and the Age of Liberal Democracies, 1870–1922* (London, 1983), pp. 36–37.

31. Duffy, *Saints and Sinners*, p. 289.

32. Ibid., pp. 293–94.

33. "Peter's Pence," *New York Times*, December 4, 1860.

34. John F. Pollard, *Catholicism in Modern Italy: Religion, Society and Politics Since 1861* (New York, 2008), p. 22; Kertzer, *Prisoner of the Vatican*, p. 24.

35. Garry Wills, *Papal Sin* (New York, 2000), p. 74.

36. Duffy, *Saints and Sinners*, p. 228.

37. Pollard, *Money and the Rise of the Modern Papacy*, pp. 32–33.

38. J. N. D. Kelly, *The Oxford Dictionary of Popes* (Oxford, 1986), pp. 314–16. On 3.5 million lire, see Duffy, *Saints and Sinners*, p. 233.

39. Pollard, *Money and the Rise of the Modern Papacy*, p. 39.
40. Kertzer, *Prisoner of the Vatican*, p. 19.
41. Ibid., p. 26.
42. Ibid., p. 31.
43. Gertrude Himmelfarb, *Lord Acton: A Study in Conscience and Politics* (London, 1952), p. 102, explains that "the Roman States" had sixty-two bishops representing 700,000 people, while a single bishop represented 1.7 million Polish Catholics. "In ecclesiastical statistics, it appeared that twenty learned Germans counted for less than one untutored Italian."
44. Wills, *Papal Sin*, pp. 249–56.
45. Ibid., p. 215.
46. Corrado Pallenberg, *Vatican Finances* (London, 1971), p. 59.
47. Hans Küng, *Infallible? An Unresolved Enquiry* (New York, 1994), pp. 145–46.
48. Pallenberg, *Vatican Finances*, p. 32.
49. Ibid., p. 33.
50. Kertzer, *Prisoner of the Vatican*, p. 132.
51. Pollard, *Money and the Rise of the Modern Papacy*, p. 51.
52. D'Agostino, *Rome in America*, pp. 61, 78.
53. Pollard, *Money and the Rise of the Modern Papacy*, p. 51.
54. Rhodes, *The Power of Rome*, p. 76.
55. Kertzer, *The Popes Against the Jews*, p. 192.
56. Pollard, *Money and the Rise of the Modern Papacy*, p. 360.
57. James M. O'Toole, *Militant and Triumphant: William Henry O'Connell and the Catholic Church in Boston, 1859–1944* (Notre Dame, IN, 1992), p. 16.
58. Ibid., p. 11.
59. Ibid., pp. 34, 39.
60. Ibid., pp. 56–57.
61. Charles R. Morris, *American Catholic: The Saints and Sinners Who Built America's Most Powerful Church* (New York, 1997), p. 114.
62. Ibid., pp. 103, 93.
63. John Cooney, *The American Pope: The Life and Times of Francis Cardinal Spellman* (New York, 1984), p. 24.
64. O'Toole, *Militant and Triumphant*, p. 182.
65. Ibid., p. 186.
66. Ibid., p. 193.
67. Kelly, *The Oxford Dictionary of Popes*, pp. 314–16; Duffy, *Saints and Sinners*, p. 333.
68. John F. Pollard, *The Unknown Pope: Benedict XV (1914–1922) and the Pursuit of Peace* (London, 1999), p. 122.
69. Christopher Duggan, *The Force of Destiny: A History of Italy Since 1796* (London, 2007), p. 399.
70. Ibid., p. 400.
71. Pollard, *The Unknown Pope*, p. 146.
72. John Henry Cutler, *Cardinal Cushing of Boston* (New York, 1970), p. 63.

73. Edward R. Kantowicz, *Corporation Sole: Cardinal Mundelein and Chicago Catholicism* (Notre Dame, IN, 1983), p. 42.

74. Ibid., p. 39.

75. Morris, *American Catholic,* pp. 163, 187.

76. Ibid., p. 168.

77. Ibid., p. 171.

78. Ibid., pp. 186–87.

79. Kertzer, *The Popes Against the Jews*, p. 241.

80. George Seldes, *The Vatican: Yesterday, Today and Tomorrow* (New York, 1934), p. 326.

81. Ibid., p. 330.

82. Ibid., p. 426.

83. Donald Sassoon, *Mussolini and the Rise of Fascism* (New York, 2007), p. 85.

84. Ibid., p. 427.

85. Duffy, *Saints and Sinners*, p. 337. Italics added.

86. Cooney, *The American Pope*, p. 39.

87. Duffy, *Saints and Sinners*, p. 339.

88. Emilio Gentile, *The Sacralization of Politics in Fascist Italy* (Cambridge, MA, 1996), p. 59.

89. Duffy, *Saints and Sinners*, p. 339.

90. Peter Godman, *Hitler and the Vatican: Inside the Secret Archives That Reveal the New Story of the Nazis and the Church* (New York, 2004), p. 27.

91. Ronald J. Rychlak, *Hitler, the War, and the Pope* (Huntington, IN, 2010), p. 73.

92. James Gollin, *Worldly Goods* (New York, 1971), pp. 439, 441.

93. John Cornwell, *Hitler's Pope: The Secret History of Pius XII* (New York, 1999), p. 190.

94. See George Seldes, *The Catholic Crisis* (New York, 1945); and D'Agostino, *Rome in America.*

95. Pollard, *Money and the Rise of the Modern Papacy*, p. 186; see also Gollin, *Worldly Goods*, pp. 449–54.

96. Duffy, *Saints and Sinners*, pp. 343–45.

97. Rabbi David G. Dalin, *The Myth of Hitler's Pope* (New York, 2005), pp. 55–56; Rychlak, *Hitler, the War, and the Pope*, p. 317.

98. Cornwell, *Hitler's Pope*, p. 295.

99. Ronald Rychlak in *Hitler, the War, and the Pope* and Rabbi David Dalin in *The Myth of Hitler's Pope* have been relentless critics of Cornwell's thesis.

100. Eric O. Hansen, *The Catholic Church in World Politics* (Princeton, NJ, 1987), p. 81.

CHAPTER 3: SEEDS OF REVOLT

1. Jack Thomas, "Scandal Darkens a Bright Career," *Boston Globe*, April 14, 2002.

2. John Allen, *Conclave* (New York, 2004), p. 29.

3. Bruce Teague, interview with the author.

4. *Boston Globe* Investigative Staff, *Betrayal: The Crisis of the Catholic Church* (New York, 2002), p. 146.

5. Andrea Estes, "Vatican Reverses Kennedy Ruling," *Boston Globe*, June 21, 2007.

6. Steve Marantz, "Law Raps Ex-priest Coverage," *Boston Globe*, May 24, 1992.

7. Channing Thieme, interview with and e-mails to the author. She has since married and now goes by Channing Penna.

8. Art Austin, e-mail to the author, March 18, 2002.

9. Jason Berry and Gerald Renner, *Vows of Silence: The Abuse of Power in the Priesthood of John Paul II* (New York, 2004), p. 89.

10. Robert Blair Kaiser, *A Church in Search of Itself: Benedict XVI and the Battle for the Future* (New York, 2006), pp. 68–69.

11. Allen, *Conclave*, p. 163.

12. John L. Allen Jr., "Vatican Defends Church's Handling of Sexual Abuse Allegations," *National Catholic Reporter*, March 29, 2002. At the press conference, Cardinal Castrillón cited a figure of 3 percent of priests with "tendencies" toward abuse and only 0.3 percent as actual pedophiles. His data were drawn from a book by Philip Jenkins, *Pedophiles and Priests* (New York, 1996), which in turn had cited a 1992 study of Chicago priests, meaning that the cardinal's figures were a decade old. *A Report on the Crisis in the Catholic Church in the United States*, by Robert S. Bennett et al., prepared by the National Review Board for the Protection of Children and Young People (Washington, DC: United States Conference of Catholic Bishops, 2004), cited data that put the figure at 4 percent of American priests.

13. On Castrillón correspondence, see Jason Berry, "Vatican Cardinal Bucked U.S. Bishop on Abuse," *National Catholic Reporter*, April 22, 2010; Patty Machelor, "Moreno Struggled to Defrock 2 Priests," *Arizona Daily Star*, April 1, 2010. See also Berry and Renner, *Vows of Silence*, 234–35; Michael Rezendes, "Ariz. Abuse Case Names Bishops, 2 Priests," *Boston Globe*, August 20, 2002. Castrillón correspondence is posted on www.natcath.org.

14. Phone interview with Lynne Cadigan, May 13, 2010.

15. Berry and Renner, *Vows of Silence*, pp. 65–66.

16. John Allen, "Catholic Vatican Summit Produces Flawed Document," *National Catholic Reporter*, May 10, 2002.

17. Berry and Renner, *Vows of Silence*, pp. 65–66.

18. Nicholas P. Cafardi, "The Scandal of Secrecy," *Commonweal*, August 13, 2010.

19. Laurie Goodstein and David M. Halbfinger, "Church Office Failed to Act on Abuse Scandal," *New York Times*, July 1, 2010.

20. The papal document was a *motu proprio*, meaning "by his own hand" or "impulse," a distinction signaling direct action by the pope. In this case

the language obscures reality. The available record on Pope John Paul II, including biographies by Jonathan Kwitny and George Weigel; his myopic support of the long-accused Father Marcial Maciel; his passive handling of Cardinal Hans Hermann Groër, who resigned as archbishop of Vienna in 1995 under accusations by former seminarians, suggest the opposite: the pope was locked in denial and viewed predatory priests as a marginal issue. A moral fundamentalist, Ratzinger abhorred the crisis—though he had no idea of its explosive impact to come in Boston—and insisted on taking canonical responsibility for such cases in the Vatican, thereby assisting the pope. In the *New York Times* article cited in note 18, journalists Goodstein and Halbfinger report that Ratzinger had greater authority that he should have used all along. They make a strong case.

21. John Thavis, "CDF Official Details Response to Sex Abuse," Catholic News Service, *National Catholic Reporter*, March 16, 2010. The official, Monsignor Charles Scicluna, said that only about 10 percent involved prepubescent children, while 60 percent involved priests who preyed on adolescent males.

22. John Thavis, "Doctrinal Congregation Takes Control of Priestly Pedophilia Cases," Catholic News Service, December 5, 2001.

23. David Gibson, *The Coming Catholic Church* (San Francisco, 2003), p. 22.

24. David France, *Our Fathers* (New York, 2004), p. 423.

25. Ibid., p. 430.

26. Jack Sullivan and Eric Convey, "Land Rich: Archdiocese Owns Millions in Unused Property," *Boston Herald*, August 27, 2002. The plaintiff attorneys had made Law, not the archdiocese, a defendant. Legally, the cardinal was a corporation sole, which meant he had power over all church assets. Massachusetts law had a $20,000 limit on damages that a charitable organization could pay. But if officers of a group drew salaries, they could be sued personally. Garabedian had therefore sued Law and other hierarchs, though the funds would come from the church and its liability insurers.

27. Michael Paulson, "After Abuse Scandals Many Priests Tread Warily," *Boston Globe*, January 13, 2002.

28. Michael Rezendes and Thomas Farragher, "Archdiocese Mortgages Law's Home to Pay Debt," *Boston Globe*, September 28, 2002.

29. For King quotation, see Stewart Burns, *To the Mountaintop: Martin Luther King Jr.'s Mission to Save America* (San Francisco, 2004), p. 27. Bowers's thoughts are from an unpublished essay used by permission.

30. Michael Paulson, "58 Priests Send a Letter Urging Cardinal to Resign," *Boston Globe*, December 10, 2002.

31. Michael Rezendes and Walter V. Robinson, "Lennon Picks Sites for Sale, Eyes Court Test in Abuse Cases," *Boston Globe*, December 23, 2002.

32. Walter V. Robinson and Matt Carroll, "Lennon Is Viewed as Skilled Manager," *Boston Globe*, December 14, 2002.

33. Kevin Cullen, "Legends on the Waterfront," *Boston Globe*, July 25, 2004. Billy Bolger was the pol; Kevin White the mayor.

34. Brian Wallace, telephone interview with and e-mail to the author, August 24, 2009; Megan Tench, "4 Accuse Bishop of Breaking Promise," *Boston Globe*, June 28, 2003.

35. Megan Tench and Anand Vaishnav, "Catholic School in South Boston to Close," *Boston Globe*, June 11, 2003.

36. V. Val Mulcahy, "The Case for a Single Parish" (unpublished), March 12, 2004, p. 3.

37. Ibid.

38. Michael Paulson, "65 Parishes to Be Closed," *Boston Globe*, May 26, 2004.

39. Michael Paulson, "Pope Names Law to Ceremonial Position in Rome," *Boston Globe*, May 28, 2004.

40. "Pastors Meet with O'Malley About Church Closings," WCVB Boston, www.thebostonchannel.com, May 27, 2004.

41. Michael Paulson, "Church Offers Guidance on Closings," *Boston Globe*, May 28, 2004.

CHAPTER 4: THE VATICAN, THE VIGILS, AND THE REAL ESTATE

1. See www.bishopaccountability.org/diocese for coverage of the Fall River, MA, scandal. See also Sean Gonsalves, "Diocese Details Abuse," *Cape Cod Times*, February 21, 2004.

2. Doyle collaborated with attorney F. Ray Mouton and the late Reverend Michael Peterson, a psychiatrist and founder of St. Luke Institute, on a ninety-three-page report in 1985 on the pedophilia crisis that Peterson sent to the bishops. See Jason Berry, *Lead Us Not into Temptation* (New York, 1992), pp. 98–103.

3. Betty Clermont, *The Neo-Catholics: Implementing Christian Nationalism in America* (Atlanta, 2009), p. 21.

4. Martin Lee, "Their Will Be Done," *Mother Jones*, July/August 1983.

5. Mary McLachlin, "Turbulent Year for Diocese, Church," *Palm Beach Post*, March 9, 2003.

6. Dan Moffett, "Bishop Symons Resigns," *Palm Beach Post*, June 3, 1998. Bishop Robert Lynch of St. Petersburg served as an interim administrator after Symons resigned, before O'Connell arrived. In 2002 the St. Petersburg diocese paid slightly more than $100,000 to the diocesan spokesman, Bill Urbanski, who accused Lynch of making sexual advances toward him. Lynch denied the allegations. For the out-of-court payment, Urbanski agreed not to press a civil lawsuit. The diocese called it a severance payment. See Chuck Murphy and Waveney Ann Moore, "Church Paid $100,000 to Bishop Lynch's Aide," *St. Petersburg Times*, March 23, 2002.

7. Jeff Brumley, "Bishop Apologizes for Abuses," *Press Journal* (Palm Beach, FL), June 14, 2003.

8. Walter V. Robinson and Stephen Kurkjian, "Boston Archdiocese Weighs Bankruptcy Filing," *Boston Globe*, December 1, 2002.

9. The figures cited are drawn from the Boston archdiocese financial statements posted on its website and from coverage in the *Boston Globe*.

10. Nicholas Cafardi, telephone interview with the author, August 24, 2009. See also Nicholas P. Cafardi, "The Availability of Parish Properties for Diocesan Debts," *Seton Hall Legislative Journal* 29, no. 2(2005), pp. 361–73.

11. Elena Curti, "Study in Scarlet," *The Tablet*, May 8, 2010.

12. John L. Allen Jr., "Vatican Disses One of Its Own on Clergy Sex Abuse," *National Catholic Reporter*, April 15, 2010.

13. Victor L. Simpson, "Vatican Reports Deficit for Third Year," Associated Press, July 7, 2004.

14. John L. Allen Jr., *All the Pope's Men: The Inside Story of How the Vatican Really Works* (New York, 2004), p. 30; and John Allen, *Conclave* (New York, 2004), p. 173.

15. Tim Weiner, *Legacy of Ashes* (New York, 2007), p. 309.

16. CIA, *Report of CIA Chilean Task Force Activities, 15 September to 3 November 1970*, Chile and the United States, Declassified Documents relating to the Military Coup, 1970–1976, November 18, 1970, www.gwu.edu.

17. Weiner, *Legacy of Ashes*, p. 315.

18. Cathy Lisa Schneider, *Shantytown Protest in Pinochet's Chile* (Philadelphia, 1995), p. 101.

19. Pamela Constable and Arturo Valenzuela, *A Nation of Enemies: Chile Under Pinochet* (New York, 1991), p. 241. Hugh O'Shaughnessy, "The Cardinal Who Stood Up to Pinochet," *The Tablet*, February 27, 1999.

20. Penny Lernoux, *People of God* (New York, 1989), p. 149.

21. John L. Allen Jr., *Cardinal Ratzinger: The Vatican Enforcer of the Faith* (New York, 2000). See chap. 4.

22. David Gibson, *The Rule of Benedict: Pope Benedict XVI and His Battle with the Modern World* (San Francisco, 2006), p. 195.

23. Paul Collins, *The Modern Inquisition: Seven Prominent Catholics and Their Struggles with the Vatican* (New York, 2002), p. 27.

24. John L. Allen Jr., "These Paths Lead to Rome," *National Catholic Reporter*, June 2, 2000.

25. www.remember-chile.org.uk/declarations/romero.htm. The website was established in 1998 when Pinochet, while in England, was placed under house arrest in response to a warrant from a Spanish judge for him to stand trial for human rights crimes. Cardinal Sodano was widely criticized for his appeal to the British government to release Pinochet; he was acting on a request from Chile's democratically elected government, which wanted its courts to be the venue for any legal recourse against Pinochet, who had negotiated a senator-for-life status and immunity from prosecution during Chile's transition to democracy.

26. George Weigel, *Witness to Hope: The Biography of Pope John Paul II* (New York, 1999), p. 531.

27. Jonathan Kwitny, *Man of the Century: The Life and Times of Pope John Paul II* (New York: 1997), p. 563.

28. Carl Bernstein and Marco Politi, *His Holiness: John Paul II and the Hidden History of Our Time* (New York, 1996), p. 465.

29. Kwitny, *Man of the Century*, p. 564.

30. Clermont, *The Neo-Catholics*, p. 77.

31. Achille Silvestrini, "Introduction," p. xx, in Agostino Casaroli, *The Martyrdom of Patience: The Holy See and the Communist Countries (1963–89)*, trans. Fr. Marco Bagnarol IMC (Toronto, 2007); Jason Berry, "Change Challenges the Church," *Chicago Tribune Perspective*, April 10, 2005.

32. Agostino Bono, "Cardinal-designate Sodano Has 3 Decades of Diplomatic Experience," Catholic News Service, January 1991.

33. Giovanni Avena, interview with the author, Rome, July 15, 2009.

34. Father Kenneth J. Doyle, "Vatican to Pay $250 Million in Ambrosiano Case, Says Cardinal Krol," Catholic News Service, March 5, 1984; Sandro Magister, "The Pope's Banker Speaks: 'Here's How I Saved the IOR,' " *L'Espresso*, June 18, 2004, www.chiesa.espressonline.it.

35. Kwitny, *Man of the Century*, p. 654.

36. Weigel, *Witness to Hope*, p. 749.

37. Magister, "The Pope's Banker Speaks." Sodano's quote is from Alan Cowell, "Challenge to the Faithful," *New York Times Magazine*, December 27, 1992.

38. Copies of the document in Latin and translation provided by Peter Borré.

39. Michael Paulson, "Church Offers Guidance on Closings," *Boston Globe*, May 28, 2004.

40. Stephen Kurkjian, "Parishes' Proceeds to Benefit Diocese," *Boston Globe*, February 2, 2004.

41. Rev. Stephen S. Josoma and Rev. John A. Dooher, pastors, Letter on Reconfiguration Process from Saint Mary Parish and Saint Susanna Parish to Monsignor Cornelius V. McRae, VF, March 8, 2004.

42. Rev. Bill Williams, pastor, Letters to St. Mary's Parish Members, April 17, 2007, and November 18, 2007.

43. Marco R. della Cava, "Santa Fe Archdiocese Learned Lessons That Could Help Others," *USA Today*, March 26, 2002; Demetria Martinez, "Diocese Sells Retreat in Sex Abuse Bailout," *National Catholic Reporter*, September 30, 1994.

44. Deposition of Archbishop Michael J. Sheehan, 134th Judicial District Court, Dallas County, Texas, case no. 93-05258-G, *John Doe I et al. v. Reverend Rudolph Kos et al.*, April 14, 1994, p. 63.

45. Brooks Egerton of the *Dallas Morning News* chronicled the Kos saga, followed by an extensive series in 2002 on international dimensions of the

clergy abuse crisis. See also Jason Berry and Gerald Renner, *Vows of Silence: The Abuse of Power in the Papacy of John Paul II* (New York, 2004), pp. 235–41.

46. Joe Feuerherd, "Diocesan Bankruptcies Raise Church Ownership Issues," *National Catholic Reporter,* September 9, 2005.

47. Samuel J. Gerdano, "Diocesan Bankruptcies: A Feast for Lawyers," *The Edge,* December 12, 2004, www.catholicexchange.com.

48. Affidavit of Nicholas P. Cafardi, U.S. Bankruptcy Court, Eastern District of Washington, case no. 04-08822, *The Catholic Bishop of Spokane Debtor, Committee of Tort Litigants v. The Catholic Bishop of Spokane, et al.,* May 27, 2005, p. 16.

49. "Bankruptcy: The Gamble That Backfired," *National Catholic Reporter,* September 9, 2005.

50. Christine Tolfree, "VOTF Mass in Response to Church Closings," *The Pilot* (Boston archdiocesan newspaper), August 23, 2004.

51. State Representative James M. Murphy, "An Argument Against Closing a Church in Weymouth," letters, *Boston Globe,* May 13, 2004.

52. Denise Leavoie, "Parishioners Refuse to Leave Church Scheduled to Close," Associated Press, August 31, 2004.

53. Bella English, "Weymouth Parishioners Stage Sit-in to Protest Closing," *Boston Globe,* August 31, 2004.

54. Mary Williams Walsh, "Parishioners in Boston Plan Suit over Priests' Pensions," *New York Times,* May 21, 2005.

55. Michael Paulson, "O'Malley Seeks Review of Closings," *Boston Globe,* October 8, 2004.

56. Kate Zezima, "Parish Closings Inspire Prayer Vigils and Sit-ins," *New York Times,* November 6, 2004.

57. Statement of Archbishop Seán O'Malley regarding Reconfiguration, BostonCatholic.org, November 13, 2004.

58. Jonathan Finer, "Boston Torn by Parish Closings," *Washington Post,* November 17, 2004.

CHAPTER 5: ITALIAN INTERVENTIONS

1. "Top Cardinal Says Media Overplay Sex Scandal," *New York Times,* October 11, 2003.

2. John L. Allen Jr., *All the Pope's Men: The Inside Story of How the Vatican Really Works* (New York, 2004), p. 327.

3. Alex Kingsbury, "A Rift over Iraq Between President and Pope," *U.S. News & World Report,* April 16, 2008.

4. John L. Allen Jr., "Vatican Asks Condoleezza Rice to Help Stop a Sex Abuse Lawsuit," *National Catholic Reporter,* March 3, 2005.

5. Source for "Court of Cassation," from Pasquale Follieri's biography on the company website, is U.S. Attorney's Office, Manhattan. On Pasquale's

legal problems, see John R. Emshwiller, "Joint Venture to Purchase Catholic Properties Sours," *Wall Street Journal*, June 15, 2007.

6. Government Sentencing Memorandum, Deposition of FBI Agent Theodore Cacioppi, Southern District of New York, case no. 08 CR00850-001 (JKG), *United States v. Raffaello Follieri*, June 23, 2008. "FOLLIERI donated hundreds of thousands of dollars of money of the Principal Investor to the Vatican without disclosing those donations . . . [and] concealed that these payments were donations by falsely representing to the Principal Investor that the money was being used for 'engineering reports,' " p. 8. The payment to Monsignor Giovanni Carrù is referenced in the letter from Castrillón to Follieri.

7. Michael Shnayerson, "The Follieri Charade," *Vanity Fair*, October 2008.

8. Joe Feuerherd, "Catholic Real Estate Bonanza," *National Catholic Reporter*, March 3, 2006.

9. Joe Feuerherd, telephone interview with the author, December 7, 2009.

10. Feuerherd, "Catholic Real Estate Bonanza."

11. Ibid.

12. Melanie Bonvicino, interviews with the author, January 2010.

13. Shnayerson, "The Follieri Charade." On the car and driver, see the Bonvicino interviews.

14. The letter, in Italian with English translation, became an exhibit in the federal prosecution in the case file, *United States v. Raffaello Follieri*.

15. Shnayerson, "The Follieri Charade," citing Hathaway interview with *Harper's Bazaar*.

16. John R. Emshwiller and Gabriel Kahn, "Presidential Connection: How Bill Clinton's Aide Facilitated a Messy Deal," *Wall Street Journal*, September 26, 2007.

17. Feuerherd, "Catholic Real Estate Bonanza."

18. Various authors, "Blinded by Love," *People*, July 14, 2008.

19. Invoices are exhibits in Government's Sentencing Memorandum, *United States v. Raffaello Follieri*.

20. Information memo of fourteen counts, for plea agreement, accompanying letter of September 8, 2008, from Assistant U.S. Attorney Reed M. Brodsky and Raymond J. Lohier to Flora Edwards, Esq., attorney for the defendant, *United States v. Raffaello Follieri*.

21. Sodano's letter is included in exhibit list with the Government Sentencing Memorandum.

22. Government Sentencing Memorandum, *United States v. Raffaello Follieri*, p. 19.

23. Government Sentencing Memorandum, Deposition of FBI Agent Theodore Cacioppi, *United States v. Raffaello Follieri*. See also Emshwiller and Kahn, "Presidential Connection."

24. " 'Great Discoveries' Awaiting in the Catacombs," Zenit News Service, July 20, 2009. Carrù's official title is Secretary of the Pontifical Commission

for Sacred Archaeology. Archbishop Gianfranco Ravasi—president of the Pontifical Council for Culture—is the official quoted.

CHAPTER 6: THE CASE OF THE MISSING MILLIONS

1. Carolyn Y. Johnson, "A Vigil of Faith, Hope Endures," *Boston Globe*, October 23, 2005.
2. Jillian Fennimore, "New Hope for Parishioners; Ruling Expected," *Scituate Mariner*, September 22, 2005.
3. Suzanne Hurley, interview with the author, December 2008.
4. Mary Williams Walsh, "Boston's Catholic Archdiocese May Cut Priests' Pensions," *New York Times*, May 12, 2005.
5. Michael Levenson, "Parishioners Seek Probe of Priests' Pension Fund," *Boston Globe*, May 22, 2005.
6. Antonio M. Enrique, "Chancellor Clarifies Use of Clergy Collections," *The Pilot* (Boston archdiocesan newspaper), June 10, 2005. The article calls the Benefit a "Fund" instead of a trust.
7. Deposition of David W. Smith, Superior Court, C.A. no. 99-0371, *Leary v. Geoghan et al.*, *Commonwealth of Massachusetts*, vol. 2, June 26, 2002.
8. Maureen Orth, "Unholy Communion," *Vanity Fair*, August 2002.
9. Boston Archdiocesan Documents Showing the Involvement of Bishop Richard G. Lennon in Abuse Cases, www.bishopaccountability.org.
10. Robin Washington and Tom Mashberg, "Lennon Tied to Priest Probe; Foster Case Memo Shows Bishop Was at Meeting," *Boston Herald*, December 26, 2002.
11. Michael Rezendes and Stephen Kurkjian, with Sacha Pfeiffer, "Lennon Gave Advice on Reassigned Priest," *Boston Globe*, February 5, 2003.
12. Boston Archdiocesan Documents Showing the Involvement of Bishop Richard G. Lennon, www.bishopaccountability.org.
13. Richard G. Lennon, Letter to Clergy Fund Members, December 8, 2003.
14. For a detailed account of Teague, see Bill Zajac, "He Remembers, He Tries to Forgive," *Springfield Sunday Republican* (Springfield, MA), September 14, 2003.
15. Sam Hemenway, "Diocese Settles Priest Abuse Case for $965,000," *Burlington Free Press*, April 20, 2006.
16. Kevin Cullen, "Priest Cites Cost for Speaking Out," *Boston Globe*, March 23, 2002; editorial, "Church History Missing in Burlington Verdict," *The Observer* (Springfield, MA), May 27, 2008.
17. Stephanie Barr, "Accused Clergy Had Influential Posts," *Springfield Republican* (Springfield, MA), March 1, 2004. See also the link to "Diocese of Springfield, MA" on www.bishopaccountability.org.
18. Michael Paulson, "Resistance Widens to Parish Closings," *Boston Globe*, May 8, 2005.

19. Michael Paulson, "Vatican Stops Diocese in Taking Parish Assets," *Boston Globe*, August 11, 2005.

20. The Parish Reconfiguration Fund Oversight Committee's Final Report, David Castaldi, chair, Roman Catholic Archdiocese of Boston, November 2007.

21. Michael Paulson, "Church Tackles $46M Gap," *Boston Globe*, April 20, 2006.

22. Laura Crimaldi, "Photographer Snaps $1.8M off Eastie Church Deal," *Boston Herald*, January 5, 2007; Laura Crimaldi, "Church Panel to Review Dubious Sale," *Boston Herald*, January 10, 2007.

23. Crimaldi, "Photographer Snaps $1.8M off Eastie Church Deal."

24. The Honorable Kevin M. Herlihy (Ret.), *Sale of Saint Mary Star of the Sea Parish, East Boston: Findings, Conclusions and Recommendations*, Roman Catholic Archdiocese of Boston, October 2007.

CHAPTER 7: FATHER MACIEL, LORD OF PROSPERITY

1. The Márquez quote is from John Allen, *Conclave* (New York, 2004), p. 190. Leonardo Boff, *Church Charism and Power: Liberation Theology and the Institutional Church* (New York, 1986), p. 9.

2. Boff, *Church Charism and Power*, p. 38.

3. Joseph Cardinal Ratzinger, Prefect, Congregation for the Doctrine of the Faith, *Instruction on Certain Aspects of the "Theology of Liberation,"* www.vatican.va, August 6, 1984.

4. Harvey Cox, *The Silencing of Leonardo Boff: The Vatican and the Future of World Christianity* (Oak Park, IL, 1988), p. 11.

5. John L. Allen Jr., *Cardinal Ratzinger: The Vatican Enforcer of the Faith* (New York, 2000), p. 160.

6. Maciel's ordination footage appeared in Legion of Christ promotional videos that are no longer used for the order's marketing. The footage is included in the documentary film *Vows of Silence* (2008), produced by Jason Berry. The film is based on the book written by Berry and Gerald Renner. See www.vowsofsilencefilm.com.

7. Alfonso Torres Robles, *La prodigiosa aventura de los Legionarios de Cristo* (Madrid, 2001), p. 18.

8. This priest and three others as background sources in the chapter were first quoted in my articles "Vatican Investigates Legion of Christ," Global Post.com, July 21, 2009, and "How Fr. Maciel Built His Empire," *National Catholic Reporter*, April 6, 2010.

9. Angeles Conde and David J. P. Murray, *The Legion of Christ: A History* (North Haven, CT, 2004), p. 121.

10. Peter Hebblethwaite, *Paul VI: The First Modern Pope* (New York/Mahwah, NJ, 1993), p. 147.

11. For an intelligent overview of the prosperity gospel associated with certain

Pentecostal groups in America, see Hanna Rosin, "Did Christianity Cause
the Crash?" *The Atlantic,* December 2009. The religious anthropologist
Elio Masferrer Kan uses the term in an explicit linkage with the Catholic Church in his treatment of Pope John Paul II's 1999 trip to Mexico
and the media furor that engulfed Mexico City's Cardinal Norberto Ri-
vera Carrera over commercial sales of papal insignias and the like by street
vendors. See *Es del César o es de Dios? Un modelo antropológico del camp
religioso* (Centro de Investigaciones Interdisciplinarias en Ciencias y Hu-
manidades, UNAM de la UNAM Ciudad Universitaria, 04510, México
D.F., 2007), p. 242.

12. The most extensive account of Maciel's fund-raising and the order's early
years is Torres Robles, *La prodigiosa aventura de los Legionarios de Cristo.*

13. The constitution of the Legion of Christ circulated in Spanish within the
order and Regnum Christi, the predominantly lay affiliate, for many years.
It apparently underwent considerable revision under Maciel. The order reportedly made its first English translation in 1990, though former Legionaries oversaw another translation, which I have quoted here. In 2007 the
Legion sued an organization of ex-members, ReGAIN—www.regainnet
work.org—in Alexandria, Virginia, alleging that it had no right to post the
constitutions; see Daniela Deane, "Outspoken Ex-Priest Sued Over Documents," *Washington Post,* September 6, 2007. The case settled out of court
after ReGAIN withdrew the document from the website and halted its discussion board. The constitutions continue to circulate. See, for example,
www.unitypublishing.com/NewReligiousMovements/Leagonaires2.html or
www.unitypublishing.com/NewReligiousMovements/Constitution%20--
%20LegionariesofChrist.htm.

14. *Envoy.* As with much of Regnum Christi materials, dating this work is
a bit of a riddle. The 230-page softcover lists no publisher or ISBN; the
preface on p. 7 lists no author but concludes "LC Rome, June 6, 1986,
Solemnity of the Sacred Heart of Jesus." Maciel routinely dictated letters
and a sort of oral history of his life and the Legion to selected Legionaries,
as recounted in Jason Berry and Gerald Renner, *Vows of Silence: The Abuse
of Power in the Papacy of John Paul II* (New York, 2004), chaps. 8 and 13,
and the citation that follows. On the founding of Regnum Christi, see Jack
Keogh, *Driving Straight on Crooked Lines: How an Irishman Found His Heart
and Nearly Lost His Mind* (IveaghodgePress.com, 2010), p. 236.

15. The Pontifical Athenaeum Regina Apostolorum has a complicated no-
menclature and history. It is a university, just barely, which awards
pontifical—meaning papally sanctioned—degrees. Regina Apostolorum has
a master's program, with a licentiate and a doctorate in philosophy and theology. It also has a department of bioethics. According to a scholar at another
pontifical university in Rome, the RA has only a few terminal degrees that
would be accepted in American universities. As an athenaeum it is one step
above an institute of higher learning, one below a full-fledged university.

16. Ed Housewright and Brooks Egerton, "Kos Jury Awards $119 Million,"
    Dallas Morning News, July 25, 1997. On the settlement particulars, see
    the 1998 Statement of Windle Turley, Attorney, & The Plaintiffs, at www
    .bishopaccountability.org. Bishop Charles Grahmann issued an apology by
    the Dallas diocese to Kos's victims and agreed to a sex abuse risk audit. In
    1999 the Vatican sent a coadjutor bishop, Joseph Galante, to take Grah-
    mann's place. But Grahmann refused to leave. A November 16, 2002, *Dal-
    las Morning News* editorial called for Grahmann's departure:

    > His misjudgments have cost the diocese millions of dollars in payments
    > to abuse victims and in legal fees, and they threaten to cost it still more. It
    > has become apparent that many Catholics feel alienated from the church
    > and are reacting by withholding financial contributions to it . . . Bishop
    > Grahmann's most recent misstep is his handling of an incident involving
    > the rector of the cathedral, about which the *Dallas Morning News* reported
    > on Monday. A 58-year-old man alleges that the rector sexually abused him
    > 11 years ago. Bishop Grahmann allowed the rector to continue in minis-
    > try even though the rector acknowledged "inappropriate contact" with
    > the man and resumed psychological counseling about "boundary issues,"
    > according to a diocesan spokesman. He allowed him to continue even
    > though a policy that he installed to prevent and to manage such scandals,
    > and that he touts as a model, declares that sexual misconduct "will not be
    > tolerated under any circumstances" and defines sexual misconduct as "any
    > kind of sexual interaction between a celibate cleric and an adult, whether
    > initiated by one or the other, and whether or not consensual."
    >
    > But that's not all. Bishop Grahmann allowed his representatives to
    > publicly assign to the man impure motives for his accusation, thereby
    > possibly discouraging other possible victims from coming forward. He
    > did not ask lay and personnel review boards to review his handling
    > of the matter. And he did not consult with co-adjutor Bishop Joseph
    > Galante, who has criticized his handling of the matter.

17. McDaid was not alone in his attitude about the sex education films. In
    1988, when I interviewed people at St. Luke Institute, the films had stirred
    a minor controversy; the hospital director refused to let me view the films.
    The late Reverend Michael Peterson, M.D., the hospital founder, was em-
    phatic about their benefits. So were staffers. See Jason Berry, *Lead Us Not
    into Temptation* (New York, 1992), p. 202.
18. Richard Owen, "Archbishop of Vienna Accuses One of Pope's Closest
    Aides of Abuse Cover-up," *Times* (London), May 10, 2010.
19. On the Groër scandal and Vatican response, see Berry and Renner, *Vows of
    Silence*, pp. 227–32.
20. George Weigel, *Witness to Hope: The Biography of Pope John Paul II* (New
    York, 1999), p. 282.

21. Conde and Murray, *The Legion of Christ*, p. 269.

22. Torres Robles, *La prodigiosa aventura de los Legionarios de Cristo*, p. 60.

23. Jose de Cordoba, "With Elite Backing, Catholic Order Has Pull in Mexico," *Wall Street Journal*, January 23, 2006.

24. Brian J. Lowney, "The Mystery in Rhode Island," *Rhode Island Catholic*, July 30, 2009.

25. Objection of Mary Lou Dauray to Motions to Quash, *In Re: Estate of Gabrielle D. Mee*, no. 20090029, Probate Court, the Town of Smithfield, State of Rhode Island, Providence, SC, July 31, 2009.

26. Dave Altimari, "Will Has Heir of Secrecy: Legionaries of Christ," *Hartford Courant*, June 28, 2009.

27. Ibid.

28. *Estate of Gabrielle D. Mee (A/K/A Gabrielle Malvina Mee)*, no. 20090029, Probate Court, the Town of Smithfield, State of Rhode Island, Providence, SC, 2008.

29. John L. Allen Jr., *Opus Dei: An Objective Look Behind the Myths and Reality of the Most Controversial Force in the Catholic Church* (New York, 2007), pp. 6–7.

30. Enrique Krauze, *Mexico: Biography of Power: A History of Modern Mexico, 1810–1996* (New York, 1997), p. 663.

31. Anthony DePalma, "As the Rules Change in Mexico, He's a Quick Study," *New York Times*, December 4, 1994.

32. My first interview with Roberta Garza was in Houston in 2002, on background, with continuing conversations and interviews on research trips to Mexico City over the next eight years. In 2010 she agreed to speak on the record. See also Jason Berry, "How Fr. Maciel Built His Empire, Part 2," *National Catholic Reporter*, April 12, 2010.

33. Jose de Cordoba, "With Elite Backing, a Catholic Order Has Pull in Mexico."

34. "Fr. Luis Garza, LC, on the Choice for a Friendship," International Resources Testimonies—Legionaries, part 17 in a series on life as a priest, no byline given, January 21, 2010, www.regnumchristi.org.

35. Fernando M. González, *La iglesia del silencio: De mártires y pederastas* (Mexico City, 2009), p. 279. See also Alma Guillermoprieto, "The Mission of Father Maciel," *New York Review of Books*, June 24, 2010.

36. For background on Cotija and Maciel's childhood, see Conde and Murray, *The Legion of Christ: A History*, pp. 14–15. The book is hardly authentic history; however, it reflects how the Legion presented itself as late as 2004. Juan Vaca, who filed the earliest allegations of abuse against Maciel, said that Maciel's father viewed him as "a sissy boy." Berry and Renner, *Vows of Silence*, profiles his victims. For a detailed biography, see Fernando M. González, *Marcial Maciel: Los Legionarios de Cristo: testimonios y documentos inéditos* (Mexico City, 2006).

37. Julia Preston and Samuel Dillon, *Opening Mexico: The Making of a Democracy* (New York, 2004), p. 45.

38. Carlos Fuentes, *The Buried Mirror: Reflections on Spain and the New World* (New York, 1992), p. 286.

39. Preston and Dillon, *Opening Mexico*, p. 47.

40. Pete Hamill, "The Casosola Archive," in *Mexico: The Revolution and Beyond; Photographs by Agustín Victor Casasola 1900–1940*, ed. Pablo Ortiz Monasterio (New York, 2003), p. 18.

41. Berry and Renner, *Vows of Silence*, p. 148.

42. Michael J. Gonzalez, *The Mexican Revolution: 1910–1940* (Albuquerque, NM, 2002), p. 211. Discussion on bishops in San Antonio is from Dr. Matthew Butler, University of Texas, Austin, telephone interview with the author, February 3, 2010.

43. Jean Meyer, *The Cristero Rebellion: The Mexican People Between Church and State, 1926–1929* (Cambridge, UK, 1976), p. 114.

44. Ibid.

45. González, *La iglesia del silencio*, pp. 53–55.

46. Carlos Monsiváis, *Mexican Postcards* (New York, 2000), p. 132.

47. Graham Greene, *Another Mexico* (New York, 1967), p. 105.

48. Berry and Renner, *Vows of Silence*, p. 158.

49. Barba teaches at Instituto Tecnológico Autónomo de México in Mexico City.

50. Torres Robles, *La prodigiosa aventura de los Legionarios de Cristo*, p. 20; González, *Marcial Maciel*, p. 126.

51. *Vows of Silence* (2008), produced by Jason Berry. See www.vowsofsilence film.com.

52. Gerald Renner and Jason Berry, "Head of Worldwide Catholic Order Accused of History of Abuse," *Hartford Courant*, February 23, 1997.

53. Torres, Robles, *La prodigiosa aventura de los Legionarios de Cristo*, pp. 27–28.

54. Berry and Renner, *Vows of Silence*, p. 1.

55. Renner and Berry, "Head of Worldwide Catholic Order Accused of History of Abuse."

56. Jason Berry, "Vatican Investigates Legionaries of Christ," GlobalPost.com, posted July 19, 2009.

57. Editorial, "Can Synod Survive Vatican Manipulation?" *National Catholic Reporter*, November 7, 1997.

58. On Neuhaus's career, see Damon Linker, *Theocons* (New York, 2006).

59. Richard John Neuhaus, *Appointment in Rome: The Church in America Awakening* (New York, 1999), pp. 2, 39.

60. Ibid., p. 110.

61. Berry and Renner, *Vows of Silence*, p. 214.

62. Jonathan Kwitny, *Man of the Century: The Life and Times of Pope John Paul II* (New York, 1997), p. 452.

63. Former Legionary Jack Keogh, who toured the chapel with his mother, describes the frescoes in *Driving Straight on Crooked Lines*, p. 269.

64. Cardinal Stanisław Dziwisz, in Conversation with Gian Franco Sviderco-schi, *A Life with Karol: My Forty-Year Friendship with the Man Who Became Pope* (New York, 2008), p. 85.

65. Jason Berry, "Money Paved the Way for Maciel's Influence in the Vatican," *National Catholic Reporter*, April 6, 2010.

66. Ibid.

67. Andrea Insunza and Javier Ortega, *Legionarios de Cristo en Chile: Dios, dinero y poder* (Santiago, Chile, 2008), p. 39.

68. Ibid., p. 41.

69. Mario Guarino, *I mercanti del Vaticano* (Milan, 2008), p. 253. Alessandro Sodano has since died.

70. Laurie Goodstein, "Vatican Declined to Defrock U.S. Priest Who Abused Boys," *New York Times*, March 24, 2010; "The Failed Papacy of Benedict XVI," *Spiegel Online International*, April 6, 2010; Paddy Agnew, "Vatican Hits Back Again at Criticism over Child Sex Abuse," *Irish Times*, April 8, 2010.

71. Berry and Renner, *Vows of Silence*, p. 218.

72. Berry, "Money Paved the Way for Maciel's Influence in the Vatican."

73. José Martínez de Velasco, *Los documentos secretos de los Legionarios de Cristo* (Barcelona, 2004), pp. 65–66.

74. Ibid., On Ruiz, see Krauze, *Mexico: Biography of Power*, pp. 784–85.

75. A report citing many of the files can be accessed on www.regainnetwork .org.

76. Jason Berry and Gerald Renner, "Sex-Related Case Blocked in Vatican," *National Catholic Reporter*, December 7, 2001.

77. Richard John Neuhaus, "Feathers of a Scandal," *First Things*, March 2002.

78. Brian Ross, ABC News, *World News Tonight*, April 26, 2002.

79. Jason Berry, "Cracks in the Wall of the Curia," Examining the Crisis, *National Catholic Reporter*, May 20, 2004.

80. John L. Allen Jr., "The Word from Rome," *National Catholic Reporter*, December 3, 2004.

81. Gerald Renner, "Vatican Revisits Abuse Charges," *Hartford Courant*, January 3, 2005.

82. "Cardinal Ratzinger's Meditations for Way of the Cross," Zenit.org, March 24, 2005; Robert Blair Kaiser, *A Church in Search of Itself: Benedict XVI and the Battle for the Future* (New York, 2006), p. 206.

83. John L. Allen Jr., "New Legionaries Intrigue: Statement on Maciel Not Issued by Agency Responsible for Sex Abuse Cases," *National Catholic Reporter*, May 25, 2005.

84. Andy Wooden, "Vatican Says Legionaries' Founder Cannot Exercise Ministry Publicly," *Catholic News Service*, May 19, 2006.

85. Daniela Deane, "Outspoken Ex-Priest Sued Over Documents"; *The Legion of Christ, Inc. v. Regain, Inc. and John Paul Lennon,* Circuit Court, City of Alexandria, VA, CL 07002920.

86. Idoia Sota and José M. Vidal, "El legionario que murió cuatro veces y no quiso confesarse," *El Mundo,* January 31, 2010. Although the article mixes opinion and some ornate prose, the Legion has not disputed the essence of the reporting.

CHAPTER 8: BORRÉ IN ROME

1. Darío Cardinal Castrillón Hoyos, Letter from Congregation of [sic] the Clergy: U.S. Bishops Wrongly Invoke Canon 123, Save Our Parish Community project, www.futurechurch.org, March 2006.

2. Eileen Markey, "Attempt to Destroy a Faith Community," *National Catholic Reporter,* February 28, 2007.

3. Elizabeth Hamilton and Eric Rich, "Egan Protected Abusive Priests," *Hartford Courant,* March 17, 2002.

4. David Gibson, "The Cardinal's Sins," *New York,* January 28, 2007.

5. Michael Powell, "At 75, a Battle-Tested but Unwavering Cardinal," *New York Times,* April 23, 2007.

6. Grant Gallicho, "Cardinal Egan Paints Himself an Unhappy Ending," *New York Observer,* June 26, 2007.

7. Monsignor Brian Ferme, dean of the canon law faculty at Pontifical Lateran University, Rome, interview with the author, November 27, 2002. See also Jason Berry and Gerald Renner, *Vows of Silence: The Abuse of Power in the Papacy of John Paul II* (New York, 2004), p. 102.

CHAPTER 9: SECRECY AND LAMENTATIONS

1. Jerry Pockar, "Clergy Crisis Forecast," *Catholic Universe Bulletin* (Diocese of Cleveland), November 8, 1991. See also a longer report by Sister Maureen Haggarty, CSJ, "Priesthood in Peril," June 22, 1990.

2. www.futurechurch.org.

3. W. A. Jurgens, *A History of the Diocese of Cleveland,* vol. 1, *The Prehistory of the Diocese to Its Establishment in 1847* (Cleveland, 1980), pp. 203, 565.

4. Ibid., p. 581.

5. Carol Poh Miller and Robert A. Wheeler, *Cleveland: A Concise History, 1796–1996* (Bloomington, IN, 1997), pp. 81–82.

6. Edward M. Miggins and Mary Morgenthaler, "The Ethnic Mosaic," in *The Birth of Modern Cleveland, 1865–1930,* ed. Thomas F. Campbell and Edward M. Miggins (Cleveland, 1988), p. 127.

7. Miller and Wheeler, *Cleveland: A Concise History,* p. 85.

8. Michael J. McTighe, "Babel and Babylon on the Cuyahoga," in *The Birth of Modern Cleveland,* p. 248.

9. Merit Brief, Court of Appeals, Third Appellate District, Seneca County, Ohio, case no. 13-08-19, *Kansas St. James Parish of Ohio, Inc., Jim and Virginia Hull v. The Catholic Diocese of Toledo in America, Bishop Leonard P. Blair,* July 14, 2008. See also *Mannix, Assignee v. Purcell, et al., 46 Ohio St.* 102 (1988).

10. Mary J. Oates, *The Catholic Philanthropic Tradition in America* (Bloomington, IN, 1995), p. 100.

11. Diocese of Cleveland, Department of Communication, *The Catholic Diocese of Cleveland Factsheet.* The one-page document cites 2002 U.S. Census estimates. See also Thomas Kelly, "Who Owns Cleveland," *Cleveland Free Times,* March 10, 2004.

12. Bishop Anthony M. Pilla, "The Moral Implications of Regional Sprawl: The Cleveland Catholic Diocese's Church in the City Vision Process," a speech given at the City Club of Cleveland, June 17, 1996, www.citc.org.

13. Diego Ribadeneira, "Bishop Discusses Woes in Church," *Boston Globe,* November 12, 1996.

14. Christine Schenk, CSJ, "Faith in the Wasteland," unpublished autobiographical essay.

15. John and Mary Evelyn Grim, "Teilhard de Chardin: A Short Biography," American Teilhard Association, www.teilharddechardin.org.

16. Pierre Teilhard de Chardin, *The Divine Milieu* (New York, 1968), p. 148.

17. Gustavo Gutiérrez, *A Theology of Liberation* (Maryknoll, NY, 1973), p. 205.

18. Schenk, "Faith in the Wasteland."

19. Tim Weiner, *Legacy of Ashes* (New York, 2007), p. 180.

20. Thomas Vail, William J. Woestendiek, and Thomas H. Greer, "The Parish Must Be Told the Truth, Bishop Pilla," *Cleveland Plain Dealer,* March 15, 1987.

21. Jason Berry, *Lead Us Not into Temptation* (New York, 1992), p. 231.

22. Vail, Woestendiek, and Greer, "The Parish Must Be Told the Truth."

23. Ibid.

24. James F. McCarty, "The Churchman at Scandal's Heart," *Cleveland Plain Dealer,* July 21, 2002.

25. Berry, *Lead Us Not into Temptation,* p. 287.

26. The entire text by the Reverend Thomas P. Doyle, F. Ray Mouton, and Dr. Michael Peterson, *The Problem of Sexual Molestation by Roman Catholic Clergy: Meeting the Problem in a Comprehensive and Responsible Manner* (May 15, 1985), is reprinted as chapter 4 in Thomas P. Doyle, A. W. R. Sipe, and Patrick J. Wall, *Sex, Priests, and Secret Codes: The Catholic Church's 2,000-Year Paper Trail of Sexual Abuse* (Los Angeles, 2006). In the original text, Mouton reported that one diocese (Lafayette, Louisiana) had seen $5 million in settlements and faced $100 million in claims; though he did not delineate how much of the settlements had been covered by insurance policies, the document addressed insurance issues. The manual guided its original readership of bishops through a series of questions about complex issues in the civil and criminal proceedings (pp. 112–13).

27. Berry, *Lead Us Not into Temptation*, pp. 236–37.

28. John Tidyman, "God-1, Newspaper Guild-0," *Cleveland Edition*, May 26, 1988.

29. Jason Berry, "Immunity: A Haven for Sensitive Files, Too?" *Cleveland Plain Dealer*, June 17, 1990. See also Berry, *Lead Us Not into Temptation*, p. 290.

30. On Quinn, see James F. McCarty, "The Churchman at Scandal's Heart," *Cleveland Plain Dealer*, July 21, 2002. On Berthiaume, see James F. McCarty and David Briggs, "Diocese Confronted Clergy Abuse in 1987," *Cleveland Plain Dealer*, March 10, 2002; Bishop Joseph Imesch, correspondence with the author.

31. Elizabeth Auster, "Rape Victims, Loved Ones Don't Get Released Early," *Cleveland Plain Dealer*, May 23, 1996. The television interview was a CBS report in which Ed Bradley was the correspondent. See David Kohn, *60 Minutes*, "The Church on Trial, Part II," July 12, 2002.

32. CARA (Center for Applied Research in the Apostolate, Georgetown University), "Understanding the Ministry and Experience: Parish Life Coordinators in the United States," Special Report, Summer 2005.

33. Joseph Cardinal Ratzinger, "Letter to the Bishops of the Catholic Church on the Pastoral Care of Homosexual Persons," Congregation for the Doctrine of the Faith, October 1, 1986, www.vatican.va. For a trenchant account on the impact of a gay culture in religious life, see Michael S. Rose, *Goodbye! Good Men: How Catholic Seminaries Turned Away Two Generations of Vocations from the Priesthood* (Cincinnati, 2002). As an alternative, see Mark D. Jordan, *The Silence of Sodom: Homosexuality in Modern Catholicism* (Chicago, 2000).

34. Elisabeth Schüssler Fiorenza, *In Memory of Her: A Feminist Theological Reconstruction of Christian Origins* (New York, 1984), pp. 170–71. For this note and the one that follows I have drawn upon Sister Christine Schenk's thesis synopsis and bibliographical list. The citations are of my own choosing.

35. Karen Jo Torjesen, *When Women Were Priests* (San Francisco, 1993), pp. 32–33.

36. John Paul II, *Ordinatio Sacerdotalis*, Apostolic Letter to the Bishops of the Catholic Church on Reserving Priestly Ordination to Men Alone, May 22, 1994, www.vatican.va.

37. Doyle, Sipe, and Wall, *Sex, Priests, and Secret Codes*, p. 11.

38. Data from the Austrian church are from the office in Vienna of Cardinal Cristoph Schönborn, courtesy of *The Tablet* correspondent Christa Pongratz-Lippitt, in correspondence with the author.

39. "Responsum ad Dubium," Congregation for the Doctrine of the Faith, October 28, 1995, publicly released November 18, 1995, www.vatican.va.

40. Nicholas Lash, "On Not Inventing Doctrine," *The Tablet*, December 2, 1995.

41. Joan Chittister, "Can't Suppress Spirit," *National Catholic Reporter*, December 8, 1995.

42. David Gibson, *The Rule of Benedict: Pope Benedict XVI and His Battle with the Modern World* (San Francisco, 2006), p. 214.

43. Jerry Filteau, "Bishop Calls Bishop-People Dialogue Key to Church's Future," Catholic News Service, October 31, 1995.

44. David Eden, "The Bishop's Lawyer: A Question of Faith," *Cleveland Free Times*, December 24, 2003.

45. McCarty and Briggs, "Diocese Confronted Clergy Abuse."

46. WJW TV, 10 p.m. news, interview with the Kodger family, May 17, 2002.

47. Testimony of Stephen Sozio, U.S. District Court, Northern District of Ohio, Eastern Division, case no. 1:06-CR-00394, *U.S. v. Joseph Smith, et al.*, cross-examination by Philip Kushner, June 10, 2008. After much prodding, Sozio said the Jones Day partner who engaged the diocese had a $650-an-hour fee that was reduced to $250 to $280 because the church was a nonprofit.

48. James F. McCarty, "Bishop Pilla Walks Tightrope in Priest Sex Abuse Scandal," *Cleveland Plain Dealer*, May 5, 2002.

49. Kohn, "The Church on Trial, Part II."

50. James F. McCarty and Joel Rutchick, "Catholic Charities Seeks Pledge from Pilla," *Cleveland Plain Dealer*, August 2, 2002.

51. Ibid.

52. John Maimone, "Current Financial Concerns of the Diocese of Cleveland: Parish Pastoral Council Chair Persons Gathering," April 28, 2007. According to Joseph Smith, the 2006 figures cited by Maimone, who delivered his white paper as the diocesan CFO, were not appreciably different from those in 2002, as referenced in the *Plain Dealer* coverage by McCarty and Rutchick.

53. Jason Berry and Gerald Renner, *Vows of Silence: The Abuse of Power in the Papacy of John Paul II* (New York, 2004), p. 286.

54. The account is based on Liturgy of Lament, which can be accessed at www.futurechurch.org. I have tightened certain passages for narrative pacing, with permission of the homilist. See also David Briggs, "Lament for Christ's Broken Body," *Cleveland Plain Dealer*, October 15, 2002.

55. James F. McCarty, "Seven Indicted in Diocesan Sex Cases," *Cleveland Plain Dealer*, December 5, 2002.

56. Laurie Goodstein, "Diocese Resists Releasing Names of Accused Priests," *New York Times*, February 28, 2003.

57. Prosecutor's Merit Brief, Court of Common Pleas, Cuyahoga County, Ohio, Special Docket no. SD 03 075617, Judge Brian J. Corrigan, *In Re: Grand Jury Investigation*, October 2003.

58. James F. McCarty, "Budget Woes Could Force Cutbacks, Pilla Warns," *Cleveland Plain Dealer*, March 5, 2003.

59. Merit Brief of Petition-Intervenor New World Communications of Ohio, Inc., on Behalf of Its Television Station, WJW-Fox 8, Court of Common Pleas, Cuyahoga County, Ohio, Special Docket no. SD 03 075617, Judge Brian J. Corrigan, *In Re: Grand Jury Investigation*, August 24, 2003.

60. Information on Zrino Jukic is taken from the transcript of his trial testimony under cross-examination by defense attorney Philip Kushner in *U.S. v. Joseph Smith*, and his testimony in U.S. District Court, Northern District of Ohio, Eastern Division, case no. 1:06CR394-02, *U.S. v. Anton Zgoznik*. Kushner provided copies of the transcripts.

61. Bill of Particulars, U.S. District Court, Northern District of Ohio, Eastern Division, case no. 1:06-CR-00394-AA, *U.S. v. Joseph H. Smith and Anton Zgoznik*, exhibit C, The Letter.

62. Government's Responses to Defendant Smith's Motion to Order Production of Documents and Additional Scheduling Motions, *U.S. v. Joseph Smith, et al.*, March 2, 2007, exhibit G, Charles D. Hassell letter to Carl M. Grant, May 3, 2004.

63. Ibid., General Allegations.

64. Dennis Mahoney, "Clevelanders Sue Columbus Diocese's Financial Chief," *Columbus Dispatch*, June 5, 2005.

65. Opinion and Judgment Entry, Judge Brian J. Corrigan, Court of Common Pleas, Cuyahoga County, Ohio, case no. 03 SD 075617, *In Re Grand Jury Investigation*, February 27, 2004, p. 10. The Ohio Supreme Court refused to grant a hearing on the federal vs. state disparities on grand jury secrecy as requested by the station attorneys, McMenamin and Zirm. See Original Action for Writ of Mandamus, case no. 04-1646, *State of Ohio, Ex Rel. New World Communication of Ohio, Inc. Relator, v. William D. Mason, Cuyahoga County Prosecutor, Respondent*, September 29, 2004.

66. "Perspectives: John Jay Sex Abuse Report," episode 726, *Religion & Ethics Weekly*, PBS, February 27, 2004.

67. David Eden, "City Chatter: Bishop Pilla Lied About Number of Accused Priests He Transferred, Former Lawyer Charges," *Cleveland Free Times*, March 3, 2004.

68. "Bishop Reaffirms Commitment to Protect Children," www.dioceseof cleveland.org, February 27, 2004.

69. Regina Brett, "Diocese Lawyers Got Court to Seal Data," *Cleveland Plain Dealer*, March 7, 2004.

70. James F. McCarty, "Catholic Reformers Contest New Edict," *Cleveland Plain Dealer*, April 26, 2004.

71. Ibid.

72. Tom Roberts, "A Map to the Future Church," *National Catholic Reporter*, July 16, 2009.

73. Dennis Mahoney, "Clevelanders Sue Columbus Diocese's Financial Chief," *Columbus Dispatch*, June 5, 2005.

74. James F. McCarty, "Diocese Ex-CFO to Get Same Job in Columbus," *Cleveland Plain Dealer*, August 20, 2004.

75. Complaint, Court of Common Pleas, Cuyahoga County, Ohio, case no. 05 565095, *Rosie Andujar, et al. Plaintiffs v. Anthony M. Pilla, et al. Defendants,*

June 13, 2005. The lawsuit also names Thomas Kelly, who was an official of the diocesan Cemeteries office; Kelly was not indicted.

76. Memorandum of Opinion and Order, Judge Stuart A. Friedman, *Rosie Andujar, et al. v. Anthony M. Pilla, et al.*, September 12, 2005.

77. "Cleveland Bishop Asks Permission of Pope to Retire," Catholic News Agency, January 6, 2006.

78. I would not have thought to ask Sister Schenk about the catacomb of Saint Priscilla were it not for a reference to the site in Garry Wills, *What Jesus Meant* (New York, 2006), p. 51. On the group's visit, see Sylvia Poggioli, "Pilgrims Trace Women's Role in Early Church," *NPR*, transcript, April 16, 2006.

CHAPTER 10: PROSECUTION AND SUPPRESSION

1. U.S. District Court, Northern District of Ohio, Eastern Division, case no. 1:06-CR-00394-AA, *U.S. v. Joseph H. Smith and Anton Zgoznik*, August 16, 2006.

2. Mike Tobin, "Lawyer Says Priest Duped by Associates," *Cleveland Plain Dealer*, August 24, 2006.

3. Ibid.

4. Conference for Pastoral Planning and Council Development, 2003 *National Study of Parish Reorganization*, www.cppcd.org.

5. David Briggs, "Local Catholic Finances 'Stretched,'" *Cleveland Plain Dealer*, February 6, 2007.

6. The dialogue is from the transcript. Courtesy Zingerplatz Pictures Inc., Joe Cultrera, producer, *Hand of God*, 2007.

7. Bishop Richard Lennon, "The Church Going Forward," City Club of Cleveland, February 16, 2007. Transcript courtesy City Club of Cleveland.

8. Defendant Joseph H. Smith's Motion to Order Production of Documents, case no. 1:06-CR-00394-AA, *U.S. v. Joseph H. Smith and Anton Zgoznik*, February 16, 2007. The motion and other documents from the case can be accessed on www.bishopaccountability.org. Hereafter referred to as case no. 1:06-CR-00394-AA.

9. Redacted FBI interview with Zrino E. Jukic, November 17, 2005, case no. 1:06-CR-00394-AA, document 51-6, exhibit E, filed March 15, 2007.

10. Defendant Anton Zgoznik's Response to Motion of United States to Quash Subpoena to Huntington Bank, case no. 1:06-CR-00394-AA, November 15, 2006.

11. Bill Frogameni, "The Scum Always Rises: An Embezzlement Scandal Closes In on Top Diocesan Officials," *Cleveland Scene*, April 4, 2007.

12. Defendant Smith's Motion Regarding Destruction of Evidence by the Diocese and Request for the Evidentiary Hearing, case no. 1:06-CR-00394-AA, August 1, 2007.

13. Smith's Motion to Order, case no. 1:06-CR-00394-AA, February 16, 2007.

14. Mike Tobin, "Fund Furnished Diocesan Home, Ex-Workers Say," *Cleveland Plain Dealer*, February 25, 2007.

15. James F. McCarty, "Catholic Diocese's Income Declines, Pilla Cutting Costs, but Church Says It Is Not in Fiscal Crisis," *Cleveland Plain Dealer*, April 5, 2004.

16. Judge Ann Aldrich, Memorandum and Order, case no. 1:06-CR-00394-AA, June 14, 2007. See also Mike Tobin, "Judge Orders Catholic Diocese to Turn Over Financial Records," *Cleveland Plain Dealer*, June 15, 2007.

17. Christopher Maag, "Cleveland Diocese Accused of Impropriety as Embezzlement Trial Nears," *New York Times*, August 20, 2007.

18. Trial transcript, testimony of Anton Zgoznik, U.S. District Court, Northern District of Ohio, Eastern Division, case no. 1:06CR394-02, *U.S. v. Anton Zgoznik*, September 24, 2007.

19. Trial transcript, testimony of Zrino Jukic, *U.S. v. Anton Zgoznik*, case no. 1:06CR394-02, August 23, 2007.

20. *U.S. v. Anton Zgoznik*, case no. 1:06CR394-02, government exhibit 72-1. The U.S. Attorney's office made available to me the CD-R of the taped conversation, and the transcript that was scrolled for jurors as the tape played during the trial. The transcript per se was admitted only as an aid for the jury. See also James F. McCarty, "Tape Evidence Splits Trials of 2 Charged with Catholic Diocese Kickbacks," *Cleveland Plain Dealer*, August 9, 2007.

21. Trial transcript, John Wright testimony, *U.S. v. Anton Zgoznik*, case no. 1:06CR394-02, August 27, 2007. All quotations from the proceedings that follow are taken from the transcript, unless otherwise indicated.

22. James F. McCarty, "Juror in Diocesan Kickback Trial Wanted to Hear More from Pilla," *Cleveland Plain Dealer*, October 5, 2007.

23. James F. McCarty, "At Church Kickback Trial, 'Roman Collar Amnesia,' " *Cleveland Plain Dealer*, September 4, 2007.

24. James F. McCarty, "Jury Now Has Diocese Kickback Case," *Cleveland Plain Dealer*, September 28, 2007.

25. Michael O'Malley, "A Fight for Churches," *Cleveland Plain Dealer*, March 2, 2009.

26. Diocesan Finances, 2008–2009, *Key Diocesan Realities—a Context for Parish Consolidation*, www.dioceseofcleveland.org.

27. Ibid.

28. Ibid.

29. Michael O'Malley and Robert L. Smith, "Parishes Get Bishop's Decision: 29 Will Close and 41 Will Merge," *Cleveland Plain Dealer*, March 15, 2009.

30. Ibid.

31. Diocesan Finances, 2008–2009, *Key Diocesan Realities*, www.dioceseof cleveland.org.

32. O'Malley, "A Fight for Churches."

33. Michael Polensek, telephone interview with the author, October 22, 2010.

34. Reverend Robert Begin, letter to Archbishop Pietro Sambi, April 6, 2009.

35. Michael O'Malley, "St. Colman to Stay Open After Bishop Reconsiders," *Cleveland Plain Dealer*, May 2, 2009. See also Michael O'Malley, "The Rev. Bob Begin, Known as the Rebel Priest, Wins His Latest Battle—to Keep St. Colman Church Open," *Cleveland Plain Dealer*, June 15, 2009.

36. Tom Roberts, "Cleveland Diocese Shaken by Seismic Shifts," *National Catholic Reporter*, May 9, 2009.

37. Tom Roberts, "Scranton's Bishop Martino Stepping Down," *National Catholic Reporter*, August 28, 2009.

38. Tim Townsend, "The St. Stanislaus Saga: Is Resolution Imminent?" *St. Louis Post-Dispatch*, May 1, 2010; Tim Townsend, "After Years of Discord, Status of St. Stanislaus's Is Coming to an End," *St. Louis Post-Dispatch*, July 31, 2010.

39. Malcolm Gay, "Renegade Priest Leads a Split St. Louis Parish," *New York Times*, August 13, 2010; Joseph Kenny, "St. Louis Parish Rejects Archdiocese's Proposal," Catholic News Service, August 24, 2010, in *National Catholic Reporter*.

40. Joan M. Nuth, Ph. D., "The Story of a Church," unpublished. Nuth, a systematic theologian at John Carroll University in Cleveland, sent the essay to Archbishop Pietro Sambi, the papal nuncio in Washington, D.C., on April 18, 2009. The essay appeared in the parish's online newsletter, which has ceased circulation on the Internet since the parish was suppressed.

41. Court of Appeals, Third District, Seneca County, *Kansas St. James Parish of Ohio, et al. Plaintiffs-Appellants v. The Catholic Diocese of Toledo in America, et al., Defendants-Appellees*, case no. 13-08-19.

42. Rachel Dissell, "Final Mass at Downtown St. Peter Catholic Church Leaves 'An Empty Tomb,' " *Cleveland Plain Dealer*, April 4, 2010.

CHAPTER 11: THE DEBTS OF APOSTOLIC SUCCESSION

1. "The Plot Thickens: Two Normas, Maciel, Consecrated and Quirece and des Andres," March 25, 2010, www.exlcblog.com; Carmen H. Moreno, "Las familias de Maciel," *Quien*, March 19, 2010.

2. George Weigel, author of a 1998 biography of John Paul, was among the pope's advisers at the Vatican during the 2002 abuse crisis. Weigel portrays the pope as a victim of Maciel's deception in *The End and the Beginning: Pope John Paul II—The Victory of Freedom, the Last Years, the Legacy* (New York, 2010). Weigel argues that John Paul was poorly informed by Vatican officials in 2002. In response to the pounding international media coverage at the time, John Paul issued a statement that condemned clergy predators yet left room for redemption of those priests (see chapter 3). The inconclusive nature of that document mirrored his ambivalence on the issue. John Paul was one of the great popes and a towering figure of the twentieth century, but his failures of church governance were substantial. By

bending over backward to absolve John Paul of responsibility in the abuse crisis, Weigel avoids—indeed, distorts—the historical record. In 1984 Father Tom Doyle wrote a forty-two-page summary of the abuse crisis, as it unfolded, for his boss, Archbishop Pio Laghi, the papal nuncio, who sent the information to Rome. In *Vows of Silence* (New York, 2004), Gerald Renner and I tracked the escalation of scandals in the 1990s, particularly the case of Cardinal Groër of Austria, whose 1995 retirement amid a flood of allegations we now know caused great tension between Ratzinger and Sodano over the Vatican's tight-lipped response to Groër's history of sexual abuses. Weigel (unlike Jonathan Kwitny in his biography *Man of the Century*) ignores the well-documented record of John Paul's passivity and inaction for years before he was weakened by Parkinson's disease. By failing to cite the interviews Maciel's victims gave to us and other journalists, Weigel approaches Maciel as if the public accusations had no merit until they became testimony with the CDF investigator, Monsignor Scicluna, whose sessions began the day John Paul died. By avoiding the public record on Maciel during John Paul's lifetime, Weigel silences himself on Cardinal Sodano's machinations and why Ratzinger waited eight years before ordering an investigation. Ignoring the evidence, Weigel places John Paul above fault, citing only the "incapacity and weakness on the part of the Pope's subordinates, who ought to have had, when circumstances demanded it, the courage to lead according to the pattern he had set" (p. 514). Regarding the abuse crisis, that "pattern" is the issue. Weigel does not identify those subordinates, which is not surprising. Hagiography is no handmaiden of history; however, a valid case for sainthood cannot be made without confronting the factual reality, and human failings, in the life of a given candidate for sainthood.

Weigel treats Maciel as a master of deception, the pope as his victim. On page 552 of *The End and the Beginning*, Weigel in footnote 139 says that he interviewed Maciel on February 19, 1998. This is remarkable. Maciel avoided journalists for most of his life; after the 1997 *Hartford Courant* report he gave an orchestrated statement to Jésus Colina, the Regnum Christi editor of Zenit, the Legion news service, for the book *Christ Is My Life* (2003), which constituted his self-defense. Weigel actually got Maciel to talk a year after the *Hartford Courant* report of February 23, 1997, that put his victims on record. What did Weigel ask him? What did Maciel say? For years thereafter, Weigel's endorsement of the Legion was prominent on the website LegionaryFacts.org, which defended Maciel against his putative enemies, the victims. In 2009, when the news broke on Maciel's daughter, Weigel used the *First Things* website to call for a Vatican investigation of the Legion. Better late than never, Weigel was also engaging in a personal form of spin control, positioning himself against his previous support of the order and his own record of whitewashing history.

3. A June 2010 editorial in *New Oxford Review*, "The Double Life of Marcial

Maciel," quoted Podles as saying that Groër "had molested almost every student he had come into contact with for decades." In response to my e-mail about his source, Podles wrote on November 20, 2010: "A German homosexual web site claimed that Groer had molested almost every student (1,000+) that he had come into contact with. I asked Cardinal [Christoph] Schönborn about this claim, and he said that Groer had made strong homoerotic gestures to most of his students, but that the gestures did not extend as far as penetration."

4. John Paul II, *Ordinatio Sacerdotalis*, Apostolic Letter, to the Bishops of the Catholic Church on Reserving Priestly Ordination to Men Alone, May 22, 1994, www.vatican.va.

5. See in particular Paul Lakeland, *The Liberation of the Laity: In Search of an Accountable Church* (New York, 2003).

6. Garry Wills, *Papal Sin* (New York, 2000), p. 190.

7. Eugene Kennedy, *The Unhealed Wound: The Church and Human Sexuality* (New York, 2001), p. 66.

8. Marco Politi, "The Church's New Age of Dissent," *The Tablet*, March 21, 2009.

9. Ibid.

10. "MG Critical Path" study, no author or release date given.

11. Avery Dulles, "What Distinguishes the Jesuits?" *America*, January 15, 2007.

12. " 'Psalter of My Hours,' the Work Plagiarized by Maciel," Catholic News Agency, December 18, 2009.

13. U.S. Federal Court, Minnesota District, case no. 0:04-CV-02895-RHK-AJB, *Sellors v. Legionaries of Christ et al.*, filed June 4, 2004, http://www.mnd.uscourts.gov/. See also Giselle Sainte Marie, "Gospel Charity Cuts Both Ways: Lifting the Veil on How the Legion Builds Their Kingdom: The Familia Saga," www.regainnetwork.org.

14. Albert Camus, "The Almond Trees," *Lyrical and Critical Essays* (New York, 1968), p. 135.

15. Jason Berry, "Legionary Founder Said to Father a Child," *National Catholic Reporter*, February 3, 2010.

16. U.S. District Court of Oregon, case no. CV 02 430 MO, *John Doe v. Holy See*.

CHAPTER 12: ANOTHER CALIFORNIA

1. Jill Hodges, "Attacking Abuse: Lawyer Finds His Niche Suing Authority Figures in Abuse Cases," *Minneapolis Star Tribune*, May 20, 1991.

2. Peter Slavin, "Jeff Anderson, Jousting with the Vatican from a Small Law Office in St. Paul," *Washington Post*, April 19, 2010.

3. U.S. District Court, Eastern District of Wisconsin, Milwaukee Division, case no. 10-CV-00346-RTR, *John Doe 16 v. Holy See*, April 22, 2010.

4. Laurie Goodstein, "Vatican Declined to Defrock U.S. Priest Who Abused Boys," *New York Times*, March 24, 2010.

5. Kim Ode, "On a Crusade," *Minneapolis Star Tribune*, April 26, 2010.

6. David Schimke, "True Believer," *St. Paul City Pages*, April 16, 2003.

7. Tim Townsend, "Abuse Scandal Puts Victims' Group Back in the Spotlight," *St. Louis Post-Dispatch*, April 20, 2010.

8. Jason Berry, *Lead Us Not into Temptation* (New York, 1992), pp. 281–86, 371–73.

9. Daniel J. Wakin, "Catholic Priest Who Aids Church Sexual Abuse Victims Loses His Job," *New York Times*, April 29, 2004.

10. Mike Davis, *City of Quartz: Excavating the Future in Los Angeles* (New York, 2006), p. 360.

11. Ibid., pp. 359–65. On Western Sequoia, see Ron Russell, "Taj Mahony," *New Times* (L.A.), December 20, 2001.

12. Msgr. Francis J. Weber, *Cathedral: Our Lady of the Angels* (Mission Hills, CA, 2004), p. 69.

13. Steve Lopez, "The Amazing 'Teflon Cardinal,' " *Los Angeles Times*, April 7, 2002.

14. The testimony cited is drawn from Lopez, "The Amazing 'Teflon Cardinal,' " unless noted otherwise.

15. Testimony cited in Jason Berry, "Church in Crisis: Mahony, in Legal Battle, Insists Church Has Right to Secrecy," *National Catholic Reporter*, March 18, 2005.

16. Margaret Leslie Davis, *Dark Side of Fortune: Triumph and Scandal in the Life of Oil Tycoon Edward L. Doheny* (Berkeley, CA, 1998), p. 277.

17. Msgr. Francis J. Weber, *A History of the Archdiocese of Los Angeles and Its Precursor Jurisdictions in Southern California, 1840–2007* (Los Angeles, 2007), pp. 9–11.

18. George J. Sánchez, *Becoming Mexican American: Ethnicity, Culture, and Identity in Chicano, Los Angeles, 1900–1945* (New York, 1993), p. 71.

19. Davis, *City of Quartz*, pp. 330–31.

20. Charles R. Morris, *American Catholic: The Saints and Sinners Who Built America's Most Powerful Church* (New York, 1997), p. 258.

21. Msgr. Francis J. Weber, *His Eminence of Los Angeles: James Francis Cardinal McIntyre*, vol. 1 (Mission Hills, CA, 1977), p. 237.

22. Msgr. Francis J. Weber, "Historical Reflections," in *Days of Change, Years of Challenge: The Homilies, Addresses, and Talks of Cardinal Timothy Manning*, ed. Francis Weber (Los Angeles, 1987), p. 107.

23. Kevin Starr, *Coast of Dreams: California on the Edge, 1990–2003* (New York, 2006), p. 17.

24. On Hawkes's financial control, see Thomas J. Reese, *Archbishop: Inside the Power Structure of the Roman Catholic Church* (San Francisco, 1989), p. 190. How priests feared Hawkes is from a background interview, Los

Angeles, November 2009. On Hawkes's probate, see Superior Court of California, Los Angeles County, P702033, filed October 17, 1985.

25. Los Angeles Archdiocese, *Report to the People of God*, February 17, 2004, lists Hawkes with two accusers. Demarco's client makes a third. Terence McKiernan of BishopAccountability.org explains further: "The archdiocese no longer has the list on their site, though they pretend to—they deleted the list, and only post the introductory essay now, without saying that the Report is bowdlerized. See our brief explanation of this situation with links at: http://www.bishopaccountability.org/AtAGlance/lists.htm."

26. Weber, *Cathedral*, p. 102.

27. Ibid., pp. 105–6.

28. Joseph Claude Harris, "Paying for Parish Programs: Archdiocese of Los Angeles," unpublished, July 2001.

29. Manny Vega, conversations with the author, Los Angeles and Pasadena, June 2005; screening of videotape of Vega's life prepared for settlement negotiations under the auspices of attorney Ray Boucher. Tom Kisken, "Officer Battles Personal Crime," *Ventura County Star*, April 27, 2003, is an exceptional report.

30. Berry, "Mahony in Legal Battle." The quotation in question was from an earlier *Los Angeles Times* article. The legal narrative in this part of the chapter is drawn from the *National Catholic Reporter* coverage.

31. Jeffrey Anderson, "Behind the Robes," *L.A. Weekly*, March 18, 2003. He is no relation to the attorney.

32. Glenn F. Bunting, Ralph Frammolino, and Richard Winton, "Archdiocese for Years Kept Accusations from Police," *Los Angeles Times*, August 18, 2002.

33. Larry B. Stammer, "One Church, Two Missions," *Los Angeles Times Magazine*, August 25, 2002.

34. Larry B. Stammer, "Mahony's Top Chiefs All Resign," October 31, 2002.

35. Thomas P. Doyle, A.W. R. Sipe, and Patrick J. Wall, *Sex, Priests, and Secret Codes: The Catholic Church's 2,000-Year Paper Trail of Sexual Abuse* (Los Angeles, 2006).

36. On Stewart's relationship with the archdiocese, see Ron Russell, "Taj Mahony," *New Times* (Los Angeles), December 20, 2001.

37. Berry, "Mahony in Legal Battle."

38. Jason Berry, "Telephone Interview with Cardinal Roger Mahony of Los Angeles on the Sexual Abuses in the Archdiocese of Los Angeles," February 12, 2005, posted *National Catholic Reporter*, March 18, 2005, as a sidebar to "Mahony in Legal Battle."

39. Berry, "Mahony in Legal Battle."

40. *Report to the People of God*, February 18, 2004, in *The Tidings*, www.archdiocese.la.org.

41. Jean Guccione, William Lobdell, and Megan Garvey, "O.C. Diocese Settles Abuse Cases," *Los Angeles Times*, December 3, 2004.

42. This section on Levada is based on my reporting for a profile of the arch-bishop, "The Man Who Kept the Secrets," *San Francisco Magazine*, September 2005.

43. Ibid., See also "Sipe Reports XX," www.richardsipe.com; Court of Appeal of California, Second Appellate District, Division Eight, B198136, *Doe v. Salesian Society*, filed January 29, 2008.

44. William Lobdell and Jean Guccione, "A Novel Tack by the Cardinal," *Los Angeles Times*, March 14, 2004.

45. Berry, "Mahony in Legal Battle."

46. Ibid.

47. Jason Berry, "Cracks in the Wall of the Curia," *National Catholic Reporter*, May 10, 2010.

48. Jason Berry, "How Fr. Maciel Built His Empire, Part 2," *National Catholic Reporter*, April 12, 2010.

49. John Spano, Paul Pringle, and Jean Guccione, "Church to Settle with 45 Accusers," *Los Angeles Times*, December 2, 2006.

50. John L. Allen Jr., "Sex Abuse Settlement, the Pope's Visit and Ecumenism: Cardinal Mahony Speaks with NCR," *National Catholic Reporter*, November 30, 2007.

51. Joe Mozingo and John Spano, "$660-Million Settlement in Abuse Cases," *Los Angeles Times*, July 15, 2007.

52. The AIB loan is referenced in a sidebar box, credited to the archdiocese. See Rebecca Trounson, "Parishes May Help Pay Sex Abuse Tab," *Los Angeles Times*, May 25, 2008.

53. Weber, *Cathedral*, p. 227.

54. Conor O'Clery, "Abuse Scandals Put Catholic Church in US in Cash and Manpower Crisis," *Irish Times*, April 13, 2002.

55. Ellie Hidalgo, "Archdiocese Outlines Financial Recovery Strategy," *The Tidings*, March 14, 2008.

56. United States Bankruptcy Court, Southern District of California, case no. 07-00939-LA 11, *In Re: The Roman Catholic Bishop of San Diego, a California Corporation Sole, Debtor*, Chapter 11, First Report of Expert R. Todd Neilson, CPA Pursuant to Appointment, dated April 30, 2007, pp. 165–66.

57. Greg Moran and Mark Sauer, "Legal Experts Fault Bankruptcy Option," *San Diego Union-Tribune*, September 10, 2007.

58. Sandi Dolbee and Mark Sauer, "Judge's Tears, Rebuke Close Case," *San Diego Union-Tribune*, November 2, 2007.

59. Trounson, "Parishes May Help Pay Sex Abuse Tab."

CHAPTER 13: AMERICA AND THE VATICAN

1. Jeffrey Anderson, "Roger's Nest," *L.A. Weekly*, March 11, 2004. The Los Angeles journalist is no relation to the attorney profiled in the previous chapter.

2. Peter Borré, "Request for Mediation," letter to the Reverend Monsignor Pietro Parolin, April 7, 2009.

3. Jerry Filteau, "Louisianans Face Long Recovery from Katrina, New Orleans Flooding," Catholic News Service, August 31, 2005.

4. Will H. Coleman, "The French Market," in Frank de Caro, editor, and Rosan Augusta Jordan, associate editor, *Louisiana Sojourns: Travelers's Tales and Literary Journeys* (Baton Rouge, LA: 1998), pp. 89–91.

5. Randy J. Sparks, " 'An Anchor to the People': Hurricane Katrina, Religious Life, and Recovery in New Orleans," arranged and edited by Tracy Fessenden and Michael Pasquier, "After the Storm: A Special Issue on Hurricane Katrina," *Journal of Southern Religion*, 2008, http://jsr.fsu.edu/Katrina/FrontKatrina.htm.

6. Peter Entell, director, *Shake the Devil Off*, Show and Tell Films, 2007. The documentary provides a poignant treatment of the protest Mass and the struggles at St. Augustine.

7. Peter Finney Jr., "Financial Recovery Continuing for Archdiocese," *Clarion Herald*, September 4, 2010.

8. Bruce Nolan, "Catholic Church Quantifies Katrina Damage," *Times-Picayune*, July 26, 2008.

9. Jason Berry, "Mass Protests," *Gambit Weekly*, November 4, 2008.

10. Andrew Walsh, "Losing Patience with the Vatican," *Religion in the News* 13, no. 1 (Summer 2010).

11. Jason Berry, "What Benedict Must Do," PoliticsDaily.com, March 30, 2010.

12. Associated Press, "Pope Celebrates Easter Mass, Hailed by Cardinal," April 5, 2010.

13. Paddy Agnew, "Vatican Hits Back Against Criticism of Child Sex Abuse," *Irish Times*, April 8, 2010.

14. David Gibson, "A 'Failed Papacy'? How Benedict XVI Got into This Mess," PoliticsDaily.com, April 18, 2010.

15. John L. Allen Jr., "Vatican Statement on Maciel, Legionaries," *NCR Today*, May 1, 2010. Allen's blog included a full translation of the "Communiqué of the Holy See," released in Italian that day.

16. Jason Berry, "Maciel's Son to Sue Legion," *National Catholic Reporter*, June 20, 2010.

17. Ibid.

18. U.S. District Court of Oregon, case no. CV 02 430 MO, *John Doe v. Holy See*, April 3, 2002.

19. Plaintiff's Memorandum in Support of Jurisdictional Discovery, *John Doe v. Holy See*, September 8, 2010.

20. *John Doe v. Holy See*, 557 F.3d 1066 (9th Civ. 2009) *cert. denied*, 130 S. Ct. 3497 (2010).

21. Borré provided his exchange of letters (translated from the Italian) with

Archbishop Sambi that reference key points of their discussion to buttress his account of their dialogue.

22. Lisa Wangsness, "Archdiocese Regaining Its Financial Footing," *Boston Globe,* June 11, 2010.

23. James P. McDonough, "Chancellor's Annual Overview," *Archdiocese of Boston Financial Report for the Year Ending June 30, 2009,* p. 7.

24. Archdiocese of Boston, "St. Francis of Assisi School to Consolidate with Cheverus School and St. Joseph School," BostonCatholic.org, May 20, 2010.

25. Katherine Q. Seelye, "For Priest, Intersection of Faith and Doubt," *New York Times,* May 16, 2010.

26. Robert Bowers, e-mail to the author.

27. Stephanie Barry, "Historical District Under Our Lady of Hope Church in Springfield Wins Backing of Federal Judge," *Springfield Republican,* January 6, 2011.

28. Christopher Lamb, "North-East Faces Steep Fall in Numbers of Priests," *The Tablet,* January 22, 2011.

29. Michael Rubinkam, "Catholics Win Rare Victories on U.S. Church Closures," Associated Press, March 6, 2011.

EPILOGUE: BENEDICT XVI: POPE OF IRONIES

1. Jason Berry, "Is the Church Really This Blind?" *Los Angeles Times,* November 11, 2007.

2. The Pew Forum on Religion and Public Life, Summary of Key Findings, *The U.S. Religious Landscape Survey,* February 25, 2008.

3. Patrick Schiltz, "The Future of Sexual Abuse Litigation," *America,* July 7, 2003.

4. Jason Berry, "Gambling with History: Benedict and the Legion of Christ," *National Catholic Reporter,* December 29, 2010.

5. Wilton Wynn, *Keeper of the Keys: John XXIII, Paul VI, and John Paul II—Three Who Changed the Church* (New York, 1988), p. 161.

6. Alessandro Speciale, "Unmasking the Vatican's Bank," *GlobalPost,* January 25, 2011.

7. Guy Dinmore, "Sicily Probe Adds to Vatican Bank Pressure," *Financial Times,* November 3, 2010.

8. Russell Chandler, "Focus of Controversy: Ratzinger: Point Man for the Vatican," *Los Angeles Times,* November 7, 1986.

ACKNOWLEDGMENTS

My literary agent, Steve Hanselman of Level Five Media, was the catalyst for this book. I was finishing a documentary when Steve suggested an investigation of church finances; he arranged a meeting with Trace Murphy, editorial director of Doubleday Religion, who had alerted Steve to his deepening interest in the subject. To these good men, my lasting thanks.

I extend my gratitude to Maureen Clark, who did a superb job as copy editor.

The reporting on Father Maciel and the Legion of Christ sent me to Mexico City many times before the final leg for this book. My cousin, Victoria Miranda de la Pena, and her husband, Willi Frehoff Evers, welcomed me into their home with a graciousness I will never forget. In March 2010 Victoria seemed to be in remission from cancer; her death the following fall is a continuing source of sorrow. To Willi, Dagmar, and Armin, and to Monica Miranda and Ignacio Gómez: *Un abrazo tierno con mucho amor. Mil gracias otra vez.*

This book straddles journalism and history. Many articles formed the building blocks for certain chapters. I had substantial help along the way.

Above all, I thank the Fund for Investigative Journalism in Washington, D.C., particularly board member Margaret Engel, for support on this book and previous projects. To the Joe Busam Foundation, notably Barb Kelly, John Busam, and the late Claire Busam, I am grateful for the grants that facilitated my research in Rome and, previously, on the documentary film *Vows of Silence*.

Esther Kaplan and Joe Conason at the Investigative Fund of the Nation Institute provided timely support for a *National Catholic Reporter* series on Father Maciel's financial history. At *NCR* I have been lucky to work closely with editor-at-large Tom Roberts, a writer's editor in the best sense. Joe Feuerherd, the publisher and editor-in-chief, was of great help on the Follieri reporting. Likewise, to editor Tom Fox and attorney David Korzenik, many thanks.

I am grateful to Special Agent Theodore V. Cacioppi of the Federal Bureau of Investigation in New York for his insights on the Follieri prosecution; to the U.S. Attorney's office, Southern District of New York, for sending documents; and to the FBI for facilitating my Freedom of Information Act request.

Jack Ruhl, professor of accountancy and associate dean of the Haworth College of Business at Western Michigan University, drew upon his extensive research on financial statements of Catholic dioceses in answering many questions; he also gave a close reading of several sections.

Joseph Claude Harris provided data from his research on diocesan collections and was unfailingly helpful. Michael W. Ryan, an authority on church embezzlements and missing funds, shared his findings and opinions with refreshing candor.

Terence McKiernan and Anne Barrett Doyle of BishopAccountability .org have done pioneering work to create this online archive, which was of great help to me. For anyone interested in the internal politics of the church, BishopAccountability is an unparalleled resource. Many thanks to Leon C. Podles, author and a founder of BishopAccountability, for support of my production work and the early research on church closings.

In like measure, a debt of lasting gratitude to Eugene Kennedy, for advice of many years, and to Merry O'Donnell, for generous friendship.

I am grateful to Peter Borré for his time and information in the interviews, e-mails, and phone calls; and to his wife, Mary Beth, and her mother, Rose Mary Piper. Likewise, to Peter's cousin, Marie Roth, for the genealogical research.

For assistance in various ways: Thomas Powers; Gerard Wimberly;

Carolyn Disco; Tim Watson of Ariel Montage; Louise Rosen and Emily Radaker of Louise Rosen Ltd; Channing Penna; Jackie Renner; Julie Anderson; Therese Gahler; Mike Finnegan; Pat Noaker; Tom Byrne; Anastasia and Will Lyman; Ann and Alan Klonowski; Pat and Bill Nordstrom; Ginny and Larry Hoenhe; the late Reverend David A. Boileau; Barbara Fortier; Harold Baquet and Cheron Brylski; Alden Hagardon; Dan Bartley, president of Voice of the Faithful; Donna Doucette, the executive director; Peg Clark and other VOTF members too numerous to mention; Steve Sheehan and Kristine Ward of National Survivor Advocates Coalition News; SNAP (Survivors Network of those Abused by Priests) leaders Barbara Blaine, David Clohessy, Barbara Dorris, and Peter Isely.

To these priests who spoke on-the-record: Bob Begin, Jon Conley, Stephen Fichter, Bruce Teague, Robert Bowers, Stephen Josoma, Robert Marrone, Thomas Reese, SJ, Jerome LeDoux, SVD. I thank certain clerics of the Curia, the Legion of Christ in Rome, and former Legionaries who remain anonymous at their request.

To those who gave substantial time for interviews and follow-up questions: Sister Christine Schenk, CSJ, Christopher Kunze, Jeff Anderson, Manny Vega, Juan Vaca, José Barba, Nicholas Cafardi, Tom Doyle, Marci Hamilton, Ginny Hull, Ray Boucher, Anthony Dimarco, Steve Rubino, Patrick Wall, John Manly, Paul Lennon, Glenn Favreau, Genvieve Kineke, Melanie Bonvicino, Santiago Feliciano Jr., Joseph Smith, Phil Kushner, Cleveland city councilman Mike Polensek, and Massachusetts state representative Brian Wallace.

A special appreciation to Clancy DuBos of New Orleans's *Gambit Weekly* for publishing my first reports on parish closings.

In my research consulting for ABC News, I've been privileged to work with Brian Ross, Rhonda Schwartz, Ron Claiborne, and Bill Blakemore.

Journalist Betty Clermont, author of *The Neo-Catholics*, provided valuable research, often on short notice; Michael J. Luke of WWL TV, New Orleans, did extensive Web research; and Alessandro Speciale in Rome, a correspondent with GlobalPost and other outlets, who helped with reporting for the second chapter and generously assisted me in the Vatican research. Thanks also to Dennis Sadowski of Catholic News Services.

For various forms of help in Rome: Robert Mickens, correspondent for *The Tablet*; Massimo Franco of *Corriere della Sera*; Sandro Magister of *L'Espresso*; Nicole Winfield of the Associated Press; Marco Politi of *La*

Repubblica; Eldio Fazi and Olimpia Ellero of Fazi Editore; Giovanni Avena of *Adista;* Gioia Avvantaggia; the Reverend Frederico Lombardi, SJ, of the Holy See Press Office; the author and journalist Philip Willan; John Phillips; Patrizia Velletri; Kristine Ward; author Michael Mewshaw; Cinzia Scagliarini; Glenn Favreau; Paul Lennon; and José Barba. For assistance in translations from the Italian, Grady Hardy and Rosy Santella.

In Mexico City, *muchisimas gracias* to Jose de Cordoba of the *Wall Street Journal* and his wife, Gina Manfredo, for invaluable assistance; author David Lida; José Barba for sharing his indefatigable research and contacts; Ciro Gómez Lleyva, the broadcast journalist and editor and columnist for *Milenio,* for his long coverage of Maciel. A special tribute to Carmen Aristegui of CNN Mexico and MVS Radio for her continuing focus on these issues and for her narration of the Spanish edition of my film. Carmen's compelling book, *Marcial Maciel: Historia de un criminal* (Grijalbo), was published as I finished this one. I owe a special debt to Roberta Garza, a *Milenio* editor who shared her family history in interviews and subsequently published articles of mine in translation. I am grateful to attorney José Bonilla for his assistance in a long and informative interview. I have profited from the scholarship of Jean Meyer, Fernando M. González, and Elio Masferrer Kan and from dialogue with each of them. Alejandro Espinosa (author of *El Legionario*), Saúl Barrales, José Antonio Pérez Olvera, Arturo Jurado, and Juan José Vaca waged a long struggle against Maciel at the Vatican. I thank them for their trust; likewise, the Reverend Félix Alarcón who spent a day with me in Madrid, opening portals to the past. The author Alfonso Torres Robles was equally helpful during my time in Madrid.

For fielding questions from Chile, thanks to journalist Pascale Bonnefoy, and to Andrea Insunza, coauthor of a valuable book on the Legion.

Charles Sennott, managing editor of GlobalPost, provided an outlet for my initial reports from Rome in 2009. A former *Boston Globe* correspondent, Charlie gave advice on the Boston chapters. Carl M. Cannon, author and executive editor of PoliticsDaily, also provided a forum for my articles, and a sharp reading of the California chapter. Thanks also to PoliticsDaily editor in chief Melinda Henneberger and PD religion correspondent David Gibson.

Michael Paulson of the *Boston Globe* was helpful at the start of my work in 2008; so were columnist Kevin Cullen, former Spotlight team editor Walter V. Robinson, reporters Stephen Kurkjian and Michael Rezendes along the way. James O'Toole, the Clough Millennium Professor in History at Boston College, gave a timely critique of the second chapter. Anthony Penna, an emeritus historian at Northeastern University, was most helpful on the Boston sections.

Professor John Tutino of the Georgetown University history department went beyond the call of duty in his advice on two chapter drafts. Harvey Cox, Hollis Research Professor at the Harvard Divinity School, offered guidance on prosperity theology at a crossroads in my research. Marcus Smith, an emeritus professor of English at Loyola University of New Orleans, used a sharp lens on this book as he has on previous ones I've done. My wife, Melanie McKay, a vice-provost at Loyola, gave a close reading, reviewing several sections more than once, providing a valuable critique for which, as always, I am in her debt.

For insights on Vatican politics and the history of Italy, thanks to author Robert Blair Kaiser; historian Howard Hunter of New Orleans; Professor David I. Kertzer of Brown University; the Reverend Thomas J. Reese, SJ, a senior fellow at the Woodstock Theological Center of Georgetown University; Professor Linda Carroll of Tulane University; and for facilitating my research in the Los Angeles archdiocesan archives, Monsignor Francis J. Weber.

James McCarty at the *Plain Dealer* and Bill Sheil of WJW TV were of great help on the Cleveland chapters. Thanks to attorney Michael McMenamin; reporter Michael O'Malley at the *Plain Dealer*; Patsy McGarry, Peter Murtaugh, Simon Carswell, and Mary Raftery of the *Irish Times*; Mick Peelo of RTE in Dublin; Bruce Nolan of the *Times-Picayune* whose insights on the New Orleans archdiocese were of great benefit. Doug Smith of the *Los Angeles Times* did an extensive search of the paper's database, culling articles that saved me days of work. Jean Guccione, a former *Los Angeles Times* reporter, shared insights from her coverage and read a chapter draft. Thanks also to Peter Pach and Bernard Davidow of the *Hartford Courant*; Christa Pongratz-Lippitt, *The Tablet* correspondent in Vienna; Elena Curti, deputy editor of *The Tablet* in London; Tim Townsend of the *St. Louis Post-Dispatch*; Marie Rohde and Tom Heinen, formerly of the *Milwaukee Journal Sentinel*; John Thavis and Dennis Sadowski of Catholic News Service; and Bruce Kelley of *San Francisco Magazine*.

To my mother, Mary Frances; my daughter, Simonette; and my wife, Melanie, thank you, each and all, for the radiance that lights my life.

INDEX

Abortion, 21, 72, 151
Adamson, Father Tom, 291–292
Adler, Louise DeCarl, 322, 323
AIG, 234, 237
Akerblom, Fredrik, 281–283
Alarcón, Father Felix, 177
Aldrich, Ann, 249, 253, 254, 258–260, 262, 263
Alemán Valdés, Miguel, 158
Allen, John L., Jr., 101, 120, 192, 320, 321
Allende, Salvador, 101, 103
Allentown, Pennsylvania, diocese, 349
Allied Irish Bank (AIB), 321–323, 353
Altimari, Dave, 167, 168
America (journal), 67, 355
American War for Independence, 29
Anderson, Jeff, 286–296, 301, 302, 304, 305, 307, 312–314, 317–319, 324, 335, 339–342, 350, 356
Anderson, Julie, 289, 290, 292
Annuario Pontificio, 118, 199
Annulment process, 34–35, 72–73, 79, 199

Anthony M. Pilla Charitable Account, 251, 252
Anti-Semitism, 2, 3, 43–45, 61, 66–67
Antonelli, Cardinal Giacomo, 45–51, 54
Apostolic Signatura, 76, 77, 80, 105, 135, 199–201, 271, 272, 325, 327, 335, 343, 349, 357
Apostolic succession, 98, 278, 317, 336, 354
Arias, Bishop Francisco González, 158, 174
Aristegui, Carmen, 317
Austin, Arthur, 74–75
Austria, 163, 219–220
Avena, Giovanni, 103–104
Aylward, Father Gregory, 314–315
Aymond, Archbishop Gregory, 334

Baltimore, Maryland, archdiocese, 230–231
Banco Ambrosiano, 15, 37, 104, 358

Banco di Roma, 52, 57, 62–64

Band, Doug, 125

Bannon, Father Anthony, 166, 167, 192

Baños, Norma Hilda, 195, 196, 278, 338

Baños, Normita, 195, 196, 278, 286, 338

Barba Martin, José de Jesús, 175–178, 180, 186, 189, 193

Barragán, Roberto, 175

Barragán de Garza, Flora, 175, 181

Barroso, Guillermo, 174

Barroso, Luis, 174

Barton, William, 340, 341

Begin, Father Bob, 206, 211, 213, 268–270

Benedict XV, 2, 56–59, 61, 62, 67

Benedict XVI, 36, 39, 40, 131, 191, 193–195, 201, 238, 278, 285, 288, 317, 320, 324, 344, 345, 354, 359

clergy abuse and, 2, 3, 268, 286, 316, 335–336, 351, 356, 357

Bennett, Robert, 235

Bennett, William, 159

Berlin, Fred, 214

Bernardin, Cardinal Joseph, 7, 200

Berthiaume, Father Gary, 212–214, 216, 223, 227, 235

Bertone, Archbishop Tarcisio, 78, 81, 190, 191, 317, 328

Bevilacqua, Cardinal Anthony, 8–9

Birth control, 78, 279

BishopAccountability.org, 10, 11, 140, 142, 145

Blaine, Barbara, 289, 354

Blair, Bishop Leonard P., 274, 275, 357

Boff, Father Leonardo, 102, 157, 186, 279

Bonvicino, Melanie, 124, 129–132

Borré, Ernesto, 24

Borré, Giuseppe Agostino, 24

Borré, Mary Albina, 25

Borré, Mary Beth, 2, 19–24, 26, 28, 33, 35, 94, 116, 135, 202, 343

Borré, Peter, 1, 2, 7, 19–28, 32–35, 69, 70, 74–76, 84, 85, 89, 92–94, 97, 105–107, 114–118, 133, 135, 136, 139, 142–143, 150, 153, 154, 197–203, 239, 265, 270–273, 325–328, 334, 335, 342–349

Borré, Peter, Sr., 24–25, 28, 32, 34

Boston, Massachusetts, archdiocese, 2, 13, 14, 17, 20–23, 30–35, 53–56, 58–59, 61, 72–75, 82–94, 96–98, 100, 105, 108–118, 126, 133–154, 197–199, 201, 235, 240, 242, 243–246, 264, 271, 321, 323, 327, 328, 334–335, 343, 345–346, 349, 351, 354

Boston College, 23, 86, 88, 210

Boston Globe, 6, 17, 20–22, 73–75, 78, 83–84, 91–93, 97, 106, 116, 118, 136, 141, 145, 150, 223, 302, 303, 345

Boston Herald, 83, 141, 154

Boston Phoenix, 22

Boucher, Ray, 302, 304, 311, 312, 318–319, 321

Bouvier, Lee, 34

Bowers, Father Bob, 32, 69–75, 83–87, 89, 91–94, 106–108, 113, 114, 116–117, 346, 350

Bozek, Father Marek, 272

Brackett, Father Christopher, 167

Brady, Dona, 270

Brett, Regina, 235

Briggs, David, 223, 243–244

Brom, Bishop Robert, 322

Brown, Bishop Tod, 311

Brown, Matt, 237

Bruening, Father Allen, 223, 227

Burke, Archbishop Raymond, 98, 272, 349

Burke, Father David, 142–143

Burkle, Ron, 125, 126, 128, 129, 132

Bush, George W., 35, 116, 119, 159, 190, 352

Bush, Jeb, 159

Cacioppi, Theodore, 129, 131
Cadigan, Lynne, 77
Cafardi, Nicholas P., 80, 112, 183, 273
Calles, Plutarco Elías, 173
Calvi, Roberto, 15, 37, 38, 358
Camden, New Jersey, diocese, 126
Canali, Cardinal Nicola, 158
Cantwell, Archbishop John, 297, 298
Cardinal's Appeal, 82, 84, 87
Carfagna, Peter, 233, 252
Carlson, Bishop Robert, 291
Carmelites, 176
Carrö, Monsignor Giovanni, 120–121,
    125, 128–132
Casaroli, Cardinal Agostino, 103–104
Casey, William J., 96, 159, 166, 211
Castaldi, David, 116, 117,
    150–154, 345
Castrillón Hoyos, Cardinal Darío
    del Niño Jesús, 76–78, 80, 81,
    97–101, 105, 120, 125, 131, 150,
    156–158, 162–164, 181, 188–189,
    197–198, 201, 278, 281, 350
Cathedraticum tax, 7
Catholic Action, 25, 26, 65
Catholic Cemeteries Association, 222,
    249–250, 257, 261, 262
Catholic Charities of Cleveland, 207,
    224–225, 229–230, 240,
    242, 248
Catholic Charities USA, 14, 264, 333
Catholic News Service, 15, 39
Catholic Universe-Bulletin,
    214–215, 250
Cavour, Count Camillo, 43, 46
Cepeda, Bishop Onésimo, 189
Chávez, César, 295, 300, 308
Chicago, Illinois, archdiocese, 13, 14,
    54, 59, 61, 64, 112, 200
Chile, 101–103, 184, 185
Chittister, Sister Joan, 220
Christian Democrats (Italy), 25, 26
CIA (Central Intelligence Agency),
    25–27, 101, 103
Cincinnati, Ohio, diocese, 205–206,
    274–275

Cipriano, Ralph, 8
Clergy abuse, 2–6, 16–17, 40
    Adamson case, 291–292
    Aylward case, 314–315
    Benedict XVI and, 2, 3, 268, 286,
        316, 335–336, 351, 356, 357
    Berthiaume case, 212–214, 216, 223,
        227, 235
    Bevilacqua case, 8–9
    Bruening case, 223
    Dupré case, 149
    emergency meeting in Rome on
        (2002), 76, 78, 79, 81
    Gauthe case, 292
    Geoghan case, 22, 82, 137, 143
    Groër case, 163, 186, 278
    Harris case, 305
    Hawkes case, 300
    Ingels case, 316
    John Paul II and, 20, 41, 75, 78–80,
        145, 163, 177, 178, 186, 191, 217,
        277–279, 353
    Kos case, 111, 162
    Law and, 74–76, 81, 82, 145
    Liturgy of Lament for the Broken
        Body of Christ and, 227–228
    Loomis case, 310
    Louis case, 217, 224
    Maciel case, 172, 175–183, 189–195,
        277–279, 286, 317, 336–339,
        353, 356
    media coverage of, 12, 20, 22, 73–76,
        79, 81–85, 97, 223–224, 229, 233,
        235–238, 289, 296, 313, 318, 323,
        335–336
    Newman case, 11–12
    O'Connell case, 96
    O'Grady case, 294–297, 300
    Picardi case, 141
    Porter case, 73, 95
    recycling of perpetrators, 5, 20, 23,
        74, 78, 139, 146, 198, 212, 214,
        216, 223, 224, 235, 279, 292, 294,
        309, 310, 313, 318, 354
    Shanley case, 84, 139–140, 143
    Silva case, 301–302, 308

Clergy abuse (*continued*)
    statute of limitations, 79–80, 149,
        229, 290, 292, 301
    Sutphin case, 309–310
    Symons case, 96
    Trupia case, 76–78, 80
    victim settlements, 6, 12, 16, 22,
        23, 70, 78, 82, 87, 88, 95, 97, 98,
        100, 110–112, 123, 135–137, 146,
        149, 212, 214–217, 224, 234–236,
        287–290, 292, 297, 305, 306, 310,
        313, 315, 316, 318, 319, 321–323,
        339, 345, 355
    Wempe case, 308–309
Clergy pension and retirement funds,
        13–14, 136–138, 143–146, 149,
        153, 276, 345
Cleveland, Ohio, diocese, 203–208,
        211–218, 221–244, 246–276, 335,
        346, 347, 349–351
Cleveland Free Times, 222, 235
Clinton, Bill, 121, 125, 128, 342
Clinton, Hillary, 121, 342
Clohessy, David, 289
Colby, William, 96
Colina, Jésus, 190–191
Collins, Paul, 102
Colombia, 99, 189, 322
Colson, Chuck, 180
Communism, 61, 65, 101, 104, 162,
        164
Community of St. Malachi,
        211–212
Conference for Catholic Facility
        Management, 122–123
Congregation for Bishops, 70–71
Congregation for the Causes of Saints,
        127, 194
Congregation for the Clergy, 3, 41,
        76–77, 80, 91, 97–100, 105,
        120–121, 125, 128, 129, 131, 132,
        136, 150, 156, 162, 163, 178, 198,
        200, 202, 216, 272, 320, 325, 327,
        343, 349, 357
Congregation for the Doctrine of the
        Faith (CDF), 80, 96, 102, 164,

        180, 181, 186, 189, 191, 193, 194,
        279, 316, 317, 327, 335
Conley, Father Jon, 314–316
Connors, Jack, 153
Convey, Eric, 83
Cooley, Steve, 308
Cooney, John, 55
Cooper, Gary, 26
Corcuera, Father Alvaro, 192, 195,
        285, 286, 337–339
Cordoba, Jose de, 171
Corinez, Leopoldo, 175
Cornwell, John, 26, 67
Corrigan, Brian, 229, 230, 234, 236
Cosgrave, Father Raymond, 185
Coughlin, Charles, 67
Cox, Harvey, 157
Coyne, Reverend Ron, 113
Crimaldi, Laura, 154
Cristeros, 173–174, 298
Crosby, Bing, 26
Cultrera, Joe, 244–246
Curran, Charles, 186, 279
Curti, Elena, 99
Cushing, Cardinal Richard, 31–32, 53,
        109, 148

Dallas, Texas, diocese, 111
Dauray, Jeanne, 168
Day, Dorothy, 70, 73
De Gasperi, Alcide, 25, 26
De Paolis, Cardinal Velasio, 356
Demarco, Anthony, 300
Department of Children and Family
        Services (DCFS), 216, 224
Deysher, Cynthia, 115, 116, 135, 136,
        153
Díaz, Porfirio, 172–173
DiMaria, Ryan, 305
Dimengo, Father Michael, 215
Dinmore, Guy, 358–359
Doheny, Edward L., 297
Doheny, Estelle, 297
Dolan, Larry, 251

Dolan, Matt, 252
Dominicans, 147, 156, 293
Donohue, Bernardine, 300
Donohue, Daniel, 300
Donohue, William, 159
Donovan, Jean, 211
Dooher, Reverend John A., 110
Dorris, Barbara, 289
Dougherty, Archbishop Dennis, 53, 59–61
Doyle, Anne Barrett, 140, 142, 145
Doyle, Father Thomas, 7, 95, 214, 215, 293–295, 305, 307, 314, 340
Drivon, Larry, 295, 301, 302
Duffy, Eamon, 45–46
Dulles, Cardinal Avery, 284
Dupré, Bishop Thomas, 149
Durant, Father Michael, 109
Dziwisz, Cardinal Stanislaw, 181–184, 192, 337

Egan, Cardinal Edward, 125, 198, 199, 200, 306, 328
Eisner, Sister Janet, 116, 117
El Salvador, 211
Emshwiller, John R., 129
Ernst & Young, 234, 237
Escobar, Pablo, 99
Escuti, Martha, 302

Fair, Jim, 282, 337
Fall River, Massachusetts, diocese, 73, 95, 100
Fallon, Jerry, 297, 300
Farrelly, Bishop John, 206
Fascism, 62–67
Favreau, Glenn, 165, 184, 185, 189, 286
FBI (Federal Bureau of Investigation), 4, 127–131, 211, 234, 240, 249
Feehan, Archbishop Patrick, 53, 54

Feliciano, Santiago "Charlie," Jr., 211–212, 214–216, 221–224, 235, 237, 238, 241, 249, 253, 257
Female priesthood, 203, 204, 217, 218–221, 278, 279
Feuerherd, Joe, 122–124, 127
Fichter, Father Stephen, 187
Finn, Joe, 82
Finnegan, Mike, 288, 341*
Flatley, Reverend Brian, 141
Fleet Bank, 84, 167, 168
Flynn, Archbishop Harry, 192
Folchi, Monsignor Enrico, 51–52
Follieri, Pasquale, 121–122, 126, 131
Follieri, Raffaello, 121–132
Follieri Foundation, 125
Follieri Group, 121–128, 185
Foreign Sovereign Immunities Act of 1976, 120, 340
Fortuna, Father Joe, 227
Fossa, Florence, 56
Foti, Anthony and Noreen, 271
Francis of Assisi, St., 133, 277
Franciscans, 11, 95
Franco, Francisco, 158
Freberg, Katherine, 305, 307, 311
Freeman, James, 7
Frogameni, Bill, 250
Fuentes, Carlos, 172, 176
FutureChurch, 203–204, 208, 217, 221, 227, 236–237, 242, 243, 265, 271, 273, 326, 349

Gallagher, Delia, 159
Gallagher Sharp, 222
Galvin, William F., 106
Garabedian, Mitchell, 22, 82, 137
García Márquez, Gabriel, 157
Garibaldi, Giuseppe, 43, 44, 46
Garrahy, John Joseph, 166
Garrahy, Marguerite, 166
Garza, Eugenio, 169
Garza, Paulina, 170
Garza, Roberta, 169–171, 175, 282

Garza Medina, Dionisio, 169, 171
Garza Medina, Luis, 169–171, 179,
    195, 282, 286
Gasparri, Cardinal Pietro, 63–65
Gauthe, Father Gilbert, 292
Gay marriage, 33, 72
Gelineau, Bishop Louis, 166
Geoghan, Father John, 22, 82,
    137, 143
George, Cardinal Francis, 122, 354
Giardiello, Doris, 116
Gibson, David, 81, 198–199, 221, 336
Glendon, Mary Ann, 159, 180
Godman, Peter, 65
Gold, Vatican ownership of, 15, 66, 67
Gollin, James, 4
González, Fernando M., 172, 174
González Lara, Raúl, 324, 339, 356
Goodstein, Laurie, 80, 288
Gordon, William H., 22, 137–138
Grahmann, Bishop Charles, 111
Grant, Mary, 310
Greeley, Andrew M., 12
Gregory, Archbishop Wilton, 82, 235
Griffin, Bishop James, 237–238, 257
Grocholewski, Zenon, 186
Groër, Archbishop Hans Hermann,
    163, 186, 219, 278
Guatemala, 211
Guccione, Jean, 316–317
Guinan, Reverend Francis, 9
Guízar Valencia, Bishop Rafael, 173, 194
Gullo, Alessia, 200
Gullo, Carlo, 199–202, 271, 273, 325,
    327, 335, 342, 344, 349
Gutiérrez, Blanca Lara, 196
Gutiérrez, Father Gustavo, 210

Haig, Al, 96
Haiti, 36
Halbfinger, David M., 80
Hamilton, Marci, 341–342
Hand of God (documentary), 244–246
Harris, Father Michael, 305

Harris, Joseph Claude, 5–6, 10
Hartford Courant, 17, 167, 177, 180,
    192, 339
Hathaway, Anne, 121, 124–126, 129,
    130, 132
Hawkes, Monsignor Robert, 300
Hayes, Patrick, 53
Helios, 129, 130, 132
Henderson, Karen, 214
Hennigan, J. Michael, 302, 304, 307,
    310, 312, 318–321
Herlihy, Kevin J., 154–155
Hickey, Bishop James, 211, 212
Hilton, Baron, 300
Hitler, Adolf, 3, 67, 68
Hitler's Pope (Cornwell), 67
Hoag, Emily, 242
Hodge, Monsignor William, 126, 130
Hodgman, William, 302, 303, 308
Hoffman, Iowana, 182
Holocaust, 67, 281
Hope, Dolores, 300
Howard, Father Maurice, 204
Howard, James, 294–295
Howard, Joh, 294–295
Hughes, Archbishop Alfred, 271, 328,
    329, 331–334
Hughes, John, 53
Hull, Virginia, 275
Hummes, Cardinal Cláudio, 99, 320
Hungary, 163–164
Hurley, Suzanne, 134
Hurricane Katrina, 243, 328–329,
    331–334

Ignatius Loyola, St., 277
Il Giornale, 78
Imesch, Bishop Joseph, 216
Immaculate Conception, 48
Immigration and Naturalization
    Service, 211
Indresano, Michael, 154
Infallibility doctrine, 47–49, 59,
    220, 279

Ingels, Father Greg, 316
Inquisition, 80, 89
Inside the Vatican: The Politics and Organization of the Catholic Church (Reese), 39
Insunza, Andrea, 184
Iraq war, 119–120
Ireland, John, 53

Jackson, Jesse, 125
Jacques, Father Michael, 330–332
Jenkins, Jim, 316
Jesuits, 147, 156, 165, 168–169, 175
Jews, 3, 43–45, 61, 66–67
John, Erica P., 4
John Paul II, 37, 38, 49, 71, 72, 92, 95, 100, 101, 157, 184, 236, 295, 300, 306, 327
    clergy abuse and, 20, 41, 75, 78–80, 145, 163, 177, 178, 186, 191, 217, 277–279, 353
    death of, 193, 280
    female priesthood and, 219, 278, 279
    finances and, 104
    health of, 105, 119
    human rights and, 3, 68
    Iraq war and, 120
    Legion of Christ and, 163, 164, 182
    Maciel and, 159, 164, 181, 337, 353
    Sodano and, 103–104
    trip to Chile (1987), 102–103
    trip to Mexico (1979), 164
    trip to Mexico (1999), 159
    trip to U.S. (1993), 216
    visit to Austria (1998), 163
John XXIII, 3, 32, 67, 176
Johns Hopkins Hospital Sexual Disorders Clinic, 214
Jones Day, 214, 221, 224, 230, 233, 237, 251, 252, 263
Josoma, Father Stephen, 92–93, 108–113, 115–116, 242
Jukic, Zrino, 232, 249–250, 254–255, 258–260, 263

Jurado, Arturo, 177, 180
Jurecki, Laurel, 227

Kagan, Elena, 341, 342
Kaifer, Father William, 209
Kaiser, Robert Blair, 193
Kalamazoo, Michigan, archdiocese, 13
Kammer, Reverend Fred, 14
Kantowicz, Edward, 59
Kasper, Cardinal Walter, 336
Kazel, Dorothy, 211
Kearns, Father Owen, 161, 166, 179, 339
Keating, Frank, 83
Keeler, Cardinal William H., 230–231
Kelly, Tom, 257, 262
Kennedy, Edward M., 72
Kennedy, Eugene, 280
Kennedy, John F., 31, 34, 83
Kennedy, Joseph, 31, 72–73
Kennedy, Robert F., 209
Kennedy, Sheila Rauch, 73
Kerry, John, 20, 35, 72, 116
Kertzer, David I., 43, 44, 61
Kineke, Genvieve, 166, 168, 190
King, Martin Luther, Jr., 85, 290, 291
Kneedler, Edwin, 341
Knights of Columbus, 23, 31, 61, 64, 84
Knights of Malta, 95–96, 100
Koh, Harold, 342
Kos, Rudy, 111, 162
Krauze, Enrique, 168
Krol, Cardinal John, 37–39
Küng, Hans, 48–49, 186, 279, 359
Kunze, Elizabeth, 165–166, 179, 195, 282
Kunze, Father Christopher, 156, 158–165, 171–172, 178–179, 181, 187–188, 190, 193, 282
Kunze, Mary, 282
Kushner, Philip, 249–251, 253, 260–261
Kwitny, Jonathan, 103, 104

La Repubblica, 78, 280–281, 336

Lafayette, Louisiana, diocese, 292

Laghi, Cardinal Pio, 184, 186, 214

Lash, Nicholas, 220

Lateran Pacts, 64, 65, 174, 199

Law, Cardinal Bernard, 6, 20–23, 32,
    70–76, 81–88, 92, 93, 96, 97, 100,
    108, 113, 117, 136, 137, 139–141,
    144–146, 149, 151–153, 191, 229,
    240, 278, 279, 303, 323, 343,
    347, 351

Law of Guarantees, 46, 51

Lead Us Not into Temptation (Berry),
    16, 177

Leahy, Father William, 108

LeDoux, Jerome, 330–332

Lee, Martin, 96

Legion of Christ, 17, 156, 158–162,
    164–172, 175–196, 237, 277, 278,
    281–286, 320, 324, 336–340, 350,
    356–357

LegionaryFacts.org, 178, 339

Lena, Jeffrey, 340, 341

Lenin, V. I., 61, 63

Lennon, Bishop Richard G., 85–93,
    98, 106–112, 114–118, 140–145,
    150, 152–155, 195, 238–248,
    263–267, 269, 270, 272–276, 278,
    323, 328, 335, 343, 346, 347,
    349, 351

Lennon, Paul, 190

Leo XIII, 50–51, 67

L'Espresso, 39, 78

Levada, Bishop William, 313–317

Liberation theology, 157, 161, 189,
    210, 279

Liturgy of Lament for the Broken Body
    of Christ, 227–228

Lo Bello, Nino, 26

Lobdell, William, 316–317

Lombardi, Father Federico, 184, 185

Lombardi, Kristen, 22

Loomis, Monsignor Richard A., 310

López, Father Gregorio, 175

Lopez, Steve, 295

López Portillo, José, 164

Los Angeles archdiocese, 13, 14, 17,
    264, 295, 297–312, 316, 318–324

Los Angeles Times, 76, 295, 303, 304,
    316–318, 321

L'Osservatore Romano, 15, 65, 336

Louis, Father Martin, 217, 224

Louis-Napoléon, Emperor, 44

Lucia, Luis, 284

Lukas, Anthony J., 29

Lumen Gentium, 279

Maciel, Maurita, 172, 173

Maciel Degollado, Father Marcial,
    3, 4, 17, 156–161, 164, 165,
    168–196, 199, 201, 277–278, 281,
    283–286, 298, 317, 320, 324,
    336–339, 350, 353, 356

Maciel Farías, Francisco, 172

MacLeish, Roderick, Jr., 22

Madero, Francisco, 172–173

Maestri, Father William, 331

Maffei, Kay, 134

Magister, Sandro, 39

Mahoney, Father Dan, 84

Mahony, Cardinal Roger M., 76,
    294–297, 300–314, 316–323, 341

Maine archdiocese, 52–53

Mainiero, Antonio, 127–129, 131

Manly, John, 300, 304–305

Manning, Bishop Timothy, 53, 300

Mannix v. Purcell (1888), 205, 206, 274

Marcinkus, Archbishop Paul, 38,
    104, 358

Married priests, 203, 204, 217, 219

Marrone, Father Robert, 273–274, 276

Marshall, Bishop John, 146–149

Martín-Artajo, Alberto, 158

Martínez de Velasco, José, 188

Martínez Somalo, Cardinal Eduardo,
    181, 184

Martino, Bishop Joseph, 271

Mason, William D., 224, 225, 229,
    230, 236

McCain, John, 126

McCall, Bill, 126
McCarrick, Cardinal Theodore, 81
McCartan, Patrick, 221, 252
McCarty, James F., 213, 223, 224, 229, 233, 252
McCone, John, 96
McCormack, Father John, 139–140
McDaid, Monsignor James Anthony, 98–99, 162–163
McDonnel, Monsignor Tom, 88
McDonough, James P., 345
McEveety, Steve, 159
McGann, Bishop John R., 177
McIntyre, Cardinal James F., 53, 298–300
McKiernan, Terence, 10–11, 140, 142
McLaughlin, Father Peter, 204
McMenamin, Michael, 230
McMenamin, Robert, 313
McMurray, William F., 120
McTighe, Michael J., 205
Meade, Peter, 116, 117
Mecir, Father Joseph, 266
Medical Mission Sisters, 210
Mee, Gabrielle Dauray, 166–168, 175
Mee, Timothy, 167
Menino, Thomas M., 106
Mexican Revolution of 1910, 172–173, 298
Meyer, Jean A., 173
Micara, Cardinal Clemente, 158, 176–177
Mickens, Robert, 15
Milano, Jay, 232, 233
Militant and Triumphant (O'Toole), 52
Miller, Sam, 221
Milos, Maria "Mitzy," 256
Modern Inquisition, The (Collins), 102
Modernism, 56, 57
Monaghan, Thomas, 159
Moody, Father Quentin, 332
Moreno, Bishop Manuel, 76–78
Morial, Jacques, 331–332
Morones, Luis Napoleón, 173, 174
Morris, Charles R., 60, 298
Morrow, Dwight, 174

Mortara, Edgardo, 45
Mouton, F. Ray, 293
Mulcahy, Val, 89, 107
Mullen, Father John, 55
Mundelein, Archbishop George, 53, 59–61, 64
Murphy, Bishop P. Francis, 220–221
Mussolini, Benito, 25, 27, 57–58, 62–68, 162, 174, 199, 201

Nagin, Ray, 271, 334
National Catholic Register, 178, 339
National Catholic Reporter, 8, 71–72, 92, 112–113, 120, 127, 180, 182, 192, 237, 270, 271, 309, 320
National Review Board for the Protection of Children and Young People, 10, 83, 235
Nazi Germany, 3, 62, 67, 68
Neilson, R. Todd, 322–323
Neuhaus, Father Richard John, 159, 180, 189–190
New Orleans, Louisiana, archdiocese, 13, 112, 243, 271, 327–334, 333
New York archdiocese, 10, 44, 327, 328
New York Times, 4, 46, 80, 136, 169, 199, 288, 318, 335, 350
Newman, Jack, 252
Newman, Reverend Charles, 11–12
Newsweek magazine, 74
Nicaragua, 211
Nicora, Cardinal Attilo, 359
Nixon, Richard M., 101, 323
Nogara, Bernardino, 66–68
Nolan, Bruce, 333
Noriega, Manuel, 103
Noyes, Dan, 313
Nuth, Joan M., 274

Obama, Barack, 343, 352
O'Brien, Archbishop Edwin, 294
O'Carroll, Father Fergus, 178

O'Connell, Bishop Anthony, 96
O'Connell, Cardinal William, 52–56,
    58–61, 81
O'Connell, Father James, 55–56,
    58, 81
O'Connell, Father Mark, 143–144
O'Connor, Cardinal John, 198–199
O'Connor, Cormac Murphy, 306
O'Grady, Father Oliver, 294–297, 300
O'Malley, Archbishop Seán, 22–23,
    88–89, 91–93, 95–100, 105–118,
    120, 133–135, 142, 143, 145,
    150–155, 198, 199, 240, 268, 272,
    306, 320, 323, 328, 335, 343–345,
    347–348, 351
O'Malley, Michael, 263
Opus Dei, 164, 168, 184, 199, 358
Orange, California, diocese, 311,
    312, 319
Ordinatio Sacerdotalis (John Paul II),
    219, 220
Ortega, Javier, 184
Orth, Maureen, 139
Ortoli, Richard, 124
O'Toole, James, 52, 53, 55
Our Lady Help of Christians,
    Concord, 106
Our Lady of Guadalupe Basilica,
    Rome, 176, 177, 181, 277
Our Lady of Vilnius, Manhattan,
    199
Our Lady Queen of Angels,
    Harlem, 198
Oxnard, California, diocese, 301

Pacelli, Eugenio, 65, 67. See also
    Pius XII
Palm Beach, Florida, diocese, 96
Panama, 103
Panetta, Leon, 10, 235
Papal Foundation, 36
Papal States, 40–46, 48, 65, 68
Paracletes' facility, New Mexico,
    214, 309

Parish assessments, 7, 73–74, 84, 88,
    109, 148, 225
Parish closures, 7, 86, 89–93, 97, 98,
    105–118, 136, 150–154, 163,
    197–202, 243–246, 263–276,
    326–328, 331–334, 343, 344,
    346–350, 357
Parolin, Monsignor Pietro, 327
Partito Popolare Italiano (Catholic
    Party), 61, 62, 64, 65, 67
Paterson, New Jersey, diocese, 141
Patton, Tom, 270
Paul IV, 43
Paul VI, 3, 68, 211, 219
Paulson, Michael, 91–92, 150
People of God concept, 279
Perpetual care, 148
Peter's Pence, 36–40, 44–47, 49–50,
    52–54, 57, 59, 68, 100, 104, 306,
    351, 353
Peterson, Father Michael, 293
Philadelphia archdiocese, 8–9, 13, 44,
    60–61
Piacenza, Monsignor Mauro, 99n, 164
Pican, Bishop Pierre, 100
Picardi, Father John, 141
Pikula, Edward M., 348
Pilla, Bishop Anthony, 204, 207–208,
    211–215, 218, 221–226, 229, 230,
    231–238, 240–243, 246, 249–253,
    255–257, 259, 262–265, 268, 350
Pilot, The (Catholic weekly), 54, 136,
    137, 139
Pinochet, Augusto, 101–103, 184, 185
Piper, Bill, 1–2, 20, 21, 33
Piper, Claudia, 20
Piper, Rose Mary (Rosie), 5, 12, 20,
    21, 32–33, 69–70, 84, 93–94, 202
Pironio, Cardinal Eduardo Francisco,
    183, 184
Piscitelli, Joey, 312, 313
Pittner, Nicholas A., 274–275
Pius IX, "Pio Nono," 40, 41–53, 56,
    59, 65, 67, 68, 201
Pius VI, 42
Pius X, 25, 56–57

Pius XI, 25, 62–67, 174
Pius XII, 3, 25, 27, 48, 67–68, 76, 158,
    174, 176, 299, 300
Plain Dealer newspaper, 212–215, 223,
    224, 229, 233, 235–237, 241,
    243–244, 251, 252, 263, 266
Podles, Leon C., 278
Polensk, Michael, 267–268
Politi, Marco, 280–281
Pollard, John F., 49–51
Ponsor, Michael A., 348, 357
Ponte, Vincent, 125
Populorum Progressio, 37
Porter, James, 73, 95
Portland, Oregon, diocese, 112–113,
    135, 321
Power and the Glory, The (Greene), 174
Prigione, Archbishop Girolamo, 165
Pumphrey, Lou, 215
Purcell, Bishop John, 205–206

Quinn, Archbishop John, 316
Quinn, Bishop A. James, 213–216,
    223, 229, 236, 237

R.F. Binder Partners Inc., 81, 82
Radziwill, Stanislaw, 34
Ratzinger, Cardinal Joseph, 2, 78, 79,
    80, 81, 83, 96, 101, 102, 145,
    157, 163, 164, 180, 186–187, 189,
    191, 193–194, 199, 217, 218, 220,
    277–281. *See also* Benedict XVI
Re, Cardinal Giovanni Battista, 71, 100
Reese, Father Thomas J., 39–40
ReGAIN Network, 190, 195
Regina Apostolorum, 185–188
Regnum Christi, Kingdom of Christ,
    161–162, 164–168, 170, 171, 177,
    179, 185, 190–192, 195, 237, 277,
    281–285, 356
Renner, Gerald, 17, 177, 192, 339
Rerum Novarum (1891), 51

Retes, Talita, 174
Rezendes, Michael, 78
Rhode Island Catholic, 166
Rhodes, Anthony, 45
Rice, Condoleezza, 119–120
Riordan, Richard, 295, 300
Roach, Archbishop John, 292
Roberts, Tom, 237, 270
Robinson, Walter V., 74
Rockefeller, John D., 204–205
Rodé, Cardinal Franc, 190, 320, 350
Rodgers, Jon and Maryellen, 133
Rodgers, Wilson, 82
Roe v. Wade (1973), 21
Roman Curia, 4, 78–79, 105, 159,
    164, 281
Romero, Archbishop Oscar, 211, 278
Roncalli, Angelo, 67. *See also*
    John XXIII
Ross, Brian, 190
Rotatori, Robert, 250, 255–257, 259,
    260, 263
Rothschild, James, 44–46
Rothschild bank, 43, 44, 46
Ruane, Marilyn, 250, 262
Rubino, Steve, 307, 311, 318, 319, 321
Ruhl, Jack, 12–13, 15, 275–276,
    333–334, 345
Ruíz, Bishop Samuel, 189, 278
Rupert Murdoch Family
    Foundations, 300
Rush, Father Tom, 299
Russell, Ron, 295, 302
Rutchick, Joel, 233
Ryan, Michael W., 10, 11, 225–226,
    351

Sacra Rota, 34
Sacred Heart of Jesus, Slavic
    Village, 266
Sahel Foundation, 37
St. Aidan's, Boston, 83
St. Albert the Great, Weymouth, 113,
    114

St. Andrew's, Cleveland, 267
St. Anselm, Sudbury, 115
St. Augustine Elementary School,
    Boston, 87–88
St. Augustine's Cemetery, Boston,
    86–87
St. Bernard, Newton, 115
St. Brigid, Amherst, 147–149
St. Casimir, Cleveland, 266
St. Catherine of Siena, Boston, 1,
    32–33, 69, 73, 74, 84, 86–87,
    89, 91, 93–94, 106, 107, 114,
    116–117
St. Colman, Cleveland, 263, 268–270
St. Emeric, Cleveland, 267
St. Frances Cabrini, Scituate, 87–88,
    106, 133–134, 346
St. Francis de Sales, Boston, 69, 84
St. Ignatius, Antioch, 263, 270
St. James, Kansas, Ohio, 274–275,
    357
St. James, Lakewood, 263
St. James, Wellesley, 134
St. Luke Institute, Maryland, 163,
    214, 309
St. Mary, Boston, 69
St. Mary of the Assumption, Dedham,
    109–110
St. Mary Star of the Sea, East
    Boston, 154
St. Peter's, Cleveland, 272–274,
    276, 346
St. Pius X, Milton, 142–143
St. Stanilaus Kostka, St. Louis, 272
St. Susanna, Dedham, 92, 108–111,
    115–116
St. Thomas the Apostle, Peabody,
    114–115
Salesians of Don Bosco, 312–313, 317,
    318, 320
Sambi, Archbishop Pietro, 37,
    268–270, 342–344, 346, 347, 350
San Bernardino, California, diocese,
    139, 140
San Diego, California, diocese,
    322–323

San Francisco, California, archdiocese,
    312–316
San Francisco Examiner, 315
Sanchez, Archbishop Robert, 111
Sanctuary movement, 211
Santa Fe, New Mexico, archdiocese,
    110–111
Santa Maria Maggiore, Rome, 92
Santorum, Rick, 159
Sawdust Caesar (Seldes), 64
Schenk, Sister Christine, 16, 203,
    208–212, 217–218, 220–221,
    226–228, 236–239, 242–243, 264,
    273, 327, 349–351
Schiltz, Patrick J., 4, 355–356
Scicluna, Monsignor Charles,
    193–194, 277, 285, 339
Secretariat of State, Vatican City, 36,
    37, 80, 100, 164
Seldes, George, 62, 64
Sellors, Paul and Libbie, 284
September 11, 2001, terrorist
    attacks, 70
Shanley, Father Paul, 84, 139–140,
    143
Shattered Faith (S. Kennedy), 73
Sheehan, Archbishop Michael,
    110, 111
Sheil, Bill, 223–224, 229, 230, 235,
    244, 245
Shnayerson, Michael, 124
Siegel, John, 254–255, 257, 259
Silva, Father Fidencio, 301–302, 308
Silva Henriquez, Cardinal Raúl, 101,
    184, 185
Silvestrini, Cardinal Achille, 103, 104
Simmons, Rick, 312, 313
Sinatra, Frank, 26, 76
Sindona, Michele, 38, 358
Sipe, Father Richard, 305, 340
60 Minutes (television show), 224
Skehan, John, 9
Skylstad, Bishop William, 197, 273
Slim, Carlos, 159, 190
Smith, David W., 137–139, 144, 152,
    154–155

Smith, Joseph H., 214, 221–226, 231–234, 237–238, 240–242, 249–258, 260–264, 276
Snyder, John, 25–26
Società Generale Immobiliare, 52
Society of St. Pius X, 281, 285, 347
Sodano, Alessandro, 185
Sodano, Andrea, 118, 120–124, 126–129, 131, 185
Sodano, Cardinal Angelo, 3–4, 100–105, 118, 119–121, 123–125, 127, 128, 131, 132, 163, 164, 181, 184–187, 191, 194, 277, 278, 281, 285, 317, 336, 350, 351, 353, 357, 359
Solidarity, 181
Sota, Idoia, 195
Sozio, Steve, 233, 234, 251, 252, 254, 263
Speciale, Alessandro, 37
Spellman, Cardinal Francis J., 26, 53, 54, 60, 64
Spence, Anne, 88
Spokane, Washington, diocese, 112, 135, 197, 273
Springfield, Massachusetts, diocese, 348, 349, 357
Stafford, Cardinal James Francis, 78, 216, 306
Stammer, Larry B., 76, 303
Starr, Kevin, 299
Statute of limitations, 79–80, 149, 229, 290, 292, 301
Steier, Don, 307
Stockton, California, diocese, 294–297, 301, 304
Stogner v. California (2003), 308
Sturzo, Father Luigi, 61–62, 64, 67
Sullivan, Jack, 83
Sunday collection figures, 5–6, 10–11, 16, 145, 225–226, 264
Survivors Network of Those Abused by Priests (SNAP), 152, 289–290, 310, 312, 354
Sutphin, Father Carl, 309–310
Sweeney, Constance, 2

Syllabus of Errors (1864), 46, 56
Symons, J. Keith, 96
Szoka, Cardinal Edmund C., 39, 104

Tablet, The (magazine), 15, 99
Tamberg, Tod, 322
Taxa fee, 7
Tayek, Bob, 235, 236, 251–252
Teague, Father Bruce, 146–149
Tedeschi, Ettore Gotti, 358
Teilhard de Chardin, Pierre, 209
Ternyak, Archbishop Csaba, 163–164
Thieme, Channing, 73
Timothy J. Mee Foundation, 167
Tobin, Mike, 251, 252
Tomashek, Monsignor George, 126, 130
Toomey, Father David, 55–56
Torjesen, Karen Jo, 218
Torres Robles, Alfonso, 164–165
Towers Perrin, 136
Treaty of Versailles (1919), 58, 66
Trivison, Father Lou, 203, 204, 217, 236, 242
Trupia, Father Robert, 76–78, 80
Tucci, Father Roberto, 102
Tucson, Arizona, diocese, 112, 135

Unhealed Wound, The (Kennedy), 280
United States Conference of Catholic Bishops (USCCB), 5, 6, 10, 37, 81, 82, 351, 354
Universal Church of the Kingdom of God, 154
USA Today, 6, 10

Vaca, Father Juan, 172, 175–179, 193, 337–339
Vairo, Georgene, 311
Valentino, Michael, 331, 332

Valeri, Cardinal Valerio, 176
Vanity Fair, 124, 139
Vatican Bank (Istituto per le Opere
    di Religione), 15, 26, 37–40, 68,
    100, 104, 131, 323, 351, 353,
    357–359
Vatican City, 48, 64
Vega, Manny, 301–302, 304, 308,
    312, 319
Vicariate of Solidarity, 102
Victim settlements, 6, 12, 16, 22, 23,
    70, 78, 82, 87, 88, 95, 97, 98, 100,
    110–112, 123, 135–137, 146, 149,
    212, 214–217, 224, 234–236,
    287–290, 292, 297, 305, 306, 310,
    313, 315, 316, 318, 319, 321–323,
    339, 345, 355
Victor Emmanuel II, 43, 46, 50
Vidal, José M., 195
Vigil movement, 113–116, 133–135,
    143, 155, 198, 199, 202, 203, 239,
    271, 326–328, 333–335, 344, 346
Villanova University, 9–11
Vlazny, Archbishop John, 112
Voice of the Faithful (VOTF), 82, 92,
    113, 115, 147, 150–152, 271,
    294, 326
Voinovich, George, 268
Vows of Silence: The Abuse of Power in
    the Papacy of John Paul II (Berry
    and Renner), 17

Wahl, Rosalie, 291
Wall, Father Patrick, 305, 314,
    326, 340
Wall Street Journal, 7, 122, 125, 129,
    165, 171, 300
Wallace, Brian, 87, 88
Walsh, Andrew, 335
Walsh, Bishop Louis, 53, 56, 58
Walsh, Mary Williams, 136
Walsh, Paul F., Jr., 230
Wangsness, Lisa, 345

Washington Post, 118, 288
Waste Land, The (Eliot), 209
Watters, Bishop Loras, 292
Weakland, Archbishop Rembert, 4–5,
    163, 288
Wegan, Martha, 105, 186, 199, 201
Weigel, George, 104, 159
Weill, Sanford, 190
Weiner, Tom, 25, 26
Wells, Monsignor Peter, 344
Wempe, Father Michael, 308–309
Westbrook, Jay, 266, 267, 270
Whelan, Father Stephen, 312–313
When Women Were Priests
    (Torjesen), 218
White, Stacie, 216–217, 224
Why Catholics Don't Give . . . and What
    Can Be Done About It (Zech), 12
Williams, Father Tom, 280
Wills, Garry, 46, 48, 279
Wilson, Elsie Maier, 210
Woolsey, Monsignor John, 9–10
Wordly Goods (Gollin), 4
World War I, 2, 57–58, 61
World War II, 3, 67
World Youth Day (1993), 216
Wright, Cardinal John, 25, 216
Wright, Father John, 214–216, 222,
    234, 236, 238, 241–242, 249, 250,
    253–263

Yucaipa Companies, 125–126, 129
Yucaipa Follieri Investments, 128

Zalkin, Irwin, 323
Zech, Charles E., 9, 12
Zenit news agency, 191, 285
Zgoznik, Anton, 231–234, 238, 240,
    241, 249, 250, 253–264
Zirm, Kenneth, 230
Zone, Matt, 270